The Life of the Sixteenth Karmapa Rangjung Rigpe Dorje

Studies in Modern Tibetan Culture

Series Editor: Gray Tuttle, Columbia University

Advisory Board
Lauran Hartley, Columbia University (literature)
Isabelle Henrion-Dourcy, Université Laval (anthropology)
Kurtis Schaeffer, University of Virginia (religion)
Emily Yeh, University of Colorado at Boulder (human geography)
The *Studies in Modern Tibetan Culture* series focuses on Tibetan culture and society from the early modern period of the seventeenth century to the present. The first series on modern Tibetan studies by a scholarly press, it explores how modernity manifests in a wide range of fields, not only religion, but also literature, history, economy, anthropology, media, and politics. It seeks to bring rarely heard and important Tibetan perspectives to a wider audience by publishing fresh analyses of yet unexplored source materials ranging from census and yearbook databases to auto/biographies and ethnographic fieldwork, as well as original translations of poetry, biography, and history.

Titles in Series
The Hidden Life of the Sixth Dalai Lama by Ngawang Lhundrup Dargyé and translated by Simon Wickham-Smith
The Disempowered Development of Tibet in China: A Study in the Economics of Marginalization by Andrew Martin Fischer
The Social Life of Tibetan Biography: Textuality, Community, and Authority in the Lineage of Tokden Shakya Shri by Amy Holmes-Tagchungdarpa
The Rise of Gönpo Namgyel in Kham: The Blind Warrior of Nyarong by Yudru Tsomu
Oral and Literary Continuities in Modern Tibetan Literature: The Inescapable Nation by Lama Jabb
Muslims in Amdo Tibetan Society: Multi-Disciplinary Approaches edited by Marie-Paule Hille, Bianca Horlemann, and Paul K. Nictupski
Tibetan Environmentalists in China: The King of Zi by Liu Jianqiang, translated by Emily Yeh
Life of the Sixteenth Karmapa Rangjung Rigpe Dorje: Transmitting the Dharma in Exile by Meng Wang

The Life of the Sixteenth Karmapa Rangjung Rigpe Dorje

Transmitting the Dharma in Exile

Meng Wang

LEXINGTON BOOKS
Lanham • Boulder • New York • London

Published by Lexington Books
An imprint of The Rowman & Littlefield Publishing Group, Inc.
4501 Forbes Boulevard, Suite 200, Lanham, Maryland 20706
www.rowman.com

86-90 Paul Street, London EC2A 4NE

Copyright © 2023 by The Rowman & Littlefield Publishing Group, Inc.

All rights reserved. No part of this book may be reproduced in any form or by any electronic or mechanical means, including information storage and retrieval systems, without written permission from the publisher, except by a reviewer who may quote passages in a review.

British Library Cataloguing in Publication Information Available

Library of Congress Cataloging-in-Publication Data

Names: Wang, Meng, 1982- author.
Title: The life of the sixteenth Karmapa Rangjung Rigpe Dorje :
   transmitting the Dharma in exile / Meng Wang.
Description: Lanham : Lexington Books, 2022. | Series: Studies in modern
   Tibetan culture | Includes bibliographical references and index.
Identifiers: LCCN 2022042081 (print) | LCCN 2022042082 (ebook) |
   ISBN 9781666913453 (cloth) | ISBN 9781666913460 (ebook)
Subjects: LCSH: Rang-byung-rig-pa'i-rdo-rje, Karma-pa XVI, 1924-1981. |
   Bka'-brgyud-pa lamas—China—Tibet Autonomous Region—Biography. |
   Tibet Autonomous Region (China)—Biography.
Classification: LCC BQ7950.R387 W36 2022 (print) | LCC BQ7950.R387 (ebook) |
   DDC 294.3/923092 [B]—dc23/eng/20220912
LC record available at https://lccn.loc.gov/2022042081
LC ebook record available at https://lccn.loc.gov/2022042082

Contents

Acknowledgements	vii
PART I: INTRODUCTION: A CROSS-CULTURAL APPROACH	**1**
1 The Tibetan Perspective	3
2 Western Context	29
PART II: RECEPTION: PERCEIVING THE KARMAPA	**57**
3 Faithful Translation	59
4 The Emergence of New Narratives	83
PART III: TRANSMISSION (I): PRESERVATION	**103**
5 Politics and Patronage	105
6 Preservation Initiative	129
PART IV: TRANSMISSION (II): EXPANSION	**149**
7 Preparing the Ground	151
8 Strategies on Tour	183
Conclusion	195
Appendix A: Rangjung Rigpe Dorje's *Rangnam*—a Brief Autobiography	201

Appendix B: Rangjung Rigpe Dorje's *Namthar*, Composed
by Thrangu Rinpoche—The Life Story of the Victorious One,
the Great Sixteenth [Karmapa]   205

Bibliography   261

Index   287

About the Author   303

Acknowledgements

First, I would like to express my gratitude to Professor Ulrich Pagel for his continued guidance and support throughout my PhD and postdoctoral research. With unwavering patience and kindness, he has helped me progress every step of the way in critical thinking, academic research and Tibetan language translation. My deepest appreciation goes to Charles Manson, my first Tibetan language teacher, who has opened my eyes to the boundless beauty and profoundness of the Tibetan language and culture. His enormous kindness and vast knowledge made each Tibetan language class an utterly enjoyable experience; it was with his excellent guidance that I was able to locate many core Tibetan sources for my research. I would like to thank Professor Marta Sernesi for her generous help with my Tibetan language translation and my research on Tibetan life-writing. I am incredibly grateful for the inspiring advice and encouragement from Dr Martin Mills during the oral examination of my doctorate, with which I was able to make a significant improvement to the structure and central argument of my thesis. I also extend my appreciation to Dr Vincent Tournier and Dr Antonello Palumbo for their thoughtful suggestions on my upgrade from MPhil to PhD.

I would like to convey my sincere gratitude to Jose Tashi Tsering (Jo sras bKra shis tshe ring). His compilation of *The Collected Works of the Sixteenth Karmapa* (*rgyal dbang karma pa bcu drug pa chen po'i gsung 'bum*) has tremendously enriched my knowledge about the Karmapa's life and activity, which greatly benefitted my research. He also shared his valuable insights into prophetic texts in Tibetan Buddhism and offered copies of rare sources on the Karmapa prophecies. Dr Raj Kotwal patiently answered all my questions and kindly sent me a rare copy of the paperback edition of his book that contains his personal records about the Karmapa unseen in any other sources, for which I feel very grateful. I would also like to thank Dr Ruth Gamble for providing me with a copy of her PhD thesis which greatly enhanced my understanding of the early history of the Karmapa lineage.

Last but not least, I would like to express immense appreciation from the bottom of my heart to my dear colleagues and friends, Dr Susan Roach, Dr Serena Biondo, Dr Jing Luo, Irene Ng, Xiaoying Chang, Michelle Tsui, Harmony DenRonden, Hannah Marianne Duggan, as well as my dear husband, John Sullivan. Their generous love, warm friendship, constant encouragement and steadfast support have been a crucial source of strength for me throughout my research. My special thanks go to Xiaoying Chang, a wonderful friend and talented artist, for the brilliant artwork that she created for the front cover of this book.

Part I

INTRODUCTION

A CROSS-CULTURAL APPROACH

The Sixteenth Karmapa, Rangjung Rigpe Dorje (Rang byung rig pa'i rdo rje, 1924–1981), was the head of the Karma Kagyu school of Tibetan Buddhism. He was the first Tibetan Buddhist leader to make extensive teaching tours to the West. His three tours to Europe and North America (1974–1975, 1976–1978 and 1980) led to the fastest global expansion of a Tibetan Buddhist school: by the 1980s, more than 300 Dharma centres spread across the world; most Tibetan Buddhist centres in Europe and the United States belonged to the Kagyu school. This was an impressive achievement, considering the short period of time of his activity in the West, over the span of less than a decade, from 1974 when he visited the West for the first time to 1981 when he died in the United States.

This study offers a close examination of the Karmapa's life, especially his transmission of Tibetan Buddhism in exile. It seeks to answer two questions: (1) How did the Karmapa achieve the fast and widespread development of his tradition? (2) What were his main contributions to the preservation of Tibetan Buddhism and its transmission to the West? It is an application of the critique of the anti-Orientalist argument; the aim is to introduce balance to the existing scholarship that privileges reception over transmission agency. To do so, it places at its core Tibetan agency and presents the transmission as a cross-cultural phenomenon. The diaspora serves as its overarching context to bring to the fore the global, transcultural character of the transmission and to underline the urgency to preserve tradition felt among Tibetan Buddhist teachers (Tibetan lamas) which explains their 'missionary spirit'. The Karmapa's role as the transmitter occupies the centre of the 'transcultural space' that geographically encompasses the Indian subcontinent, Europe and North America. Consistency (continuity with tradition) and change (adaptation), both seen as integral parts of the Karmapa's transmission strategies, constitute two main themes. The study draws on a wide range of data from both Tibetan and English language sources, including written accounts, collections of photographs, recordings of interviews and documentaries, dating from 1976 to 2020. They contain historical evidence as well as collective and individual memories from the Karmapa's disciples.

To observe the Karmapa's activity through the lens of cross-cultural interaction, one must first understand the perspectives of both the transmitter and the receiver. For this reason, this part of the book explores the traditional values of the lineage that inform the transmitter's perspective and the Western sociocultural factors that shape the reception of Tibetan Buddhism. Both topics are treated as equally important to allow the complex and dynamic nature of the transmission to be fully recognised. Chapter 1 contextualises the portrayal of the Karmapa within the Tibetan literature of Buddhist life-writing. It explains how the Karmapa is perceived by the Tibetans as well as the reason and meaning behind such perception. Chapter 2 examines two specific phenomena in the West, the idealisation of Tibet and the introduction of other Buddhist traditions. It aims to create a good foundation for understanding the Karmapa's Western disciples and their role as the receiver in the transmission of the Karma Kagyu lineage.

Chapter 1

The Tibetan Perspective

The Karmapa lineage started in the twelfth-century Tibet. It ranks among the most ancient lines of tulkus (*sprul sku*).[1] A tulku lineage is sustained through the process of identification and enthronement of a lama's reincarnation. Such process began to be formalised during the time of the Third Karmapa, Rangjung Dorje (Rang 'byung rdo rje, 1284–1339). His predecessor, Karma Pakshi (1204/1206–1283), came to be known as the reincarnation of the First Karmapa, Düsum Khyenpa (Dus gsum mkhyen pa, 1110–1193), only by virtue of his own recollection at the age of fifty.[2] The death of Düsum Khyenpa (1193) and the birth of Karma Pakshi (1204/1206) are eleven or thirteen years apart; thereafter, the gap between every two subsequent Karmapa incarnations is no more than four years.[3] Rangjung Dorje was the first to receive formal identification as a tulku; official enthronement started with the Seventh Karmapa, Chödrak Gyatso (Chos grags rgya mtsho, 1454–1506).[4] The concepts essential to the formation of the Tibetan tulku system were in constant change throughout history, interwoven with new ideas that developed among different schools.[5] Rangjung Dorje established the authority of the tulku lineage of the Karmapas through the integration of such concepts, including 'lineage' (*brgyud*, *rgyud*), 'manifestation' (*sprul*, *'phrul*), 'rebirth' and 'recognition', into a meaningful edifice.[6] This created 'a symbiotic relationship between the tradition of reincarnation and the institution of the Karmapas'.[7]

The origin of the title 'Karmapa' has its footing in both religious and historical contexts. Popular belief connects the title with the Sanskrit word *karma* and the Tibetan nominalising particle *pa*, and interprets it as 'one who performs the activity of a buddha'. Accordingly, the Kagyu tradition considers the Karmapa to be 'the embodiment of buddha activity'.[8] This interpretation of the title was a key element in the introduction of the Karmapa to the West.[9] Furthermore, Richardson refers to an episode in *A Scholar's Feast of Doctrinal History* (*Chos 'byung mkhas pa'i dga' ston*) to account for the name 'Karmapa'. At the age of sixteen, during his haircutting ceremony, Düsum Khyenpa perceived the assembly of Cakrasaṃvara placing on his head the Black Crown made from the hair of *ḍākinī*s; since he was the embodiment of the activities of all buddhas, they bestowed on him the name 'Karmapa'.[10] Both the crown and the name were essential to maintain continuity in the Karmapa lineage since its early formation.[11]

Ogyen Trinley Dorje cites the same text. He argues that since a monk could hold different Dharma names, given on different occasions, it is possible that 'Karmapa' was but one of many names of Düsum Khyenpa. The name was kept secret because he received it through a spiritual vision. In the lineage of the Karmapas, the secret name of one incarnation usually becomes the name that is publicly known of the next. Since 'Karmapa' was the secret name of Düsum Khyenpa, his successor Karma Pakshi became widely known as the 'Karmapa'.[12] Richardson offers a second explanation: he links the title to Karma Monastery that Düsum Khyenpa founded in 1147.[13] Manson too draws on this link.[14] He even proposes a third interpretation: the man of karma. This derives from a remark that Pomdrakpa (sPom brag pa, 1170–1249) made to Karma Pakshi: 'You are someone with good karmic propensity, aren't you? (*khyod las 'phro yod pa gcig e ma yin*)'.[15] Düsum Khyenpa was one of the primary disciples of Gampopa (sGam po pa, 1079–1153), the lineage holder of the Kagyu school. He himself founded a sub-school, the Karma Kagyu, also known as Kamtsang Kagyu or Karma Kamtsang, and Tsurphu Kagyu.[16] This lineage has continued through seventeen successive Karmapas and their primary disciples up to the present day.

Like most Tibetan Buddhist schools, the Karma Kagyu has an established tradition of Buddhist life-writing. It records the spiritual accomplishment of historical lineage holders and presents an uninterrupted line of transmission from its founder to each subsequent teacher. This type of literature is used as a means to invoke devotion which is crucial to the disciples' spiritual progress; its core function is to produce an exemplary model of spiritual perfection. Historical and spiritual components coexist within one narrative, creating a multi-layered structure of storytelling. To develop an in-depth understanding of the Tibetan narratives of the Sixteenth Karmapa, this chapter presents a survey of life-writing in Tibetan Buddhism; the multilayered narrative structure serves as the framework for discussing the portrayal of the Karmapa in the lineage texts.

1.1. OVERVIEW OF LIFE-WRITING IN TIBETAN BUDDHISM

The most common forms of Buddhist life-writing in Tibet are *namthar* (*rnam thar*) and *rangnam* (*rang rnam*). *Namthar* is the abbreviation of *rnam par thar pa*. It means 'complete liberation', translated from the Sanskrit term *vimokṣa. The Great Tibetan Dictionary (Tshig mdzod chen mo)* gives a standard definition of *namthar*[17] which establishes its principal purpose: to demonstrate the spiritual accomplishment of a revered teacher. The Seventeenth Karmapa, Ogyen Trinley Dorje, points out three primary characteristics of *namthar*: 'the subject must be a great being; the topic must be directly connected to the true dharma; it must be able to instil longing and inspiration in people of all levels'.[18] According to him, *namthar* refers to the life story of a teacher who developed spiritual qualities through listening, contemplation and meditation; it is intended to strengthen the disciples' faith and devotion so that they would aspire to follow the teacher's example.[19]

In Tibetan literature, *namthar* can be traced to the translation of Śāntideva's *A Guide to the Bodhisattva's Way of Life (Bodhisattvacaryāvatāra)*. In its fifth chapter, the text mentions 'The Liberation of *Śrīsambhava*' which refers to Sudhana's encounter with fifty-three teachers in the *Gaṇḍavyūha Sūtra*. There, Sudhana received from each teacher a *vimokṣa*, that is, a method to attain liberation.[20] *Namthar* came to refer to the life stories of renowned lamas during the 'era of fragmentation' (*sil bu'i dus*), that is, the post-imperial time in Tibetan history.[21] The term also appears in the titles of the earliest life stories of Kadampa teachers, including Atiśa (982–1054) and Rinchen Zangpo (Rin chen bzang po, 958–1055), as well as Gampopa's accounts of early Kagyu lineage teachers. Soon after, the four major schools of Tibetan Buddhism began their own *namthar* traditions, mainly in textual form but, in some cases, also in iconographic and oral forms.[22]

The *namthar* literature has a variety of functions: it expresses beliefs, illustrates theories, comments on doctrinal issues, authenticates a teaching, serves as a didactic tool, presents models to be emulated, inspires faith, circumscribes and affirms group identity, or legitimises behaviour and norms.[23] These functions can be understood within the larger context of the composition of Tibetan texts in general which relies on several factors apart from the individual author's intentions. These include intellectual trends, community needs and support, economic and political circumstances, cultural preoccupations, lineage association and personality.[24] In the same way, the functions of *namthar* reflect the shared values and expectations of a community. Such text shapes the identity of the community and serves its changing needs of collectivity.[25] Moreover, a teacher's *namthar* may differ in content and style as the religious, sociocultural and political conditions change over time. Take the 'Mila *namthar*' tradition for example. It started with sketches of Milarepa's (Mi la ras pa, 1052–1135) life in Gampopa's account and developed into a sophisticated drama in Tsangnyön Heruka's (gTsang smyon Heruka, 1452–1507) work nearly four centuries after the yogin's death. The portrayal of the yogin varies due to each author's own agenda within the specific historical context.[26]

Another type of Tibetan life narrative is *rangnam* (*rang rnam*). The name literally means one's own liberation. It refers to a teacher's own account of his/her spiritual achievements or 'spiritual memoir',[27] autobiography in other words. The tradition of *rangnam* began in the eleventh century. It proliferated since the sixteenth century and developed on a larger scale in the nineteenth and twentieth centuries,[28] even though in the majority of Buddhist countries, sacred autobiography does not exist because of the commonly held Buddhist idea of non-self.[29] Gyatso identifies over 100 book-length *rangnam* texts, many of which are over 200 pages long.[30] She makes a possible link between Tibet's prolific *rangnam* literature and its Tantric tradition.[31] *Rangnam* aims to demonstrate the teacher's own spiritual progress, to contextualise and legitimate his/her works, or to attract students and patrons.[32] Unlike *namthar* which may involve several authors writing about the same teacher, each at a different time and with a different agenda, *rangnam* is simply a teacher's own account. However, its production may still be a complex process. For example, the Fifth Dalai Lama's (Ngawang Lobsang Gyatso, 1617–1682) *rangnam* is comprised of nine different types of materials and stages of composition.[33] The diversity of sources, elaborate procedures and participation of experts signify the mature stage of the development of *rangnam* at that time.

To understand *namthar* and *rangnam*, two issues need to be addressed. First is the tendency to compare this genre to the European sacred auto/biography or hagiography. On the one hand, Tibetan *namthar* and *rangnam* do share certain features with European sacred auto/biography or hagiography: the topic is the life of a religious teacher; the purpose is to inspire devotion and provide a model for the disciples' spiritual path.[34] On the other, they vary significantly in both style and content; they may even belong to other European literary genres.[35] Roesler suggests 'life story' and 'life-writing' as more neutral designations; she also views *namthar* as 'a Tibetan form of novel writing'.[36] Moreover, *namthar*, albeit the most commonly known, is not the only form of life-writing in the Tibetan Buddhist tradition. Schaeffer has conducted a survey on *namthar* in TBRC[37] database and identified 1,225 texts produced between the twelfth and twentieth centuries.[38] However, one can also find a teacher's life story in other literary forms. These include diaries, travelogues (*lam yig*), songs (*mgur*), devotional prayers (*gsol 'debs*), invocations (*smon lam*), historical treatises (*chos 'byung*), story about former lives (*sku 'phreng* or *'khrungs rabs*), 'the succession to an abbatial seat' (*gdan rabs*), eulogies (*bstod pa*),[39] doctrinal works, poems,[40] Tantric instructions for empowerment rituals,[41] letters and catalogues.[42] Therefore, static typology does not apply to Tibetan life-writing; each text is subject to its unique historical conditions.[43] Ascribing it to 'biography' or 'autobiography' without considering its original context may cause one to overlook its essential features.[44]

The divide between autobiographies, biographies and hagiographies is also problematic.[45] Gyatso and Roesler have both observed the blurring of the boundaries between *namthar* and *rangnam*. In the oral tradition, a Tibetan lama recounts to the disciples his/her life story which the disciples then use as part of their own compositions of the teacher's *namthar*.[46] Moreover, Kalu Rinpoche (1905–1989) of the Kagyu school composed a *namthar* prayer (*rnam thar gsol 'debs*) in which he refers to himself in the second person so that his disciples would be able to pray to him when reciting it.[47] In these cases, a *rangnam* comes in the form of *namthar*. In addition, some disciples may also present the life story of the teacher in the first person, in which case, the text becomes a *rangnam*.[48] The Fifth Dalai Lama's use of his *namthar* in the production of his *rangnam* serves as another example.[49]

The second issue is the assumed division between fact and fiction which arose during the early application of historical methodology. Vostrikov describes some *namthar* texts as 'full of legends and are interesting not from the historical but only or almost only from the folkloristic and literary standpoint'.[50] He considers these 'legends' as a shortcoming; to him, only the texts that contain 'basically important and fully authentic historical monuments' are 'real biographies'.[51] His notion of biography is under the influence of the historical-critical methodology that aims to 'filter' historical facts from a text. This renders the spiritual purpose of *namthar* irrelevant. Such approach posits a clear-cut boundary between what is real/factual and what is imagined/fictional.

Scholars have long dismissed the exclusive use of such method;[52] some critique it for its bias towards historical facts.[53] Roesler offers a more nuanced perspective for the study of biography and history positioning both within a broad spectrum between fact and fiction.[54] This points to the need for a more contextualised approach that takes note of the dynamics of each text. Conermann and Rheingans argue that the dualism of fact and fiction is in itself culturally relative.[55] Robinson expresses a similar view in his study of the life stories of the eighty-four Indian *mahāsiddha*s. He questions the use of 'rationality of common sense' as a way to discern whether a miraculous event is factual or not. He believes that the so-called rationality is 'the accustomed and familiar', 'a cultural postulate and an assumption'.[56] Furthermore, reality, in the ideal sense of the term, is extremely hard to capture.[57] In any given text, the author always has to make choices of what to write and how despite his/her intention to present what is factual. By examining these choices, one can identify the author's specific strategies and techniques[58] which, in turn, reflect his/her sociocultural, political and religious background. The 'fact or fiction' approach causes one to lose sight of this underlining connection between a text and its wider context.

Schaeffer suggests 'a wide-angle point of view' for the study of Tibetan life-writing.[59] He identifies four sets of perspectives with regard to a given text in a layered structure ranging from the content of the text itself to the broader historical context.[60] Roesler explores the context of a text through three basic narrative patterns[61] that reveal the correlation between an individual life story and the author's narrative strategies embedded in a wider religious context. Particularly, she cautions against the tendency to classify the stories of a teacher's former lives as fiction in literary criticism, for the reason that the Buddhist readership does not make such distinction and considers them just as real.[62] That is to say, one should not ignore the intended readers, but see them as an integral part of the specific context of the text. In addition, Roesler points out that the scholars themselves are not completely detached observers, but rather participants in the biographical process.[63]

A *namthar* or *rangnam* text does not necessarily contain one single perspective of truth or reality. Several truths and realities can coexist in the life story of one and the same person. Among them, historical truth is only one type out of several. This is evident in the basic textual structure that contains three layers of narrative, each corresponding to a different perspective. The outer (*phyi*) provides a chronological account of the teacher's life, the inner (*nang*) focuses on his/her spiritual transmission and accomplishment, and the secret (*sang*) reveals his/her prophetic dreams and spiritual visions.[64] Many texts incorporate more than one layer.[65] Hence, one may find tension between the different perspectives about a teacher's life within the same narrative.

The method that Robinson proposes in his study of Indian *mahāsiddha*s offers a possible solution to resolve this tension. He suggests a three-dimensional system: the historical, hagiographical and mythological. The first is concerned with the historical narrative. The last two deal with the mystical aspect of the *mahāsiddha*s.[66] The hagiographical dimension builds a bridge between history and symbolic literature. The mythological dimension has two features. On the one hand, the saint 'humanises' the supernatural/mystical; he/she demonstrates to ordinary people what it means to be enlightened and how. It creates a living example for disciples to follow on their spiritual path. On the other hand, the saint maintains the continuity of spiritual transmission and legitimates the purity of a lineage.[67] Here, the historical perspective remains valuable. It provides the historical context for the life of the teacher. The mystical aspect is equally non-dismissible. It demonstrates the spiritual qualities of the teacher, and hence fulfils the religious purpose of the text. This approach harmonises the different types of reality within one narrative and offers flexibility in understanding and interpreting the teacher's life through different levels of perception.

Based on this method, I shall now analyse the portrayal of the teacher in Tibetan life-writing from two aspects: (1) the spiritual qualities that relate to the hagiographical and mythological dimensions; (2) the interplay between spirituality and history which involves also the historical dimension.

1.2. SPIRITUAL QUALITIES OF THE TEACHER

The portrayal of the teacher as an ideal serves to invoke devotion. In Tibetan Buddhism, especially its Tantric tradition, the role of the teacher in the disciple's spiritual progress is of vital importance; thus, devotion to the teacher and his/her lineage holds special significance to the disciple.[68] Through devotion, the disciple's commitment to the teacher and lineage strengthens. Then, the transmission of the lineage teachings dependent on the deep personal connection[69] between teacher and disciple is possible to take place. Devotion to lineage teachers becomes crucial to the success of the disciple's training. It is the first step in the spiritual path[70] and one of the 'three entry-ways' for all disciples of the Vajrayāna.[71]

In the Kagyu school, the practice of devotion is an essential part of the training process that prepares the disciple to accomplish the highest practice—Mahāmudrā.[72] Since *namthar* serves as a means to engender devotion, it plays a fundamental role in the spiritual path of the disciples. By hearing or reading the teacher's *namthar*, the disciple develops faith. At that point, 'the seed of liberation' is planted in their mind; he/she aspires to develop the same spiritual qualities as the teacher.[73] The life stories of lineage teachers shape their understanding of the principal value of the lineage; the bestowal of the reading transmission of a *namthar* text is seen as the preliminary step of their practice.[74] For example, the Lineage Wish-Fulfilling Gem (*brGyud pa yid bzhin nor bu*) constitutes the first cycle of the Aural Transmission of Saṃvara (*bDe mchog snyan brgyud*) in the early Kagyu school. This cycle aims to establish the characteristics of teacher and disciple or to introduce the *namthar* of lineage teachers; it legitimates the authenticity of the lineage, whereby guarantees the effectiveness of the teachings.[75] The fact that *namthar* forms part of key lineage texts shows the high status it holds in the tradition.

As the Kagyu school continued to grow over time, the *namthar* collection of lineage teachers, named as 'Golden Rosaries' (*gser 'phreng*), developed further. In a 'Golden Rosaries' collection, one can trace an uninterrupted line of transmission within the context of the teacher-disciple relationship. It begins with the founder and passes on to each lineage holder who, by virtue of the lineage teachings, achieved 'complete liberation'. Such collection of writing aims to help disciples generate devotion, to confirm the legitimacy of lineage teachings and also to reflect historical preoccupations.[76]

With the purpose of invoking devotion, *namthar* is meant to create an exemplary model for others to emulate. In general, there are three types of role models in Buddhism that capture the ideal image of the teacher: the *arhat* in Theravāda Buddhism, the *bodhisattva* in the Mahāyāna and the *mahāsiddha* in the Vajrayāna.[77] In his study of the Eighth Karmapa, Mikyö Dorje (Mi bskyod rdo rje, 1507–1554), Rheingans notes that tradition holds the Karmapa to be an embodiment of all these three ideals and presents him as an accomplished scholar and realised meditator (*mkhas sgrub*).[78] The most influential of the three models is the bodhisattva. Here, the common purpose of great teachers is to bring all sentient beings to enlightenment. Their activities which correspond to the deeds of buddhas or bodhisattvas express the perfect union of wisdom and compassion. Yet, ordinary people are unable to understand this. Therefore, many *namthar* texts compare the life story of the teacher to a mere drop from the ocean of his/her enlightened activity. The teacher is not only a historical figure but also an emanation of a buddha or bodhisattva.[79] Disciples view the *namthar* of their teacher, often produced after his/her death, as sacred relics with the power to liberate those who see, hear, remember or touch it.[80] Accordingly, one should not expect the life story of a teacher to merely display historical facts but understand the significance of its hagiographical/mythological dimensions.

Like *namthar*, the function of *rangnam* is also to demonstrate an exemplary life to the disciples. Gyatso considers the motive to present oneself as a role model as the key reason for a teacher to write *rangnam*; narration of one's own life is only meaningful insofar as it provides a good example for the disciples to follow.[81] However, such motive manifests differently in three principal modes of self-representation: the self-deprecating, the straightforward and the self-glorifying.[82] One may not immediately recognise which mode a *rangnam* text employs, because the Tibetan literary convention calls for an apologetic introduction to show humility.[83] It is only after the opening lines that the real style of the text unfolds.

Among the three modes, self-glorification is the most robust model to create an ideal image of the teacher. It promotes the teacher's spiritual qualities, often comparing him/her as equal to the Buddha. The author positions his/her own life as an object of reverence for the disciples. Kalu Rinpoche's *namthar* prayer mentioned earlier belongs to this type. Speaking in the second person, he praises himself as a highly realised teacher who benefits many. In its commentary, Kalu tells that any connection with him will become the seed of higher rebirth and liberation.[84] In this way, the author teaches his disciples the specific way to perceive him that helps them make spiritual progress. Understanding the spiritual qualities of the teacher becomes a necessary training method for devotion. This brings the hagiographical and mythological dimensions of the teacher's life to the foreground.

The other two modes of self-representation are less significant to the creation of the ideal image of the teacher. Yet, they contain certain features that are worth mentioning to achieve a more nuanced understanding. In the self-deprecation mode, the teacher shows reluctance to tell anything about his/her life and only agrees to do so after repeated pleas from the disciples who insist it will benefit future generations. Many Tertöns (*gter ston*) adopt this style in their *rangnam* texts. They openly express doubts about the legitimacy of their own visions which they refer to as 'deluded appearance' (*'khrul snang*).[85] However, one should not take the author's words at face value. The intention to benefit disciples is still there, even though projected through the lens of humility.

In the straightforward mode, a teacher discusses his/her life matter-of-factly. The historical dimension is at the centre of the narrative. This renders the text historically valuable.[86] Such approach is favoured by some Tibetans, including Gyalwa Yungtönpa, Drukpa Kunley and Je Barawa. To them, *rangnam* has a special advantage over *namthar*. When writing the *namthar* of their teacher, disciples tend to fixate on praises, exaggerating, sometimes even fabricating, the teacher's spiritual qualities. This causes the life story of the teacher to be untruthful; the reader may dismiss the teacher as a charlatan and develop a feeling of contempt instead. The teacher's own account, *rangnam*, in contrast, paints a more complete and accurate picture of his/her life.[87] For example, in his *rangnam*, the Eighth Karmapa presents himself as 'an ordinary person, an ordinary monk' who 'worked hard to make his life be in harmony with the dharma'.[88] The Fifth Dalai Lama also applies this mode to his *rangnam* collection. He declares: 'there is no sin in telling with a straight story how this drama of body, speech, and mind transpired with its happiness, suffering, and in between'.[89] Still, he does not completely shun self-deprecation. When introducing his own spiritual visions, he practises self-critique and discourages scholars from even reading them.[90] He shows reluctance to make public the inner (*nang*) and secret (*sang*) layers of his *rangnam* and seeks to avoid promoting a mystical image of himself. Roesler describes his style as a representation of the 'historically minded, scholarly forms of life-writing'.[91]

A standard *namthar* begins with the teacher's previous lives and prophecies from various sources.[92] The teacher is portrayed as the reincarnation of renowned Indian/Tibetan scholars/*siddha*s in history; his/her efforts to benefit others span many lifetimes. The link between the present and past lives in *namthar* sheds light on the particular emphasis on tradition in Tibetan Buddhism. Tradition ensures continuity and consistency, which stresses the importance of the 'unbroken lineage'. All Tibetan Buddhist schools trace their origin to India in order to establish their own authenticity.[93] They hold Indian gurus in the highest esteem; their own role, in comparison, is to merely transmit lineage teachings.[94] This is attested in *The Lives of the Eighty-Four Siddhas*. The text serves as a key link between Tibetan and Indian Buddhism. The life stories of Indian *mahāsiddha*s legitimise the authority of a Tibetan

Buddhist lineage. The belief that a Tibetan lama is a reincarnation of past Indian masters adds to this process.

The stories of a teacher's former lives in *namthar* and *rangnam* help shape the mystical image of the teacher. The paradigm of these stories originated from the *jātaka*s in Indian Buddhism. They convey the doctrinal message of karma and illustrate the qualities of a bodhisattva that lead to enlightenment.[95] Appleton uses the *Jātakatthavaṇṇanā*, the semi-canonical *jātaka* collection, to chart the historical development of this genre. The Pāli *jātaka* was originally associated with the Buddha and his ability to recount the stories of past lives to his audiences. The overall rationale is that *jātaka* tales "'illuminate the unimaginable magnificence of the deeds of a Great Man" who "brought to fruition over a long time the endless condition for *bodhi*'".[96] Nonetheless, the earliest *jātaka*s preserved in *sutta*s, as well as the *Jātakatthavaṇṇanā*, characterise the Bodhisatta in different ways. Some present him as an exemplar of good conduct, while others reveal his immoral behaviour or place him in a rather insignificant role in the narrative.[97]

Later, the Bodhisatta's path to buddhahood through the practice of perfections came to the fore as the *bodhisatta* ideal emerged in the Theravāda tradition in the *Apadāna*, *Buddhavaṃsa* and *Cariyāpiṭaka*.[98] Then, *jātaka*s became a form of Bodhisatta- and Buddha-biography with didactic functions.[99] They provide examples to the Buddhists, demonstrate the Bodhisatta's perfections and lead to a variety of practices, such as the artistic display of *jātaka*s at *stūpa* sites and temples or the inclusion of *jātaka*s in *paritta* collections, manuscripts and inauguration ceremonies of Buddha images.[100] They not only highlight the magnificence of the Buddha and his path to enlightenment but also become objects of worship, equivalent to the Buddha himself.[101]

The *Cariyāpiṭaka*, *Apadāna* and *Jātaka-Nidāna* contain stories of the Buddha's recollection of his previous lives. They all claim that the Buddha's deeds in his past lives contribute to his realisation of a particular perfection.[102] Descriptions of these deeds are rich, beautiful and heroic; they portray an inspiring and commendable personage for the path to buddhahood.[103] They also contain narrative elements that express morally equivocal behaviour, personal deliberation and debate. The Bodhisatta had been born as an animal, king, outcast, sailor, and so on. In these different lives, he sometimes possessed nobility, wisdom and kindness, but at other times, also encountered ethical dilemmas and personal spiritual conflict.[104] Hence, these tales tend to be more captivating than the classical life story of the Buddha. They aim to demonstrate the long path of the Bodhisatta replete with all kinds of challenges, thereby constructing a much more diverse character than the one portrayed in the story of his final life.[105] In a sense, these narratives depict a more complete picture of the journey to enlightenment. In addition, the *jātaka*s hold soteriological value. The standard formulae at the end of the texts report that after hearing these tales, many attained various stages of the path, even enlightenment.[106]

Later on, *jātaka*s appeared in Sanskrit texts, most notably the *Jātakamālā* ascribed to Āryaśūra. The focus here is on the practice of the 'six perfections' (*pāramitā*) of a bodhisattva.[107] The title *Jātakamālā* literally means garlands of birth-stories. Similar to their Pāli counterparts, they serve as religious discourse, either to glorify the Buddha or to illustrate the Buddhist doctrines and precepts.[108] Nearly all thirty-four stories in this text have parallels in other collections, in Pāli and Sanskrit alike. The author took great care to conform to tradition.[109] Nonetheless, the narratives are more sophisticated than the Pāli version, in both style and language, filled with lofty conception and artistic elaboration.[110] The epilogue of each story contains elements of moral maxim embedded within the account of the Bodhisattva's miraculous deeds. It is unclear whether the author added these elements himself or someone else did this at a later time. In any case, the purpose of edification is clear.[111]

These Indian *jātaka*s became a prototype for the Buddhist life-writing in Tibet. Many were included in the *Mūlasarvāstivādavinaya* brought from India to Tibet to govern its monastic community. Tibetans also translated Āryaśūra's and Kṣemendra's compositions of *jātaka*s and added them to the Tibetan Buddhist canon.[112] Through these sources, they grew familiar with the genre of *jātaka*s. As the institution of reincarnate lamas came to be established in the thirteenth and fourteenth centuries, the Kadam and Kagyu schools began to compose and compile stories of their own teachers that resemble the *jātaka*s. In due course, rebirth stories came to be a common feature in Tibetan life-writing.[113] A genre, called 'histories of incarnations' (*'khrungs rabs*), describes, in sequence, the former lives of a teacher. Rebirth stories constituted 'the ideological background for the development of an incarnate hierarchy in Tibet'.[114] In *rangnam* literature, authors who intend to create a glorified self-image[115] often begin with narratives of their former lives. This, to some extent, gives them their own sense of identity.[116] The Fifth Dalai Lama criticised this strategy. To him, stories of one's own previous incarnations are conceited tales; writing about them would lead one to break his/her vows.[117] His disapproval suggests that the influence of rebirth stories in *rangnam* had become prevalent by the seventeenth century.[118]

1.3. INTERPLAY BETWEEN THE SPIRITUAL AND THE HISTORICAL

To the disciples, the teacher's life story represents spiritual perfection. Unsurprisingly, possession of auspicious marks and abilities to perform miracles, to give prophecies and to experience revelatory visions are routine narrative elements in both *namthar* and *rangnam*. Any weakness of the teacher, such as a short lifespan or illness, is interpreted to be the result of feeble merit or negative karma of the people in this world.[119] The archetype of the teacher in the 'Golden Rosaries' (*gser 'phreng*) of the Kagyu school is Vajradhāra. He is the Tantric representation of enlightenment and is believed to be the origin of the school. All subsequent human Kagyu teachers are emanations of Vajradhāra.[120] This establishes the authenticity of the lineage teachings as well as the authority of the teachers. Meanwhile, the worldly aspect of the teacher's life anchors him/her as a historical figure. The spiritual image of the teacher often coexists with the historical portrayal in a single narrative. The interplay between the two completes the life story. This multilayered pattern is not uniquely Tibetan; it goes back to Indian Buddhism. I shall, in the following paragraphs, give a brief sketch of its development in Theravāda Buddhism, the Mahāyāna and the Vajrayāna (Tantric Buddhism).

The Pāli canon sometimes describes the Buddha as a charismatic teacher endowed with miraculous signs and powers. At other times, it portrays him as an ordinary person.[121] Shaw gives several examples that are worth mentioning here: in DN II (142–178), the Buddha possesses the thirty-two marks and the voice of Brahma; he shines like the lord of devas—Sakka; in Paṭis I (125–126) and Ja IV (263–267), he performs miracles. Meanwhile, in the *Sāmaññaphala Sutta* (DN I 50), the Buddha appears so normal that others describe him to King Ajātasattu as merely one sitting by a pillar; in the *Dhātuvibhaṅga Sutta* (MN III 238–247), a monk who shares lodging with the Buddha mistakes him for an ordinary bhikkhu.[122] Shaw argues that these varied portrayals do not contradict each other. The Buddha simply chooses to manifest differently depending on each specific occasion. This understanding not only resolves the tension between the spiritual and the worldly aspect of the Buddha. It also indicates his ability to present himself in accordance with different situations.

The Mahāyāna sūtras speak of this ability as skilful means.[123] Both *Lokānuvartanā* and *Upāyakauśalya* tell that the Buddha, though already enlightened, lives a human life in this world for the benefit of ordinary beings. At birth, the Buddha declared that he was the greatest in the world; yet, as a young adult, he encountered scenes of old age, illness and death, which led to his decision to renunciate worldly life and enter the spiritual path. These two episodes are seemingly in tension with each other. The *Lokānuvartanā Sūtra* describes this tension as the Buddha's 'conformity with the world'.[124] The *Upāyakauśalya Sūtra* considers the Buddha's statement at birth to be a method to tame the pride of the gods who were present at the time; his encounter with the scenes of suffering later in life is intended to help ordinary beings.[125]

The *Lokānuvartanā* also speaks of the Buddha's *dharmakāya*, *saṃbhogakāya* and *nirmāṇakāya*. The *nirmāṇakāya*, especially the emanations of enlightened beings in a human form, shapes the idea that a guru is an emanation. The idea that the Buddha can produce multiple manifestations to help sentient beings, together with the notion of 'skilful means', serves as the theoretical basis for the multilayered teacher portrayal in *namthar* and *rangnam* texts. To the Tibetans, a realised teacher is an embodiment of a buddha or an advanced bodhisattva. He/she chooses to be born in Tibet to guide beings of a particular time and place; his/her human life is a compassionate display of conduct that the disciples should make efforts to emulate on their spiritual path.[126]

In Tantric Buddhism, there are life stories of Indian *mahāsiddha*s who, though ordinary people, became enlightened in one lifetime. The *siddha* tradition came into being in Medieval India.[127] The *siddha*s were often of diverse social backgrounds, especially of low caste. Their life stories convey the same message: those at the periphery of society can achieve liberation. *The Lives of the Eighty-Four Siddhas* included a shoemaker (Camaripa), a bird-catcher (Gorura), a gambler (Tandhepa), and so on. They all, in their lifetime, accomplished Mahāmudrā, the highest attainment of meditation leading directly to enlightenment. Such rapid progression testifies to the supremacy of the Tantric path. As Tantric Buddhism took hold in Tibet, the narrative features of the *siddha* literature developed a notable impact on the life stories of Tibetan lamas.

The 'Mila *namthar*' tradition[128] best represents the influence of Indian Buddhism on the portrayal of the teacher in Tibetan life-writing. As the Kagyu lineage developed over time, the portrayal of Milarepa became increasingly dynamic and complex. This is because the agenda of each *namthar* author differs due to the specific religious, sociocultural environment of his time. One key feature is the tension between the image of Milarepa as an emanation and the narrative that portrays him as an ordinary human. The former relates to the hagiographical and mythological dimensions of his life, intended to legitimise the unbroken lineage. Devotional content is evident. Many accounts identify the yogin with the Buddha. Some consider him to be an emanation of Nāgārjunagarbha[129] or Mañjuśrīmitra.[130] Particularly, the miraculous events around the yogin's death portray him as a buddha in his own right. These all correspond to the supramundane aspect of the Buddha in the Mahāyāna doctrine.

Most *namthar* texts also portray Milarepa as an ordinary person. The historical dimension dominates the narrative prior to the yogin's enlightenment. The early *namthar* authors, including Gampopa and Dönmo Ripa (Don mo ri pa), talk openly about Milarepa's shortcomings. Dorje Dze Ö (rDo rje mdzes 'od) offers more detail on the yogin's early life. In Gyalthangpa's (rGyal thang pa) work, the themes of revenge and purification become manifest. The Twelve Great Disciples (Bu chen bcu gnyis) accentuates the yogin's experience of tragedy in his early life and the hardships that Marpa put him through during his training. Both elements are further dramatised in Tsangnyön Heruka's (gTsang smyon Heruka) account. The author conveys a clear message: Milarepa was an ordinary person who managed to achieve buddhahood in one lifetime. Even the yogin himself is said to criticise the idea that he is an emanation and considers his own life as proof of the efficacy of the Dharma.[131] Such portrayal is not very different from the life stories of Indian *mahāsiddha*s where even the most flawed people can reach enlightenment in one life.

1.4. PORTRAYAL OF THE KARMAPA

The *namthar* tradition of the Karmapas can be traced to Tibetan chronicles, including *The Red Annals* (*Deb ther dmar po*), *The Blue Annals* (*Deb ther sngon po*)[132] and *A Scholar's Feast of Doctrinal History*.[133] The Second Shamar Khachö Wangpo (Zhwa dmar mKha' spyod dbang po, 1350–1405) compiled the life stories of the Karmapas as part of a *namthar* collection of the Kagyu school.[134] Based on this text, the Eighth Situ Chökyi Jungne (Si tu Chos kyi 'byung gnas, 1699/1700–1774) and his disciple, Tsewang Kunkyab (Tshe dbang kun khyab, 1718–1790), co-authored the *namthar* of the first seven Karmapa incarnations in elaborate detail.[135] More recently, Rinchen Palsang (Rin chen dpal bzang) compiled the *namthar* of the seventeen Karmapas in *A Completely Clear Mirror, the Catalogue of Tsurphu*.[136] Thrangu (Khra 'gu) Rinpoche published the longest *namthar* collection of the Karmapa incarnations to date,[137] encompassing the lives of all sixteen Karmapas. This contains Karma Ngedön Tengye's (Karma nges don bstan rgyas)[138] account of the fourteen Karmapas, Palpung Khyentse Özer's (dPal spungs mKhyen brtse 'od zer)[139] account of the Fifteenth Karmapa and Thrangu's own account of the Sixteenth Karmapa. My analysis here draws mainly on Thrangu's compilation.

Karma Ngedön Tengye's account of the fourteen Karmapa incarnations conveys a core message: the Karmapa has already attained enlightenment; the purpose of his human life is to help others. On one level, the Karmapa is both a buddha and a bodhisattva. He is able to produce countless manifestations to benefit beings. His wisdom reaches beyond the understanding of ordinary people. His life story is as vast as an ocean, of which Karma Ngedön Tengye is able to describe only a fraction. Even bodhisattvas are unable to fully understand the inner (*nang*) and secret (*gsang*) aspects of his life.[140] This very idea appears also in Khyentse Özer's account of the Fifteenth Karmapa.[141] The *namthar* of the Sixteenth Karmapa often deploys the word 'inconceivable' (*bsam gyis mi khyab pa*) to describe his attributes. For instance, Thrangu describes him as the unique manifestation of the inconceivable wisdom (*bsam mi khyab pa'i ye shes gcig gi 'phrul*) transforming whomever he trains in an inconceivable way, like a miraculous play (*gang 'dul sprul pa'i zlos gar bsam gyis mi khyab pa'i tshul du bsgyur*).[142] Near the end of his account, Thrangu reveals that he only wrote down the outer (*phyi*) *namthar*, because: 'If the greater qualities of the extraordinary form [of the Karmapa] were read out loud, apart from [what is] widely known [about him] in the perception of ordinary [people, he] would not be very pleased.'[143] Tashi Tsering states that since the outer qualities of the Karmapa are vast, he can only capture a tiny account; his inner and secret life stories are difficult for even the noble ones to understand.[144]

On another level, the Karmapa lives a human life; his presence on earth is held to be extraordinary. Karma Ngedön Tengye explains that the Karmapa is willingly reborn in samsara, and yet remains without taint.[145] The Karmapa[146] corroborates this attribution: he is not reborn in this world without purpose; due to the virtue he accumulated in the past, he benefits others in an indescribable way.[147] The Karmapa's birth is intentional. This contrasts with ordinary beings' lack of control over their future destinies; it reflects his spiritual achievement and commitment to helping others. Even though the Karmapa's life story identifies his teachers and says that he studied, took vows and nurtured good qualities, such conduct is a display of his skilful means (*thabs mkhas*) for the sake of his disciples.[148] Karma Ngedön Tengye quotes from the Karmapa's[149] own words when he says that the miraculous aspect of his life only constitutes what humans are able to perceive of his existence; his activity for the purpose of liberating the beings without form remains unknown.[150]

The Karmapa's life is best viewed through layered perspectives. Karma Ngedön Tengye argues that the Karmapa's human life manifests on a level of Expedient Meaning (*drang pa'i don*). At the level of Definitive Meaning (*nges pa'i don*), he realised already the enlightened body, speech and mind of a buddha many aeons ago. His enlightened activity is effortless and beyond conception, arising spontaneously in all places and at all times.[151] The Expedient Meaning is connected to ordinary perception, whereas the Definitive Meaning points to an enlightened state. Since the Karmapa is believed to be a real buddha with the highest accomplishment, he is beyond change or transition. Nonetheless, in the perception of ordinary people, he still appears to be reborn, grow old and die.[152] Karma Ngedön Tengye compares the worldly life of the Karmapa to the life of the Buddha unfolding through his Twelve Deeds.[153] The proposition that the Karmapa is a buddha/bodhisattva does not contradict his human aspect; they constitute two different perspectives of his life. The paired concepts of expedient/definitive meaning provide a useful lens to observe the multilayered portrayal of the Karmapa.

Although the Karmapa is considered to be a buddha/bodhisattva, his life unfolds within the perception of ordinary disciples. The way he is perceived reflects the disciples' own state of mind. Karma Ngedön Tengye quotes the Kagyu forefathers:

> The lama is the mirror of [your] own mind
> Observe whether [his] bodily form changes or not
> As long as [it changes] between life and death
> Still purify [your] own mind in devotion.[154]

Here, the perception of the teacher serves as a benchmark that measures the disciple's training of mind. Devotion becomes a means to purify one's own mind through the production of pure perception about the teacher. Karma Ngedön Tengye explains further:

> The disciple's devotion [is like] a profound mantra of a wrathful deity that summons the lama's mind. Then, [the disciple's] own mind is no longer obscured [and becomes] inseparable from dharmakāya. [At that point,] it is sufficient to rely on [the instruction] that there is no need to look for the lama elsewhere rather than one's own mind. Thus, [the mind of the disciple] is inseparable from the lama. That moment is called the mind of the lama and the mind of the disciple merge together. [The disciple] has obtained the [spiritual] state of the perfect lama.[155]

Devotion to the teacher is an effective method that allows the disciple to see, and to experience, that his/her own nature of mind is no different from that of the teacher. Above all, *namthar* serves to inspire devotion in disciples. Especially in the Kagyu school, the practice of devotion forms an integral part of the disciples' training. In that sense, the Karmapa's life reaches beyond the historical context. Its spiritual aspect inspires devotion which is closely connected to the disciple's inner development instead of the external world. While the historical perspective is a necessary part of the Karmapa's *namthar*, it is the spiritual component that fulfils the seminal purpose.

NOTES

1. Several Tibetan accounts consider the Karmapa lineage to be *the most* ancient tulku lineage: Khra 'gu rin po che, *rgyal ba'i dbang po dpal karma pa sku 'phreng bcu drug pa tshun rim par byon pa'i rnam thar phyogs bsgrigs* (Varanasi: Vajra Vidya Institute Library, 2008), 326.10–326.11; bKra shis tshe ring, "'jig rten dbang phyug mthing mdog cod paN 'chang ba bcu drug pa chen po'i phyi yi rnam thar rgya mtsho ltar tshad med pa las chu thigs tsam gyi sa bon bzhugs so," *Bulletin of Tibetology: Karmapa Commemoration Volume*, no. 1 (1982): 25.2–25.5; Shes bya, "bzod par

dka' ba'i ches yid gdung gi gnas tshul," in *rgyal dbang karma pa bcu drug pa chen po'i gsung 'bum 1*, ed. Jo sras bkra shis tshe ring (Dharamsala: Tshurphu Labrang; The Amnye Machen Institute, 2016), 227.9–227.10; 'Ju chen thub bstan rnam rgyal, "rgyal dbang karma pa sku phreng 16 pa rang byung rig pa'i rdo rje mchog dgongs pa chos dbyings su thim pa'i tshul bstan pa," in *'Ju chen thub bstan gyi sku tshe'i lo rgyus* (9) (Chauntra: Juchentsang, 2014), 321.13–321.14.

Such belief has been disputed elsewhere:

Richardson reports, though without reference, that the Drikung Kagyu lineage has challenged this claim. See Hugh Richardson, "The Karmapa Sect. A Historical Note," in *High Peaks, Pure Earth: Collected writings on Tibetan history and culture*, ed. Michael Aris (London: Serindia, 1998), 337.

Gamble argues that the Third Karmapa Rangjung Dorje himself drew on several precedents to show that the lineage of the Karmapa incarnations was no invention. See Gamble, "View from Nowhere," 90.

Further evidence includes claims of memories of former lives and identification of reincarnations that already existed before the Karmapa lineage. See Leonard W. J. van der Kuijp, "The Dalai Lamas and the Origins of Reincarnate Lamas," in *The Dalai Lamas: A visual history*, ed. Martin Brauen (Chicago: Serindia Publications, 2005), quoted in Ruth E Gamble, "The View from Nowhere: The travels of the Third Karmapa, Rang byung rdo rje in story and songs" (PhD diss., The Australian National University, 2013), 90; Daniel A Hirshberg, "Karmic Foreshadowing on the Path of Fruition: Narrative devices in the biographies of Nyang ral nyi ma 'od zer," *Bulletin of Tibetology* 45, no. 1 (2009), quoted in Ruth E Gamble, "The View from Nowhere: The travels of the Third Karmapa, Rang byung rdo rje in story and songs" (PhD diss., The Australian National University, 2013), 90; Daniel A Hirshberg, "Delivering the Lotus-Born: Historiography in the Tibetan renaissance" (PhD diss., Harvard University, 2012), quoted in Ruth E Gamble, "The View from Nowhere: The travels of the Third Karmapa, Rang byung rdo rje in story and songs" (PhD diss., The Australian National University, 2013), 90.

2. Ngawang Zangpo, Introduction to *Enthronement: The recognition of the reincarnate masters of Tibet and the Himalayas*, trans. Ngawang Zangpo (New York: Snow Lion Publications, 1997), 17.

3. Charles E Manson, "Introduction to the Life of Karma Pakshi (1204/6–1283)," *Bulletin of Tibetology* 45, no. 1 (2009): 31.

4. Ngawang Zangpo, Introduction, 18–19.

5. Gamble, "View from Nowhere," 89–115.

6. Gamble, "View from Nowhere," 89–115.

7. Gamble, "View from Nowhere," 90.

8. *The Lion's Roar: The Classic Portrait of the 16th Gyalwa Karmapa*, DVD, directed by Mark Elliott (USA: Festival Media, 2006).

9. For example, by Jamgon Kongtrul in a television interview in the United States in 1976: Interview with the Sixteenth Karmapa and Jamgon Kongtrul on the American television programme "Vermont Report" (December 1976), in *Recalling a Buddha. Memories of the Sixteenth Karmapa: The life and death of an awakened being*, DVD, directed by Gregg Eller Nydahl (USA: Tendrel Media, 2009).

10. gTsug lag 'phreng ba, "sgrub rgyud karma kam tshang gi chos byung rgyas pa (pa)," in *chos 'byung mkhas pa'i dga' ston*, TBRC W28792. 2 (Delhi: Delhi karmapae chodey gyalwae sungrab partun khang, 1980), 3.3–3.5. See Richardson, "The Karmapa Sect."

Detail varies in other accounts. Some report that it was the *ḍākinīs* who presented the crown to Düsum Khyenpa: bKra shis tshe ring, "'jig rten dbang phyug," 48; 噶玛善莲, and噶玛宝阳, "黑宝冠缘起:杜松虔巴剃度圣地呷拉觉空," 法露 *(Dharma Nectar)* 5, no. 3 (2019): 50, Karmapa Office; 噶玛钨金 et al., eds., "第一世噶玛巴:杜松虔巴. 开启九百年传承," 法露 *(Dharma Nectar)* 2, no. 2 (2016): 9, Karmapa Office. In Karma Thinley's account, Düsum Khyenpa received the crown from the *ḍākinīs* at the time when he achieved enlightenment (See Karma Thinley, "Rangjung Rigpe Dorje," 28).

In addition, according to the oral history in his birthplace, the Third Karmapa Rangjung Dorje received, at a very young age, a black crown from 100,000 *ḍākinīs* that they made from their own hair (噶玛善喜, "三世噶玛巴出生地:吉隆镇崩巴村. 飞越'抗秀磨'," 法露 *(Dharma Nectar)* 3, no. 2 (2017): 67, Karmapa Office).

11. Gamble, "View from Nowhere," 97, 113.

12. Kagyu Office, "Four-Session Guru Yoga Session One," reported February 11, 2017, http://kagyuoffice.org/four-session-guru-yoga-session-one/.

13. Richardson, "Karmapa Sect," 337.

14. Manson, "Life of Karma Pakshi," 31.

15. Manson, "Life of Karma Pakshi," 32.

16. The lineage came to be known as 'Karma Kagyu', 'Kamtsang Kagyu' and 'Tsurphu Kagyu' on account of the three monastic seats that Düsum Khyenpa founded, that is, Karma Monastery in 1147, Kampo Nenang in 1164 and Tsurphu Monastery in 1189, respectively. See 噶玛钨金, "杜松虔巴," 15–16; 噶玛钨金 et al., eds., "噶玛寺朝圣：月亮山峰前的圣地," 法露 *(Dharma Nectar)* 2, no. 2 (2016): 92, Karmapa Office.

Ogyen Trinley Dorje explains the meaning of 'Kamtsang' as follows:

'Kam comes from Kampo Gangra, the name of a place in Lithang in Eastern Tibet; Tshang literally means "nest" and by extension, "dwelling or place". . . . This sacred place of Chakrasamvara is where Gampopa told Dusum Khyenpa to practice, and if he did, his activity would spread throughout Tibet. Dusum Khyenpa's final realization was also here at Kampo Gangra.' See Kagyu Office, "Gyalwang Karmapa's Teachings on the Vajradhara Lineage Prayer Session One: Great masters of the Karma Kamtshang lineage," reported February 26, 2012, https://kagyuoffice.org/gyalwang-karmapas-teachings-on-the-vajradhara-lineage-prayer-session-one-great-masters-of-the-karma-kamtshang-lineage/.

According to him, the name 'Karma Kagyu' came to be used to refer to this sub-school during or after the time of the Second Karmapa Karma Pakshi who restored the three principal monasteries founded by Düsum Khyenpa and propagated the teachings. See Kagyu Office, "The Life of the Eighth Karmapa. Year One. Day Four: A Historical Examination of the First Eight Karmapa Reincarnations," reported February 19, 2021, https://kagyuoffice.org/life-of-mikyo-dorje//#4.

17. (1) *skyes bu dam pa'i mdzad spyod lo rgyus kyi gzhung ngam | rtogs pa brjod pa'i bstan bcos* | (2) *rnam grol*.

18. Kagyu Office, "The Life of the Eighth Karmapa. Year Two. Day 1: Remembering Our Good Fortune and the Purpose of Liberation Stories," reported March 19, 2022, https://kagyuoffice.org/life-of-mikyo-dorje/#21.

19. Kagyu Office, "Purpose of Liberation Stories."

20. Peter A Roberts, "The Evolution of the Biographies of Milarepa and Rechungpa," in *Lives Lived, Lives Imagined: Biography in the Buddhist traditions*, eds. Linda Covill, Ulrike Roesler, and Sarah Shaw (Boston: [Oxford]: Wisdom Publications, 2010), 182.

21. Ruth E Gamble, "The View from Nowhere: The travels of the Third Karmapa, Rang byung rdo rje in story and songs" (PhD diss., The Australian National University, 2013), 37–38.

22. Kevin Garratt, "Biography by Instalment: The Tibetan periodicals *Sheja* and *Trunggö Böjong* on the lives of reincarnate lamas," in *Religion and Biography in China and Tibet*, ed. Benjamin Penny (Richmond: Curzon, 2002), 189–190.

23. Ulrike Roesler, Introduction to *Lives Lived, Lives Imagined: Biography in the Buddhist traditions*, eds. Linda Covill, Ulrike Roesler, and Sarah Shaw (Boston: [Oxford]: Wisdom Publications, 2010), 3.

24. Steven D Goodman and Ronald M. Davidson, eds., *Tibetan Buddhism: Reason and revelation* (Albany: State University of New York Press, 1992), 4–5.

25. Marta Sernesi, "Biography and Hagiography: Tibet," *BEB*, no. 1 (2015): 741.

26. This is explained in more detail in 1.3. Interplay between the Spiritual and the Historical.

27. Jim Rheingans, "Narratives of Reincarnation, Politics of Power, and the Emergence of a Scholar: The very early years of Mikyö Dorje," in *Lives Lived, Lives Imagined: Biography in the Buddhist traditions*, eds. Covill, Linda, Ulrike Roesler, and Sarah Shaw (Boston: [Oxford]: Wisdom Publications, 2010), 253.

28. Janet B Gyatso, "From the Autobiography of a Visionary," in *Religions of Tibet in Practice*, ed. Donald S. Lopez (Princeton: Princeton University Press, 2007), 275.

29. Roesler, Introduction, 5; Ulrike Roesler, "Operas, Novels, and Religious Instructions: Life-stories of Tibetan Buddhist masters between genre classifications," in *Narrative Pattern and Genre in Hagiographic Life Writing: Comparative perspectives from Asia to Europe*, eds. Stephan Conermann and Jim Rheingans (Gottingen: Hubert & Co., 2014), 115.

30. Janet B Gyatso, "Autobiography in Tibetan Religious Literature: Reflection on its modes of self-presentation," in *Tibetan studies: Proceedings of the 5th seminar of the International Association for Tibetan Studies NARITA 1989 vol.2*, eds. Ihara Shōren and Yamaguchi Zuihō (Japan: Naritasan Shinshoji, 1992), 466.

31. Gyatso, "Autobiography in Literature," 477.

32. Gyatso, "Autobiography of a Visionary," 275.

33. K. R. Schaeffer, "Tibetan Biography: Growth and criticism," in *Edition, éditions: L'écrit au Tibet, évolution et devenir*, eds. A. Chayet, C. ScherrerSchaub, F. Robin, and J.-L. Achard (Munich: Indus Verlag, 2010), 273.

34. Roesler, "Operas, Novels," 117.

35. Roesler, "Operas, Novels," 117; Sernesi, "Biography and Hagiography," 734.

36. Roesler, "Operas, Novels," 118.
37. Tibetan Buddhist Resource Center, now renamed as Buddhist Digital Resource Center.
38. Schaeffer, "Tibetan Biography," 267.
39. Sernesi, "Biography and Hagiography," 734–735, 740.
40. Roesler, Introduction, 5–6; Roesler, "Operas, Novels," 117.
41. Rheingans, "Narratives of Reincarnation," 251–252.
42. Schaeffer, "Tibetan Biography," 270.
43. Roesler, Introduction, 5–6.
44. Rheingans, "Narratives of Reincarnation," 253.
45. Stephan Conermann and Jim Rheingans, "Narrative Pattern and Genre in Hagiographic Life Writing: An introduction," in *Narrative Pattern and Genre in Hagiographic Life Writing: Comparative perspectives from Asia to Europe*, eds. Stephan Conermann and Jim Rheingans (Gottingen: Hubert & Co., 2014), 11.
46. Gyatso, "Autobiography in Literature," 469.
47. Gyatso, "Autobiography in Literature," 472.
48. Roesler, "Operas, Novels," 132.
49. Schaeffer, "Tibetan Biography," 272.
50. A. I. Vostrikov, *Tibetan Historical Literature* (Surrey: Curzon Press, 1994), 188–189.
51. Vostrikov, *Tibetan Historical Literature*, 289–290.
52. Goodman and Davidson, *Tibetan Buddhism*, 1.
53. Rheingans, "Narratives of Reincarnation," 255.
54. Roesler, Introduction, 6.
55. Conermann and Rheingans, "Narrative Pattern," 11.
56. James B Robinson, "The Lives of Indian Buddhist Saints: Biography, hagiography and myth," in *Tibetan Literature: Studies in genre*, eds. José Ignacio Cabezón and Roger R. Jackson (New York: Snow Lion Publications, 1996), 64.
57. Conermann and Rheingans, "Narrative Pattern," 12.
58. Conermann and Rheingans, "Narrative Pattern," 12.
59. Schaeffer, "Tibetan Biography," 270.
60. Schaeffer, "Tibetan Biography," 270.
61. Roesler, "Operas, Novels," 119–132.
62. Roesler, "Operas, Novels," 128.
63. Roesler, Introduction, 2.
64. Sernesi, "Biography and Hagiography," 736.
65. Peter Schwieger, "From Hagiography to Modern Short Story: How to get rid of old social ideals and literary stereotypes," in *Tibetan Literary Genres, Texts, and Text Types: From genre classification to transformation*, ed. Jim Rheingans (Leiden; Boston: Brill, 2015), 272.
66. Robinson, "Indian Buddhist Saints," 61.
67. Robinson, "Indian Buddhist Saints," 67.
68. Marta Sernesi, "A Prayer to the Complete Liberation of Mi la ras pa," in *Narrative Pattern and Genre in Hagiographic Life Writing: Comparative perspectives from Asia to Europe*, eds. Stephan Conermann and Jim Rheingans (Gottingen: Hubert & Co., 2014), 146.

69. Francis V Tiso, *Liberation in One Lifetime: Biographies and teachings of Milarepa* (Isernia: Proforma, 2010), 79.
70. Sernesi, "Biography and Hagiography," 741.
71. Tiso, *Liberation in One Lifetime*, 277.
72. Sernesi, "Complete Liberation," 147.
73. Kagyu Office, "Purpose of Liberation Stories."
74. Sernesi, "Biography and Hagiography," 741.
75. Marta Sernesi, "To Establish the Qualities of the Master: Considerations on early bKa' brgyud hagiographical writings," in *Tīrthayātrā: Essays in honour of Stefano Piano*, eds. Pinuccia Caracchi, Antonella Serena Comba, Alessandra Consolaro, and Alberto Pelissero (Alessandria: Edizioni dell'Orso, 2010), 405.
76. Sernesi, "Biography and Hagiography," 735, 741.
77. Rheingans, "Narratives of Reincarnation," 254.
78. Rheingans, "Narratives of Reincarnation," 254.
79. Sernesi, "Biography and Hagiography," 736.
80. Sernesi, "Biography and Hagiography," 741.
81. Gyatso, "Autobiography in Literature," 469–470.
82. Gyatso, "Autobiography in Literature," 470, 473.

Roesler identifies another mode of self-representation in the *rangnam* of the 'crazy saints' (*smyon pa*) of fifteenth-century Tibet which displays little interest in historical events and contains unorthodox, provocative traits and lyrical elements. See Roesler, "Operas, Novels," 136.

83. Roesler, "Operas, Novels," 133.
84. Kalu Rinpoche, *The Chariot for Travelling the Path to Freedom: The life story of Kalu Rinpoche*, trans. Kenneth I. McLeod (Kagyu Dharma, 1985), 49.

Gyatso explains in a footnote: The English version of the entire prose has been adjusted to the first person; the original Tibetan text, however, includes the versified prayer in the second person. See Gyatso, "Autobiography in Literature," 15.

85. Gyatso, "Autobiography in Literature," 470–471.
86. Gyatso, "Autobiography in Literature," 470–473.
87. Kagyu Office, "Purpose of Liberation Stories."
88. Kagyu Office, "The Life of the Eighth Karmapa. Year One. Day One: The Black Hat Lama," reported February 15, 2021, https://kagyuoffice.org/life-of-mikyo-dorje/#1.
89. Schaeffer, "Tibetan Biography," 275.

The original Tibetan is not referenced.

90. Schaeffer, "Tibetan Biography," 274.
91. Roesler, "Operas, Novels," 134.
92. Sernesi, "Biography and Hagiography," 736.
93. David Templeman, "The Mirror of Life: The structure of a 16th century Tibetan hagiography," in *Religion and Biography in China and Tibet*, ed. Benjamin Penny (Richmond: Curzon, 2002), 132.
94. Robinson, "Indian Buddhist Saints," 57.
95. Roesler, "Operas, Novels," 128.
96. Naomi Appleton, *Jātaka Stories in Theravāda Buddhism: Narrating the Bodhisatta path* (Surrey, VT: Ashgate Publishing, 2010), 21.

97. Appleton, *Jātaka Stories*, 21–39.
98. Appleton, *Jātaka Stories*, 83, 86.
99. Appleton, *Jātaka Stories*, 108.
100. Appleton, *Jātaka Stories*, 122, 145–146.
101. Appleton, *Jātaka Stories*, 147, 156.
102. Sarah Shaw, "And That was I: How the Buddha himself creates a path between biography and autobiography," in *Lives Lived, Lives Imagined: Biography in the Buddhist traditions*, eds. Linda Covill, Ulrike Roesler, and Sarah Shaw (Boston: [Oxford]: Wisdom Publications, 2010), 34.
103. Shaw, "And That was I," 34.
104. Shaw, "And That was I," 37.
105. Shaw, "And That was I," 30.
106. Shaw, "And That was I," 38.
107. Roesler, "Operas, Novels," 128.
108. J. S Speyer, Introduction to *Jātakamālā or Garland of Birth-Stories*, trans. J. S. Speyer, ed. F. Max Muller (Ancient Buddhist Texts, 2010), xx.
109. Speyer, Introduction, xx.
110. Speyer, Introduction, xviii, xx, xxi.
111. Speyer, Introduction, xxiii.
112. Roesler, "Operas, Novels," 128; Speyer, Introduction, xxvi.

For example, Āryaśūra's *Jātakamālā* was translated into Tibetan as *skyes rabs 'phreng ba*.

113. Roesler, "Operas, Novels," 128–129.
114. Matthew Kapstein, "The Indian Literary Identity in Tibet," in *Literary Cultures in History: Reconstructions from South Asia*, ed. Sheldon Pollock (Berkeley: University of California, 2003), quoted in Ruth E Gamble, "The View from Nowhere: The travels of the Third Karmapa, Rang byung rdo rje in story and songs" (PhD diss., The Australian National University, 2013), 42.

On the Karmapa lineage, one of the earliest lineages of reincarnate lamas in Tibet, Gamble discusses the rebirth stories of the first three Karmapas, Düsum Khyenpa, Karma Pakshi and Rangjung Dorje, and the way in which wider cultural trends influenced their storytelling (See Gamble, "View from Nowhere," 108–110). Especially, Rangjung Dorje's approach to rebirth stories was 'exceedingly thorough, organised and multi-pronged', which corresponds to the systemisation of the Karmapa institution at that time (See Gamble, "View from Nowhere," 43).

115. That is, the self-glorification mode.
116. Gyatso, "Autobiography in Literature," 474.
117. Schaeffer, "Tibetan Biography," 276.
118. Roesler, "Operas, Novels," 131.
119. Schwieger, "From Hagiography," 270–273.
120. Khenpo Konchog Gyaltsen, Introduction to *The Great Kagyu Masters: The golden lineage treasury*, ed. Victoria Huckenpahler (Ithaca, NY: Snow Lion Publications, 1990), 9; Tiso, *Liberation in One Lifetime*, 108.
121. Shaw, "And That was I," 33.
122. Shaw, "And That was I," 33.

123. The following discussion on skilful means, Trikāya, *mahāsiddha*s and the 'Mila *namthar*' tradition, is based on the findings in Meng Wang, "The Tension Between the Narratives of Mi La Ras Pa as an Emanation and an Ordinary Person in the Mi La rNam Thar Tradition of Tibetan Buddhism" (MA diss., SOAS, University of London, 2014).

124. Tibetan: *'di ni 'jig rten 'thun 'jug yin*. See Jonathan A Silk, "The Fruits of Paradox: On the religious architecture of the Buddha's life story," *Journal of the American Academy of Religion* 71, no. 4 (2003): 875.

125. See Silk, "Fruits of Paradox," 876.

126. Sernesi, "Complete Liberation," 149.

127. See Ronald M Davidson, *Indian Esoteric Buddhism: A social history of the tantric movement* (New York: Columbia University Press, 2002).

128. That is, the *namthar* collection of Milarepa.

In "The Tension Between the Narratives of Mi La Ras Pa as an Emanation and an Ordinary Person in the Mi La rNam Thar Tradition of Tibetan Buddhism," I examine the following *namthar* accounts that represent the different stages in the evolution of the 'Mila *namthar*' tradition: sGam po pa bsod nams rin chen, "The Biographies of Marpa and Milarepa," in *Liberation in one lifetime: biographies and teachings of Milarepa*, trans. Francis V. Tiso (Isernia: Proforma, 2010), 240–254; Dorje Dze Öd, *The Great Kagyu Masters: The golden lineage treasury*, trans. Khenpo Könchog Gyaltsen, ed. Victoria Huckenpahler (Ithaca, NY: Snow Lion Publications, 1990), 123–144; rGyal thang pa bde chen rdo rje, "The biography of Milarepa," in *Liberation in one lifetime: biographies and teachings of Milarepa*, trans. Francis V. Tiso (Isernia: Proforma, 2010), 161–240; Bu chen bcu gnyis, "bZhad pa'i rdo rje'i rnam thar mgur mchings dang bcas pa" in *The Yogin And The Madman*, trans. Andrew Quintman (New York: Columbia University Press, 2014), 91–104; Tsangnyön Heruka, *The Life of Milarepa*, trans. Andrew Quintman (London: Penguin Books, 2010); gTsang smyon Heruka, "The Treasure Trove of Blessings," trans. Marta Sernesi, in *Narrative Pattern and Genre in Hagiographic Life Writing: Comparative perspectives from Asia to Europe*, eds. Stephan Conermann and Jim Rheingans (Gottingen: Hubert & Co., 2014), 181–185.

129. rGyal thang pa bde chen rdo rje, "Biography of Milarepa," 168.

130. Bu chen bcu gnyis, "bZhad pa'i rdo rje'i," 92.

131. Andrew Quintman, *The Yogin and the Madman: Reading the biographical corpus of Tibet's great saint Milarepa* (New York: Columbia University Press, 2014), 149.

132. For example, gZhon nu dpal, "sgam po ba'i dngos slob kyi skabs," in *deb ther sngon po*, TBRC W7494. 1 (New Delhi: International Academy of Indian Culture, 1974), 414.

133. For example, gTsug lag 'phreng ba, "karma kam tshang."

134. mKha' spyod dbang po, *bka' brgyud rin po che'i rnam par thar pa chos tshan bcu bdun* (TBRC W3CN2636).

135. Chos kyi 'byung gnas and Tshe dbang kun khyab, *sgrub brgyud karma kaM tshang gi brgyud pa rin po che'i rnam par thar pa rab 'byams nor bu zla ba chu shel gyi phreng ba* (TBRC W24686).

鄔金欽列多傑 (O rgyan phrin las rdo rje, or Ogyen Trinley Dorje) gives an overview of the Tibetan texts that contain the life stories of the Karmapa incarnations, from the *Deb ther dmar po, sngon po* up to the *Zla ba chu shel*. See 鄔金欽列多傑, "序言," in 上師之師, trans. 比丘尼洛卓拉嫫 (台灣: 眾生文化, 2016), 3.

136. See Rin chen dpal bzang, *mtshur phu dgon gyi dkar chag kun gsal me long*, TBRC W20850. 1 vols (pe cin: mi rigs dpe skrun khang, 1995).

137. That is, Khra 'gu rin po che, *rgyal ba'i dbang po*.

138. Born in the nineteenth century, his title was Mandong Tsampa (sMan sdong mtshams pa) Rinpoche. See "karma nges don bstan rgyas (b. 18uu,)," TBRC P926., 2011, http://tbrc.org/link?RID=P926.

139. The Second Jamgon Kongtrul ('Jam mgon kong sprul), the son of the Fifteenth Karmapa, Khakyap Dorje (mKha' khyab rdo rje, 1871–1922). See "mkhyen brtse 'od zer (b. 1904, d. 1953/1954)," TBRC P937, 2011, http://tbrc.org/link?RID=P937.

140. Karma nges don bstan rgyas, "chos rje karma pa sku phreng rim byon gyi rnam thar mdor bsdus dpag bsam khri shing /(1–14)," in *karma pa sku 'phreng bcu drug pa tshun rim par byon pa'i rnam thar phyogs bsgrigs*, TBRC W1KG3815. (Delhi: konchhog lhadrepa, 1994), 6.4–6.5, 8.1–9.2, 12.2–12.4.

141. mKhyen brtse 'od zer, 1994, 473.2–473.3, 475.3–475.4.

142. Khra 'gu rin po che, *rgyal ba'i dbang po*, 322.14, 323.7–8.

143. *thun mong gi mthun snang la yongs su grags pa tsam las | thun min sku'i che ba'i yon tan bsgrags na de tsam thugs mnyes po mi gnang bar brten |* (Khra'gu rin po che, *rgyal ba'i dbang po*, 386.)

144. bKra shis tshe ring, "'jig rten dbang phyug," 24.5–24.8.

145. Karma nges don bstan rgyas, "rnam thar mdor bsdus," 447.4–448.1.

146. The Tibetan text only addresses *chos rje karmapa* (See Karma nges don bstan rgyas, "rnam thar mdor bsdus," 448.4–448.5). The Chinese translation identifies this to be the Fourteenth Karmapa. See 勉東倉巴仁波切, 八蚌欽哲仁波切, 堪千創古仁波切, 上師之師：歷代大寶法王噶瑪巴的轉世傳奇, trans. 比丘尼洛卓拉嫫 (台灣：眾生文化, 2016), 248.

147. Karma nges don bstan rgyas, "rnam thar mdor bsdus," 449.1–449.3.

148. Karma nges don bstan rgyas, "rnam thar mdor bsdus," 448.1–448.3.

149. Identified to be the Fourteenth Karmapa in the Chinese translation. See 勉東倉巴仁波切, 八蚌欽哲仁波切, 堪千創古仁波切, 上師之師：歷代大寶法王噶瑪巴的轉世傳奇, trans. 比丘尼洛卓拉嫫 (台灣：眾生文化, 2016), 248–249.

150. Karma nges don bstan rgyas, "rnam thar mdor bsdus," 449.5–449.6.

151. Karma nges don bstan rgyas, "rnam thar mdor bsdus," 450.3–450.6.

152. Karma nges don bstan rgyas, "rnam thar mdor bsdus," 452.4–452.5, 453.2–453.3.

153. Karma nges don bstan rgyas, "rnam thar mdor bsdus," 453.3–453.4.
    The Twelve Deeds (*mdzad pa bcu gnyis*, Skt. *dvadaśabuddhakārya*).

154. *bla ma 'di rang rgyud kyi me long yin | sku 'gyur ba mnga'am mi mnga' ltos | ji srid du 'das grong yod kyi bar | da dung du gus par rang rgyud sbyong |* (Karma nges don bstan rgyas, "rnam thar mdor bsdus," 453.)

155. *slob ma'i mos gus drag sngags zab mo des | bla ma'i thugs yid dbang du bsdus nas ni | rang sems sgrib bral chos kyi sku nyid dang | dbyer med bla ma rang gi sems nyid las | gzhan du tshol mi dgos par bsten chog pas | bla ma nyid dang 'bral ba med pa yin | de tshe dpon slob thugs yid gcig 'dres zhes | bla ma dam pa'i go 'phang thob pa yin |* (Karma nges don bstan rgyas, "rnam thar mdor bsdus," 460–461.)

Chapter 2

Western Context

The Western perception of the Karmapa that began to form in the 1960s and 1970s was shaped and influenced by two important phenomena in the broader sociocultural context. First, the idealisation of Tibet had by then been crystallised through three main stages of change and reinforcement in history. The first two, spanning from the European colonial presence in Asia during the nineteenth century to the end of World War II, were dominated by the Western perspective. In the third stage, starting from the rise of the Tibetan diaspora, Tibetan agency moves to the foreground. The Tibetans, participating in the intercultural exchange with the West on the largest scale ever, created a collective identity and promoted a romantic construction of Tibet for their own political goals. The idealisation of Tibet, reinvigorated by the Tibetans themselves, had a long-lasting impact on the Western adherents of Tibetan Buddhism. Their interest in paranormal activities and mystical experiences largely facilitated the reception of the Karmapa's spiritual image. Second, prior to the arrival of Tibetan Buddhism in the West, two other Buddhist traditions, Theravāda and Zen, had already been introduced to the Western audience, integrated with the dominant social, religious movements, including the counterculture, new religious and New Age movements. The development of these traditions set the background for the transmission of Tibetan Buddhism. Here, the discussion focuses on two specific countries: the United States and Great Britain. These two countries are connected to the activities of two outstanding agents of the Karma Kagyu lineage, Chögyam Trungpa and Akong Tulku; they each pioneered the transmission of Tibetan Buddhism to North America and Europe and played an instrumental role in the Karmapa's tours there, respectively.

2.1. IDEALISATION OF TIBET

In the West, Tibet once symbolised the fountain of youth and a place of secret wisdom, peace and power.[1] Some even believed that Tibetans were a long-lost Jewish population or descendants of a forgotten Christian kingdom; the Nazis considered Tibetans to be the Aryans.[2] To Lopez, fantasies about Tibet are examples of Romantic Orientalism.[3] He even uses Oscar Wilde's theory of the 'art of lying' as a point of reference.[4] He regards the Western perception of Tibet as 'a work of art, fashioned through exaggeration and selection into an ideal with little foundation in history';[5] in a sense, Western adherents of Tibetan Buddhism appear to be more 'authentic' than the Tibetans themselves in that 'they are more intimate with the simulacrum of Tibet that is the invention, that is the artifice'.[6] Such a statement brings to one's attention the role of Westerners in the modern representation of Tibet. Nonetheless, it is also important to acknowledge the shift that has already taken place in the post-colonial period moving from predominantly Orientalist interpretations to a more critical and nuanced discourse that recognises Tibetan agency. In the following, I shall examine this shift by identifying key agents in the construction of the modern image of Tibet in three important periods.

2.1.1. Western Imagination

The first period falls into the late nineteenth century. Tibet's peripheral location, at the edge of the European imperial influence in Asia, boosted romantic imaginations. Bishop considers these imaginations as Europeans' attempt to escape from the 'rigid rational censorship' in the West; Tibet came to possess the 'qualities of a dream, a collective hallucination', far removed from reality.[7] This phenomenon arose from the Great Game between Britain and Russia: 'Tibet was thus an object of imperial desire, and the failure of the European powers to dominate it politically only increased European longing and fed the fantasy about the land beyond the Snowy Range.'[8] Although Tibet was never colonised by any European country, it was still under the influence of Britain's imperial rule in Asia. Adjacent to British India, Tibet was incorporated into the European projections of Asian cultures.[9] Tibet and Tibetan Buddhism became important examples of 'otherness' bearing the imprint of nineteenth-century Romanticism. Opposite to the romantic imagination was the intellectual attitude of rationalism that saw Tibetan Buddhism as a degeneration from the original Buddhism, a 'fossilized, despotic aberration'.[10] These two very different projections led to a complex imagining of Tibet. Yet, the romantic projection began to gather momentum with the rapid development of the Theosophical Society.

The Theosophical Society was founded by Helena Blavatsky and Henry Steele Olcott in 1875. Its purpose was to study 'Occult science' in response to rationalism and scientific domination in the West: 'Many people were distressed by positivist science and aggressive materialism and had little faith in the ability of Christianity to guard human spirituality and protect its true place in the universe.'[11] European colonialism and Christian missionary endeavour in Asia also shaped the development of the Theosophical Society.[12] The society attempted to explain religious dogma in rational terms with a particular interest in the mystical experience of Asian religions. Blavatsky introduced to the public 'a complex evolutionary theory linking cosmic evolution to human spiritual growth—a comprehensive psychology, or "science of the soul"';[13] she defined Theosophy as a synthesis of science, religion and philosophy.[14]

Tibet was at the centre of Blavatsky's theosophical imagination and promotion of 'Oriental wisdom'. She claimed to have been contacted by a 'Tibetan mahatma', then travelled to Tibet to train in Occult science and received the instruction to create the Theosophical Society. While Western Buddhologists were dismissing Tibetan Buddhism as a degenerated, corrupted form of what they called 'Pure Buddhism', Blavatsky promoted it to be the world's greatest wisdom.[15] Despite that Blavatsky faced accusations of fraud,[16] the Theosophical Society continued to thrive up to the late 1920s. Its imagination of Tibet propelled the Western construction of Tibet and Tibetans as 'imaginary objects' in scholarly works, travelogues and occult, esoteric books.[17] Theosophy became a source of inspiration for travellers, writers and scholars who continued to mould the image of Tibet in Western consciousness. The most notable among them were Alexandra David-Neel, W. Y. Evans-Wentz, Lama Anagarika Govinda and Edward Conze. It also prepared the ground for the coming of 'New Age Orientalism'.[18] At the turn of the twentieth century, the exotic presentation of Tibet found its way into popular novels, including Rudyard Kipling's *Kim* and Conan Doyle's *The Adventure of the Empty House*.[19] To sum up, in the period from the late nineteenth to the early twentieth century, Europeans and Americans exercised active agency in the idealisation of Tibet; the Tibetans played no role in this. Such exclusively Western practice, as Lopez points out, draws 'a distinction between the Tibetans' own religious practice and the secret knowledge of occult masters'.[20]

The second period in the construction of Tibet spans from the Anglo-Tibetan imperial encounter at the beginning of the twentieth century to the end of World War II. Several groups of agents, including Tibetans, interpreted Tibetan culture from various perspectives. The first group consists of British colonial officers stationed in Tibet after the Younghusband expedition (1903–1904). To begin with, these officers held negative views about Tibet in an attempt to justify their mission. However, as their relationship with the local ruling class improved, they began to paint a more positive picture of Tibetan society. An intention for objectivity notwithstanding, their discovery still bore the influence of their own imperial education and training. In the 1920s, these officers started to restrict the entry of European travellers and conduct censorship on their travel accounts. In doing so, they controlled the European representation of Tibet. They also wrote their own accounts that served the political interest of British India. Tibet, in their accounts, turned into a modern nation-state and a friendly, admirable neighbour, and the Tibetans worthy allies of the British. The publishers of these accounts, driven by commercial incentives, contributed to a further idealised Tibet.[21] The romantic image of Tibet in the officers' accounts served three purposes: the political agenda of the British colonial government, the commercial aspiration of the publishers and the officers' personal interest in mysticism. Their representation of Tibet helped shape the collective identity of the Tibetan diaspora decades later.[22]

The second group of agents in this period comprised members of the ruling class in Lhasa. After the expedition, the British introduced modern culture which transformed the life of the Tibetan aristocracy between the 1920s and 1940s. In Lhasa, they installed a telephone line and a diesel generator for electricity. In Darjeeling, they provided education to young Tibetan officials who then became fluent in English and offered them access to English language books, newspapers and magazines. They helped the Tibetans publish the first Tibetan-language newspaper. They trained the Tibetan army, even equipped it with a fife and drum band; the band presented itself to the Dalai Lama in the tune of 'God Save the King'.[23] These examples of modernisation suggest a good relationship between the British colonial government and the Tibetan ruling class. Furthermore, in this period, the British Empire began to use cinema to educate the population of their colonies. In Tibet, this led to the production of documentary films which emerged as a result of the intercultural dialogue between the British filmmakers and the Lhasa government. These films reflect the Western imagination of Tibet as well as the ambition of the Tibetan ruling class to shape the Western perception of their own country. This created the 'cinematic myths of Tibet' that emphasised Tibetan Buddhist rituals over the reality of daily life.[24] The Tibetans, for the first time, came to engage in the modern construction of Tibet.

The third group consists of European travellers and writers. Most travellers in this period were British on account of British imperial rule in India and its diplomatic relationship with Tibet. Their interpretations of what they discovered in Tibet, be it positive or negative, captured the political climate at the time. In 1924, the British colonial government started to monitor travellers' accounts. Some accounts produced before then described Tibetan Buddhism as 'devil worship and ruin of Tibetan society' and Tibetans as 'despotic, licentious, and dirty'.²⁵ Post-1924, the representation of Tibet grew more nuanced. Some travellers praised Tibet for its 'merry people, a tranquil environment, their peaceful spirituality, and their intelligence'; others condemned it for its 'violence, danger, superstition, backwardness, and xenophobia'.²⁶

The most remarkable traveller of this time was the French mystic-scholar Alexandra David-Neel. She made two journeys to Tibet in 1916 and 1924 and became a renowned figure in the European construction of Tibet, partly because she demonstrated that Tibetan Buddhism was not all about mysticism. To her, Tibet was a land of joyful people; its Buddhist tradition represented the pinnacle of human culture.²⁷ Still, she maintained a deep interest in the 'Occult Tibet' and recounted many magical and mysterious experiences that signify the influence of Blavatsky's Theosophy. At the same time, she was also critical of the image of Tibet as mysterious and exotic:

> For many Westerners Tibet is wrapped in an atmosphere of mystery. The 'Land of Snows' is for them the country of the unknown, the fantastic and the impossible. What superhuman powers have not been ascribed to the various kinds of lamas, magicians, sorcerers, necromancers and practitioners of the occult who inhabit those high tablelands, and whom both nature and their own deliberate purpose have so splendidly isolated from the rest of the world? And how readily are the strangest legends about them accepted as indisputable truths!²⁸

To Bishop, this critique shows that '[c]reating and deflating all-encapsulating visions of Tibet was a common pastime among contemporary writers'.²⁹ In any case, David-Neel's version of Tibet was not very distant from the existing romantic imagination. Lopez considers her to be among the 'Great Mystifiers' who projected their own fantasies onto Tibet.³⁰

The romantic imagination of Tibet reached a new level in James Hilton's *Lost Horizon* (1933). This book built the foundation for the myth of Shangri-la. Here, the appeal of Shangri-la has nothing to do with its indigenous people. It stems from a fantasy that Tibet preserves what is good in European culture.³¹ Tibet becomes a secret hidden place that upholds the treasures of the long-lost wisdom of Western civilisation. The book soon became a best-seller; Hollywood made it into a film.³² Its popularity attests to the shared longing for an exotic Tibet in the West. Such sentiment derived from Europeans' disillusionment with the industrial culture post–World War I. In Hilton's own words: 'The Dark Ages that are to come will cover the whole world in a single pall; there will be neither escape nor sanctuary, save such as are too secret to be found or too humble to be noticed. And Shangri-La may hope to be both of these.'³³ Hilton's vision of Shangri-la carried on with the fantasy and myth of Tibet from Blavatsky and Kipling.³⁴ It was based on the late nineteenth-century legacy of Romanticism; the critical reflections of Western culture after World War I accentuated it further. It appealed to

Europeans to view Tibet as a place of refuge that provided cures to the plight of their own societies.

Tibet underwent significant change between the two world wars. However, Western writers and filmmakers refused to acknowledge this, but instead, continued to imagine Tibet to be an otherworldly fantasy, a repository of wisdom and a remedy against the world's ills. This is so because: 'These Westerners lived in a split world. Quite clearly they knew about the turmoil of Tibetan history in the twentieth century, yet at the same time, they disavowed it. The West seemed to need at least one place to have remained stable, untouched, an unchanging centre in a world being ripped apart.'[35] The wars in the West intensified the need to believe in a utopian Tibet. Therefore, Tibet became a dreamlike projection of fears, desperations and spiritual quests of the disillusioned Europeans and Americans.[36]

These circumstances led to an increasing interest in psychic research and psychoanalysis which, in turn, gave rise to the fourth group of agents in the representation of Tibet. The period between the two world wars was 'a time of psychological awakening in the West' when religion and science began to interact.[37] Carl G. Jung pioneered the psychological explanation of Tibetan Buddhism. He shared the same idea with Blavatsky's Theosophy and interpreted Eastern religions in psychological terms.[38] To him, Tibetan Buddhism had much to offer on the workings of the human psyche. His interpretation of *The Tibetan Book of the Dead* (Bardo Thödol, Tib. *bar do thos grol*) turned the text into one of the most popular books about Tibetan Buddhism in the West. The text was seen as 'a powerful symbol of highly organized spiritual attainments, an affirmation of a pure spiritual science'.[39] This romantic projection, however, discarded without a trace the historical context of the Tibetan text itself.

Later, in the 1960s, *Bardo Thödol* became a popular material to explore psychedelic experiences. This contributed to the belief in the compatibility of Buddhism and science.[40] Popular interest in *Bardo Thödol* facilitated the introduction of the seemingly exotic concepts, such as reincarnation and reincarnate lamas of Tibet, to the West. The psychological interpretation of Buddhism led to two general trends: 'One was that ideas of Eastern religion and psychology became more clearly defined in terms of current Western psychological paradigms. The other was that various Eastern religious practices—and in particular meditation—would be seen as techniques for the attainment of mental health or, in other words, as psychotherapy.'[41] The Tibetan lamas who came to Europe and North America in the later decades, the 1960s and 1970s, adapted to these trends. Some borrowed psychological terminology to explain Buddhist ideas and concepts and created new methods and practices to address mental health issues in the West. To many Westerners, Tibetan Buddhism came to be both spiritual and scientific.

The third period in the construction of Tibet began in the 1950s, encompassing the Cold War and the formation of the Tibetan diaspora. On the one hand, the Chinese military conquest of Tibet created a sense of loss among Europeans and Americans who had eagerly believed Tibet to be a timeless sacred place. Their idealisation of Tibet, however, intensified even further: Tibet became a utopia, purely imaginary without physical form.[42] The fear of communism provoked a sense of urgency for such imagination:[43] 'Communism was already mythologized, already the Antichrist, the bearer of the West's unadulterated shadow. Tibet was merely drawn into the mythic drama as the other side of the equation: the "Most peaceful nation on earth" versus "this soulless regime."'[44] The West saw Tibet and China in opposition: 'the pristine and the polluted, the authentic and the derivative, the holy and the demonic, the good and the bad'.[45] The Chinese rule of Tibet was perceived as 'an undifferentiated mass of godless Communists overwhelming a peaceful land devoted only to ethereal pursuits'.[46] This is so because: 'China must be debased in order for Tibet to be exalted; in order for there to be a spiritual and enlightened Orient, there must be a demonic and despotic Orient.'[47] This perception of Tibet was, to a large degree, a strategic reaction to communist propaganda.[48] Accordingly, Tibetan Buddhism came to be portrayed as a victim of the communist hegemony.[49]

The interest in the spiritual aspect of Tibetan culture, the 'Occult Tibet' favoured by Blavatsky and David-Neel, grew in prominence. The West regarded Tibetan Buddhism as 'another artefact of Shangri-La from an eternal classical age, set high in a Himalayan keep outside time and history'.[50] The appeal of Tibet continued to strengthen: 'Tibet is seen as the cure for an ever-ailing Western civilization, a tonic to restore its spirit. And since the Tibetan diaspora that began in 1959 there seems an especial urgency about taking this cure, before it is lost forever.'[51] Once in exile, Tibetan Buddhism was, for the first time, acknowledged as a living tradition.[52] The few Tibetan lamas who made their way into the Indian subcontinent became the only remaining embodiment of the mysterious quality of Tibet: 'Even Tibetan religion as a whole had ceased to be the object of fascination; now only the spiritual masters and their most advanced techniques excited Western fantasies.'[53]

On the other hand, in the diaspora, Tibetans, both ordinary people and lamas, strove to preserve their own culture. The exile situation created opportunities for them to make frequent contact with Westerners. Organisations and individuals in the West provided them with financial aid; young Europeans and Americans visited the lamas to either fulfil their spiritual quests or pursue their academic interests. In this way, Tibetans found themselves in a constant intercultural exchange with the West as they carried out their own cultural preservation. Collectively, they engaged in the image-making of Tibet and reinforced its idealisation, though with a different set of objectives and interests. Tibetan agency was no longer limited to a specific social class as in the second period; it now encompassed the entire exile community and operated under rather different circumstances from pre-1959. The construction of Tibet was no longer a predominantly Western matter; it became a hybridised product of cross-cultural encounters between the Europeans/Americans and Tibetans in exile. This significant shift in power relations requires a change of point of reference from the West to the Tibetan diaspora.

2.1.2. Tibetan Contribution

In 1959, more than 60,000 Tibetans fled into exile and arrived in India.[54] The Tibetan diaspora came into being. The damage caused to Tibetan culture within Tibet, especially during the Chinese Cultural Revolution, from 1966 to 1976, created among Tibetans in exile a sense of urgency to save their culture from extinction.[55] Anand draws on the history of the Jewish diaspora to explain the Tibetan situation: the diaspora experience features the 'conscious cultivation of collective memory of the homeland, with a strong emphasis on ultimate return' and 'preservation of culture through a patrolling of communal boundaries'.[56] This explains the reason why the exile government prioritised cultural preservation. Dharamsala serves as 'a temporary home preserving historical culture in its pure form'.[57] This is achieved through education and construction of monasteries.[58]

The Tibetans also created among themselves a collective identity, namely 'Tibetan-ness'. This is an innovation of the diaspora,[59] a concept unheard of in pre-modern Tibet: 'Ethnic Tibet, despite the unifying effects of Buddhism, trade, and a common written language, has never been a particularly homogeneous region. The major provinces of Kham, Amdo, Central Tibet, and western Tibet have different histories and have been shaped in many ways by those histories.'[60] In exile, however, it was necessary for all Tibetans to share a common goal and act as one community: '[T]he focus of identification has now shifted from local contexts to a national one—instead of individual localities and regions, it is to the "Tibet" that is collectively imagined as the homeland that the refugees hope to return one day.'[61] With this purpose in mind, many Tibetans held on to their refugee status and refused to obtain citizenship from the host countries.[62]

Meanwhile, to be Tibetan also calls for flexibility; one needs to stay in tune with the norms of the host culture: '[I]t is fruitful to look at Tibetanness as a product of the creative negotiations conducted by diasporic Tibetans with the dominant representational regime and as a process of selective resistance to and appropriation of dominant identity concepts, including (trans)nationalism, sovereignty, indigeneity, universal human rights, and Diaspora.'[63] Tibetan-ness represents a 'hybridized diasporic subjectivity' that emerges from two primary concerns: to identify oneself with the imagined homeland and to adapt to the host societies.[64] It invokes patriotism but, at the same time, creates a modern, transnational and intercultural experience.[65]

For the cultural preservation in the diaspora, Tibetan-ness triggers tension between the Tibetans' need for adaptation and their resolve to maintain traditional values. This presents a challenge for Tibetan Buddhism which is at the centre of the preservation. Back in Tibet, Buddhism was an integral part of Tibetan life; Tibetans committed a remarkable amount of time, energy and resources to developing the Buddhist institution.[66] The diaspora continued with such effort, though within a very different sociocultural and political environment, dedicating substantial funds to the construction of monasteries.[67] Buddhism became the foundation of a shared identity among the Tibetans. The lamas and monks played a pivotal role in its preservation. Most focused on safeguarding tradition and its values. Their conservatism set the tone for the activities of those who travelled to the West to propagate the Dharma. While introducing their tradition to the West, many relied on traditional methods despite the evident sociocultural differences. Attempts to modernise and adapt Buddhist teachings to Western culture often led to censure and alienation from the Tibetan circle.

External help was also crucial to the Tibetans' cultural preservation. The Government of India provided much-needed support for the resettlement of Tibetan refugees. However, resettlement camps soon became overcrowded, and their limited resources overstretched.[68] The fragile status of the Indian economy further exacerbated the situation. The biggest difficulty for the exile community, though, was the need to adapt its social organisation. In pre-modern Tibet, the fundamental structure of society was built on property. The upper strata accumulated wealth through land ownership and acted as patrons for monasteries. The monastic institutions too were sustained through property: large monasteries gained substantial yield from their estates. In exile, the upper class and the monastics could no longer rely on the traditional estate system; the Tibetans were not allowed by law to own land in India.[69] Tibetan lamas found new patronage from the West.

Initial support came from aid agencies and sympathetic individuals. Substituting the traditional patrons of pre-modern Tibet, they played a vital role in rebuilding Tibetan cultural and religious institutions in exile. Many continued their support for decades.[70] For the Tibetans: 'The value of the support of Western donors extends beyond the economic: their donations have, from the Tibetan perspective, the quality of offerings *sbyin-bdag* make, given in the spirit of belief, compassion, and encouragement for all that Tibetans in their refugee circumstances represent of and for old Tibet.'[71] During this time, the countercultural movement gained influence in the West. Young hippies began to travel to the Himalayas to fulfil their spiritual quests. Some developed an interest in Tibetan Buddhism and became the first Western students of Tibetan lamas in exile. In due course, they invited the lamas to their home countries and helped them build institutions and communities there, laying the foundation for the spread of Tibetan Buddhism in the West. As a result, the Tibetans, for the first time in history, openly welcomed and engaged with Westerners at the collective level: '[T]he Western quest for spiritualism and the exile government's need to promote the Tibetan cause in the world, to keep alive Tibetan religion and culture, to continue its age-old tradition of seeking patronage, has inevitably led Tibetans to open their hearth and homes to Westerners.'[72] It was from this collective openness within the diaspora that the cross-cultural exchange between the Tibetans and Westerners unfolded on a large, global scale.

Support came also from within Western academia. From the 1960s, interest in Tibetan culture developed at American and European universities. The turmoil in Tibet at that time engendered a sense of urgency to preserve its culture.[73] Many Western scholars considered Tibetan Buddhism as an untainted, authentic ancient wisdom, valuable to the modern world.[74] This clearly contrasts with the intellectual attitude in the nineteenth century that considered the Tibetan tradition to be a degenerated form of Buddhism. The new, positive attitude led to the founding of departments of Tibetan Studies and the recruitment of Tibetan lamas as teachers.[75] These Tibetan lamas encouraged their students to pursue academic careers in Buddhist Studies; they did not set out to propagate Buddhism in the West. It was only later that they began to establish Dharma centres and teach in public.[76] Through the combined effort of Western scholars and Tibetan lamas, Tibetan Buddhism soon became a legitimate field of academic research.[77] Meanwhile, the Library of Congress in the United States sponsored large-scale printing of Tibetan texts and distributed them to university libraries across the country.[78] As Tibetan lamas came to work in American and European universities, young graduates and scholars also travelled to India to work with the exile lamas there. Many sought to translate Buddhist texts from Tibetan into English. They considered themselves to be best suited to preserve Tibetan culture.[79] Their focus was on classical scriptures instead of the living tradition; their priority was philosophy over ritual, community and history. Some struggled with the authority of the texts over the oral commentaries of Tibetan lamas.[80]

The academic interest in Tibetan culture played a role in the early spread of Tibetan Buddhism in the West. It was rare, however, for its impact to extend beyond the university campus. This was achieved by a small group of publishing houses, each associated with one Tibetan lama, producing and distributing a large number of Buddhist books to the public. These include Shambhala Publications founded in 1969, Dharma Publishing in 1971,[81]

Wisdom Publications in 1975 and Snow Lion Publications in 1980. Together, they contributed to the popularisation of Tibetan Buddhism in the West.

The discussion so far has shown that the preservation of Tibetan culture in exile was driven by two constituents: the Tibetans themselves and the interested Westerners. They each had a different understanding and interpretation of Tibet and Tibetans, hence creating two distinct metanarratives: 'The Tibetan Metanarrative, in essence, values Tibetans as a whole over individual experience and describes Tibet as pure and traditional like nowhere else. The American/European Metanarrative is focused on individuals and views Tibet as the home of an exotic people with a mystical repository of aged learning.'[82] On the one hand, the American/European interpretation of Tibet bore the imprint of Western cultural values, political agenda against communism as well as a yearning for spirituality. It portrays Tibetans as worthy recipients of aid and prompts Western patrons to be committed to the reconstruction of Tibetan culture and religion.[83] The support from these patrons not only derived from humanitarian concern but also fed on the Western imagination of Tibet.[84]

On the other hand, the Tibetans utilised the romantic representation of Tibet to serve their own political cause of self-determination.[85] They exercised active agency in the modern construction of Tibet. Harle identifies two contrasting trends in the literature about Tibet since 1959. Books sympathetic to the Tibetan cause develop a romantic vision of pre-modern Tibet as a land of peace and harmony, to bring into sharp relief the destruction under Chinese rule. Books aligned with China celebrate the liberation of Tibet from its oppressive theocracy.[86] As the division between the two trends increased, the Tibetan diaspora welcomed the former, subscribing to the Shangri-la myth, and dismissed the latter as serving the interest of Communist China. For example, the Tibetan government-in-exile rejected Goldstein's study of pre-modern Tibet, because it reveals extensive factionalism and sectarianism which undermine its own version of Tibet's history.[87] The Tibetans instead created an image of Tibet as a 'modern, liberal Shangri-la':[88] '[N]ew Tibetan exile identity claims represent, at least in part, an appropriation of Western discourse by the objectified Tibetan "Other" and its creative reflection back to the West. Exile identity claims are often so appealing to, and uncritically accepted by, many Westerners precisely because of such feedback.'[89] The cultural destruction in Tibet, coupled with the hardship and frustration in exile, led the Tibetans to remember their homeland as a Buddhist Pure Land, an imagined alternative to reality.[90] This imagination allowed them to maintain hope for a future return.[91] Their utopian version of Tibet is very similar to the Western idealisation. Just as the Tibetans and Westerners contributed to the preservation of Tibetan culture, they also, for different reasons, co-created a romantic image of Tibet.

2.2. INTRODUCTION OF BUDDHISM

The development of Buddhism in the West has its roots in the modernisation of the Theravāda and Zen Buddhist traditions in Asia. During the nineteenth century, Buddhist leaders of these traditions formulated strategies of reform in response to colonialism. 'Modernist Buddhism' came thus into being. While 'Traditionalist Buddhism' advocates devotion, ritual and established pattern of authority, 'Modernist Buddhism' stresses the importance of meditation, text reading and rationalist interpretation. As Theravāda and Zen Buddhism spread to Europe and North America, their modernised form drew many Western followers. The traditional form, on the other hand, remained within the immigrant communities. Tamney identifies five aspects of the modernisation process: individualism, religious purification, a concern about mental health, the wish for religion to be consistent with one's lifestyle and the sense of entitlement to be able to borrow from different cultures.[92] The modernisation of Buddhism, it is easy to see, promoted the role of the laity in a multicultural society. It privileged meditation aimed to achieve spiritual fulfilment, mental health and a contented life.

'Modernist Buddhism' then gave way to 'Postmodernist Buddhism' which further secularised and psychologised Buddhism. Springing from the 'non-rational basement of the mind', postmodernism brought forth a 'free market place of ideas', a space where alternative religions could blossom, where the potential of the mind and personal revelation of divinity could unfold.[93] This feature of postmodernism nourished the counterculture and new religious movements in the 1960s. It revitalised the romantic imaginations created through the Orientalist gaze of Buddhism during the nineteenth century. Tibetan Buddhism connected to this, through a revival of the myth of Shangri-la, as a result of the joint effort of the Europeans/Americans and the Tibetan diaspora in the idealisation of Tibet. It appealed to the Western audience as a means of spiritual fulfilment at a profound level.[94]

Both modernist and postmodernist interpretations of Buddhism became popular among the early Western 'converts'.[95] They led Asian Buddhist teachers to mould their teachings to suit local expectations and values.[96] In the case of Tibetan Buddhism, they inspired some lamas to distinguish the traditional and fixed from the adaptable elements in their teachings. Already in the 1970s, they 'began exploring what in their religion was universally valid, and what was merely "Himalayan dogma" and which therefore could go'.[97] Yet, this was a difficult task, not without risk and controversy, because: 'The process of adapting the dharma to a new culture is highly complicated, involving the adaptation of religious practices to a new environment, the association of formerly unrelated ideas, and the recasting of received values into new ethical language.'[98] At the same time, Western converts began to contribute to the spread of Buddhism. Baumann maintains that Buddhism took root in the West because of the efforts of its sympathisers and initial followers who translated and published Buddhist texts, adopted Buddhist ideas and practices, and invited Buddhist teachers to deliver lectures.[99] The converts also adapted Buddhism in ways that were quite alien to tradition; 'Western Buddhism' came thus to be discussed as an emerging phenomenon. In the following, I shall discuss, in particular, the development of Buddhism in the United States and Great Britain.

2.2.1. The United States

The popularity of Buddhism in the United States sprang from two sources: the Theosophical Society and the World's Parliament of Religions. Blavatsky's Theosophy largely influenced the Western interpretation of Buddhism. Orientalism endemic within the academia and popular culture projected European/American values onto Buddhism, and in so doing, undermined the position of Asian Buddhists.[100] For decades, Orientalism sustained a strong impact on the American interpretation of Buddhism, even after Asian Buddhist teachers had settled in the country. The Asian teachers, in response, created strategies to communicate Buddhist ideas to their new audience. The launch of the World's Parliament of Religions in Chicago in 1893 offered the first opportunity for Theravāda and Zen teachers to introduce a modernist form of Buddhism.[101] This event became a landmark for 'Modernist Buddhism' in the United States. It informed Asian Buddhist teachers' modernisation strategy reaching into the twentieth century.

The modernised Zen Buddhism in the first half of the twentieth century had a particular impact on the early transmission of Tibetan Buddhism. The Japanese were the first to teach Buddhism to American converts; they also pioneered the dialogue between Buddhism and psychology. The form of Zen teaching they articulated stemmed from the modernisation in Japan. Upon its arrival in the West, Zen Buddhism soon developed its appeal to the Western audience: 'Zen appeared in the West at the right historical moment because its purported anti-intellectualism, anti-ritualism and iconoclasm, and its emphasis on unmediated experience of ultimate truth, confirmed and hardened the "hermeneutic of experience" characterising Western scholarship of religion at the turn of the last century.'[102]

From the 'Zen boom' in the 1950s, teachers, such as D. T. Suzuki, together with the Beat poets, introduced Buddhism to popular culture with a distinctive approach. Their introduction shaped the way in which Buddhism developed in the following decades. Their adaptation to host culture drew on various strategies: '[T]ranslating key ideas; simplifying or de-emphasizing elements unacceptable to the host culture; tolerating previously unacceptable customs in the host culture; reinterpreting teachings or practices; absorbing elements of the host culture into rituals or systems of meaning; and assimilating converts into foreign practices.'[103] The Zen teachers created new teaching styles and methods aligned with American values. In the process, Buddhism became 'Americanised', removed from its historical context. Still, from the converts' point of view, it was necessary to shed the 'ethnic and cultural trappings',[104] because:

> Their introduction to the dharma was largely through books, and they easily drew from them the conclusion that the pursuit of enlightenment could be highly individualized and personalized, filtered through humanistic psychology, augmented through the use of mind-altering substances, pursued without sustained discipline, and divorced from institutions.[105]

Buddhism appealed to the Americans because it seemed to 'offer a more effective way of realizing values that are already held in the culture', such as 'self-realization, freedom, transforming relationships, getting in touch with one's experience, living more fully in the moment or the world, healing, and so forth'.[106] The converts came to know Buddhism through the lens of their own sociocultural values, without sufficient understanding of its historical background.

From the mid-1960s to the mid-1970s, American converts grew into a larger community associated with diverse Buddhist traditions. The number of meditation centres increased fivefold in this period.[107] The multicultural and pluralist religious setting, combined with the 1965 Immigration Act opening the door to Asian political refugees, propelled the diffusion of different Buddhist traditions within American society. The counterculture, new religious and New Age movements provided fertile ground for them to flourish. Most young Americans discovered Buddhism first through books. Some then travelled to Asia to seek spiritual guides while others found their teachers in the United States. They became the driving force to promote Buddhism in popular culture. As a result: 'Prior to and through the 1950s, the dharma had remained more or less confined to bohemian quarters and was the preoccupation of a small handful of spiritual seekers. In the course of the next decade, however, Buddhism began to turn into something that resembled a mass religious movement.'[108]

The counterculture movement spread across the country expressing the young generation's escalated discontent with society.[109] It signalled the end of 'American Dream' that promised 'a secular version of salvation' with economic success, a happy family and opportunities for self-expression.[110] The young people, especially those associated with the hippie subculture, openly challenged mainstream values through radical action.[111] They rejected society, sought alternative values in Asian cultures and indulged in various

Asian religions in pursuit of different kinds of enlightenment. The converts' radical social aspirations rendered their involvement in, and interpretation of, Asian religions problematic:

> Stressing less the basic doctrine and painstaking practice, they usually base their attraction on the promise of something new, frequently centered on the personal charisma of a flamboyant leader. In other words, they replace the old social order, now in decay or disfavor, with a new one, replete with the same sort of trappings, but transmuted into what is thought to be a more profoundly 'relevant' religious foundation. By nature flashy, opaquely exotic, and 'hip', these movements gain much attention in the press but are unstable. Some . . . do endure, but only after the pandemonium has passed and they have adopted a more solid working basis.[112]

The close ties with the counterculture youths caused instability in the Buddhist community:

> In many ways, Buddhists' infant community life in America was more seriously disrupted than were those of more established communities in the mainstream of American culture. Consequently, through its association with the counterculture, Buddhist community life was to some extent a hot-bed of current or defunct radicals, practicing everything from do-it-yourself macrobiotics to various forms of multi-lateral marriage.[113]

In the end, the young rebels' countercultural ambitions turned out to be fruitless. They retreated from confrontation with society to inner development.[114]

During this time, the new religious movement too gathered influence and played an important part in the early development of Buddhism in the United States. The movement allowed Asian religions to find a place in American society. Although some had already existed long before, they remained within the immigrant communities. Now for the first time, they began to attract American followers. This created a good timing for the arrival of Tibetan Buddhism: 'at no other time, before or since, could Tibetan Buddhism have thus landed on American shores and enjoyed such a welcoming reception'.[115] American converts, instead of Tibetan immigrants, made up the largest part of its community.[116] Mullen describes this phenomenon as 'the American "occupation" of the Vajrayāna'.[117] Tibetan lamas created teaching methods tailored to middle-class Americans with the purpose of preserving the Dharma. The American converts, in turn, gathered around Tibetan lamas to help them build communities and institutions.[118] Ordinary Tibetans, in contrast, formed self-reliant communities to attract American support for their political cause.

The convert communities of Tibetan Buddhism were shaped also by another phenomenon called the New Age movement. While the period between the 1920s and 1960s witnessed religious pluralism and experimentation, the New Age movement became increasingly popular during the 1970s. It combined Eastern mysticism with Native American spirituality and other practices.[119] Its seekers readily incorporated Tibetan Buddhism into their shopping baskets for alternative religious experiences. Tibet again represented a dreamlike fantasy: an isolated, mysterious and sacred place with an inaccessible treasure of spiritual masters and esoteric teachings.[120] This led to a revival of the myth of Shangri-la, known as 'New Age Orientalism'.[121] The mythologisation of Tibet influenced the ways in which the converts approached Tibetan Buddhism. In some cases, it distorted the teacher-disciple relationship, turning it into a personality cult. Near the end of the decade, with the rise of the 'anti-cult movement', religious groups displaying abuse of power faced criticism in the media. The convert communities of Tibetan Buddhism came under close public scrutiny; some underwent leadership crises, and in response, began a period of critical self-reflection.

As the 1970s saw Buddhism taking root in American society, the first generation of American Buddhist teachers emerged in the 1980s. This was an important transitional period: as Asian teachers who had played a pivotal role in the early transmission of Buddhism died, American converts stepped forward to propagate Buddhism themselves. Now approaching middle age, they had re-entered mainstream society; some became Buddhist scholars, Dharma teachers and leaders of Buddhist communities.[122] A new term, 'American Buddhism', emerged to highlight the converts' role in creating new expressions of Buddhism.[123] Between 1975 and 1984, the number of meditation centres doubled.[124] By the end of the 1980s, Tibetan Buddhist communities had founded 184 centres across the country.[125]

Alongside the new religious and New Age movements, two other forces allowed Tibetan Buddhism to prosper in mainstream society. First, the Free Tibet campaign promoted the cause of the Tibetan diaspora, and in the process, embedded Tibetan Buddhism within its politically motivated narrative. Second, the commercialisation of Tibetan culture, with its roots in the New Age movement, built on consumerism and targeted white, middle-aged wealthy Americans who pursued their spiritual path through purchase.[126] The lavish events and pricey lectures, seminars and exhibitions organised at Tibetan Buddhist and cultural institutions in New York, such as Tibet House, serve as good examples.[127] Tibet had now turned into a fancy commodity for self-expression among affluent Americans, be it spiritual or political, largely divorced from real Tibet or Tibetans. Tibet came to be seen as a brand that is mysterious, spiritual, remote, trendy and supernatural, deployed to evoke images of wealth, salvation, morality and a spiritual lifestyle.[128]

2.2.2. Great Britain

The introduction of Buddhism to England was, in Mellor's view, a 'cultural translation'.[129] It was deeply embedded within Theosophy, modernity and the Protestant discourse of individualism and dismissal of religious formality.[130] This proposition, though criticised for its exaggeration of the impact of the Protestant values,[131] identifies key factors that shaped the development of Buddhism in Britain. For example, the popular 'Modernist Buddhism' features individualism and rationalist interpretation. Waterhouse considers personal experience to be one of the 'authority sources' that different Buddhist traditions draw on to justify their efforts of adaptation,[132] which points again to individualism. Bell describes the spread of Buddhism as a result of 'active collaboration' between British converts and Asian Buddhists.[133] Similar to their American counterparts, British converts played an important part in the adaptation of Buddhism to the local context: they promoted Buddhism based on an interpretation defined by British culture and social norms. This, in turn, impacted Asian Buddhist teachers' transmission strategies. Above all, the Orientalist view about Asian religions that prevailed in society, coupled with an individualistic mindset among the converts, came to be a defining feature of 'British Buddhism': 'The lure of the mysterious East, a scholarly and reserved approach, with personal (rather than institutional) choices about what to retain or discard, all appear characteristic of a British attitude towards spiritual practice in a materialistic age.'[134]

During the nineteenth century, British churches began to lose authority as religion became privatised. This, together with Christian missionary activity and the British imperial rule in Asia, kindled an intellectual interest in Buddhism. The British studied Buddhism through the lens of Christian ideas, British values and Orientalism. They considered the Buddha to be 'an ideal Victorian gentleman'[135] and Buddhism a 'religion of reason'; a new term, 'original Buddhism', as a product of Romantic Orientalism, was coined.[136] Consequently, Buddhist teachings and practices were often misinterpreted and misrepresented. In 1881, Rhys Davids founded the Pali Text Society to study the ancient Buddhist texts of the Theravāda tradition. Anti-Catholic and of Victorian rationalist predisposition, he presented Theravāda Buddhism as the most authentic, original and purest form of Buddhism. He criticised the Mahāyāna school as superstitious and Tibetan Buddhism as resembling Romanism. Meanwhile, popular works, such as Edwin Arnold's *The Light of Asia* (1879), and Blavatsky's Theosophy drove some of those who had begun to lose faith in Christianity towards Buddhism.[137] The appeal of Buddhism rested, in part, on its compatibility with the rationalist critique of Christianity and a romantic yearning unsatisfied in either Christianity or science.[138] Buddhism provided 'a source of spiritual renewal'.[139]

In 1907, Rhys Davids founded the Buddhist Society of Great Britain and Ireland. Tension soon developed between Buddhist scholars and practitioners. In the period between the two world wars, the authority of Christian churches continued to decline. In 1924, a London branch of the Theosophical Society came into being, called 'Buddhist Lodge'. Christmas Humphreys served as its president. The Theosophical Society demonstrated hostility towards Christianity; it emphasised practice in contrast to the scholarly orientation of Rhys Davids's Buddhist Society. At this time, Theravāda and Zen teachers began to visit Britain. Their lectures left a long-lasting impact on the public reception of Buddhism. Zen teacher D. T. Suzuki, through his *Essays in Zen Buddhism* (1927) and meetings with the British members of the Theosophical Society, introduced Mahāyāna Buddhism to a large audience. In 1943, the Buddhist Lodge was renamed as the Buddhist Society. It became a centre of Buddhist teaching and represented Buddhism in Britain.[140]

Moving on to the 1950s, as Christianity lost further its appeal to the public, the Buddhist Society expanded its reach. Humphreys even sought to propagate its 'Twelve Principles of Buddhism' in Asian Buddhist countries as the basis of all Buddhist traditions. The society's publication, *The Middle Way*, began to discuss the future of 'Western Buddhism'. Yet, the society also gave prominence to Asian Buddhist traditions. It invited Suzuki, as well as Buddhologists Edward Conze, I. B. Horner and Maurice Walshe, to deliver lectures. Humphreys's *Buddhism: An introduction and guide* and Conze's *Buddhism: Its essence and development*, both published in 1951, increased public interest in Buddhism.[141]

In the 1960s, Buddhism gained wider influence on account of the significant social change in British society.[142] This led to an increase in religious pluralism; the appeal of Buddhism to the public grew. However, the Buddhist Society remained conservative. Towards the end of the 1960s, its status as a driving force for the spread of Buddhism in Britain declined. Now, young British converts began to approach Buddhism in a different manner: many sought a more personal and direct encounter with Buddhism, either on their travels through Asia or in the newly established Dharma centres in Britain.[143] At this point, Buddhism embarked on a much more ambitious expansion:

> The pattern of Buddhism in Britain between 1945 and 1965 is one of gradually increasing complexity, including awareness of a wider range of teaching and practice, early attempts to establish a monastic *saṅgha* and the growth of lay groups. The emergence of separate schools, the possibility of a westernized Buddhism and the tensions between progressive and conservative Buddhists all suggest that the subsequent development of Buddhism in Britain should be traced in a rather different format.[144]

Buddhism, between the 1960s and 1970s, was associated with the counterculture and new religious movements. Barker regards their followers as first-generation enthusiasts attracted to charismatic leadership.[145] Nonetheless, Kay cautions against the tendency to overestimate the impact of new religious movements on the popularity of Buddhism in Britain. British converts, in his view, possessed 'high educational levels . . . and the discriminating and reasoned manner in which they negotiate their spiritual paths'.[146] At any rate, from this time onwards, Buddhism developed at a more rapid pace, driven by the Britons' disillusionment with their own culture and religion. The number of Buddhist groups associated with various Buddhist traditions increased from 22 in 1966 to 100 by 1978, and then 140 in 1981.[147]

Buddhism in Britain was also closely connected to the New Age movement. This movement was seen as a 'mainstream adaptation of the 1960s counterculture' and 'one of the foremost religious expressions of postmodernity'.[148] According to Cush, the link between 'British Buddhism' and the New Age movement goes back to Blavatsky's Theosophy which found a warm reception among the early converts.[149] Her data shows that the adherents of Tibetan Buddhism in the 1970s mostly came from alternative cultures. They became attracted to Tibetan Buddhism for its rituals, meditation and esoteric teachings. However, from the mid-1980s, Buddhism began to disaggregate itself from New Age. The convert community of Tibetan Buddhism, for example, was by then comprised of serious and respectable practitioners.[150]

New Buddhist movements too emerged during this time. They claimed independent authority, separated themselves from their Asian origins and recruited members from wider social strata that extended beyond the middle-class converts of the traditional Asian Buddhist schools.[151] Bluck identifies ten areas where traditional Buddhist schools and new Buddhist movements coalesce: (1) traditional silent meditation, (2) largely traditional devotional activities, (3) traditional teachings, (4) some emphasis on textual study, (5) a programme of retreats and courses, (6) ancient and contemporary narratives, (7) a common ethical code for all members, (8) an important teacher-pupil relationship, (9) mostly Western teachers and (10) increased lay participation.[152] The first three plus eight reveal their shared emphasis on tradition. The fourth stresses the sophistication of Buddhist teaching and a textual preference. The fifth and sixth express concern with continuity of tradition and flexibility to incorporate modern elements. The seventh and tenth highlight the role of the laity and a shared religious code. The ninth signals the rise of Western Buddhist teachers.

Many of these factors apply to the development of Tibetan Buddhism in Britain. It puts forth traditional approaches to meditation and devotional activities, grants authority to contemporary teachers within the lineage narrative, advocates a group of basic precepts for all practitioners and allocates a critical role to the teacher in one's spiritual progress. While Tibetan lamas are given much prominence, Western Buddhist teachers and lay members are gradually gaining a more important role in the community. Nonetheless, it is also flexible in methods of teaching, open to secular elements, such as therapy, and prioritises practice over formal study.[153]

NOTES

1. Martin Brauen, *Dreamworld Tibet: Western illusions* (Trumbull, CT: Weatherhill, 2004), 216–217.
2. Lee Feigon, *Demystifying Tibet: Unlocking the secrets of the land of the snows* (Chicago: Ivan R. Dee, 1996), 15.
3. Donald S Lopez, "New Age Orientalism: The case of Tibet," *Tricycle* 3, no. 3 (1994): 43.
4. In Wilde's opinion: 'Art takes life as part of her rough material, recreates it, and refashions it in fresh forms, is absolutely indifferent to fact, invents, imagines, dreams, and keeps between herself and reality the impenetrable barrier of beautiful style, of decorative or ideal treatment.' Oscar Wilde, *Complete Works of Oscar Wilde* (New York: Harper & Row, 1989), quoted in Donald S Lopez, "New Age Orientalism: The case of Tibet," *Tricycle* 3, no. 3 (1994): 183.
5. Lopez, *Prisoners of Shangri-La*, 183.
6. Lopez, *Prisoners of Shangri-La*, 184.
7. Peter Bishop, *Dreams of Power: Tibetan Buddhism and the western imagination* (London: Athlone, 1993), 16.
8. Lopez, *Prisoners of Shangri-La*, 5–6.
9. Tsering Shakya, "Who are the Prisoners?" *Journal of the American Academy of Religion* 69, no. 1 (2001): 183–189.
10. Per Kvaerne, "Tibet Images Among Researchers on Tibet," in *Imagining Tibet: Perceptions, projections, and fantasies*, eds. Thierry Dodin and Heinz Räther (Boston: Wisdom Press, 2001), 48.
11. Poul Pedersen, "Tibet, Theosophy, and the Psychologization of Buddhism," in *Imagining Tibet: Perceptions, projections, and fantasies*, eds. Thierry Dodin and Heinz Räther (Boston: Wisdom Press, 2001), 152.
12. Jeannine M Chandler, *Hunting the Guru: Lineage, culture and conflict in the development of Tibetan Buddhism in America* (State University of New York at Albany, 2009).
13. Pedersen, "Tibet, Theosophy," 152.
14. Pedersen, "Tibet, Theosophy," 152.
15. Pedersen, "Tibet, Theosophy," 156.
16. In 1884, the Society for Psychical Research exposed Blavatsky's claim of connection with Tibetan masters as fraud. It declared: '[S]he has achieved a title to permanent remembrance as one of the most accomplished, ingenious, and interesting

impostors in history.' See Maria Carlson, *No Religion Higher Than Truth: A history of the Theosophical movement in Russia, 1875–1922* (Princeton: Princeton University Press, 1993), quoted in Poul Pedersen, "Tibet, Theosophy, and the Psychologization of Buddhism," in *Imagining Tibet: Perceptions, projections, and fantasies*, eds. Thierry Dodin and Heinz Räther (Boston: Wisdom Press, 2001), 156, 164.

17. Pedersen, "Tibet, Theosophy," 152–157.
18. Pedersen, "Tibet, Theosophy," 157.
19. Rudyard Kipling, *Kim* (London: Macmillan, 1963); Arthur C Doyle, *The Adventure of the Empty House* (Createspace independent publishing platform, 2012).
20. Lopez, "New Age Orientalism," 38.
21. Alex C McKay, "'Truth,' Perception, and Politics: The British construction of an image of Tibet," in *Imagining Tibet: Perceptions, projections, and fantasies*, eds. Thierry Dodin and Heinz Räther (Boston: Wisdom Press, 2001), 76.
22. McKay, "'Truth,' Perception, and Politics," 71–84.
23. Peter Bishop, *The Myth of Shangri-La: Tibet, travel writing and the western creation of sacred landscape* (London: Athlone, 1989), 192.
24. Peter H Hansen, "Tibetan Horizon: Tibet and the cinema in the early twentieth century," in *Imagining Tibet: Perceptions, projections, and fantasies*, eds. Thierry Dodin and Heinz Räther (Boston: Wisdom Press, 2001), 92–97.
25. Diana Martinez, "The Journey of an Image: The western perception of Tibet from 1900–1950" (MA diss., The University of Texas at El Paso, 2009), 108.
26. Martinez, "Journey of an Image," 109.
27. Jeffrey Paine, *Re-Enchantment: Tibetan Buddhism comes to the West* (New York and London: W.W. Norton, 2004), 33–49.
28. Alexandra David-Neel, *Magic and Mystery in Tibet* (New York: Dover Publications, 1971), quoted in Peter Bishop, *The Myth of Shangri-La: Tibet, travel writing and the western creation of sacred landscape* (London: Athlone, 1989), 199.
29. Bishop, *Myth of Shangri-La*, 199.
30. Donald S Lopez, "The Image of Tibet of the Great Mystifiers," in *Imagining Tibet: Perceptions, projections, and fantasies*, eds. Thierry Dodin and Heinz Räther (Boston: Wisdom Press, 2001), 183–184.
31. Lopez, "New Age Orientalism," 39.
32. See *Lost Horizon*, DVD, directed by Frank Capra, 1937 (USA: Sony Pictures Home Entertainment, 2001).
33. James Hilton, *Lost Horizon* (London: Pan Books, 1947), quoted in Peter Bishop, *The Myth of Shangri-La: Tibet, travel writing and the western creation of sacred landscape* (London: Athlone, 1989), 211.
34. Bishop, *Myth of Shangri-La*, 211.
35. Bishop, *Myth of Shangri-La*, 206.
36. Alex C McKay, "'Truth,' Perception, and Politics: The British construction of an image of Tibet," in *Imagining Tibet: Perceptions, projections, and fantasies*, eds. Thierry Dodin and Heinz Räther (Boston: Wisdom Press, 2001), 76.
37. Bishop, *Dreams of Power*, 62.
38. Pedersen, "Tibet, Theosophy," 159–160.
39. Bishop, Dreams of Power, 73.

40. Lopez, *Prisoners of Shangri-La*, 76.
41. Pedersen, "Tibet, Theosophy," 160.
42. Bishop, *Myth of Shangri-La*, 216.
43. Bishop, *Myth of Shangri-La*, 203.
44. Bishop, *Myth of Shangri-La*, 209.
45. Lopez, *Prisoners of Shangri-La*, 4.
46. Donald S Lopez, *Curators of the Buddha: The study of Buddhism under colonialism* (Chicago and London: University of Chicago Press, 1995), 293.
47. Lopez, "New Age Orientalism," 40; 1995: 293.
48. Fisher, "Dialogical Construction."
49. Bishop 2001: 217.
50. Lopez, *Prisoners of Shangri-La*, 7.
51. Lopez, *Prisoners of Shangri-La*, 10.
52. Dodin & Räther 2001: 399.
53. Bishop, *Myth of Shangri-La*, 244.
54. *From the Roof of the World: Refugees of Tibet* (Berkeley: Dharma Publishing, 1992); quoted in Peter G Harle, "Thinking with Things: Objects and identity among Tibetans in the Twin Cities" (PhD diss., Indiana University, 2003), 40.
55. Dibyesh Anand, "A Contemporary Story of 'Diaspora': The Tibetan version," *Diaspora: A Journal of transnational studies* 12, no. 2 (2003): 214; Harle, "Thinking with Things," 2.
56. Anand, "Contemporary Story of 'Diaspora'," 214.
57. Dibyesh Anand, "A Guide to Little Lhasa: The role of symbolic geography of Dharamsala in constituting Tibetan diasporic identity," in *Tibet, Self and the Tibetan Diaspora: Voices of difference*, ed. C. Klieger (Leiden: E. J. Brill, 2002), quoted in John Robertson, "Semiotics, Habitus and Music in the Transmission of Tibetan Culture in Toronto" (MA diss., Liberty University, 2011), 2.
58. Harle, "Thinking with Things," 41.
59. Lopez, *Prisoners of Shangri-La*; Anand, "Contemporary Story of 'Diaspora'"; Yosay Wangdi, "Agonized Nation."
60. Geoffrey Samuel, *Civilized Shamans: Buddhism in Tibetan societies* (Washington and London: Smithsonian Institution Press, 1993), 112.
61. Anand, "Contemporary Story of 'Diaspora'," 215.
62. McLagan, "Mobilizing for Tibet," 204–205; Anand, "Contemporary Story of 'Diaspora'," 218.
63. Anand, "Contemporary Story of 'Diaspora'," 222.
64. Anand, "Contemporary Story of 'Diaspora'," 220.
65. Anand, "Contemporary Story of 'Diaspora'," 220.
66. Harle, "Thinking with Things," 1–2.
67. McLagan, "Mobilizing for Tibet," 96.
68. Harle, "Thinking with Things," 44.
69. McLagan, "Mobilizing for Tibet," 40–41.
70. McLagan, "Mobilizing for Tibet," 208–210.
71. Dorsh Marie de Voe, "Keeping Refugee Status: A Tibetan perspective," in *People in Upheaval*, eds. Scott Morgan and Elizabeth Colson (New York: Center

for Migration Studies, 1987), quoted in Margaret J McLagan, "Mobilizing for Tibet: Transnational politics and diaspora culture in the post-cold war era" (PhD diss., New York University, 1996), 210.

72. Yosay Wangdi, "Agonized Nation," 11.

73. Lopez, *Curators of the Buddha*; Kvaerne, "Tibet Images"; Heather Stoddard, "The Development in Perceptions of Tibetan Art: From golden idols to ultimate reality," in *Imagining Tibet: Perceptions, projections, and fantasies*, eds. Thierry Dodin and Heinz Räther (Boston: Wisdom Press, 2001); Jeffrey Hopkins, "Tibetan Monastic Colleges: Rationality versus the demands of allegiance," in *Imagining Tibet: Perceptions, projections, and fantasies*, eds. Thierry Dodin and Heinz Räther (Boston: Wisdom Press, 2001).

74. Lopez, "New Age Orientalism," 41; Lopez, *Curators of the Buddha*, 266–267; Lopez, *Prisoners of Shangri-La*, 42.

75. Amy Lavine, "The Politics of Nostalgia: Social memory and national identity among diaspora Tibetans in New York City" (PhD diss., The University of Chicago, 2001), 37–38.

76. For example, Dezhung Rinpoche and Geshe Lhundub Sopa. See David P Jackson, *A Saint in Seattle: The life of the Tibetan mystic Dezhung Rinpoche* (Boston: Wisdom Publications, 2003); Geshe Lhundub Sopa and Paul Donnelly, *Like a Waking Dream: The autobiography of Geshe Lhundub Sopa* (Boston: Wisdom Publications, 2012).

77. Lopez, *Curators of the Buddha*, 265.

78. Lopez, *Curators of the Buddha*, 265.

79. Lopez, *Curators of the Buddha*, 268.

80. Lopez, *Curators of the Buddha*, 270–282.

81. Dharma Publishing was founded by Tarthang Tulku in India in 1963 and moved to California in 1971.

82. Ryan Fisher, "The Dialogical Construction of Tibetan-ness: Narratives of Tibetan identity and memory" (PhD diss., Southern Methodist University, 2011), 160.

83. Margaret J McLagan, "Mobilizing for Tibet: Transnational politics and diaspora culture in the post-cold war era" (PhD diss., New York University, 1996), 208–209.

84. McLagan, "Mobilizing for Tibet," 208.

85. McLagan, "Mobilizing for Tibet"; Yosay Wangdi, "Echoes of an Agonized Nation: Transformations in Tibetan identity in diaspora" (PhD diss., University of Nevada, Reno, 2003); Fisher, "Dialogical Construction."

86. Peter G Harle, "Thinking with Things: Objects and identity among Tibetans in the Twin Cities" (PhD diss., Indiana University, 2003), 23.

87. McLagan, "Mobilizing for Tibet," 28.

88. Huber, "Shangri-La in Exile," 368.

89. Huber, "Shangri-La in Exile," 358–359.

90. Lavine, "Politics of Nostalgia," 2.

91. Lavine, "Politics of Nostalgia," 31–32.

92. Joseph B Tamney, Afterword to *North American Buddhists in Social Context*, ed. Paul D. Numrich (Leiden and Boston: Brill, 2008), 226–230.

93. Robert S Ellwood, *The Sixties Spiritual Awakening: American religion moving from modern to postmodern* (New Brunswick, NJ: Rutgers University Press, 1994), quoted in Elizabeth C Cleland, "The Vajrakilaya Sadhana: An Euro-American experience of a Nyingma ritual" (MA diss., Carleton University, 2001), 24.

94. Cleland, "Vajrakilaya Sadhana," 26.

95. The term 'converts' is often found in the study of the typology of Buddhism. Notable works include: Emma M Layman, *Buddhism in America* (Chicago, IL: Nelson-Hall, 1976); Prebish, *American Buddhism*; Charles. S Prebish, "Two Buddhisms Reconsidered," *Buddhist Studies Review* 10, no. 2 (1993): 187–206; Jan Nattier, "Visible and Invisible: The politics of representation in Buddhist America," *Tricycle: The Buddhist Review* 5 (1995): 42–49; Jan Nattier, "Buddhism Comes to Main Street," *Wilson Quarterly* (Spring 1997): 72–80; Jan Nattier, "Who is a Buddhist? Charting the Landscape of Buddhist America," in *The Faces of Buddhism in America*, eds. Charles S. Prebish and Kenneth K. Tanaka (Berkeley, CA: University of California Press, 1998); Paul D Numrich, *Old Wisdom in the New World: Americanization in two immigrant Theravada Buddhist temples* (Knoxville, TN: University of Tennessee Press, 1996); Paul D Numrich, "How the Swans Came to Lake Michigan: The social organization of Buddhist Chicago," *Journal for the Scientific Study of Religion* 39, no. 2 (2000): 189–203; Paul D Numrich, "Two Buddhisms Further Considered," *Contemporary Buddhism* 4, no. 1 (2003): 55–78; Paul D Numrich, "Two Buddhisms Further Considered," in *Buddhist Studies from India to America: Essays in honor of Charles S. Prebish*, ed. D. Keown (New York: Routledge, 2006); Amy Lavine, "Tibetan Buddhism in America: The development of American Vajrayāna," in *The Faces of Buddhism in America*, eds. Charles S. Prebish and Kenneth K. Tanaka (Berkeley, CA: University of California Press, 1998); Thomas A Tweed, "Night-Stand Buddhists and Other Creatures: Sympathizers, adherents, and the study of religion," in *American Buddhism: Methods and findings in recent scholarship*, eds. Duncan Ryuken Williams and Christopher S. Queen (London: Curzon Press, 1999); Thomas A Tweed, *The American Encounter with Buddhism, 1844–1912: Victorian culture and the limits of dissent* (Chapel Hill, NC: University of North Carolina Press, 2000); Thomas A Tweed, "Who is a Buddhist? Night-Stand Buddhists and Other Creatures," in *Westward Dharma: Buddhism beyond Asia*, eds. Charles S. Prebish and Martin Baumann (Berkeley: University of California Press, 2002); Peter N Gregory, "Describing the Elephant: Buddhism in America," *Religion and American Culture: A journal of interpretation* 11 (2001): 233–263; Donald Swearer, "Tensions in American Buddhism," *Religion and Ethics Newsweekly*, July 6, 2001. http://www.pbs.org/wnet/religionandethics/week445/buddhism.html; Martin Baumann, "Protective Amulets and Awareness Techniques, or How to Make Sense of Buddhism in the West," in *Westward Dharma: Buddhism beyond Asia*, eds. Charles S. Prebish and Martin Baumann (Berkeley: University of California Press, 2002); Richard H Seager, "American Buddhism in the Making," in *Westward Dharma: Buddhism beyond Asia*, eds. Charles S. Prebish and Martin Baumann (Berkeley: University of California Press, 2002).

The theory of 'Two Buddhisms' draws division between converts and Asian immigrants while 'Three Buddhisms' claims to offer an alternative to the ethnic-based classification. There are also critiques of both models and suggestions for a more nuanced approach. For the period between the 1960s and 1980s that this study focuses on, the binary of converts and immigrants was still evident. To avoid confusion, the term 'converts' here refers to those of non-Asian origin who adopted 'a religious world view different from that of their ethnic heritage and of the mainstream culture in which they were raised' (see Numrich, "Two Buddhisms Further Considered," 63).

96. Baumann, "Buddhism in the West," 55–61.
97. Paine, *Re-Enchantment*, 15.
98. Seager, *Buddhism in America*, 33.
99. Baumann, "Buddhism in the West," 52.
100. Nattier, "Visible and Invisible," quoted in Elizabeth C Cleland, "The Vajrakilaya Sadhana: An Euro-American experience of a Nyingma ritual" (MA diss., Carleton University, 2001), 17.
101. Seager, *Buddhism in America*, 36–37.
102. Kay, *Tibetan and Zen Buddhism*, 15.
103. Wakoh S Hickey, "Two Buddhisms, Three Buddhisms, and Racism," *Journal of Global Buddhism* 11 (2010): 15.
104. Gregory, "Describing the Elephant," 248.
105. Seager, *Buddhism in America*, 43.
106. Gregory, "Describing the Elephant," 250.
107. Don Morreale ed., *The Complete Guide to Buddhist America* (Boston: Shambhala, 1998), quoted in Peter N Gregory, "Describing the Elephant: Buddhism in America," *Religion and American Culture: A journal of interpretation* 11 (2001): 239.
108. Seager, *Buddhism in America*, 40.
109. Eldershaw, "Shambhala International," 187.
110. Paine, *Re-Enchantment*, 212.
111. Wade C Roof, "A Time When Mountains were Moving," in *Cults in Context: Readings in the study of new religious movements*, ed. Lorne Dawson (Toronto: Canadian Scholars' Press, 1996), quoted in Lynn. P Eldershaw, "Collective Identity and the Post-Charismatic Fate of Shambhala International" (PhD diss., University of Waterloo, 2004), 79–80.
112. Charles S Prebish, "Reflections of the Transmission of Buddhism to America," in *Understanding the New Religions*, eds. Jacob Needleman and George Baker (New York: Seabury Press, 1978), quoted in Wakoh S Hickey, "Two Buddhisms, Three Buddhisms, and Racism," *Journal of Global Buddhism* 11 (2010): 6.
113. Prebish, *American Buddhism*, quoted in James C Browning, "Tarthang Tulku and the Quest for an American Buddhism" (PhD diss., Baylor University, 1986), 181.
114. Eldershaw, "Shambhala International," 187.
115. Paine, *Re-Enchantment*, 13.
116. Seager, *Buddhism in America*, 114.
117. Eve L Mullen, "Tibetan Buddhism, American Interests: Influences upon the lay and monastic relationship in New York's Tibetan Buddhist immigrant community" (PhD diss., Temple University, 1999), 55.
118. Seager, *Buddhism in America*, 124.

119. Frank J Korom, "The Role of Tibet in the New Age Movement," in *Imagining Tibet: Perceptions, projections, and fantasies*, eds. Thierry Dodin and Heinz Räther (Boston: Wisdom Press, 2001), 177–178.

120. Korom, "Role of Tibet," 181.

121. Lopez, "New Age Orientalism."

122. Seager, *Buddhism in America*, 10.

123. Seager, *Buddhism in America*, 235.

124. Morreale ed., *Buddhist America*, quoted in Peter N Gregory, "Describing the Elephant: Buddhism in America," *Religion and American Culture: A journal of interpretation* 11 (2001): 239.

125. Korom, "Role of Tibet," 160.

126. Lisa Aldred, "Plastic Shamans and Astroturf Sun Dances: New Age commercialization of native American spirituality," *American Indian Quarterly* 24, no. 3 (2000): 329–352, quoted in Darinda J Congdon, "'Tibet Chic': Myth, marketing, spirituality and politics in musical Representations of Tibet in the United States" (PhD diss., University of Pittsburgh, 2007), 72–73.

127. Mullen, "Tibetan Buddhism, American Interests."

128. Congdon, "'Tibet Chic'," 76–77.

129. Philip A Mellor, "The Cultural Translation of Buddhism: Problems of theory and method arising in the study of Buddhism in England" (PhD diss., University of Manchester, 1989), quoted in David N Kay, *Tibetan and Zen Buddhism in Britain: Transplantation, development, and adaptation* (London and New York: RoutledgeCurzon, 2004), 9.

130. Mellor, "Cultural Translation of Buddhism," 9.

131. Kay, *Tibetan and Zen Buddhism*, 10.

132. Helen J Waterhouse, "Authority and Adaptation: A case study in British Buddhism" (PhD diss., University of the West of England, 1997).

133. Bell, "Buddhism in Britain," 11.

134. Bluck, *British Buddhism*, 190.

135. Philip C Almond, *The British Discovery of Buddhism* (Cambridge: Cambridge University Press, 1988), quoted in Robert Bluck, *British Buddhism: Teachings, practice and development* (London and New York: Routledge, 2006), 5.

136. Lopez, *Prisoners of Shangri-La*, 37.

137. Bluck, *British Buddhism*, 5–6.

138. Kay, *Tibetan and Zen Buddhism*, 6.

139. Stephen Batchelor, *The Awakening of the West: The encounter of Buddhism and western culture* (Berkeley, CA: Parallax Press, 1994), 252.

140. Bluck, *British Buddhism*, 7–8.

141. Bluck, *British Buddhism*, 8–10.

Christmas Humphreys, *Buddhism: An introduction and guide* (London: Penguin Books, 1951); Edward Conze, *Buddhism: Its essence and development* (Oxford: Bruno Cassirer Ltd., 1951).

142. Bluck, *British Buddhism*, 10.

143. Bluck, *British Buddhism*, 10.

144. Bluck, *British Buddhism*, 10.

145. Eileen Barker, "New Religious Movements: Their incidence and significance," in *New Religious Movements: Challenge and response*, eds. Bryan Wilson and Jamie Cresswell (London: Routledge, 1999), quoted in Robert Bluck, *British Buddhism: Teachings, practice and development* (London and New York: Routledge, 2006), 11.

146. Kay, *Tibetan and Zen Buddhism*, 5.

147. Bluck, *British Buddhism*, 12.

The data is collected from the *Middle Way* of the Buddhist Society, among other sources.

148. M York, "The New Age in Britain Today," *Religion Today* 9, no. 3 (1994): 14–21, quoted in Denise Cush, "British Buddhism and the New Age," *Journal of Contemporary Religion* 11, no. 2 (1996): 196.

149. Cush, "British Buddhism," 204.

150. Cush, "British Buddhism," 196–199.

151. Bluck, *British Buddhism*, 190.

152. Bluck, *British Buddhism*, 192.

153. Bluck, *British Buddhism*, 193–194.

Part II

RECEPTION

PERCEIVING THE KARMAPA

The Karmapa's transmission of Tibetan Buddhism to the West began with his encounters with young Europeans and North Americans in the 1960s and 1970s. Many of them became his followers, either during the early years of his resettlement in the Indian subcontinent or, as in most cases, on his extensive Dharma tours in their home countries. Despite their distinctively different upbringings from the Tibetans, they had no difficulty embracing the traditional spiritual image of the Karmapa. Their accounts, written or spoken, portray him as a highly realised being endowed with miraculous powers, drawing on either conventional beliefs within the Karma Kagyu lineage or purported personal experience of supernatural incidents. The consistency with the Tibetan perspective in their perception of the Karmapa is an indication of successful reception of tradition which, in turn, attests to the effectiveness of the Karmapa's strategies in transmitting the lineage in its traditional form. This part of the book examines the Western reception of the Karmapa, intended to provide context for understanding his role as the transmitter and his transmission strategies. The two chapters herein each discuss one particular aspect of the Western devotees' perception of the Karmapa, based on a comparison between Tibetan and English language accounts to identify continuity and change.

Chapter 3

Faithful Translation

This chapter investigates two spiritual attributes of the Karmapa. First, each Karmapa incarnation is believed to be a buddha and bodhisattva manifestation, especially the Sixth Buddha of Fortunate Aeon Siṃha and Bodhisattva Avalokiteśvara. Tradition holds that these identifications originate from Sūtra, Tantra and Terma (*gter ma*) texts in the form of prophecy. Second, the Karmapas are also believed to be able to predict their own reincarnations. The testament letter of the Fifteenth Karmapa, Khakyap Dorje (mKha' khyab rdo rje, 1871–1922), which contains the prediction of his reincarnation played a vital role in the identification of Rangjung Rigpe Dorje as the Sixteenth Karmapa. Both attributes are reproduced faithfully in the English sources. They highlight the Karmapa's spiritual accomplishment and legitimate his authority as the spiritual head of the lineage. The continuity in their reception helped establish such authority in his Western community.

3.1. IDENTIFICATION WITH ENLIGHTENED BEINGS

Karma Ngedön Tengye, in his *namthar* of the fourteen Karmapa incarnations, engages with various metaphors and ideas found in different *yāna*s to convey the enlightened state of the Karmapas. In the opening praise,[1] he portrays the Karmapa as embodying the enlightened body, speech, mind, quality and activity of all the buddhas of the ten directions and three times. He characterises him as the source of the Dharma; the chief of the noble sangha; the protector of sentient beings; a great physician who cures afflictions of desire, hatred and ignorance; and an excellent steersman who guides beings across the ocean of samsara. To him, the Karmapa is the essence of the holy teachers, *vidyādhara*s and *siddha*s, the main deity of all *maṇḍala*s and the master of the assembly of *ḍāka*s and *ḍākinī*s.² He possesses three bodies: *dharmakāya*, *saṃbhogakāya* and *nirmāṇakāya*.³ The metaphors of physician, steersman and buddha embodiment through *Trikāya* stem from the Sūtrayāna;⁴ the reference to *vidyādhara*, *siddha*, *maṇḍala*, *ḍāka* and *ḍākinī* symbolises high spiritual accomplishment in the Mantrayāna.⁵

Karma Ngedön Tengye argues that the Karmapa's attainment of buddhahood is best understood in two different ways. To those of the Causal Vehicle (*rgyu'i theg pa*, Skt. hetuyāna),⁶ the Karmapa has already become a buddha through the bodhisattva path that begins with the generation of *bodhicitta* and culminates in the realisation of the wisdom of all-encompassing awareness (*ji lta ji snyed mkhyen pa'i ye shes*).⁷ His life accommodates two aspects: the outer and the inner. Outer aspect: he is a great *arhat* who perfectly upholds the 250 vows of the *Prātimokṣa*.⁸ Inner aspect: he is a great bodhisattva who has developed *bodhicitta* by accomplishing the ten perfections (*pāramitā*).⁹ To those of the Resultant Vehicle (*'bras bu'i theg pa*, Skt. phalayāna),¹⁰ he fulfilled accumulations and obtained buddhahood instantly.¹¹ This constitutes the secret aspect of his life. Here, he is a supreme *siddha* who has attained Great Bliss (*bde ba chen po*, Skt. *mahāsukha*) through the threefold process of ground, path and fruition in Tantric practice.¹²

Both Karma Ngedön Tengye and Khyentse Özer portray the Karmapa incarnations as the embodiment of the activity of the buddhas in the past, present and future.¹³ They also identify the Karmapas with specific buddhas. Karma Ngedön Tengye states that, for ordinary people, the Karmapa manifests as buddhas in the past, such as Shenpen Namrol (gZhan phan rnam rol); as buddhas in the future, such as the Sixth Buddha Siṃha (*seng ge*); and as buddhas of the present, such as Amitābha.¹⁴ He also reports that Śākya Śrī and Lama Zhang both believed the Karmapa to be the emanation of Buddha Siṃha.¹⁵ Khyentse Özer, in his *namthar* of the Fifteenth Karmapa, refers to him as Shenpen Namrol and Siṃha, but he identifies him with a different present buddha—Akṣobhya.¹⁶

In the same way, Thrangu considers the Sixteenth Karmapa to be a buddha (*rgyal ba*), the lord of the Victorious Ones (*rgyal dbang* or *rgyal ba'i dbang po*) and the embodiment/unifier of the activity of all the buddhas (*rgyal ba thams cad kyi phrin las kyi rang gzugs*; *rgyal ba thams cad kyi phyin las gcig tu bsdus*).¹⁷ Tashi Tsering views the Karmapa as the embodiment of the activity of the buddhas in the three times (*dus gsum rgyal ba'i 'phrin las kyi spyi gzugs*) and master of the activity of all the buddhas and bodhisattvas in the ten directions (*phyogs bcu'i sangs rgyas dang byang chub sems dpa' thams cad kyi 'phrin kyi bdag po*).¹⁸ He explains that the Sanskrit word *karma* means action or activity; since the Karmapa performs the activity of all buddhas, he carries this title.¹⁹ Additionally, Thrangu and Tashi Tsering both quote the same verse from the *Tantra of the Blazing, Wrathful Meteorite*

(*Khro bo gnam lcags 'bar ba' rgyud*)[20] to account for the Karmapa's buddha embodiment.[21]

Lodrö Dönyö (Blo gros don yod) shares Karma Ngedön Tengye's view on the Karmapa's buddhahood through the lens of the three *yāna*s.[22] He holds that the Karmapa attained the thirteenth Vajradhāra *bhūmi* (*mthar phyin pa bcu gsum rdo rje 'dzin pa'i sa*) which marks buddhahood in Mahāmudrā.[23] Geleg Tenzin (dGe legs bstan 'dzin) considers the Karmapa to be a real buddha who appeared in human form;[24] his disciples believe him to possess the thirty-two major and eighty minor marks of a buddha[25] and to be able to see the past, present and future.[26] The former Dharamsala government official, Juchen Thupten Namgyal ('Ju chen thub bstan rnam rgyal), directly addresses the Karmapa as a buddha (*rgyal ba*).[27] The Sixteenth Karmapa himself, as well as several other authors, all compare the monastic seat of Tsurphu to Akaniṣṭha and the *maṇḍala* of Cakrasaṃvara.[28] In Tibetan Buddhism, Akaniṣṭha is connected to buddhas' three *kāya*s or buddha fields. Hence, to make such comparison is to assert that the Karmapa is a buddha. In the Tantric tradition, Cakrasaṃvara belongs to the Anuttarayoga Tantra; this deity is specifically associated with the Karma Kagyu school and Düsum Khyenpa who founded Tsurphu.[29] To identify Tsurphu as the *maṇḍala* of Cakrasaṃvara is to equate the Karmapa with the deity.

Tashi Tsering, in both his *namthar* account of the Sixteenth Karmapa[30] and his compilation of the Karmapa's *Collected Works* (*gsung 'bum*),[31] identifies him with the buddhas, Shenpen Namrol, Akṣobhya, Amitābha and Siṃha. Thrangu explains in detail the identification with the Sixth Buddha.[32] The story taps into the Mahāyāna teaching of the 1,000 buddhas in Fortunate Aeon. According to the *Bhadrakalpika Sūtra*,[33] there are 1,004 buddhas in this aeon. Among them, the present Buddha Śākyamuni ranks fourth, followed by Maitreya. In this *sūtra*, the name of the Sixth Buddha is Siṃha (*seng ge*), rather than Siṃhanāda given in Thrangu's account; Legpakye (Legs pa skyes) does not feature in this source. The period of 70,000 years refers to the Buddha Siṃha's lifespan, not the length of time during which he turns the Wheel of Dharma. Still, the birthplace and the names of the parents match.[34] Thrangu may have relied on a different source. The events depicted in his account align with the Twelve Deeds of Śākyamuni. They include the first deed (descent from Tuṣita Heaven; *dga' ldan gyi gnas nas 'pho ba*), the third deed (rebirth in a royal family; *sku bltams pa*), the tenth deed (becoming fully enlightened; *mngon par rdzogs par sangs rgyas pa*) and the eleventh deed (turning the Wheel of Dharma; *chos kyi 'khor lo bskor ba*). The Karmapa performs 'vast deeds' of a bodhisattva that span from the generation of *bodhicitta* to the attainment of buddhahood, as is standard practice in the bodhisattva path of the Mahāyāna.[35]

Tashi Tsering draws on a variety of sources to support his claim that the Karmapa is the Sixth Buddha.[36] He lists the sūtras which speak of the thousand buddhas of Fortunate Aeon and singles out the Sixth Buddha Siṃha to draw a link to the Karmapa. However, none of his sources connects Siṃha with the Karmapa; they do not confirm his view that the Karmapa is the Sixth Buddha. Furthermore, he refers to the predictions of Śākya Śrī and Lama Zhang that identify the Karmapa with the Sixth Buddha.[37] Martin quotes a short verse attributed to the *Root Tantra of Manjushri* that predicts the coming of a master with the name *ka* and *ma*,[38] which tradition links to the Karmapa. She also mentions that Situ Panchen, Chökyi Jungne, identified the Karmapa to be the Sixth Buddha.[39] The fact that such proposition is found in both Tibetan and English sources sheds light on its popularity.

Karma Ngedön Tengye and Khyentse Özer also identify the Karmapa incarnations as Avalokiteśvara.[40] Karma Ngedön Tengye claims further that Songtsen Gampo (Srong btsan sgam po) himself predicted that Düsum Khyenpa would appear as an emanation of Avalokiteśvara.[41] Such identification is repeated in the Sixteenth Karmapa's *namthar*. Thrangu points out that the Karmapa is Avalokiteśvara.[42] Tashi Tsering, through the title of his account,[43] identifies the Karmapa as *Lokeśvara* ('*jig rten dbang phyug*), another name of Avalokiteśvara. He also states, 'In the form of bodhisattvas, such as the protector Avalokiteśvara, [the Karmapa] guides the beings of the six realms.'[44] Like Karma Ngedön Tengye, he too includes Songtsen Gampo's prediction of Düsum Khyenpa.[45] He recounts how the Karmapa, as an emanation of Avalokiteśvara, obtained the vajra-like *samādhi* (*rdo rje lta bu'i ting 'dzin*) that manifests on the tenth stage of the bodhisattva path in preparation to become a buddha.[46] Shamar (Zhwa dmar) does not identify the Karmapa as Avalokiteśvara but portrays him as a bodhisattva in a more general sense. He explains that there are three types of *bodhicitta*: the highest is the herdsman-like *bodhicitta*, the middling is the ferryman-like *bodhicitta* and the lowest is the king-like *bodhicitta*; the Karmapa has raised the highest—herdsman-like *bodhicitta*.[47]

Karma Ngedön Tengye further extends the manifestations of the Karmapa. He includes also *śrāvaka*s and *pratyekabuddha*s, *paṇḍita*s and *siddha*s, bhikshus and brahmans, gods and spirits, animals and inanimate objects, such as plants, food, boats and natural elements. The list becomes inexhaustible, inconceivable to ordinary people.[48] Especially, the Karmapa incarnations appeared as Indian and Tibetan *vidyādhara*s, *paṇḍita*s and *siddha*s. These include Padmasambhava, Saraha, Aśvaghoṣa, Padampa Sangye (Pha dam pa sangs rgyas), Gyalwa Chokyang (rGyal ba mchog dbyangs), Potowa,[49] Shākya Chokden (Shākya mchog ldan) and Karma Chakmé Rāga Asya (Karma chags med Rā ga a sya). He was also reborn as Buddhist monarchs, including Songtsen Gampo and the Chinese emperor Yongle of the Ming Dynasty.[50] Khyentse Özer identifies the Karmapa with Padmasambhava, and again with countless saints, including Saraha.[51] This is carried over in the *namthar* of the Sixteenth Karmapa. He manifests in countless forms to serve the spiritual needs of the people he sets out to liberate.[52] Thrangu and Rumtek (Rum bteg) connect the Sixteenth Karmapa to similar personalities.[53] Tashi Tsering adds Barwe Gyaltsen ('Bar ba'i rgyal mtshan), Kharag Gomchung (Kha rag sgom chung), and the Indian king Bimbisara to the list.[54] Martin mentions Lha'i Pu Drime Karpo, Luyang Nyingpo and Karma Denu.[55] Holmes speaks of him as King Indrabhuti.[56]

According to tradition, the identification of the Karmapa incarnations with enlightened beings can be traced to various prophecies in Sūtra, Tantra and Terma.[57] Some of the prophecies establish an explicit link to the Karmapas; others are connected to the Karmapas through interpretation. Khyentse Özer believes that Buddha Śākyamuni himself predicted the coming of the Karmapa. In a verse that he ascribes to an unnamed Mahāyāna sūtra, the Buddha announces the following:

> Two thousand years after my passing
> The teaching will appear in the country of the red-faced [people]
> [They] will become the disciples of Avalokiteśvara
> At the time when the teaching declines there
> Bodhisattva Siṃhanāda
> Will appear, known as the Karmapa
> Having obtained the power of *samādhi*, [he] tames beings
> [And will have] placed [those who] see, hear, remember
>   and touch [him] in [the state of] happiness.[58]

It is difficult to establish the origin of this verse. Above all, the verse legitimises the spiritual authority of the Karmapa through the Buddha's own words. It identifies the Karmapa as the bodhisattva Siṃhanāda and speaks of his ability to help beings through sensory contact. Thrangu and Tashi Tsering both incorporate this passage in their accounts of the Sixteenth Karmapa.[59] Thrangu interprets the verse to be an indication that the Karmapa will become the Sixth Buddha of Fortunate Aeon.[60] This is so probably because he considers Siṃhanāda (*seng ge'i sgra*) to be interchangeable with Siṃha (*seng ge*). Tashi Tsering seems to hold the same opinion.[61] He also comments: 'Among all the great Buddhist masters [who have] appeared in Tibet, [those] foretold in prophecies are regarded as authentic.'[62] This lends authority to the lineage of the Karmapas. Both authors say that this verse comes from the *Samādhirāja Sūtra*. However, I have not been able to locate it in the editions of the Kangyur available to me.[63] Nor have I been able to trace any other purported Sūtra or Tantra verse about the Karmapa quoted in this chapter. There are two possible reasons: (1) the verses are included in a different edition of the Kangyur that is yet to be discovered or made available to the public; (2) the authors quoted them from another source without checking their origin.

Karma Ngedön Tengye and Khyentse Özer also draw on the Karmapa prophecies found in Padmasambhava's treasure texts (Terma). It turned out to be impossible to trace the origin of the Terma prophecies quoted here either; their authenticity is not easy to test. Still, they feature in the *namthar* of the Sixteenth Karmapa and shape the popular perception of him. As with the Sūtra and Tantra verses, these Terma prophecies may have been circulated in the lineage based on faith rather than historical record. Karma Ngedön Tengye's summary of Padmasambhava's prediction of the Karmapa[64] seems to convey three messages. First, the Karmapa is equal to Padmasambhava; this lends spiritual authority to him. Second, the Karmapa incarnations appear in succession in an unbroken lineage. Third, those who see, hear, remember or touch him will attain liberation; this is widely held to be a characteristic of the Karmapa's spiritual power. Martin quotes from Padmasambhava's *Hidden Predictions* (*mDo byang gud sbas*)[65] which corresponds to the first and second messages.

Khyentse Özer quotes several of Padmasambhava's prophecies in detail. For example:

> Protecting the [enlightened] activity of Avalokiteśvara
> Düsum Khyenpa will emerge in a place called Tsurphu.[66]

And,

> Through the emanation of the [enlightened] speech of Avalokiteśvara
> [He will have] descended from Tuṣita heaven for the sake of sentient beings
> [He will] be known firstly as Düsum Khyenpa, [one
>   who engages in] the secret practice
> Wearing the Black Hat, the crown of the buddha families,
>   [which is] the sign of empowerment
> He guides countless beings in each moment
> Those who see, hear, remember and touch [him]
> Will be reborn after that life in the presence of the Noble One.[67]

In these verses, Padmasambhava predicts the First Karmapa and his monastic seat Tsurphu. He also identifies the Karmapa as an emanation of Avalokiteśvara. His descent from Tuṣita corresponds to the first of Buddha Śākyamuni's Twelve Deeds. The Karmapa's famous Black Crown symbolises his spiritual lineage and power. The last three lines mirror the second and third messages from Karma Ngedön Tengye's summary. Both Thrangu and Tashi Tsering quote these verses. Thrangu combines the first verse with the fourth and fifth lines of the second into a single prophecy about the monastic seat and the Black Crown of the Karmapa.[68] Tashi Tsering cites the second verse in full.[69] He considers it proof that the Karmapa is an emanation of Avalokiteśvara and that he can control his rebirth and liberate beings through sensory contact.[70] Moreover, Martin refers to the Terma of Nyang Ral Nyima Özer that identifies the First Karmapa as an emanation of Avalokiteśvara.[71] Shamar recalls a Terma prophecy (*gter lung*) that the Sixteenth Karmapa showed him in person.[72] It says that the Karmapa called Rangjung Rigpe Dorje has a birthmark on his right foot which is a sign of bodhisattva; if someone who has accumulated the five inexpiable actions sees the Karmapa, he/she will not suffer lower rebirth in seven lifetimes.[73]

There are Terma prophecies discovered by Chokgyur Lingpa (mChog gyur gling pa, 1829–1870) that connect the Karmapa with Padmasambhava's primary disciple, Gyalwa Chokyang.[74] Khyentse Özer cites a secret prophecy (*gsang lung*):

> Translator Gyalwa Chokyang, listen to me
> In the semi-circular palace [which is] the holy site of [enlightened] speech
> Twenty-one of your reincarnations will appear in future
> [You are] the emanation of Avalokiteśvara, the
>   one who knows all the three times.[75]

This verse does not contain any explicit reference to the Karmapa. Yet, Khyentse Özer speaks of it as a prophecy about the Karmapa, seemingly on the basis of two assumptions. First, the Karmapa was, in a past life, Gyalwa Chokyang. Second, he is an emanation of Avalokiteśvara. Khyentse Özer does not clarify the reason for his proposition. The link to the Karmapa may be indicated in the last line: *dus gsum kun mkhyen pa* can be interpreted as the name of the First Karmapa Düsum Khyenpa. In addition, the prediction of twenty-one births coincides with Chokgyur Lingpa's vision of the twenty-one Karmapa incarnations. Tradition holds that Chokgyur Lingpa had such vision during a visit to Karma Monastery, one of the monasteries that Düsum Khyenpa founded in Tibet. He described this vision to the abbot who transferred it into painting; his disciples recorded it in writing.[76] The Karma Kagyu lineage holds this vision in high regard. In this specific vision, Padmasambhava is surrounded by twenty-one Karmapas.[77] It would appear to set out to provide legitimacy and authority to the lineage. The very same verse is also found in the Sixteenth Karmapa's *namthar*. Thrangu interprets it as a prophecy of the Karmapa's twenty-one incarnations.[78] Moreover, Martin cites the Terma of Sangye Lingpa (Sangs rgyas gling pa, 1340–1396) that identifies Gyalwa Chokyang as the Sixth Buddha. Through the belief that Gyalwa Chokyang was the previous incarnation of the Karmapa, she connects the Karmapa with the Sixth Buddha.[79]

Khyentse Özer lists two more Terma prophecies discovered by Chokgyur Lingpa.[80] One predicts the names of the Fifteenth to the Eighteenth Karmapas[81] and indicates a link between the Karmapa and Padmasambhava.[82] The other appears to echo the same assumption that Khyentse Özer makes about Chokgyur Lingpa's secret prophecy (*gsang lung*) discussed earlier: the Karmapa was Gyalwa Chokyang in a past life.[83] Thrangu draws on the first verse to account for the name of the Sixteenth Karmapa.[84]

3.2. SELF-PREDICTION OF REBIRTH

The Karmapa incarnations are believed to hold the ability to foresee the circumstances of their future rebirth.[85] Some issue predictions through conversations with their disciples; others write them down in letters.[86] Particularly, the prediction letter serves as the instruction that guides the search for the Karmapa's reincarnation. This ability was an important component in the introduction of the Karmapa and his lineage to the West. For example, it was highlighted by Jamgon Kongtrul in a television interview in the United States during the Karmapa's 1976 tour.[87] The *namthar* of the Sixteenth Karmapa claims that this ability testifies to his special, high spiritual attainment. Both Thrangu[88] and Tashi Tsering[89] argue that the Karmapas' 'self-prediction' is unique to their own lineage. It sets them apart from other tulkus and confers an element of distinctiveness.[90] Rumtek reports that the letter is handed over and kept safe until the search for the next Karmapa commences. The time when the Karmapa delivers the letter varies. Sometimes, he seals the letter and entrusts it to a particular disciple without revealing its content. The letter is kept confidential because when a part is publicised, danger may befall those who know about it.[91]

The prediction letter, often called the testament (*zhal chems*), of the Fifteenth Karmapa played a key role in the identification of the Sixteenth Karmapa.[92] The authors who cite this letter all interpret it in similar ways. Take Thrangu for example.[93] The first three lines of the letter[94] indicate the place of birth. To him, 'the region seized by the brave archer' refers to Dankhok (mDan khog) in Derge (sDe dge) near 'the golden river' ('Bri klung); 'the poised majestic lion' refers to Senge Namdzong (Seng ge rnam rdzong). He links Dankhok with two famous kings: Gesar of Ling (Ge sar of gLing) and Songtsen Gampo.[95] Shamar reports that 'the brave archer', the local lord Danma ('Den ma/mDan ma), was in fact Gesar's minister, known as an emanation of the Indian *mahāsiddha* Saraha.[96] Martin identifies him to be an emanation of Padmasambhava.[97] Tradition considers all these figures, except for Gesar of Ling, to be the Karmapas' former incarnations.[98] Moreover, Dzogchen Thubten Chökyi Dorje (rDzogs chen Thub bstan chos kyi rdo rje) already identified the Karmapa as a bodhisattva during his mother's pregnancy and prophesied that the Karmapa's place of birth would be Senge Namdzong.[99] Shamar and Drakpa Yongdü (Grags pa yongs 'dus) both believe Senge Namdzong to be a sacred site connected with *siddha* Langkönpa (gLang dgon pa);[100] others associate it with Padmasambhava.[101] All these interpretations bring to the fore the sacred landscape of the Karmapa's birthplace which, in turn, highlights the spiritual significance of his birth.

The next three lines of the letter[102] concern the Karmapa's parents. Thrangu's explanation[103] reveals the Karmapa's family to be the ruling class of Derge.[104] According to Tashi Tsering, the Athub family descended from a chief minister of Derge; it was one of the seven households of Danma.[105] Shamar has more to say about the Karmapa's family history. The first generation of Athub was an exiled Mongolian prince who served the Derge king. After winning a battle for the king, he was granted the status of a Derge prince and conferred a local lordship. The father, Tsewang Phuntsok (Tshe dbang phun tshogs), was also treated as a prince; the mother, Kalsang Chödrön (sKal bzang chos sgron), was both a *ḍākinī* and a member of an aristocratic family.[106] Finally, the last four lines[107] of the prophecy set out the time of the Karmapa's birth, his name and spiritual qualities.

Apart from the prediction letter, two other sources also contributed to the identification of the Sixteenth Karmapa: a dream vision of the Fifteenth Karmapa's close disciple, Situ Pema Wangchok Gyalpo (Si tu Padma dbang mchog rgyal po, 1886–1952), and the formal recognition through the Thirteenth Dalai Lama Thubten Gyatso (Thub stan rgya mtsho, 1876–1933). Situ's vision[108] took place before he received the letter but concurs with its content: it noted the Athub family as the point of reincarnation. Such consistency, coupled with the other details in the letter itself, as deciphered by Palpung Khyentrul (dPal spungs mKhyen sprul), led to the discovery and eventual enthronement. The formal recognition through the Dalai Lama mattered as well. Such procedure goes back to the Eleventh Karmapa, Yeshe Dorje (Ye shes rdo rje, 1676–1702). During the rule of the Ganden Palace since 1642, all major tulkus discovered within its territorial reach required formal endorsement through the Dalai Lama or his regent.[109] Since Tsurphu operated under the jurisdiction of the Lhasa government, such recognition was needed.[110] In the case of the Sixteenth Karmapa, acknowledgement through the Thirteenth Dalai Lama was not without complications. By the time the Tsurphu administration located the testament letter, the Dalai Lama had already endorsed a rival candidate, the son of a minister in the Lhasa government. Tsurphu repeatedly petitioned the government to reconsider its choice, but to no avail. It was only when the Lhasa candidate died in an accident that the government accepted Tsurphu's nomination. The Dalai Lama then issued his formal recognition, four years after Situ had identified the Karmapa.[111]

NOTES

1. 堪布卡塔仁波切 (Khenpo Karthar Rinpoche) gives a commentary on this praise, from *om swa sti* to *drang du gsol* in Karma nges don bstan rgyas, "rnam thar mdor bsdus," 2.1–7.1. See 堪布卡塔仁波切, "前言," in 上師之師：歷代大寶法王噶瑪巴的轉世傳奇, trans. 比丘尼洛卓拉嫫 (台灣：眾生文化, 2016), 8–14.
2. Karma nges don bstan rgyas, "rnam thar mdor bsdus," 2.1–4.4.
3. Karma nges don bstan rgyas, "rnam thar mdor bsdus," 4.6–5.2.
4. Sūtrayāna refers to Śrāvakayāna and Mahāyāna.
5. Also known as Vajrayāna.
6. That is, Sūtrayāna.
7. Karma nges don bstan rgyas, "rnam thar mdor bsdus," 7.3–7.6.
8. Karma nges don bstan rgyas, "rnam thar mdor bsdus," 451.3–451.4.
9. Karma nges don bstan rgyas, "rnam thar mdor bsdus," 451.4–452.1.
10. That is, Mantrayāna/Vajrayāna.
11. Karma nges don bstan rgyas, "rnam thar mdor bsdus," 7.6–8.6.
12. Karma nges don bstan rgyas, "rnam thar mdor bsdus," 452.1–452.4.
13. Karma nges don bstan rgyas, "rnam thar mdor bsdus," 7.1; mKhyen brtse 'od zer, "dpal ldan kun bzang chos kyi nyi ma chen po phrin las mkha' khyab rdo rje'i rnam thar mdor bsdus/_(15)," in *karma pa sku 'phreng bcu drug pa tshun rim par byon pa'i rnam thar phyogs bsgrigs*, TBRC W1KG3815. (Delhi: konchhog lhadrepa, 1994), 473.1.
14. Karma nges don bstan rgyas, "rnam thar mdor bsdus," 9.2–9.5.
15. Karma nges don bstan rgyas, "rnam thar mdor bsdus," 12.6–13.1. See also 噶玛钨金, "杜松虔巴," 16.

According to Gamble, the claim that the Karmapas are manifestations of Bodhisattva Siṃha, who is to become the Sixth Buddha, emerged during the time of Düsum Khyenpa; Lama Zhang was the first to make this claim (Gamble, "View from Nowhere," 104).

Lama Zhang's prophecy has been translated into English in Michele Martin, *Music in the Sky: The life, art & teachings of the 17th Karmapa Ogyen Trinley Dorje* (New York: Snow Lion Publications, 2003), 272.

16. mKhyen brtse 'od zer, "mkha' khyab rdo rje'i," 473.3–473.5.
17. Khra 'gu rin po che, *rgyal ba'i dbang po*, 322.1–323.7.
18. bKra shis tshe ring, "'jig rten dbang phyug," 19.5–21.11.
19. bKra shis tshe ring, "'jig rten dbang phyug," 21.14–21.16.

The author gives his reference: *Karma 'phrin las 1456–1539 pas mgur dang dris lan sna tshogs | 1975 lor ngag dbang stobs rgyal nas ldi lir gsar bskrun zhus ba de'i shog grangs | 162* (bKra shis tshe ring, "'jig rten dbang phyug," 48.)

20. Skt. *Krodharājagujvarājavajramaṇḍala vidhī-nāma*.

The English translation of the title in Martin, "*Music in the Sky*," 271.

21. *yongs su dag pa'i dkyil 'khor du || phyogs bcu'i sangs rgyas gcig bsdus pa'i || tshe 'dir grub pa ston pa'i ched || karma pa zhes yongs grags 'byung ||* (Khra 'gu rin po che, *rgyal ba'i dbang po*, 324.)

Translated into English in Appendix B (page 207 from 'In the completely pure *maṇḍala*' to 'The renowned one called the Karmapa will emerge').

This verse is also cited in bKra shis tshe ring, "'jig rten dbang phyug," 20.15–20.17 (spelling difference: *grub* as *sgrub*) and 'Ja' tshon snying po, *rgyal dbang karma pa'i che brjod mdo rgyud lung 'dren padma'i chun po 'ja'i ming can gyis sbyar ba bzhugs so* (n.d.), 2.5–3.1 (*bsdus pa'i* as *bsdus pa*, and *ched* as *phyir*). Both ascribe it to the same source.

Michele Martin gives an English translation of this verse in Martin, "*Music in the Sky*," 271.

22. Blo gros don yod, "karma pa rang byung rig pa'i rdo rje'i rnam thar," in *dus 'khor chos 'byung indra nI la'i phra tshom*, TBRC W00EGS1016994. 1 (Mirik: 'bo dkar nges don chos 'khor gling gi bla spyi spar bskrun zhus, 2005), 553.14–554.6.

23. Blo gros don yod, "rig pa'i rdo rje'i," 548.9.

24. dGe legs bstan 'dzin, "bod nas 'brug brgyud 'bras ljongs su phebs pa," in *rgyal dbang karma pa bcu drug pa chen po'i gsung 'bum 1*, ed. Jo sras bkra shis tshe ring (Dharamsala: Tshurphu Labrang; The Amnye Machen Institute, 2016), 146.4–146.5.

25. dGe legs bstan 'dzin, "'brug brgyud 'bras ljongs," 158.22–159.1.

26. dGe legs bstan 'dzin, "'brug brgyud 'bras ljongs," 159.19–159.20.

27. 'Ju chen thub bstan rnam rgyal, "rgyal dbang karma pa," 316.7, 316.10–316.11.

28. Rang byung rig pa'i rdo rje, "rang rnam bsdus pa," in *rgyal dbang karma pa bcu drug pa chen po'i gsung 'bum 1*, ed. Jo sras bkra shis tshe ring (Dharamsala: Tshurphu Labrang; The Amnye Machen Institute, 2016), 65.23; Rang byung rig pa'i rdo rje, "skabs su bab pa'i snang glu rkang drug bung ba'i lding dbyangs," in *rgyal dbang karma pa bcu drug pa chen po'i gsung 'bum 3*, ed. Jo sras bkra shis tshe ring (Dharamsala: Tshurphu Labrang; The Amnye Machen Institute, 2016), 3.4–3.6; Khra 'gu rin po che, *rgyal ba'i dbang po*, 334.2–334.3; Blo gros don yod, "rig pa'i rdo rje'i," 546.13; dGe legs bstan 'dzin, "'brug brgyud 'bras ljongs," 145.8; Rin chen dpal bzang, "sku phreng bcu drug pa rig pa'i rdo rje byon pa ni," in *rgyal dbang karma pa bcu drug pa chen po'i gsung 'bum 1*, ed. Jo sras bkra shis tshe ring (Dharamsala: Tshurphu Labrang; The Amnye Machen Institute, 2016), 279.9; Dzogchen Ponlop, "The Sixteenth Karmapa Rangjung Rigpe Dorje," in *Music in the Sky: The life, art & teachings of the 17th Karmapa Ogyen Trinley Dorje*, by Michele Martin (New York: Snow Lion Publications), 301, 305.

29. According to his *namthar*, Düsum Khyenpa had special visions of Cakrasaṃvara. See Dusum Khyenpa, *The First Karmapa: The life and teachings of Dusum Khyenpa*, trans. David Karma Choephel and Michele Martin (New York: KTD Publications, 2012), 175, 181, 227.

Ogyen Trinley Dorje tells: 'Chakrasamvara is the main yidam for the Karma Kamtsang, and for all Kagyu lineages. He is also one of the sets of five great deities in the practices from the First Karmapa, Dusum Khyenpa.' See Kagyu Office, "Completing His Teachings, the Gyalwang Karmapa Speaks of the Chakrasamvara Empowerment," reported January 22, 2017, https://kagyuoffice.org/completing-his-teachings-the-gyalwang-karmapa-speaks-of-the-chakrasamvara-empowerment/.

30. *'das pa'i dus na rdzogs pa'i sangs rgyas gzhan phan rnam rol sogs zhing khams rgya mtshor mdzad pa bcu gnyis gcig car du bstan nas sangs rgyas zin kyang*

slar yang 'gro ba'i don du thugs bskyed de da lta'i dus na de ba can sogs zhing khams rgya mtshor rdzogs pa'i sangs rgyas 'da [sic:'od] dpag med sogs mdzad pa bcu gnyis gcig car du ston bzhin pa dang | (bKra shis tshe ring, "'jig rten dbang phyug," 19.)

In English:

'In the past, [the Karmapa] simultaneously demonstrated the Twelve Deeds in vast buddha-fields [as buddhas, such as] the perfect buddha Shenpen Namrol. Then, although [he had] become enlightened, [he] generated *bodhicitta* again for the benefit of beings. At present, [he] is simultaneously demonstrating the Twelve Deeds in vast buddha-fields, [for instance,] Sukhāvatī, [as] the perfect buddha Amitābha.'

31. *'das pa'i sangs rgyas gzhan phan rnam rol dang ma byon pa'i sangs rgyas drug pa seng ge* | *da lta'i rgyal ba mi 'khrugs pa dang mgon po 'od dpag med la sogs pa'i rnam sprul* | bKra shis tshe ring, "bka' 'bum rim po che thog mar 'tshol bsdu byed pos mjug bsdu'i snyan bsgron ma bcos gnyug ma'i rang sgra bzhugs lags," in *rgyal dbang karma pa bcu drug pa chen po'i gsung 'bum 3*, ed. Jo sras bkra shis tshe ring (Dharamsala: Tshurphu Labrang; The Amnye Machen Institute, 2016), 307.

In English:

'[The Karmapa] was the past buddha, Shenpen Namrol, and [will become] the Sixth Buddha of the future, Siṃha. [He is] the manifestation of the present [buddhas,] such as Buddha Akṣobhya and Protector Amitābha.'

32. *thog mar skyes rabs kyi dbang du byas na* | *de bzhin gshegs pa dgra bcom pa yang dag pa rdzogs pa'i sangs rgyas nga ro snyan pa'i drung du* | *phyag dar khrod kyi gos phul nas dang por byang chub mchog tu thugs bskyed pa nas brtsam* | *ma 'ongs par bskal bzang gi rnam 'dren lnga pa'i rgyal tshab tu dga' ldan lha yi gnas su* | *lha yi bu legs pa skyes zhes bya bar skye ba bzhes nas* | *slar yang 'dzam bu'i gling du gzigs pa rnam pa bzhis gzigs te* | *me tog lha yi grong khyer zhes bya ba na* | *yab rgyal po seng ge stag zhes bya ba dang* | *yum lha mo dga' ba'i nga ro zhes bya ba gnyis kyi sras su byon nas* | *bskal bzang gi rnam 'dren drug pa seng ge'i sgra* | *zhes bya bar mngon par rdzogs pa sangs rgyas nas* | *lo bdun khrir dam pa'i chos kyi 'khor lo bskor bar mdzad pa'i bar* | *byang chub sems dpa'i spyod pa rgya mtsho lta bu la brtson par mdzad cing* | *bskal bzang gi rnam 'dren 'di'i bstan pa la'ang* | (Khra 'gu rin po che, *rgyal ba'i dbang po*, 325.)

Translated into English in Appendix B (page 208 from 'regarding the beginning of the story about [his] previous lives' to 'endeavours to [undertake] the vast deeds of a bodhisattva').

The Karmapa's future life as the Sixth Buddha is also described in two other works with varied details: 'Ja' tshon snying po, *padma'i chun po*, 21.2–22.3; sKyabs gnas dam pa dpal 'byor don grub, *rgyal ba karma pa na rim gyi sngon byung dang ma 'ongs pa dang da ltar gyi tshul mdo rgyud dang gter yig rnams su lung bstan tshul kun gsal me long zhes bya ba bzhugs so*, ed. bkra shis tshe ring (Dharamsala: Library of Tibetan Works & Archives, 1982), 8.3–8.14. Both texts give the name of the Buddha as seng ge, and the period of 70,000 years is his lifespan. 'Ja' tshon snying po identifies his source as a *shog ser*; for sKyabs gnas dam pa dpal 'byor don grub, the source is *bskal bzang* which possibly refers to the *Bhadrakalpika Sūtra*. Moreover, 'Ja' tshon snying po, citing different sources, also gives the name of the Sixth Buddha as *seng ge sgra* (See 'Ja' tshon snying po, *padma'i chun po*, 3.4, 67.1).

33. The Tibetan name of the sūtra:*'phags pa bskal pa bzang po pa zhes bya ba theg pa chen po'i mdo bzhugs so*||

For the Tibetan-English edition of this sūtra, see Dharma Publishing, *Fortunate Aeon*.

34. See Dharma Publishing, *Fortunate Aeon*, 522.8–522.15.

35. According to *Thub chog byin rlabs gter mdzod kyi rgyab chos padma dkar po*, Śākyamuni practised the six *pāramitā*s from the moment he generated *bodhicitta* up to his last life as the Buddha. See Mi pham rgya mtsho, "thub chog byin rlabs gter mdzod kyi rgyab chos padma dkar po," in *gsung 'bum/_mi pham rgya mtsho*, TBRC W2DB16631. 8 (khreng tu'u: [gangs can rig gzhung dpe rnying myur skyobs lhan tshogs], 2007); 全知麦彭仁波切, 释迦佛广传, trans. 堪布索达吉 (显密宝库).

36. *de yang bskal ba bzang po 'di la sangs rgyas stong 'byon par gsungs pa'i rnam 'dren bzhi ba ni rang cag gi ston pa thub pa'i dbang po 'di nyid yin la | lnga pa ni byams pa mgon po yin cing rgyal ba byams pa'i rjes su de bzhin gshegs pa seng ges mdzad pa bcu gnyis kyi tshul btsan nas sems can gyi don mdzad par gong smos kyi lung khag dang | mdo sde skal bzang | lang kar gzhegs pa'i mdo | gsang ba bsam gyis mi khyab pa'i mdo | snying rje pad dkar sogs las gsungs pas bskal bzang gi sangs rgyas stong gi nang nas drug pa yin zhing mtshan la seng ge zhes bya bas drug pa seng ger grags so |* (bKra shis tshe ring, "'jig rten dbang phyug," 21.)

In English:

'It is said that 1000 buddhas will appear in this Fortunate Aeon. [Among them], the fourth buddha is our teacher Śākyamuni; the fifth is Maitreya. After Maitreya, Tathāgata Siṃha will perform the Twelve Deeds [of a buddha] and benefit sentient beings. [This] is said in the above-mentioned scriptures [i.e., Samādhirāja Sūtra (mdo ting 'dzin rygal po) and Krodharājagujvarājavajramaṇḍala vidhī-nāma (khro bo gnam lcags 'bar ba'i rgyud)], as well as in the Bhadrakalpika Sūtra, the Laṅkāvatāra Sūtra, the Tathāgata-acintya-guhya- nirdeśa Sūtra, the Karuṇapuṇḍarīka Sūtra, and so on. Hence, [the Karmapa] is the sixth among the thousand buddhas of Fortunate Aeon, called Siṃha. Therefore, [he] is known as the sixth, Siṃha.'

The author gives reference: *Karma 'phrin las 1456–1539 pas mgur dang dris lan sna tshogs | 1975 lor ngag dbang stobs rgyal nas ldi lir gsar bskrun zhus pa de'i shog grangs | 162* (bKra shis tshe ring, "'jig rten dbang phyug," 48.)

37. bKra shis tshe ring, "'jig rten dbang phyug," 24.3–24.4.

The author gives reference: *gnas nang dpa' po [sic:bo] sku phreng gnyis pa gtsug lag phreng ba 1504–1566 zhabs kyis 1565 lor mdzad pa'i chos 'byung mkhas pa'i dga' ston gyi sde tshan pa pa'i shog grangs dang po'i rgyab shog dang | sman sdong mtshams pa'i dpag bsam khre shing ge grangs | 14* (bKra shis tshe ring, "'jig rten dbang phyug," 49.)

38. This possibly refers to *'Jam dpal rtsa rgyud* which, according to 'Ja' tshon snying po, contains the following verse:

ming ni ka dang ma yi thog mtha' can | bstan pa gsal byed skyes bu 'byung |

('Ja' tshon snying po, *padma'i chun po*, 3.)

39. Martin, *"Music in the Sky,"* 271–272.

40. Karma nges don bstan rgyas, "rnam thar mdor bsdus," 5.2–5.3; mKhyen brtse 'od zer, "mkha' khyab rdo rje'i," 473.1, 473.5.

According to Gamble, the first three Karmapas, Düsum Khyenpa, Karma Pakshi and Rangjung Dorje, identified themselves to be Avalokiteśvara; during the time of the Seventh Karmapa, Chödrak Gyatso, the belief that the Karmapa incarnation is a manifestation of Avalokiteśvara became widespread (Gamble, "View from Nowhere," 102–103).

41. Karma nges don bstan rgyas, "rnam thar mdor bsdus," 12.5–12.6.

42. *bskal bzang gi rnam 'dren 'di'i bstan pa la'ang | ri bo ta lar snying rje'i rang gzugs 'jig rten dbang phyug |* (Khra 'gu rin po che, *rgyal ba'i dbang po*, 325.)

Translated into English in Appendix B (page 208 from '[in the period when] the teaching of Buddha' to 'Avalokiteśvara').

43. *'jig rten dbang phyug mthing mdog cod paN 'chang ba bcu drug pa chen po'i phyi yi rnam thar rgya mtsho ltar tshad med pa las chu thigs tsam gyi sa bon bzhugs so ||* (bKra shis tshe ring, "'jig rten dbang phyug," 19.)

44. *mgon po spyan ras gzigs sogs byang chub sems dpa'i tshul gyis 'gro ba rigs drug 'dren pa* (bKra shis tshe ring, "'jig rten dbang phyug," 19.)

45. bKra shis tshe ring, "'jig rten dbang phyug," 24.2–24.3.

The author gives reference: *gnas nang dpa' po [sic:bo] sku phreng gnyis pa gtsug lag phreng ba 1504–1566 . . . sman sdong mtshams pa'i dpag bsam khre shing ge grangs | 14* (bKra shis tshe ring, "'jig rten dbang phyug," 49.)

46. bKra shis tshe ring, "'jig rten dbang phyug," 21.16–22.1.

47. Zhwa dmar, *dpal rgyal ba karma pa rig pa'i rdo rje'i sku tshe'i rnam thar la bstod pa kunda'i phreng ba zhes pa las lo rgyus dang 'brel ba'i tshig don rnams gsal bar bkral ba kunda'i dri bsung shes bya ba bzhugs so* (Kalimpong: Diwakar Publications, 2013), 8.3–8.7.

See also Mila Khyentse Rinpoche, Introduction to *History of the Karmapas: The odyssey of the Tibetan masters with the black crown*, ed. Maureen Lander (New York: Snow Lion Publications, 2012), 1.

48. Karma nges don bstan rgyas, "rnam thar mdor bsdus," 10.3–11.2.

49. 'Pu to ba' possibly refer to Po to ba.

50. Karma nges don bstan rgyas, "rnam thar mdor bsdus," 9.5–10.3.

51. mKhyen brtse 'od zer, "mkha' khyab rdo rje'i," 473.5–474.1.

The link to Saraha goes back to the Second Karmapa, Karma Pakshi, who, in his prophecy about the Fourth Karmapa, identifies Düsum Khyenpa as Saraha's manifestation. See 噶玛钨金 et al., eds., "第四世噶玛巴:若必多杰. 持律利苍生," 法露 (*Dharma Nectar*) 2, no. 2 (2016): 42, Karmapa Office.

52. *mdor na sangs rgyas byang sems nyan rang dang de bzhin du rgyal blon khyim bdag sogs gang la gang 'dul gyi mdzad pas sems can la phan pa de dang bde bar gyur pa'i sgyu 'phrul bsam gyi mi khyab pa ni rang cag tshur mthong byis pa'i blo'i ra ba las 'das pas na su zhig gis tshad 'dzin par nus |* (bKra shis tshe ring, "'jig rten dbang phyug," 20.)

In English:

'In brief, [the Karmapa] tames beings according to their needs through inconceivable manifestations, including buddha, bodhisattva, *śrāvaka* and *pratyekabuddha*, and similarly, minister and householder. By doing so, [he] benefits beings and brings happiness to them. [This is] beyond our immature ordinary perception. If [this is the case,] who is able to measure [the limit of his manifestations]?'

53. *rgya gar 'phags pa'i yul du grub pa'i slob dpon sa ra ha dang | klu yi byang chub sogs pan grub mang po dang | bod gangs can gyi ljongs 'dir yang lo tsā ba*

rgyal dbang mchog dbyangs | *po to ba rin chen gsal* | *sha ra ba sogs mkhas shing grub pa brnyes pa mang po dang* |

gzhan *yang chos skyong ba'i rgyal po srong btsan sgam po sogs bstan pa'i sbyin bdag chen po rnams su skye ba bzhes* (Khra 'gu rin po che, *rgyal ba'i dbang po*, 325–326.)

Translated into English in Appendix B (page 208 from 'In the noble land India' to 'King Songtsen Gampo').

Rum bteg, "rgyal dbang karma pa chen po'i dgongs rdzogs mjug mchod," in *rgyal dbang karma pa bcu drug pa chen po'i gsung 'bum 1*, ed. Jo sras bkra shis tshe ring (Dharamsala: Tshurphu Labrang; The Amnye Machen Institute, 2016), 233.6–233.7.

54. bKra shis tshe ring, "'jig rten dbang phyug," 19.12–20.6; bKra shis tshe ring, "thog mar 'tshol bsdu," 307.16–307.18.

55. Martin, *"Music in the Sky,"* 273.

56. Ken Holmes, *His Holiness the 17th Gyalwa Karmapa Urgyen Trinley Dorje* (Forres, Scotland: Altea Publishing, 1995), 137.

57. Prophecies about the Karmapas are found in different sources with varied details. In this study, I draw on the accounts of Karma Ngedön Tengye and Khyentse Özer. One can also consult the following two texts:

'Ja' tshon snying po, *padma'i chun po*.
sKyabs gnas dam pa dpal 'byor don grub, *kun gsal me long*.

For the first text, since the composer is Tertön Jatson Nyingpo ('Ja' tshon snying po, 1585–1656), the time of the composition would possibly fall in the first half of the seventeenth century. The edition that I have access to does not give the date of publication, but it mentions in the colophon the name of the publisher Zimpön Tsewang Paljor (gzim dpon Tshe dbang dpal 'byor) who, according to Tashi Tsering (through his email to author, December 20, 2019), was connected to the Sixteenth Karmapa. Of all the Tibetan texts about the Karmapa prophecies available to me, this is the earliest and most elaborate, comprised of eighty-two pages. The many Sūtra, Tantra and Terma references in the second text listed above and in the various sources discussed in this chapter are found in this text, including, for example, the identification of the Karmapa with the Sixth Buddha, Avalokiteśvara, Padmasambhava, Saraha, Nāgabodhi, Aśvaghoṣa, King Bimbisara, Potowa, Kharag Gomchung and Songtsen Gampo, as well as the prophecies about Düsum Khyenpa, Tsurphu and the Black Crown.

58. *nga 'das lo ni nyis stong na* | *gdong dmar yul du bstan pa 'byung* | *spyan ras gzigs kyi gdul byar 'gyur* | *de'i bstan pa'i snyigs ma la* | *byang chub sems dpa' seng ge'i sgra* | *karma ka* [sic:pa] *zhes bya ba 'byung* | *ting 'dzin dbang thob 'gro ba 'dul* | *mthong thos dran reg bde la bkod* (mKhyen brtse 'od zer, "mkha' khyab rdo rje'i," 474.)

This verse is also found in 'Ja' tshon snying po, *padma'i chun po*, 3.3–3.5 (spelling difference: *gyi* as *gyis*, *ge'i* as *ge*, and *bya ba 'byung* as *bya bar 'gyur*), which ascribes it to *ding 'dzin rgyal po'i rgyud*.

59. The spelling difference in comparison to mKhyen brtse 'od zer's text: *de'i* as *de yi*.

Khra 'gu's quotation does not include the last two lines (Khra 'gu rin po che, *rgyal ba'i dbang po*, 323.18–324.2); bKra shis tshe ring, "'jig rten dbang phyug," 20.11–20.14, quotes almost the entire verse except for the first line.

Michele Martin gives an English translation of this verse in Martin, "*Music in the Sky*," 271.

60. Following the verse, Khra 'gu states: *zhes ma 'ongs par bskal bzang gi rnam 'dren drug par 'tshang rgya bar 'gyur ba | byang chub sems dpa' seng ge'i sgra yi rnam 'phrul du lung bstan pa dang |* (Khra 'gu rin po che, *rgyal ba'i dbang po*, 324)

61. bKra shis tshe ring, "'jig rten dbang phyug," 20.10–21.9.

62. *bod gangs can gyi ljongs su bstan 'dzin gyi skye chen ji snyed gcig byon pa dag las lung gis zin pa ni tshad mar byed do |* (bKra shis tshe ring, "'jig rten dbang phyug," 20–21.)

63. These include the Derge, Lhasa, Lithang, dpe bsdur ma and Jiang editions from the following three online sources:

"Literature," The Tibetan & Himalayan Library, accessed March 6, 2017, http://www.thlib.org/encyclopedias/literary/canons/kt/catalog.php#cat=d/k.

"Full-text search in electronic versions of the Kanjur," University of Vienna, accessed March 6, 2017, https://www.istb.univie.ac.at/kanjur/rktsneu/ekanjur/.

"Jiang Kangyur," ADARSHA, accessed March 6, 2017, https://adarsha.dharma-treasure.org/kdbs/jiangkangyur.

64. *slob dpon chen po gu ru padmas zhal lung dri bral rnams su | gangs can gyi ljongs 'dir nyid dang tha mi dad pa'i rdo rje slob dpon bdag po chen po zhwa nag gi cod pan 'chang ba mtshan gyi nges pa gsal ba dang mi gsal ba rgyun mi chad du 'byon pa dang | de rnams mthong thos dran reg thams cad ngan song med par mtho ris dang thar pa'i lam sna zin par rdo rje'i lung bstan yang yang rtsal ba |* (Karma nges don bstan rgyas, "rnam thar mdor bsdus," 11.)

In English:

'According to the faultless prophecies of the great master Padmasambhava, a great Tantric master wearing a black crown, [who] is no different from [Padmasambhava] himself, will appear in Tibet in an uninterrupted fashion, with or without a certain name. All those who see, hear, remember or touch [him] will not suffer lower rebirth, [but instead,] attain higher rebirth and the path of liberation.'

Footnote 10, added by the Chinese translator 比丘尼洛卓拉嫫, in 上師之師 explains that mtshan gyi nges pa gsal ba refers to the Kar- mapa, and mi gsal ba his manifestations, such as gods and serpents (【具名的】指噶瑪巴；【不具名的】指他的化現,像天人、龍等). See 勉東倉巴仁波切,八蚌欽哲仁波切,堪千創古仁波切, 上師之師, 19.

65. 'The teachings of my emanation, the Karmapa, will not come to an end until the teachings of the fortunate kalpa have come to a close' (Martin, "*Music in the Sky*," 276).

66. *spyan ras gzigs kyi phrin las skyong byed cing || mtshur phu zhes byar dus gsum mkhyen pa 'byung ||* (mKhyen brtse 'od zer, "mkha' khyab rdo rje'i," 474.)

This verse is also found in 'Ja' tshon snying po, *padma'i chun po*, 18.5–19.1 (spelling difference: *byed cing* as *byed pas*), and sKyabs gnas dam pa dpal 'byor don grub, *kun gsal me long*, 7.4–7.5 (*byed cing* as *byed pa*). Both ascribe it to Sangye Lingpa (Sangs rgyas gling pa, 1340–1396).

67. *spyan ras gzigs kyi gsung gi rnam 'phrul las* || *dga' ldan gnas nas sems can don du 'phos* || *dang po'i gsang spyod dus gsum mkhyen zhes grags* || *dbang rtags rigs kyi cod pan zhwa nag 'dzin* || *skyad cig re la sems can dpag med 'dren* || *de dag mthong thos dran reg 'gro ba rnams* || *skye ba de 'phos 'phags pa'i drung du skye* || (mKhyen brtse 'od zer, "mkha' khyab rdo rje'i," 474.)

This verse is also found in 'Ja' tshon snying po, *padma'i chun po*, 29.2–34.2 (spelling difference: *rnam 'phrul* as *rnams 'phrul*, *don du* as *don la*, *gsang spyod* as *sa spyod*, *sems can* as *'gro ba*, *dran reg* as *reg pa'i*, and *'phags pa'i* as *byams mgon*), which ascribes it to Sangye Lingpa and contains a more complete version of the verse.

68. Khra 'gu rin po che, *rgyal ba'i dbang po*, 324.12–324.16.

69. bKra shis tshe ring, "'jig rten dbang phyug," 23.13–23.17.

There are four minor spelling differences: *spyan ras gzigs* as *sbyan ras gzigs*, *rnam 'phrul* as *rnam sprul*, *dang po'i* as *dang po* and *cod pan* as *cod paN*.

70. bKra shis tshe ring, "'jig rten dbang phyug," 23.17–24.2.

The author gives reference: *tshogs gnyis gru gzings kyi shog grangs 10* (bKra shis tshe ring, "'jig rten dbang phyug," 49.)

71. Martin, "*Music in the Sky*," 272–273.

72. According to Shamar, this happened during the Karmapa's visit to Bhutan in 1968. Queen Kesang Choden (bsKal bzang chos sgron) invited the Karmapa to consecrate a new Padmasambhava temple built next to Kyichu Lhakhang (sKyid chu lha khang) in Paro. At that time, a Khampa lama presented this Terma prophecy to the Karmapa. Shamar, who was present, read the text. The Karmapa also showed it to Dilgo Khyentse (Dil mgo mkhyen brtse) and the queen (See Zhwa dmar, *sku tshe'i rnam thar*, 16.5–17.13).

73. Zhwa dmar, *sku tshe'i rnam thar*, 17.11–17.13, 18.1–18.2.

'Ja' tshon snying po, *padma'i chun po*, 56.2–58.1, cites a Terma source that contains similar details: a birthmark on the right thigh which is a sign of bodhisattva; by seeing him, one will purify the karmic obscuration of seven lifetimes. However, the source does not specify which Karmapa incarnation it refers to.

74. Besides the sources quoted here, 'Ja' tshon snying po cites various Terma texts and other sources to make the same connection (e.g., 'Ja' tshon snying po, *padma'i chun po*, 27, 34, 35, 44, 49, 61, 65).

75. *lo tsā rgyal ba mchog dbyangs bdag la gson* || *gsung gi gnas mchog zla gam pho brang du* || *ma 'ongs khyed kyi skye ba nyer gcig 'byung* || *spyan ras gzigs sprul dus gsum kun mkhyen pa* || (mKhyen brtse 'od zer, "mkha' khyab rdo rje'i," 474–475.)

Michele Martin also gives an English translation in Martin, "*Music in the Sky*," 276.

76. Photographs of both the painting and the text are documented in Thomas Pardee, Susan Skolnick, and Eric Swanson, *Karmapa: The sacred prophecy*, eds. Willa Baker, Elisabeth Deran, Robert Kelly, and Jane Madill (New York: The Kagyu Thubten Chöling Publications Committee, 1999), 58–60.

77. The number of the Karmapa incarnations varies in other prophecies. See sKyabs gnas dam pa dpal 'byor don grub, *kun gsal me long*; Kagyu Office, "Karma Kamtshang lineage."

78. Khra 'gu rin po che, *rgyal ba'i dbang po*, 324.17–325.2.

The spelling difference in comparison to mKhyen brtse 'od zer's text: *gnas mchog* as *sprul pa.*

79. Martin, "*Music in the Sky,*" 272, 276.

80. *theg mchog mya ngan 'das 'og dgos pa'i mtshan* || *bde ba'i bdag nyid rig pa'i rdo rje dang* || *o rgyan phrin las bsam gtan la sogs 'byung* || . . . *nga yi sprul pa karma'i bstan pa ni* || *bskal bzang bstan pa rdzogs bar mi rdzogs so* || (mKhyen brtse 'od zer, "mkha' khyab rdo rje'i," 475.)

mchog dbyangs sprul pa sngags rig 'dzin || *rta'am lug gi lo pa ni* || (mKhyen brtse 'od zer, "mkha' khyab rdo rje'i," 476.)

In English:
'The names [of those] that must [come] after the nirvana of Thekchok [Dorje]
Dewe Dagnyi, Rigpe Dorje
Ogyen Trinley, Samten, and so on, will emerge
[. . .]
The teaching of my [own] emanation, Karma
Will not come to an end until the teaching of Fortunate Aeon is completed
And,
The emanation of Chokyang, the *Vidyādhara* of mantra
[Will be] born in the horse or sheep year.'

For Michele Martin's English translation, see Martin, "*Music in the Sky,*" 276.

81. Footnotes 3–5 in 勉東倉巴仁波切，八蚌欽哲仁波切，堪千創古仁波切，上師之師, 258, and Martin, "*Music in the Sky,*" 276, identify the names of the following Karmapas:

The Fifteenth Karmapa referred to as Dewe Dagnyi, the Sixteenth Karmapa Rigpe Dorje, the Seventeenth Karmapa Ogyen Trinley and the Eighteenth Karmapa Samten.

82. In the fourth line ('The teaching of my [own] emanation, Karma'), though the name here is Karma rather than Karmapa.

83. In the first line ('The emanation of Chokyang, the *Vidyādhara* of mantra'), Chokyang is probably an abbreviation of Gyalwa Chokyang.

84. The first three lines of the verse. See Khra 'gu rin po che, *rgyal ba'i dbang po,* 325.2–325.7.

85. The Karmapas' 'self-prediction' is often supported by visions and predictions of their primary disciples and accomplished masters, for example, in the *namthar* of the Second, Sixth to Eighth, Twelfth, Thirteenth and Fifteenth Karmapas (Karma nges don bstan rgyas, "rnam thar mdor bsdus"; mKhyen brtse 'od zer, "mkha' khyab rdo rje'i").

86. In Karma nges don bstan rgyas, "rnam thar mdor bsdus" and mKhyen brtse 'od zer, "mkha' khyab rdo rje'i," most Karmapas, from the Second to Ninth, Eleventh to Thirteenth and the Fifteenth, made predictions of their next reincarnation in one or both ways. According to Lhundup Damchö, when the Karmapa did not leave a specific letter, his primary disciples would look for clues in his correspondence, spiritual songs and poems, or their own memories of his remarks, even signs in their dreams. See Lhundup Damchö, *Karmapa: 900 years* (Himachal Pradesh: Karmapa 900 Organizing Committee; New York: KTD Publications, 2011), 99.

For each Karmapa's prediction of his future reincarnation(s), see also 噶玛善莲, "按图索骥: 重绘古" 哲霍 "圣迹地图," 法露 *(Dharma Nectar)* 5, no. 3 (2019): 22–33, Karmapa Office; 噶玛善莲, "历代噶玛巴与则拉岗," 法露 *(Dharma Nectar)* 5, no. 3 (2019): 66–75, Karmapa Office; 噶玛善喜, "七世噶玛巴出生地:扑朔迷离岗岗巴村. 消失的脚印岩石," 法露 *(Dharma Nectar)* 3, no. 2 (2017): 96–103, Karmapa Office; 噶玛善喜, "七世噶玛巴出生地:边坝县金岭乡金达村. 阿玛拉千诺'," 法露 *(Dharma Nectar)* 4, no. 2 (2017): 6–15, Karmapa Office; 噶玛善喜, "十二世噶玛巴出生地:汪布顶乡卓格村. 隔了十世重回故地," 法露 *(Dharma Nectar)* 4, no. 2 (2017): 40–47, Karmapa Office; 噶玛善莲, "四世噶玛巴出生地:边坝县加贡乡. 世外桃源小山岗," 法露 *(Dharma Nectar)* 3, no. 2 (2017): 72–79, Karmapa Office; 噶玛善宝, "五世噶玛巴出生地:工布江达镇娘当村. 掩藏在枯叶下的圣石," 法露 *(Dharma Nectar)* 3, no. 2 (2017): 80–87, Karmapa Office; 噶玛善莲, and 噶玛善宝, "九世噶玛巴出生地:卡瓦岭神山达桑山谷. 鹰巢底下手印石," 法露 *(Dharma Nectar)* 4, no. 2 (2017): 20–29, Karmapa Office; 噶玛善宝, and噶玛善莲, "十、十一世噶玛巴出生地:班玛县多日麻村. 莲花藏乡八吉祥," 法露 *(Dharma Nectar)* 4, no. 2 (2017): 30–39, Karmapa Office; 噶玛宝阳, "十四世噶瑪巴出生地:噶玛乡达那村," 法露 *(Dharma Nectar)* 4, no. 2 (2017): 56–63, Karmapa Office; 噶玛钨金, "杜松虔巴"; 噶玛钨金 et al., eds., "第二世噶玛巴:噶玛拔希. 降服外道蒙古汗王," 法露 *(Dharma Nectar)* 2, no. 2 (2016): 20–29, Karmapa Office; 噶玛钨金 et al., eds., "第三世噶玛巴:让炯多杰. 把爱放在月亮上," 法露 *(Dharma Nectar)* 2, no. 2 (2016): 30–39, Karmapa Office; 噶玛钨金, "若必多杰"; 噶玛钨金 et al., eds., "第五世噶玛巴:德新谢巴. 佛光播撒汉地,"法露 *(Dharma Nectar)* 2, no. 2 (2016): 50–61, Karmapa Office; 噶玛钨金 et al., eds., "第六世噶玛巴:通瓦敦滇. 善逝前往香巴拉,"法露 *(Dharma Nectar)* 2, no. 2 (2016): 62–69, Karmapa Office; 噶玛钨金 et al., eds., "第七世噶瑪巴:确札嘉措. 带领嘎千大营去修行," 法露 *(Dharma Nectar)* 2, no. 2 (2016): 70–79, Karmapa Office; 噶玛钨金 et al., eds., "第八世噶瑪巴:米觉多杰. 青绿山水中的不动金刚," 法露 *(Dharma Nectar)* 2, no. 2 (2016): 80–89, Karmapa Office; 噶玛钨金 et al., eds., "第九世噶玛巴:旺秋多杰. 广行尊胜佛行事业," 法露 *(Dharma Nectar)* 3, no. 2 (2017): 6–17, Karmapa Office; 噶玛钨金 et al., eds., "第十一世噶玛巴:耶谢多杰. 八瓣莲花出生智慧金刚," 法露 *(Dharma Nectar)* 4, no. 2 (2017): 88–93, Karmapa Office; 噶玛钨金 et al., eds., "第十二世噶玛巴:蒋秋多杰. 出世大士无方游乡国," 法露 *(Dharma Nectar)* 4, no. 2 (2017): 94–100, Karmapa Office; 噶玛钨金 et al., eds, "第十三世噶玛巴:敦督多杰. 以诸音而说法的伏魔金刚," 法露 *(Dharma Nectar)* 5, no. 3 (2019): 82–89, Karmapa Office; 噶玛钨金 et al., eds, "第十四世噶玛巴:特秋多杰. 无量法调无边众," 法露 *(Dharma Nectar)* 5, no. 3 (2019): 90–97, Karmapa Office.

87. Interview with the Sixteenth Karmapa and Jamgon Kongtrul on the American television programme 'Vermont Report' (December 1976) in *Recalling a Buddha*.

88. *'phags chen 'di rnams ngos 'dzin gnang ba'i tshe yang | mo brtag lung zhu tsam ma yin par | sku phreng snga mas 'byung 'gyur mkhyen pa'i ye shes kyis | gnas dang | dus 'di lta bur srid pa nye bar bzung ba'i nges pa gzigs nas lung bstan bstsal ba'i shog dril gnang srol yod pa dang | de nyid khyer nas brtsal bas mchog sprul 'khrul bral nges rnyed 'gyur ba ltar |* (Khra 'gu rin po che, *rgyal ba'i dbang po*, 326.)

Translated into English in Appendix B (page 209 from 'When these great noble [Karmapa incarnations]' to 'the true supreme reincarnation will definitely be found').

89. bod nang snga bar phyis byon sprul sku su dang yang ma 'dra bar 'phags chen 'di rnams ngos 'dzin pa'i tshe yang mo brtag lung zhu tsam ma yin par mdzad pa thun min gcig ni kar rabs bdun pa tsam nas sku phreng snga mas 'byung 'gyur mkhyen pa'i ye shes kyis gnas dang dus 'di lta bur phyi ma'i srid pa bzung ba'i nges pa gzigs shing | de yang rigs kyi mtshan dang | yul dang | dgung rtags sogs gsal bar bkod pa'i 'da' kha'i zhal chems gzim 'og shog dril zhes pa'i bka' rgya can zhes bris nas so so'i sku skye gar 'khrungs ngos 'dzin dang thog nang srol yod pa'i ngo mtshar gyi rnam thar mang dag yod pa (bKra shis tshe ring, "'jig rten dbang phyug," 25.)

In English:

'Unlike [other] past, present and future tulkus in Tibet, these great noble [Karmapa incarnations have] an unusual method of identification, rather than mere divination, [spiritual] examination or prophecy. Since [his] seventh incarnation, [in the case of all the following Karmapas,] the previous incarnation perceives [with] certainty [his] future birth, such as place and time [of birth], through the wisdom of knowing what is to arise. Furthermore, [he] writes down the letter of testament, called 'the scroll underneath the house', that mentions clearly the name of the family, the place, the sign of the year [when he will be reborn], and so on, with the seal of secrecy. Having done so, [he] identifies in advance where the individual rebirth will take place. There are many miraculous stories about [this] tradition.'

The word *nang* (*nang srol*) in bKra shis tshe ring may be a typographical error or variant spelling of *gnang*. Khra 'gu's passage cited above gives *shog dril gnang srol yod pa*. bKra shis tshe ring's own English translation, '*how* they recognized in advance', suggests the same. See Tashi Tsering, "A Biography of His Holiness The 16th Karmapa Entitled 'A Droplet from the Infinite Ocean-Like Outer Biography of Lokeshvara: The great sixteenth holder of the black crown'," *The Tibet Journal* 9, no. 3 (1984): 6.

bKra shis tshe ring gives reference for this method of self-prediction: *sgrub brgyud karma ka [sic:kam] tshang brgyud pa rin po che's rnam thar rab 'byams nor bu zla ba chu shel gyi phreng ba | si tu chos 'byung gis mdzad 'phro 'be lo karma tshe dbang kun khyab nas kha skong gnang ba de yi nang gsal yod snyam yang da lta gser phreng lag tu med stobs zhib bsdur bya dgos pas dpyad par mdzod* | (bKra shis tshe ring, "'jig rten dbang phyug," 49.)

90. See also Martin, "*Music in the Sky*," 275; Reginald A Ray, *Secret of the Vajra World: The Tantric Buddhism of Tibet* (Boston: Shambhala Publications Inc., 2001), 388.

91. Rum bteg, "dpal karma pa bcu drug pa chen po'i rnam thar lo rgyus mdor bsdus bzhugs," in *rgyal dbang karma pa bcu drug pa chen po'i gsung 'bum 1*, ed. Jo sras bkra shis tshe ring (Dharamsala: Tshurphu Labrang; The Amnye Machen Institute, 2016), 223.11–223.18.

92. For the discovery of the testament letter, see Grags pa yongs 'dus, "karma pa bcu drug pa rig pa'i rdo rje'i rnam thar," in *kam tshang gser phreng gi rnam thar kha skong*, TBRC W19988. (New Delhi: Topga Yulgyal, 1993), 385.4–386.13; 'Ju chen thub bstan rnam rgyal, "rgyal dbang karma pa," 321.14–322.8; Lea Terhune, *Karmapa: The Politics of Reincarnation* (Massachusetts: Wisdom Publications, 2004), 97; Holmes, *Gyalwa Karmapa*, 46–47; Pemo Kunsang and Marie Aubèle, "The Sixteenth Karmapa, Rangjung Rigpe Dorje (1924–1981)," in *History of the Karmapas: The odyssey of the Tibetan masters with the black crown* (New York: Snow Lion

Publications, 2012), 204; Mick Brown, *The Dance of 17 Lives: The incredible true story of Tibet's 17th Karmapa* (London: Bloomsbury, 2004), 38.

On the decoding of the letter, see Grags pa yongs 'dus, "bcu drug pa," 386.14–388.3; Terhune, *Karmapa*, 97; Holmes, *Gyalwa Karmapa*, 47.

93. There are minor differences in the content of the letter presented in different Tibetan accounts, mostly variant spellings of the same word or the use of different case markers. These differences do not change the meaning of the verse. My discussion here is based on Thrangu's version:

'di nas shar phyogs gser ldan chu yi 'gram || mda' bsnun dpa' bos bzung ba'i ljongs kyi char || lhun chags seng ge 'gyings pa'i phang pa ru || dpal gyi ri la a dang thub kyis brgyan || sa yi khyim du chos dkar rje'u'i rigs || 'jig rten mkha' 'gro'i lhums su gnas mal mthong || glang gi nya'am byi ba lo pa zhig || a ti khyab brdal kun bzang mkha' dbyings las || snang rig zung 'jug ye shes sgron me che || rang byung khyab bdag rig pa'i rdo rjer 'bod || (Khra 'gu rin po che, *rgyal ba'i dbang po*, 326–327.)

Translated into English in Appendix B (page 209 from '[In] the eastern direction from here' to 'Called Rangjung Khyabdak Rigpe Dorje').

According to bKra shis tshe ring, "'jig rten dbang phyug," 25, the title of the letter is *'da' kha'i glu skye po'i cha rgyan chu shing gi me tog brda' thim*. His English translation: 'A Dying Song—The Hidden Significance of a Bamboo Flower, An Ornament for the People' (See Tashi Tsering, "Outer Biography," 6). Martin's translation: 'The Last Song: A Reed's Flower to Embellish the Ear' (See Martin, *"Music in the Sky,"* 275).

94. See Appendix B (page 209 from '[In] the eastern direction from here' to 'On the lap of the poised majestic lion').

95. *gling rje ge sar skyes bu don grub byon pa'i skabs su skyen po'i mda' la rang dbang thob pa | tsha zhang mdan ma byang khras skyong ba'i yul ljongs mdan khog | chos rgyal srong btsan sgam pos bzhengs pa'i mtha' 'dul gyi gtsug lag khang bzhi'i ya gyal | glang thang byang chub sgrol ma'i gtsug lag khang gi nye zhol du |* (Khra 'gu rin po che, *rgyal ba'i dbang po*, 327.)

Translated into English in Appendix B (page 209 from 'at the time of the arrival [of] the accomplished one' to 'built by Dharma King Songtsen Gampo').

The two words, *mdan ma* and *mdan khog*, are spelled differently in other accounts:

In bKra shis tshe ring, "'jig rten dbang phyug", Jam dbyangs tshul khrims, "karma pa rig pa'i rdo rje," in *karma pa sku phreng rim byon gyi mdzad rnam*. TBRC W18133. (Lan kru'u: kan su'u mi rigs dpe skrun khang, 1997), Zhwa dmar, *sku tshe'i rnam thar*, and 'Ju chen thub bstan rnam rgyal, "rgyal dbang karma pa": *'dan ma* and *'dan khog*; in Grags pa yongs 'dus, "bcu drug pa": *'dan ma* and *ldan khog*. To maintain consistency, I use Khra 'gu's spelling.

96. Zhwa dmar, *sku tshe'i rnam thar*, 13.12–13.15.

The Tibetan name of Saraha, *mda' bsnun*, appears in the second line of the verse. This may be the link on which Zhwa dmar draws for his claim.

97. Martin, *"Music in the Sky,"* 301.

This identification is found in the commentary of the Karmapa's spiritual songs, produced under the guidance of Thrangu Rinpoche (Martin, *"Music in the Sky,"* 295).

98. See 3.1. Identification with Enlightened Beings.

99. *rdzogs chen mchog sprul lnga pa thub bstan chos kyi rdo rjes* | *thog mar lhums su bzhugs skabs nas kyang byang chub sems dpa'i sprul pa zhig yin par ngos 'dzin dang* | *sku bltams pa'i gnas skye bo mi nag pa'i khyim du ma yin par* | *gtsang zhing dben pa seng ge rnam rdzong gi ngogs su sku 'khrungs dgos par lung bstan gnang ba ltar* | *gnas de nyid du sku 'khrungs pa ni* | *lhun chags seng ge 'gyings pa'i phang pa ru zhes gong ma'i zhal chems dang mthun zhing* | (Khra 'gu rin po che, *rgyal ba'i dbang po*, 328.)

Translated into English in Appendix B (page 210 from 'At first, even when [he] was' to 'the testament of the previous Karmapa: "On the lap of the poised majestic lion"').

See also rDzogs chen dpon slob, "karma pa sku phreng bcu drug pa rig pa'i rdo rje," in *rgyal dbang karma pa bcu drug pa chen po'i gsung 'bum 1*, ed. Jo sras bkra shis tshe ring (Dharamsala: Tshurphu Labrang; The Amnye Machen Institute, 2016), 277.9–277.14; mKhas btsun bzang po, "rje karma pa rig pa'i rdo rje ni," in *rgyal dbang karma pa bcu drug pa chen po'i gsung 'bum 1*, ed. Jo sras bkra shis tshe ring (Dharamsala: Tshurphu Labrang; The Amnye Machen Institute, 2016), 134.13–134.14; Shes bya, "bzod par dka' ba'i," 226.16–226.17; 'Ju chen thub bstan rnam rgyal, "rgyal dbang karma pa," 323.6–323.8; Dzogchen Ponlop, "Rangjung Rigpe Dorje," 290; Terhune, *Karmapa*, 96; Jamgon Kongtrul Rinpoche, "Life Story of His Holiness the XVI Gyalwa Karmapa," *Bulletin of Tibetology: Karmapa commemoration volume*, no. 1 (1982): 6; Nik Douglas and Meryl White comp., *Karmapa: The black hat lama of Tibet* (London: Luzac & Company Ltd., 1976), 107; Karma Thinley, "Karmapa Rangjung Rigpe Dorje," in *The History of the Sixteen Karmapas of Tibet*, ed. David Stott (Boulder: Prajñā Press, 1980), 129; Holmes, *Gyalwa Karmapa*, 23; Kunsang and Aubèle, "Sixteenth Karmapa," 203; Brown, *Dance of 17 Lives*, 38; 噶玛善池, "十六世噶玛巴出生地:石渠县洛须镇. 每一次峰回路转都是修炼," 法露 *(Dharma Nectar)* 4, no. 2 (2017): 76, Karmapa Office.

Douglas and White also mention another person who made the same prophecy: Siddha Gyal Je. Dzogchen Ponlop and 噶玛善池 both report that several masters in Derge told the Karmapa's mother that her future son was a great bodhisattva.

100. Zhwa dmar, *sku tshe'i rnam thar*, 15.12–15.14; Grags pa yongs 'dus, "bcu drug pa," 360.2–360.3.

101. Dzogchen Ponlop, "Rangjung Rigpe Dorje," 290; Karma Thinley, "Rangjung Rigpe Dorje," 129; Nydahl, *Entering the Diamond Way*, 72; Holmes, *Gyalwa Karmapa*, 23; Kunsang and Aubèle, "Sixteenth Karmapa," 203; 噶玛善池, "洛须镇," 76–77.

102. See Appendix B (page 209 from 'On the mountain of glory' to 'in the womb of a worldly *ḍākinī*').

103. *sa skyong sde dge'i mdun na 'don* | *chos la dkar ba'i rje'u'i rigs* | *A thub zhes pa'i 'khrungs gzhis su* | *yab rje sde dge chos rgyal chen po'i sras kyi go gnas can tshe dbang phun tshogs dang* | *yum 'jig rten mkha' 'gro mi mo'i tshul du bzung ba skal bzang chos sgron* (Khra 'gu rin po che, *rgyal ba'i dbang po*, 327.)

Translated into English in Appendix B (page 209–210 from '[The Karmapa] was born in a family called Athub' to '*ḍākinī* in human form').

104. According to bKra shis tshe ring, "'jig rten dbang phyug," 26.9–26.10, and Kunsang and Aubèle, "Sixteenth Karmapa," 204, *chos dkar rje'u* in the letter refers to the name of the Karmapa's family lineage.

105. bKra shis tshe ring, "'jig rten dbang phyug," 26.9–26.10.

106. Zhwa dmar, *sku tshe'i rnam thar*, 14.2–15.12.

The Karmapa's family is also briefly introduced in Grags pa yongs 'dus, "bcu drug pa," 359.13–359.15, 'Ju chen thub bstan rnam rgyal, "rgyal dbang karma pa," 323.1–323.2; Jamgon Kongtrul Rinpoche, "XVI Gyalwa Karmapa," 6; Douglas and White, *Black Hat Lama*, 107; Karma Thinley, "Rangjung Rigpe Dorje," 129.

The names of the Karmapa's parents vary in Jamgon Kongtrul Rinpoche, Douglas and White, and Karma Thinley.

107. See Appendix B (page 209 from '[I will be] born on a full moon day' to 'Called Rangjung Khyabdak Rigpe Dorje').

108. *ngos 'dzin gnang skabs* | *si tu padma dbang mchog rgyal po'i gzim lam du* | *rgyal dbang mkha' khyab rdo rje* | *phyag rdor dril bsnol thabs* | *zhabs rdo rje'i skyil mo krung gis* | *'khrungs gzhis a thub kyi gzim khang thog tu bzhugs pa gzigs pa dang* | *rje gong ma'i 'da' ka'i zhal chems ang yig tu yod pa gzhan gyis shes ma nus kyang* | *dpal spungs mkhyen sprul rin po ches zhib gzigs kyis gtan 'bebs gnang ba gnyis dgongs pa gcig tu gyur nas ngos 'dzin gsal bar byung yang* | (Khra 'gu rin po che, *rgyal ba'i dbang po*, 328–329.)

Translated into English in Appendix B (page 210 from 'On the occasion of granting recognition' to '[the child was] clearly identified [as the Karmapa reincarnation]').

Situ's vision is also mentioned in 'Jam dbyangs tshul khrims, "rig pa'i rdo rje," 230.13–230.14; Blo gros don yod, "rig pa'i rdo rje'i," 545.16; mKhas btsun bzang po, "rig pa'i rdo rje," 134.14–134.16, rDzogs chen dpon slob, "rig pa'i rdo rje," 277.15–277.17; Shes bya, "bzod par dka' ba'i," 226.17–226.18, Sherap Phuntsok, "Rangjung Rigpe Dorje," 171; Terhune, *Karmapa*, 97; Douglas and White, *Black Hat Lama*, 107; Kunsang and Aubèle, "Sixteenth Karmapa," 204.

Douglas and White also report that the Second Jamgon Kongtrul had a similar vision.

109. Lhundup Damchö, *Karmapa: 900 Years*, 104; Brown, *Dance of 17 Lives*, 206.

110. Terhune, *Karmapa*, 98.

111. Erik Pema Kunsang and Marcia Schmidt, *Blazing Splendor: The memoirs of the Dzogchen yogi Tulku Urgyen Rinpoche* (Kathmandu, Nepal: Rangjung Yeshe Publications, 2005), 59–61; Brown, *Dance of 17 Lives*, 38–39; Terhune, *Karmapa*, 96; Holmes, *Gyalwa Karmapa*, 46–47.

Chapter 4

The Emergence of New Narratives

The *namthar* of the Karmapa places much emphasis on supernatural phenomena (or miracles). The Tibetans share a strong fascination with them which they view as auspicious signs of a teacher's spiritual accomplishment (*siddhi*). The Karmapa was born in miraculous circumstances and possessed supernatural powers, such as clairvoyance and the ability to manipulate natural elements. The English language sources discuss two particular topics at length based on personal experience. First, the Black Crown Ceremony, the most well-known ritual that the Karmapa performed in the West, is described by Western devotees as a significant event in which they reportedly experienced memorable moments of 'spiritual awakening' through what appear to be supernatural occurrences or intuitive visions. Second, the Karmapa died in a medical facility in the United States where, following his clinical death, he remained in a meditative absorption (Thukdam, Tib. *thugs dam*) for three days, during which time his doctors detected no physical decay. This, his Western disciples consider to be a testimony from medical science to his spiritual accomplishment. The English accounts of these events demonstrate a high consistency with tradition and enrich the Tibetan narrative, strengthening the Karmapa's spiritual authority in his Western community.

4.1. BLACK CROWN CEREMONY

The Karmapa's Black Crown is connected to an established belief in the tradition: all Karmapas are able to liberate those who see, hear, touch or remember them.[1] In particular, liberation-through-seeing (Thongdrol, Tib. *mthong grol*) is held to be a foremost characteristic of the Karmapas' spirituality. The Black Crown is a prominent representation of Thongdrol. The Karmapas are often referred to as Shanagpa (Zhwa nag pa),[2] a bearer of the Black Crown; the crown itself is seen as the hallmark of their activity. Several Terma prophecies in the previous chapter already point out the significance of the crown. For instance, in Khyentse Özer's quote, 'Wearing the Black Hat, the crown of the buddha families, [which is] the sign of empowerment, he guides countless beings in each moment', the crown symbolises the Karmapa's spiritual lineage and power.

The *namthar* of the Sixteenth Karmapa contains a similar viewpoint. Tashi Tsering cites a verse that he ascribes to the *Laṅkāvatāra Sūtra* to express the idea that the Black Crown is a distinctive attribute of the Karmapas.[3] Martin adds Sangye Lingpa's Terma text and the *Root Tantra of Manjushri*. The former depicts the First Karmapa wearing the Black Crown; the latter identifies the crown as 'the ornament of the buddhas' emanation'.[4] Tashi Tsering explains further the meaning of the crown and its role in the liberation of others. He argues that, according to the Mahāyāna sūtras, the buddhas use ornaments, instruments or sensual objects to benefit beings, implying that the Black Crown falls in this category. The crown is also one of the 'six liberating factors' (*grol pa drug ldan*) cited in the old and new Tantras.[5] He then compares the Black Crown to a crown that Dampatok Karpo (Dam pa tog dkar po, Skt. Śvetaketu) places on the head of Maitreya when he anoints him as future buddha in Tuṣita heaven.[6] Through this comparison, he suggests that the Karmapa's spiritual state matches that of the future buddha; the Black Crown symbolises buddha succession.

Regarding the origin of the Black Crown, an episode in *A Scholar's Feast of Doctrinal History*, as mentioned at the beginning of Chapter 1, traces it to Düsum Khyenpa. The most popular story, however, points to a far more distant past. According to Karma Ngedön Tengye, the Karmapa obtained the crown in a former life when he was a sage called Gönpakye (dGon pa skyes). The buddhas conferred empowerment and presented him with a crown made from the hair of 320,000,000 *ḍākinī*s. Only those with little defilement perceive this crown on the head of each Karmapa incarnation.[7] Tashi Tsering offers more detail, with some differences:[8] the one called Könpakye (dKon pa skyes) is an emanation of Avalokiteśvara; he receives his crown as he embarks on the vajra-like *samādhi*. The crown is 'the natural manifestation of wisdom'. Other authors give similar accounts.[9] They all speak of the Karmapa as a highly accomplished spiritual master bearing the crown as a symbol of his realisation. The crown is, nonetheless, not perceived by all. Tashi Tsering, echoing Karma Ngedön Tengye, states: '[A]part from a few fortunate people with very thin karmic residues, the miraculous story [about the crown] has been beyond all [the others'] perception. Thus, [it is] incomprehensible to ordinary people.'[10] According to Lhundup Damchö, the crown is only visible to those able to perceive the Buddha's *saṃbhogakāya*.[11] By this statement, she compares the Karmapa to a buddha and the crown to a *saṃbhogakāya* ornament.

A handful of people have reportedly caught a glimpse of the crown on the head of the Sixteenth Karmapa. The most famous is the Thirteenth Dalai Lama. His vision occurred when he performed the haircutting ceremony for the young Karmapa. The detail of this event varies. One version tells that during the ceremony, even though the Karmapa did not wear his material crown, the Dalai Lama saw one on top of his head. A senior council minister asked the Karmapa's father why his son did not take off his hat; clearly, he too saw the invisible crown.[12] In another version, the Dalai Lama asked why the Karmapa wore two crowns, one on top of the other. A minister reported that the Karmapa had forgotten to take off his crown when making prostrations, even though the Karmapa's retinue remembered that an attendant had kept the crown at that time. It is believed that the Dalai Lama perceived the crown through vision springing from omniscient wisdom; the minister perceived it on account of his good karma.[13]

The history of the material Black Crown is both interesting and complex. The most well-received account tells that, for ordinary people to perceive the crown, the Chinese emperor Yongle (1360–1424), a disciple of the Fifth Karmapa, Deshin Shekpa (De bzhin gshegs pa, 1384–1415), had a material Black Crown manufactured. For this, he drew on a vision. In 1407, at the invitation of the emperor,[14] Deshin Shekpa, twenty-three years of age, visited the city of Nanjing to preside over a memorial ceremony for Yongle's parents.[15] The ceremony lasted for fourteen days. During that time, the emperor and his ministers witnessed miraculous phenomena each day, which they had recorded in painting and writing.[16] Through these miracles, Yongle developed devotion towards Deshin Shekpa. One day, he noticed a crown above Deshin Shekpa's head. With Deshin Shekpa's consent, Yongle commissioned a replica.[17] This replica became the physical representation of the Karmapa's spiritual crown. Others report that the emperor of Jang,[18] offered a second replica to the Tenth Karmapa, Chöying Dorje (Chos dbyings rdo rje, 1604–1674). The succeeding Karmapas kept the first replica in Tsurphu and carried the second on their travels.[19]

Ogyen Trinley Dorje proposes a revised account of the history of the crown. According to him, the crown goes back to the time of Düsum Khyenpa. *A Scholar's Feast of Doctrinal History* records that Düsum Khyenpa created a Black Crown based on his vision of a black hat worn by Saraha.[20] The colour of the crown is not black but dark blue or blue-black (*mthing nag*). This is so because the Karmapa belongs to the buddha family of Akṣobhya who is blue in colour and represents the enlightened mind of all buddhas. Hence, the Black Crown represents the buddhas' mind.[21] The Second Karmapa, Karma Pakshi, speaks of this crown as 'a symbol of the unchanging dharma nature ... representing the unrepresentable through co-emergent wisdom mahamudra and through various symbols'.[22] Karma Pakshi himself also had a crown; it has survived to this day, kept in Karma Monastery. Compared to the lavish replica gifted by the Chinese emperor, the crowns of the early Karmapa incarnations were quite simple, made from ordinary materials.[23] The Third Karmapa, Rangjung Dorje, describes the symbolism of the Black Crown in close detail:

> The base being slightly dark
> Is a symbol of the unchanging dharmakaya.
> The sides being square is a symbol
> Of the four immeasurables.
> Having two garuda wings
> Is a symbol of the inseparability of means and prajna.
> Having three points is a symbol
> Of the three kayas being complete in him.
> Having four colours is a symbol
> Of accomplishing the four activities.
> Being adorned with five silks
> Is a symbol of the five families dwelling above the head.
> Having the parasol, sun, and moon
> Is a sign that the guru is a wish-fulfilling jewel
> And always accompanies, never apart.
> Having a blaze on the forehead
> Is a symbol of knowing the one dharma that liberates all
> And understanding everything known to be one.[24]

Ogyen Trinley Dorje then identifies three other crowns. The first belonged to the Fourth Karmapa, Rolpe Dorje (Rol pa'i rdo rje, 1340–1383), offered by the Mongol emperor Timur Khan.[25] The second, called 'Dzamling Yezhwa' (*'dzam gling ye zhwa*), was offered by a Ming emperor to the Sixth Karmapa, Thongwa Dönden (mThong ba don ldan, 1416–1453).[26] Of the third crown, he only knows its name 'Thongwa Dönden' (*mthong ba don ldan*); its origin he has not been able to trace.[27]

The Karmapa incarnations wore the material crown in a ritual ceremony called the Black Crown Ceremony.[28] The earliest Black Crown Ceremony in historical records took place during the time of Karma Pakshi who received a black crown from the Mongol emperor Möngke Khan in 1256, and then composed praise of the crown at a gathering on his way back to Tibet.[29] Nonetheless, Martin and Karma Thinley both believe that the ceremony only began from the time when Yongle offered the replica to the Fifth Karmapa.[30] Ogyen Trinley Dorje dates the first performance of this ceremony to the time of the Seventh Karmapa Chödrak Gyatso and the Eighth Karmapa Mikyö Dorje.[31] Lhundup Damchö reports that the ceremony became widely known during the life of the Ninth Karmapa, Wangchuk Dorje (dBang phyug rdo rje, 1556–1603).[32] When the Karmapa dons the Black Crown, he enters a deep meditative absorption in which he is believed to have transformed himself into Avalokiteśvara. To those present, the ceremony helps accumulate great merit, prevents lower rebirth, ripens their karma and leads to swift attainment of enlightenment.[33] Lhundup Damchö asserts: 'Although witnesses to the crown ceremony may be but ordinary beings, the experience of seeing the Karmapa wearing the material crown anticipates a time in the future when their purified minds will be able to perceive the full qualities of enlightened beings, without the aid of any external supports.'[34] Since the crown is a symbol of the enlightened mind of all buddhas, for those who possess the merit, 'through the play of outer and inner interdependence and the interdependent relationship between symbol and that symbolized',[35] they are able to recognise the nature of mind.[36] This ritual is the Karmapa's unique method to liberate beings through visual contact; thus, many speak of it as the precious crown that liberates upon sight.[37]

Like his predecessors, the Sixteenth Karmapa performed the Black Crown Ceremony on multiple occasions. It affected the participants and their perception of their surroundings. When he conducted the ritual for the first time, at Gina (sGi rna) monastery in Nangchen, people witnessed rainbow clouds and a rain of flowers.[38] In Dzongsar (rDzong gsar) monastery, Khyentse Chökyi Lodrö (mKhyen brtse Chos kyi blo gros, 1893–1959) saw the Karmapa appear as Düsum Khyenpa; the crown itself rose to about one cubit above his head.[39] Later, at Rumtek Monastery in Sikkim, his Indian disciple Goodie Oberoi also saw him assume the form of Düsum Khyenpa.[40] When he performed the ceremony on a visit to Bhutan, King Jigme Wangchuck ('Jigs med dbang phyug, 1905–1952) saw a rainbow light encircling the crown and his face.[41]

The Sixteenth Karmapa was the first to introduce the Black Crown Ceremony to the West. He performed it in the presence of Hugh Richardson, the head of the British Mission in Tibet, who at the time visited Tsurphu.[42] In Richardson's own words:

[The Sixteenth Karmapa] conducted for my benefit the ceremony of wearing the magical black hat of Dus-gsum mkhyen-pa, which confers 'Deliverance on Sight'. The lama seated himself on his throne and the hat was brought in a silk-covered box. Two monks took it out, holding it firmly all the time, for they say that if it is let go it will fly away by itself. They placed it on the lama's head and he grasped it with one hand and held it for the time it took to count the beads of his rosary as he recited the special prayer for the occasion. When the hat was restored to its box the ceremony ended with a blessing from the lama.[43]

Richardson does not comment on the meaning of the ceremony procedure; his account is possibly the first record of this ritual in the English language.

After settling in exile, the Karmapa continued to perform the Black Crown Ceremony. Many Westerners attended the ceremony, first in Rumtek and then during his visits to North America and Europe where he would perform it on frequent occasions, sometimes two or three times in a single day, often in front of a large audience.[44] Jamgon Kongtrul explains that the ceremony benefits all beings, not only Buddhists.[45] Thrangu says that its blessing, even to those disinterested in the Dharma, generates faith and devotion.[46] The ceremony can thus be observed without the requirement of prior Buddhist knowledge. In this way, the Karmapa reached out to the widest audience possible. The ceremony was promoted as a public event,[47] even at some point, to attract the 'flower children', that is, the hippies.[48] A radio advert, aired during the Karmapa's 1977 tour to the United States, introduced it as a 'sacred Buddhist rite' that 'communicates directly the intelligence of the awakened state of mind'.[49] According to Chögyam Trungpa:

> The Black Crown Ceremony is not regarded as just [a] display [of] authority and power and glory alone. When he [i.e., the Karmapa] puts [on] the Black Crown, he transforms himself into the Buddha of Compassion [i.e., Avalokiteśvara], and it creates various wonders in the people's mind. And they begin to become part of His Holiness's mind.[50]

The Karmapa's Western disciples shared new stories and interpretations, adding to the traditional narrative, based on personal experience. Many claim that the ceremony transformed their mind and their life.[51] Some even had visions of the Karmapa in the form of Avalokiteśvara.[52] Tenga Rinpoche, who accompanied the Karmapa on his 1974 tour in North America, recalls that through the ceremony, some participants recognised the nature of mind, while others noted light above the crown.[53] Trungpa's student, Judith Lief, reflects on her own experience: '[The Karmapa was] visually imprinting on us the kind of pith instructions that we have received from the Vidyadhara [Trungpa] about the nature of mind.'[54] Tenzin Palmo describes her inner tension during the ceremony at Rumtek:

> One part of me was saying: 'This is all just theatre. . . . They just have this whole theatre worked out on how to get your emotions going.' And the other part of me was: tears streaming down my face, so I could hardly see the hat [i.e., the crown] . . . and it's an incredible sense of total devotion. . . . I was so blissed out. . . . I couldn't move.[55]

Norma Levine who had attended the ceremony in Wales, England (1977) recalls:

> Time was standing still. There was a feeling of expansion, everything stretching like elastic; a sense of openness as if nothing were fixed or substantial. It was the

experience of 'the world in a grain of sand ... infinity in the palm of your hand and eternity in an hour.'. ... The experience of being fully complete, of oneness, in the eternal present was mystical: Karmapa showed it to us so powerfully that it was hard to miss.[56]

Ole Nydahl reports the effects of high drama: 'Sometimes during the ceremonies everything would explode into golden-yellow lights, and only the Crown would be clearly visible. At other times an energy moved up through the center of my body, which was so strong that I nearly fainted and was dazed for hours.'[57]

In addition to the different, individual feelings expressed in the accounts before, there are also allegedly collective visions. Levine and Baker both report an unusual experience during the ceremony that they attended in the Welsh farmhouse. The room was merely 12 by 12 feet. More than half of the space was taken by the Karmapa's throne and the rest by his monks and ritual instruments. Still, it appeared sufficiently spacious to accommodate another seventy-five people.[58] Willems recalls that, during the ceremony in the Netherlands, the Karmapa seemed to display a small crown underneath the material crown, which, according to him, many in the audience perceived.[59] Sightings of the invisible crown are very rare, afforded only to those of high spiritual accomplishment and great merit, such as the Thirteenth Dalai Lama and his minister. In the Netherlands, it is said, many of modest spiritual development came across this rarefied vision.

4.2. DEATH AND THUKDAM

In *namthar* literature, death is the episode in which the spiritual portrayal of the teacher reaches its pinnacle. Tradition believes that the death of an accomplished master is meant to demonstrate impermanence to the disciples and to urge them to persist with their spiritual path.[60] In the eyes of the disciples, this is the final stage of their teacher's enlightened activity. Accordingly, the narrative about the death of the Karmapas is usually described with elaborate details of miracles. Devotees would expectedly observe rainbows, rains of flowers and earth tremors, among other unusual displays, at the time of death and during the cremation.[61] After the cremation, relics would emerge from within the crematorium, such as the heart, tongue and eyes that survived the scorching heat of the fire,[62] pearl/crystal-like substances,[63] sacred symbols and deity images on bones.[64] These are considered the very signs of a saintly death.[65] For example, the heart and tongue indicate the teacher's continued presence in samsara as a bodhisattva and pearl/crystal-like substances represent his highly developed *bodhicitta*.[66] Although the precise significance of these signs is debatable,[67] most Tibetans interpret them to be indicators of a teacher's spiritual attainment.

The episode of death in the life story of the Sixteenth Karmapa displays some similar patterns but also introduces distinctively new content. His illness is viewed as a deliberate act to teach others impermanence,[68] to absorb their sufferings[69] and to instruct them how best to relate to mortality.[70] His death marked the moment when he withdrew from the *rūpakāya* to enter into the *dharmakāya*.[71] It likewise stems from a compassionate intention to purify others' bad karma,[72] to cleanse negative energies in the world,[73] to sever his disciples' attachment to permanence[74] and to prepare them for their own death.[75] To his primary disciples, such as Situ Rinpoche, it is 'the highest form of transmission and blessing'.[76]

Nonetheless, the circumstances in which the Karmapa fell ill and then died differed considerably from what would have happened in pre-modern Tibet. The Karmapa was first diagnosed with stomach cancer in 1979 in Delhi. In September 1981, after a brief recovery, his health deteriorated.[77] At his disciples' insistence,[78] he received treatment overseas, first in Hong Kong, and then in Illinois (United States), over eight weeks; he died on 5 November.[79] His death took place in a modern, secular setting, that is, the Intensive Care Unit of the American International Clinic in Zion. In this advanced medical facility, his sacred status played no role. The teaching and practice he is held to embody were tested through modern medical science and observed through the lens of biological knowledge. Yet, his doctors witnessed a series of events, from his treatment to his death, that they deemed uncommon. This has been recorded, in writing or through interviews, by his close disciples present at the time and, more significantly, by his two physicians, Mitchell Levy and Raj Kotwal.[80]

Several accounts report the Karmapa's ability to control pain through meditation. In Delhi, Hong Kong and Zion, he was able to fall asleep at ease without the need for anaesthetics. This would be impossible for normal patients in his condition. Shamar, who witnessed this on his daily hospital visits in Delhi,[81] explains that the Karmapa appeared to be sleeping, while in fact he was in a meditative state of luminosity, thus not feeling pain.[82] Kotwal noticed the same, both in Hong Kong and Zion.[83] He also reports another incident: one day after coming out of surgery, the Karmapa said that he 'watched from above' when the doctors were operating on his abdomen and saw how the disease had spread in his body, even though he was under deep anaesthesia at the time. Kotwal was baffled: as biologically impossible as it was, what the Karmapa had described of the state of his illness matched the doctors' observation at the operation table, Kotwal himself included.[84] Both Kotwal and Levy recount that the Karmapa never complained about pain but instead appeared happy and concerned about others.[85] According to Jamgon Kongtrul:

> Enlightened beings possess power over appearances. I have been able to see this with my own eyes when His Holiness the Karmapa was ill. All the doctors

agreed that the illness was very serious, and His Holiness manifested the apparent symptoms. However, until his death, not only did His Holiness never state that he suffered, but he also behaved exactly as usual, just as if he were in good health, with the same kindness and marvelous sense of communication. Enlightened beings like His Holiness never feel any suffering, even if they manifest the exterior signs of illness.[86]

Kotwal and Levy each makes a similar observation of the reaction from the medical staff. At Zion, Kotwal noted:

All of us—doctors, nurses and paramedics who attended on him—were affected by his presence—even if most of the attending staff were Christian by faith. I could see that they all were very kind and extremely careful while entering his room so that they did not disturb him in the slightest. None of them could speak to him, but they were all affected by his smile. And they tended to him with gentleness and caution.[87]

Levy detected a clear sense of surprise:

[They felt] wonderment and also confusion about why he [i.e., the Karmapa] wasn't following what we thought he should be doing, and amazement at his warmth and concern for others, no matter what was happening to him. . . . Most of them were Christian, and none of them knew the first thing about Buddhism, but they had no hesitancy whatever in calling him His Holiness.[88]

Kotwal also recalls how one of the main doctors treating the Karmapa, Ranulfo Sanchez, was struck by his unusual trance, finding it difficult to reconcile his emotional contentedness with his serious illness.[89] A Drukpa Kagyu master, Dorzong Rinpoche, noticed the doctors' perplexity when visiting the Karmapa in the hospital.[90] Within a few days, some members of the medical staff grew curious about the Karmapa's background and began to enquire about Buddhism and Tibet.[91] They wished to explore: 'What was it that he practiced and believed that kept him smiling and generated so much compassion for others despite his being gravely ill.'[92]

The Karmapa died at 11:30 p.m. on 5 November 1981.[93] Following his clinical death, Situ and Jamgon Kongtrul who remained by his side announced that he had entered Thukdam; this lasted for three days.[94] The medical staff exceptionally allowed his body to remain, undisturbed.[95] Two days later, on 7 November, while he was still in Thukdam, Situ explained: 'He [i.e., the Karmapa] is presently in contemplation or state of awareness, more than just the wisdom of mahamudra or the ultimate truth. Another way to say it is dharmakaya. For this reason there is heat on his heart; his skin and flesh and everything is just like that of a living person . . . we are waiting for him to complete that contemplation.'⁹⁶ According to Rumtek, the Karmapa's Thukdam revealed his attainment of the vajra-like *samādhi* (*rdo rje lta bu'i ting nge 'dzin*) and clear light Mahāmudrā (*'od gsal phyag rgya chen po*).⁹⁷ Since it happened in an American hospital, it was exposed, perhaps for the first time, to the scrutiny of Western medical science.

Kotwal and Levy each examined the Karmapa's body post-mortem during this period. Kotwal carried out two examinations at the interval of 48 hours:

> Very delicately I touched his whole chest even the upper abdomen. The area around the mid chest was very warm while the rest of the area was cold. I touched the Karmapa's face and nose especially both the [*sic*] nostrils. I also pinched skin and lifted it. There were no signs of Rigor mortis. Then Situpa Rinpoche told me to look at the Karmapa's nose. Rinpoche explained that the nostrils normally get flabby and lose their shape after a person dies. But since these signs showed otherwise—the Karmapa was in Dhayana [*sic*] (meditation).⁹⁸
>
> On the evening of the 7th when I was in the hospital again, to my surprise His Holiness's body looked the same as before—rigor mortis had not set in. The chest area around his heart was still warm after 48 hours of clinical death. Both nostrils remained in perfect shape just as I had seen them the 6th morning.⁹⁹

Kotwal was undecided about the cause of what he had witnessed: meditation or medication—'I was split about what to believe? [*sic*] To me both were true.'¹⁰⁰ Levy was similarly puzzled:

> So once or twice a day, they'd bring me in to put my hand over his heart, or feel his skin texture. And for three days I could feel there was some warmth coming from his heartcentre. [Three days is] a little bit too long to explain from a medical point of view. Also, there's a pliancy, a resilience to normal skin, and that was definitely still there after three days. As a physician I have no explanation. And as far as the heart sons [i.e., the Karmapa's primary disciples] were concerned I was the scribe, the witness.¹⁰¹

The Karmapa's Thukdam ended on 8 December 1981.¹⁰² His bodily remains were then flown back to India. A forty-nine-day funeral ceremony was performed in Rumtek, attended by over 12,000 people.¹⁰³ The ceremony concluded on 20 December with a cremation ritual.¹⁰⁴ Tibetan and Western devotees claim to have spotted, on this occasion, certain occurrences that resemble the traditional narrative of miraculous signs connected with a saintly death. These included a rainbow encircling the sun in a clear sky;¹⁰⁵ an image of the Karmapa in the halo around the sun;¹⁰⁶ rainbow lights; vultures hovering in the sky; and sun, moon and stars appearing simultaneously.¹⁰⁷ At one point, a burning mass rolled out of the north portal of the crematorium, reportedly constituting the Karmapa's heart, tongue and eyes. It became an object of worship, now enshrined in the golden stupa in Rumtek,[108] believed to be a manifestation of the Karmapa's compassion towards his disciples,[109] and according to Situ, a symbol of his heart transmission to his primary disciples.[110] Rumtek compares it to the relic of heart, tongue and eyes of Gampopa,[111] thereby equating the Karmapa's level of realisation with that of the Kagyu forefather. Also discovered inside the crematorium were pearl/crystal-like substances and the image of a deity or mantras on bones.[112] A footprint found on the top layer of the deity *maṇḍala* is seen as a sign of *siddha*; its location in the northern part of the *maṇḍala* is said to imply that the Karmapa would be reborn in Tibet.[113]

NOTES

1. This spiritual attribute has been briefly mentioned in 3.1. Identification with Enlightened Beings. See Karma nges don bstan rgyas, "rnam thar mdor bsdus," 11, 454; mKhyen brtse 'od zer, "mkha' khyab rdo rje'i," 474; 'Ja' tshon snying po, *padma'i chun po*, 3, 28, 33–34, 39–40, 51; Khra 'gu rin po che, *rgyal ba'i dbang po*, 326; bKra shis tshe ring, "'jig rten dbang phyug," 20, 23–24.

2. Richardson, "Karmapa Sect," 337.

3. *rab byung chas la zhwa nag can | stong gi bstan pa ma rdzogs par | 'gro ba'i don la rgyun chad med |* (bKra shis tshe ring, "'jig rten dbang phyug," 23.)

In English:
'[The one] with the Black Crown [and] in monastic robes
Until the teaching of one thousand [buddhas] comes to an end
[He will] benefit beings without interruption.'

Other English translations in Tashi Tsering, "Outer Biography," 5; Nydahl, *Entering the Diamond Way*, 71; Martin, "*Music in the Sky*," 271; Holmes, *Gyalwa Karmapa*, 138.

4. Martin, "*Music in the Sky*," 273.

5. bKra shis tshe ring, "'jig rten dbang phyug," 23.1–23.7.
The author does not refer to any specific text.

6. bKra shis tshe ring, "'jig rten dbang phyug," 23.7–23.9.

7. Karma nges don bstan rgyas, "rnam thar mdor bsdus," 454.3–454.6.

8. *mthong grol zhwa nag de la ni 'ga' zhig gis sngon sbyan ras gzigs kyi rnam 'phrul drang song [sic:srong] dkon pa skyes zhes bya ba rdo rje lta bu'i ting 'dzin mnga' brnyes pa'i tshe phyogs bcu'i rgyal ba sras dang bcas pas mkha' 'gro ma 'bum gyi dbu skra las byas pa'i dbang rtags kyi cod paN spyi bor bcings pa nas bzung sa ra ha pa sogs dang | dpal ldan dus gsum mkhyen pa sogs skye ba'i phreng ba kun tu ye shes rang snang gi tshul du dbu zhwa 'di nyid 'bral med bzhugs* (bKra shis tshe ring, "'jig rten dbang phyug," 21–22.)

In English:
'Regarding the liberation-through-seeing Black Crown, some people [say that] in the past, an emanation of Avalokiteśvara called Sage Könpakye (dKon pa skyes)

obtained the vajra-like *samādhi*. At that time, the buddhas and bodhisattvas in the ten directions placed upon [his] head a crown, which is a sign of empowerment, made from the hair of 100,000 *ḍākinī*s. From then on, in all [his] lives as Saraha [up to] the glorious Düsum Khyenpa, and so on, this very crown, the natural manifestation of wisdom, has remained inseparable [from him].'

Similar accounts about this event are also found in 'Ja' tshon snying po, *padma'i chun po*, and sKyabs gnas dam pa dpal 'byor don grub, *kun gsal me long*.

9. Including Zhwa dmar, *sku tshe'i rnam thar*, 26.12–27.1; *Recalling a Buddha*; *Entering the Diamond Way*, 70–71; Zhanag Dzogpa Tenzin Namgyal, "Wondrous Activities," 31; Martin, "*Music in the Sky*," 273; Lhundup Damchö, *Karmapa: 900 years*, 112; Holmes, Gyalwa Karmapa, 137.

Detail varies in these accounts. For example, Tenzin Namgyal and Martin specify the length of time of Konpakye's *samādhi*, and state that the *ḍākinī*s gave the crown. Zhwa dmar gives a different spelling for the name (dkon pa can). Holmes discovers that this story resembles an episode in the *Laṅkāvatāra Sūtra*.

10. *bag chags srab pa'i las can re zung tsam las kun kyi spyod yul du ma gyur ba sprul pa'i rnam thar de so sa skye bo dag gi ni slos dpogs pa'i yul min no* | (bKra shis tshe ring, "'jig rten dbang phyug," 22.)

11. Lhundup Damchö, *Karmapa: 900 years*, 112.

12. Khra 'gu rin po che, *rgyal ba'i dbang po*, 334.6–334.11; rDzogs chen dpon slob, "rig pa'i rdo rje," 279.13–279.18; Sherap Phuntsok, "Rangjung Rigpe Dorje," 172; Zhanag Dzogpa Tenzin Namgyal, "Wondrous Activities," 32–33.

13. Zhwa dmar, *sku tshe'i rnam thar*, 26.1–26.10; bKra shis tshe ring, "'jig rten dbang phyug," 28.12–28.18; 'Jam dbyangs tshul khrims, "rig pa'i rdo rje," 232.6–232.7; mKhas btsun bzang po, "rig pa'i rdo rje," 136.8–136.13; Douglas and White, *Black Hat Lama*, 109–110; Kunsang and Aubèle, "Sixteenth Karmapa," 206; Terhune, *Karmapa*, 99; Jamgon Kongtrul Rinpoche, "XVI Gyalwa Karmapa," 8; Karma Thinley, "Rangjung Rigpe Dorje," 130; Holmes, *Gyalwa Karmapa*, 24, 137; Pardee, Skolnick and Swanson, *Sacred Prophecy*, 45; Lhundup Damchö, *Karmapa: 900 years*, 83; Damchö D Finnegan, *Dharma King: The life of the 16th Gyalwang Karmapa in images* (New York: KTD Publications; Himachal Pradesh: Altruism Press, 2014), 11; Brown, *Dance of 17 Lives*, 39–40; Dzogchen Ponlop, "Rangjung Rigpe Dorje," 291; Tsering Namgyal Khortsa, "The Holder of the Vajra Crown: The Sixteenth Karmapa," in *His Holiness the 17th Karmapa Ogyen Trinley Dorje: A biography* (New Delhi: Hay House, 2013), 80.

14. Emperor Yongle's letter of invite to Deshin Shekpa in Chinese in 噶玛钨金, "德新谢巴," 60. The Tibetan translation of the letter in gTsug lag 'phreng ba's *chos 'byung mkhas pa'i dga' ston*. Richardson gives the transliteration of the text in Richardson, "Karmapa Sect," 368–369. A summary of the letter in English in Kagyu Office, "The Life of the Eighth Karmapa. Year One. Day Nine: The Fifth Karmapa Deshin Shekpa and the Ming Emperor Yongle," reported February 26, 2021, https://kagyuoffice.org/life-of-mikyo-dorje/#9.

15. For detail on this visit and the close connection between Yongle and Deshin Shekpa, see 噶玛善莲, "史诗般的相遇：五世噶玛巴与明成祖," 法露 (*Dharma Nectar*) 1, no. 1 (2014): 73–77, Karmapa Office; 噶玛善莲, ed., "穿越六百年的光芒," 法露 (*Dharma Nectar*) 1, no. 1 (2014): 86–91, Karmapa Office; 噶玛钨金,

"德新谢巴," 54, 56–58, 60; Kagyu Office, "Ming Emperor Yongle"; Kagyu Office, "The Life of the Eighth Karmapa. Year One. Day Ten: Karmapa Deshin Shekpa, Karmapa Mikyö Dorje and China," reported February 27, 2021, https://kagyuoffice.org/life-of-mikyo-dorje/#10.

16. The painting is titled 《普度明太祖長卷圖》 or 《噶瑪巴為明太祖薦福圖》. It features forty-nine illustrations with descriptions in five different languages. It was first kept in Tsurphu and is now housed in Tibet Museum (西藏博物館) in Lhasa. See 噶玛善莲, ed., "灵谷瑞云有迹：《荐福图》实录," 法露 (Dharma Nectar) 1, no. 1 (2014): 78–85, Karmapa Office; 噶玛钨金, "德新谢巴," 56–60; 大寶法王噶瑪巴官方中文網 (Kagyu Office), "《普度明太祖長卷圖》," accessed March 29, 2022, https://www.kagyuoffice.org.tw/c-reference/pudu-ming-taizu-changjuantu; Kagyu Office, "Fifth Karmapa Deshin Shekpa"; Kagyu Office, "Karmapa Deshin Shekpa".

Richardson gives a list of Tibetan and Chinese sources that describe this event, as well as his translation and transliteration of the Tibetan text on the scroll (See Richardson, "Karmapa Sect," 345, 361–363, 369–375). The documentary *Recalling a Buddha* includes the photographs that he took of the painting at Tsurphu in 1949.

17. bKra shis tshe ring, "'jig rten dbang phyug," 22.9–22.17.

See also Lhundup Damchö, *Karmapa: 900 years*, 111–112; Terhune, *Karmapa*, 259; Zhanag Dzogpa Tenzin Namgyal, "Wondrous Activities," 32; Kunsang and Aubèle, "Sixteenth Karmapa," 258–259; Martin, "Music in the Sky," 275; Holmes, *Gyalwa Karmapa*, 138; Karma Thinley, "Rangjung Rigpe Dorje," 28–29; Nydahl, *Entering the Diamond Way*, 70; *The Lion's Roar*; *Recalling a Buddha*; 噶玛钨金, "德新谢巴," 60; 噶玛善莲 and噶玛宝阳, "黑宝冠," 50.

18. Jang was a small kingdom to the southeast of Tibet; its territory, as in the present day, is in Lijiang of Yunnan Province in China. Its emperor Mu Yi (木懿) was a disciple of the Tenth Karmapa; at his invitation, the Karmapa lived there for many years after being forced into exile following a serious conflict between the Karma Kagyu and the Gelug school. See 噶玛钨金 et al., eds., "第十世噶玛巴：确映多杰," 法露 (Dharma Nectar) 3, no. 2 (2017): 24–28, Karmapa Office.

19. bKra shis tshe ring, "'jig rten dbang phyug," 22.8–22.9; Holmes, *Gyalwa Karmapa*, 138; Terhune, *Karmapa*, 111; Brown, *Dance of 17 Lives*, 34; Kunsang and Aubèle, "Sixteenth Karmapa," 303.

It is uncertain as to which replica the Sixteenth Karmapa brought with him into exile. bKra shis tshe ring and Kunsang and Aubèle presume that the second one was left behind in Tsurphu. This replica, according to Holmes, is kept in Potala Palace.

20. Kagyu Office, "Four-Session Guru Yoga." See also Kagyu Office, "Black Hat Lama."

21. Kagyu Office, "Akshobhya the Undisturbed: Paradigm of patience," reported August 29, 2015, http://kagyuoffice.org/akshobhya-the-undisturbed-paradigm-of-patience/; Kagyu Office, "Four-Session Guru Yoga"). See also Kagyu Office, "Black Hat Lama."

22. Kagyu Office, "Black Hat Lama."

23. Kagyu Office, "Black Hat Lama."

96   Chapter 4

24. Kagyu Office, "Black Hat Lama."
25. Kagyu Office, "Black Hat Lama."
26. There were five emperors of Ming during the lifetime of the Sixth Karmapa, from Yongle to Jingtai. Ogyen Trinley Dorje, citing Karma Thinley, specifies the emperor who offered the crown to be Qing Ha (See Kagyu Office, "Black Hat Lama"). However, this name does not match any of the names of the five emperors. The *namthar* of the Sixth Karmapa available to me does not mention this event either. Karma Ngedön Tengye speaks of a Chinese emperor's invitation and offerings to the Karmapa sent through his messengers (See Karma nges don bstan rgyas, "rnam thar mdor bsdus," 230–241). 噶玛钨金 identifies this emperor to be Yongle, but the Karmapa turned down his invitation; Yongle died before his messengers returned to China (噶玛钨金, "通瓦敦滇," 67–69). It is unclear whether the Ming emperor who offered the crown did so through his messengers or in person at his court, if the Karmapa did visit there, which again has yet to be verified.
27. Kagyu Office, "Four-Session Guru Yoga."
28. According to Ogyen Trinley Dorje, the two of the crowns that he identified, "Meaningful to See" (i.e. Thongwa Dönden) and "Dzamling Yeshak" (i.e. Dzamling Yezhwa), were used in the Black Crown Ceremony (Kagyu Office, "Black Hat Lama").
29. 《〈贤者喜宴〉译注（四）》巴卧.祖拉陈哇著，黄颢译注。载于《西藏民族学院学报》社会科学版1987年第2期，第59页. See 噶玛善莲, and 噶玛宝阳, "黑宝冠," 50.
30. Martin, *"Music in the Sky,"* 275; Karma Thinley, "Rangjung Rigpe Dorje," 29.
31. Kagyu Office, "Four-Session Guru Yoga"; Kagyu Office, "Black Hat Lama."
32. Lhundup Damchö, *Karmapa: 900 years*, 113. See also Kagyu Office, "Black Hat Lama."
33. Terhune, *Karmapa*, 260; Brown, *Dance of 17 Lives*, 66; Nydahl, *Entering the Diamond Way*, 75; Ole Nydahl, *Riding the Tiger: Twenty years on the road: The risks and joys of bringing Tibetan Buddhism to the west* (California: Blue Dolphin Publishing, 1992), 44.
34. Lhundup Damchö, *Karmapa: 900 years*, 112.
35. Ogyen Trinley Dorje, "Akshobhya the Undisturbed."
36. Ogyen Trinley Dorje, "Akshobhya the Undisturbed."
37. *dbu zhwa mthong grol rin po che* (Khra 'gu rin po che, "*rgyal ba'i dbang po*.") or *mthong grol dbu zhwa rin po che* (bKra shis tshe ring, "'jig rten dbang phyug.").
38. Khra 'gu rin po che, *rgyal ba'i dbang po*, 332.14–332.15; 'Jam dbyangs tshul khrims, "rig pa'i rdo rje," 232.1–232.2; rDzogs chen dpon slob, "rig pa'i rdo rje," 279.1–279.3; mKhas btsun bzang po, "rig pa'i rdo rje," 135.22–136.1; Douglas and White, *Black Hat Lama*, 109; Brown, *Dance of 17 Lives*, 39; Levine, Introduction, xxii; Nydahl, *Entering the Diamond Way*, 73.
39. Khra 'gu rin po che, *rgyal ba'i dbang po*, 340.12–340.14; bKra shis tshe ring, "'jig rten dbang phyug," 30.2–30.4; 'Jam dbyangs tshul khrims, "rig pa'i rdo rje," 234.5–234.6; mKhas btsun bzang po, "rig pa'i rdo rje," 138.5–138.7; Jamgon Kongtrul Rinpoche, "XVI Gyalwa Karmapa," 9; Karma Thinley, "Rangjung Rigpe Dorje,"

131; Douglas and White, *Black Hat Lama*, 111; Kunsang and Aubèle, "Sixteenth Karmapa," 211; Zhanag Dzogpa Tenzin Namgyal, "Wondrous Activities," 33.

40. Oberoi, "Dusum Khyenpa," 79.

41. Zhwa dmar, *sku tshe'i rnam thar*, 66.9–66.11.

See also mKhas btsun bzang po, "rig pa'i rdo rje," 138.23–139.1; bKra shis tshe ring, "'jig rten dbang phyug," 32.13–32.14; 'Jam dbyangs tshul khrims, "rig pa'i rdo rje," 235.6; Finnegan, *Dharma King*, 34; Douglas and White, *Black Hat Lama*, 113.

42. Finnegan, *Dharma King*, 20; Tsering Namgyal Khortsa, "Sixteenth Karmapa," 82.

According to Gene Smith, the Karmapa was one of Richardson's three Tibetan Buddhist teachers. Smith himself became interested in the Karmapa through Richardson's articles, and thereafter visited the Karmapa in Rumtek (See *Recalling a Buddha*).

43. Richardson, "Karmapa Sect," 358.

The procedure of the ceremony is also introduced in Nydahl, *Entering the Diamond Way*, 75; Holmes, *Gyalwa Karmapa*, 138–140; Brown, *Dance of 17 Lives*, 65–66), Terhune, *Karmapa*, 260; Lhundup Damchö, *Karmapa: 900 years*, 113.

44. Finnegan, *Dharma King*, 144–145, 204, 228, 303; Norma Levine, *The Spiritual Odyssey of Freda Bedi: England, India, Burma, Sikkim, and beyond* (Arcidosso: Shang Shung Publications, 2018), 256, 264, 274.

According to Levine, the first Black Crown Ceremony in the United States attracted 3,000 people; the first in Europe was participated by over 1,000.

Video recordings of the ceremony in *The Lion's Roar* and *Recalling a Buddha*.

45. *Recalling a Buddha*.
46. *Recalling a Buddha*.
47. *Recalling a Buddha*.
48. *Recalling a Buddha*.
49. *Recalling a Buddha*.
50. *The Lion's Roar*.
51. Ayang Rinpoche, "Light of the World," in *The Miraculous 16th Karmapa: Incredible Encounters with the Black Crown Buddha*, comp. Norma Levine (Arcidosso: Shang Shung Publications, 2013), 67.
52. Brown, *Dance of 17 Lives*, 66–67; Lama Palden, "Emperor of Love," in *The Miraculous 16th Karmapa: Incredible Encounters with the Black Crown Buddha*, comp. Norma Levine (Arcidosso: Shang Shung Publications, 2013), 132–133.
53. *Recalling a Buddha*.
54. *Recalling a Buddha*.
55. *Recalling a Buddha*.
56. Norma Levine, "Black Crown, Black Mountains," in *The Miraculous 16th Karmapa: Incredible Encounters with the Black Crown Buddha*, comp. Norma Levine (Arcidosso: Shang Shung Publications, 2013), 328.
57. Nydahl, *Entering the Diamond Way*, 75.
58. Levine, Introduction, xviii–xix; Diane Barker, "A Shrine Room in the Black Mountains of Wales," in *The Miraculous 16th Karmapa: Incredible Encounters with the Black Crown Buddha*, comp. Norma Levine (Arcidosso: Shang Shung Publications, 2013), 322.

59. Joost Willems, "Under Karmapa's Black Crown," in *The Miraculous 16th Karmapa: Incredible Encounters with the Black Crown Buddha*, comp. Norma Levine (Arcidosso: Shang Shung Publications, 2013), 357.

60. Garratt, "Biography by Instalment," 197.

61. For example, in the *namthar* of the First to Eleventh, Thirteenth and Fourteenth Karmapas: Karma nges don bstan rgyas, "rnam thar mdor bsdus"; mKhyen brtse 'od zer, "mkha' khyab rdo rje'i"; 噶玛钨金, "耶谢多杰"; 噶玛钨金, "旺秋多杰"; 噶玛钨金, "确映多杰"; 噶玛钨金, "杜松虔巴"; 噶玛钨金, "通瓦敦滇"; 噶玛钨金, "敦督多杰"; 噶玛钨金, "特秋多杰"; 噶玛钨金, "若必多杰"; 噶玛钨金, "米觉多杰"; 噶玛善莲, "明成祖"; 噶玛善莲, "则拉岗."

62. For example, in the *namthar* of the First, Second and Sixth Karmapas: Karma nges don bstan rgyas, "rnam thar mdor bsdus."

63. For example, in the *namthar* of the First to Third, Fifth to Seventh, Eighth and Thirteenth Karmapas: Karma nges don bstan rgyas, "rnam thar mdor bsdus"; 噶玛善莲, "明成祖"; 噶玛善莲, "则拉岗"; 噶玛钨金, "确札嘉措"; 噶玛钨金, "米觉多杰."

64. For example, in the *namthar* of the First to Third, Fifth and Seventh Karmapas: Karma nges don bstan rgyas, "rnam thar mdor bsdus"; 噶玛善莲, "明成祖"; 噶玛善莲, "则拉岗"; 噶玛钨金, "确札嘉措"; 噶玛钨金, "让炯多杰."

65. Dan Martin, "Pearls from Bones: Relics, chortens, tertons and the signs of saintly death in Tibet," *Numen* 41, no. 3 (1994): 273.

66. Dan Martin, "Crystals and Images from Bodies, Hearts and Tongues from Fire: Points of relic controversy from Tibetan history," in *Tibetan Studies: Proceedings of the 5th seminar of the International Association for Tibetan Studies NARITA 1989 vol.1*, ed. Ihara Shōren and Yamaguchi Zuihō (Japan: Naritasan Shinshoji, 1992), 184; Martin, "Pearls from Bones," 281–282, 290.

67. Martin, "Crystals and Images"; Martin, "Pearls from Bones."

68. Jamgon Kongtrul Rinpoche, "XVI Gyalwa Karmapa," 19.

69. Kunsang and Aubèle, "Sixteenth Karmapa," 203, 229; Holmes, *Gyalwa Karmapa*, 31.

70. Holmes, *Gyalwa Karmapa*, 32.

71. bKra shis tshe ring, "'jig rten dbang phyug," 43.13; Tshul khrims rgya mtsho, "rgyal dbang karma pa sku phreng bcu drug pa rang byung rig pa'i rdo rje," in *'bras ljongs su deng rabs bod kyi bla ma rnams kyis mdzad pa dang rnam thar bsdus pa*, TBRC W1KG852 (Gangtok, Sikkim: Namgyal Institute of Tibetology, 2008), 48.4–48.5.

72. Brown, *Dance of 17 Lives*, 82–83.

73. Nydahl, *Entering the Diamond Way*, 237.

74. rDzogs chen dpon slob, "rig pa'i rdo rje," 288.4–288.5. See also Jamgon Kongtrul Rinpoche, "XVI Gyalwa Karmapa," 19; *The Lion's Roar*.

75. Kunsang and Aubèle, "Sixteenth Karmapa," 230.

76. *Recalling a Buddha*.

77. Raj Kotwal, *God's Own Death* (Gangtok, Sikkim: Dr. M.R. Kotwal, M.D. 'Shunyata', 2013), 99–105, 106–108.

See also Grags pa yongs 'dus, "bcu drug pa," 378.12–378.15, 378.17–379.3; Zhwa dmar, *sku tshe'i rnam thar*, 110.15–111.3, 111.4–111.5, 132.16–133.1; Terhune, *Karmapa*, 120–121; Kunsang and Aubèle, "Sixteenth Karmapa," 229;

Finnegan, *Dharma King*, 383, 404; CBSN, "Modern Masters of Religion," *YouTube* video, 26:55, June 29, 2014. https://www.youtube.com/watch?v=oChBG73iUHI; *Recalling a Buddha*; Jamgon Kongtrul Rinpoche, "XVI Gyalwa Karmapa," 18; Gelongma Ani Ea, "Karmapa Becomes Vegetarian," in *The Miraculous 16th Karmapa: Incredible encounters with the Black Crown Buddha*, comp. Norma Levine (Arcidosso: Shang Shung Publications, 2013), 389–390.

78. 'Ju chen thub bstan rnam rgyal, "rgyal dbang karma pa," 315.15–316.4; Grags pa yongs 'dus, "bcu drug pa," 379.4–379.7; Zhwa dmar, *sku tshe'i rnam thar*, 111.3–111.5; Terhune, *Karmapa*, 121; Brown, *Dance of 17 Lives*, 77.

79. Kotwal, *God's Own Death*, 39, 89, 95–96, 108–112, 138, 163–170.

See also Rum bteg, "dgongs rdzogs mjug mchod," 234.3–234.6; Grags pa yongs 'dus, "bcu drug pa," 379.10–379.12; rDzogs chen dpon slob, "rig pa'i rdo rje," 288.6–288.8; Terhune, *Karmapa*, 121; Jamgon Kongtrul Rinpoche, "XVI Gyalwa Karmapa," 19; Brown, *Dance of 17 Lives*, 78, 79; Ani Ea, "Karmapa Becomes Vegetarian," 391–392; Tsering Namgyal Khortsa, "Sixteenth Karmapa," 86.

80. Mitchell Levy: Chögyam Trungpa's student and personal physician. Levy served as the Karmapa's physician from his 1980 visit to the United States until his death in Illinois (1981). Being both a devotee and a doctor gave him special access and media privilege. He was interviewed on more than one occasion over the years. Records of his interviews are documented in Ray, *Vajra World*; Lhundup Damchö, *Karmapa: 900 years*; Kunsang and Aubèle, "Sixteenth Karmapa"; Brown, *Dance of 17 Lives*; *The Lion's Roar*; *Recalling a Buddha*.

Raj Kotwal: a member of the Indian Army Medical Corps, stationed in Gangtok since 1980. In 1981, the Government of Sikkim assigned him to be the Karmapa's physician; at that time, he had no knowledge of Tibetan Buddhism. He was the only physician to accompany the Karmapa throughout the last two months of his life. In December 1981, following the Karmapa's death, the General Secretary of Rumtek Monastery acknowledged Kotwal's work and recognised him as an honorary personal physician to the Karmapa (See Kotwal, *God's Own Death*, 263–264, 272). Kotwal's book-length account of the illness and death of the Karmapa is the most comprehensive report on this matter. He declares therein his impartiality: 'I witnessed everything that his [i.e., the Karmapa's] sick body went through neither as a Buddhist nor as a believer of any particular religious faith, but as an open-minded doctor and a scientist' (Kotwal, *God's Own Death*, 41).

81. Zhwa dmar, *sku tshe'i rnam thar*, 133.1–133.13.

82. Zhwa dmar, *sku tshe'i rnam thar*, 138.16–138.17, 139.2–139.8.

83. Kotwal, *God's Own Death*, 112, 173–174.

84. Kotwal, *God's Own Death*, 113–114.

85. Kotwal, *God's Own Death*, 112, 116, 152, 173–174, 180, 182, 191, 200–202; Ray, *Vajra World*, 467–480.

See also Rum bteg, "dgongs rdzogs mjug mchod," 235.1–235.3; Zhwa dmar, *sku tshe'i rnam thar*, 138.16–138.17; Ani Ea, "Karmapa Becomes Vegetarian," 391; Finnegan, *Dharma King*, 453; Tsering Namgyal Khortsa, "Sixteenth Karmapa," 86; *The Lion's Roar*; *Recalling a Buddha*.

86. Jamgön Kongtrul, *La Nature de Bouddha* (Hui, Belgium: Kunchab, 1993), quoted in Pemo Kunsang and Marie Aubèle, *History of the Karmapas: The odyssey of*

the Tibetan masters with the black crown (New York: Snow Lion Publications, 2012), 230–231.
87. Kotwal, *God's Own Death*, 191.
88. Ray, *Vajra World*, 468, 470–472.
See also Terhune, *Karmapa*, 122.
89. Kotwal, *God's Own Death*, 173.
90. Dorzong Rinpoche, "As He Is," 403.
91. Rum bteg, "dgongs rdzogs mjug mchod," 235.4–235.6; Zhwa dmar, *sku tshe'i rnam thar*, 139.1; Ray, *Vajra World*, 472, 479; Kotwal, *God's Own Death*, 201–202.
92. Kotwal, *God's Own Death*, 201.
93. Kotwal, *God's Own Death*, 39.
94. Kotwal, *God's Own Death*, 39–40, 220–221; Grags pa yongs 'dus, "bcu drug pa," 379.17; Rum bteg, "dgongs rdzogs mjug mchod," 234.19; rDzogs chen dpon slob, "rig pa'i rdo rje," 288.8–288.9; Shes bya, "bzod par dka' ba'i," 225.3–225.4; Sherap Phuntsok, "Rangjung Rigpe Dorje," 176; Terhune, *Karmapa*, 122; Jamgon Kongtrul Rinpoche, "XVI Gyalwa Karmapa," 19; Holmes, *Gyalwa Karmapa*, 32; Kunsang and Aubèle, "Sixteenth Karmapa," 231; Lhundup Damchö, *Karmapa: 900 years*, 94; Finnegan, *Dharma King*, 453; Brown, *Dance of 17 Lives*, 81; Steve Roth and Norma Levine, "USA Introduction," in *The Miraculous 16th Karmapa: Incredible Encounters with the Black Crown Buddha*, comp. Norma Levine (Arcidosso: Shang Shung Publications, 2013), 156; Norma Levine, "Parinirvana of His Holiness the 16th Karmapa," in *The Miraculous 16th Karmapa: Incredible Encounters with the Black Crown Buddha*, comp. Norma Levine (Arcidosso: Shang Shung Publications, 2013), 384.
95. Rum bteg, "dgongs rdzogs mjug mchod," 235.7–235.10; Kotwal, *God's Own Death*, 220–221; Terhune, *Karmapa*, 122; Kunsang and Aubèle, "Sixteenth Karmapa," 231; Brown, *Dance of 17 Lives*, 81; Levine, "Parinirvana of His Holiness," 383; Finnegan, *Dharma King*, 453; Tsering Namgyal Khortsa, "Sixteenth Karmapa," 89; *The Lion's Roar; Recalling a Buddha*.
96. Levine, "Parinirvana of His Holiness," 382.
97. Rum bteg, "dgongs rdzogs mjug mchod," 234.19–234.22.
98. Kotwal, *God's Own Death*, 223.
99. Kotwal, *God's Own Death*, 224.
100. Kotwal, *God's Own Death*, 40.
101. Brown, *Dance of 17 Lives*, 81.
Another interview of Levy with similar detail in *The Lion's Roar*.
See also Terhune, *Karmapa*, 122; Holmes, *Gyalwa Karmapa*, 32; Ray, *Vajra World*, 477; Pardee, Skolnick and Swanson, *Sacred Prophecy*, 45; Kunsang and Aubèle, "Sixteenth Karmapa," 231; Levine, Introduction, xxix; Roth and Levine, "USA Introduction," 156; Nydahl, *Entering the Diamond Way*, 239; Finnegan, *Dharma King*, 453.
rDzogs chen dpon slob and Khenpo Sherap Phuntsok report rainbow clouds and earth tremors during the Karmapa's Thukdam (See rDzogs chen dpon slob, "rig pa'i rdo rje," 288.9–288.11; Sherap Phuntsok, "Rangjung Rigpe Dorje," 176).
102. Kotwal, *God's Own Death*, 228.

103. Rum bteg, "dgongs rdzogs mjug mchod," 240.6–252.8; Grags pa yongs 'dus, "bcu drug pa," 380.1–380.7; Kotwal, *God's Own Death*, 34–36; Finnegan, *Dharma King*, 453–459; Terhune, *Karmapa*, 126–127, 130; Jamgon Kongtrul Rinpoche, "XVI Gyalwa Karmapa," 19; Kunsang and Aubèle, "Sixteenth Karmapa," 231; Brown, *Dance of 17 Lives*, 83–84; Norma Levine, *Chronicles of Love and Death: My years with the lost spiritual king of Bhutan* (Kathmandu: Vajra Publications, 2011), 121–122; Levine, "Parinirvana of His Holiness," 385; MJ Bennett, "The Last Blessing," in *The Miraculous 16th Karmapa: Incredible Encounters with the Black Crown Buddha*, comp. Norma Levine (Arcidosso: Shang Shung Publications, 2013), 399.

104. Rum bteg, "dgongs rdzogs mjug mchod," 247.5–248.14; Kotwal, *God's Own Death*, 36–39; Terhune, *Karmapa*, 130–131; Jamgon Kongtrul Rinpoche, "XVI Gyalwa Karmapa," 19; Kunsang and Aubèle, "Sixteenth Karmapa," 231–232; Brown, *Dance of 17 Lives*, 84; Levine, *Love and Death*, 122–123; 2013: 385; Finnegan, *Dharma King*, 454–459; Tsering Namgyal Khortsa, "Sixteenth Karmapa," 86–87; *Recalling a Buddha*.

A video recording of the funeral and cremation ceremony in *The Lion's Roar*.

105. Zhwa dmar, *sku tshe'i rnam thar*, 145.9–145.11; Grags pa yongs 'dus, "bcu drug pa," 382.13–382.14; 'Jam dbyangs tshul khrims, "rig pa'i rdo rje," 239.4–239.5; rDzogs chen dpon slob, "rig pa'i rdo rje," 288.13–288.15; Rum bteg, "dgongs rdzogs mjug mchod," 248.20–248.21; Kotwal, *God's Own Death*, 39; Pardee, Skolnick and Swanson, *Sacred Prophecy*, 46; Kunsang and Aubèle, "Sixteenth Karmapa," 232; Levine, *Love and Death*, 123; Lama Surya Das, "Black Crown Lama: The 16th Gyalwang Karmapa," in *The Miraculous 16th Karmapa: Incredible Encounters with the Black Crown Buddha*, comp. Norma Levine (Arcidosso: Shang Shung Publications, 2013), 11; Levine, "Parinirvana of His Holiness," 385–386; Brown, *Dance of 17 Lives*, 84; Finnegan, *Dharma King*, 453, 457; Nydahl, *Entering the Diamond Way*, 239; Nydahl, *Riding the Tiger*, 206; *The Lion's Roar*.

106. Zhwa dmar, *sku tshe'i rnam thar*, 145.11–146.4; rDzogs chen dpon slob, "rig pa'i rdo rje," 288.16–288.17; Sherap Phuntsok, "Rangjung Rigpe Dorje," 176; Pardee, Skolnick and Swanson, *Sacred Prophecy*, 46; Oberoi, "Dusum Khyenpa," 82.

107. Rum bteg, "dgongs rdzogs mjug mchod," 249.5–249.9; Kotwal, *God's Own Death*, 39; Nydahl, *Riding the Tiger*, 208; Brown, *Dance of 17 Lives*, 84.

108. rDzogs chen dpon slob, "rig pa'i rdo rje," 288.17–288.22; Terhune, *Karmapa*, 131; Holmes, *Gyalwa Karmapa*, 32; Kunsang and Aubèle, "Sixteenth Karmapa," 232; Tsering Namgyal Khortsa, "Sixteenth Karmapa," 87.

109. Rum bteg, "dgongs rdzogs mjug mchod," 249.21–250.2; 'Jam dbyangs tshul khrims, "rig pa'i rdo rje," 239.5; rDzogs chen dpon slob, "rig pa'i rdo rje," 288.12–288.13; Sherap Phuntsok, "Rangjung Rigpe Dorje," 176; Kotwal, *God's Own Death*, 39; Terhune, *Karmapa*, 131; Holmes, *Gyalwa Karmapa*, 32; Kunsang and Aubèle, "Sixteenth Karmapa," 232; Pardee, Skolnick and Swanson, *Sacred Prophecy*, 45; Brown, *Dance of 17 Lives*, 84; Zhanag Dzogpa Tenzin Namgyal, "Wondrous Activities," 48; Levine, "Parinirvana of His Holiness," 387; Finnegan, *Dharma King*, 453, 459; Tsering Namgyal Khortsa, "Sixteenth Karmapa," 87.

110. Brown, *Dance of 17 Lives*, 85.

111. Rum bteg, "dgongs rdzogs mjug mchod," 250.2–250.4.

112. Holmes, *Gyalwa Karmapa*, 33; Pardee, Skolnick and Swanson, *Sacred Prophecy*, 46; Kunsang and Aubèle, "Sixteenth Karmapa," 232; Surya Das, "Black Crown Lama," 11; Levine, "Parinirvana of His Holiness," 387; Finnegan, *Dharma King*, 10–11; Nydahl, *Entering the Diamond Way*, 240; Nydahl, *Riding the Tiger*, 211.

113. Rum bteg, "dgongs rdzogs mjug mchod," 250.16–250.19; 'Jam dbyangs tshul khrims, "rig pa'i rdo rje," 239.5; Holmes, *Gyalwa Karmapa*, 32; Pardee, Skolnick and Swanson, *Sacred Prophecy*, 46; Kunsang and Aubèle, "Sixteenth Karmapa," 232; Nydahl, *Riding the Tiger*, 211.

Part III

TRANSMISSION (I)

PRESERVATION

The Karmapa left Tibet in 1959. Soon after resettling in the Himalayan kingdom, Sikkim, he began to rebuild his lineage in exile. This he did in two phases: (1) preservation in the Indian subcontinent and (2) expansion to the West. The success of the first phase paved the way for the second, which, in turn, led to the fastest global expansion of a Tibetan Buddhist school in the early transmission of Tibetan Buddhism to the West. This part of the book discusses the Karmapa's transmission strategy in the first phase. Chapter 5 examines his strategies in relation to the specific political and economic context of the early diaspora, intended to better understand his efforts to preserve tradition. Chapter 6 discusses his preservation initiative. He prioritised the re-establishment of the monastic community and maintained non-sectarian accommodation, both of which demonstrate consistency with his strategies in Tibet pre-1959, yet with a heightened sense of urgency to revive Tibetan Buddhism in exile.

Chapter 5

Politics and Patronage

The Karmapa was among the first Tibetan Buddhist leaders to begin to preserve their tradition in exile. To do so, he developed two key strategies. First, he adopted an apolitical stance, distancing himself from the exile government. This made it possible for him to concentrate on religious matters. Second, he strengthened his connections with Bhutan, Sikkim and India whose patronage allowed him to achieve financial stability when most Tibetan Buddhist lineages were still struggling for survival in the diaspora. Both strategies together created a good foundation for his preservation initiative.

5.1. DISSOCIATION FROM THE EXILE GOVERNMENT

In history, the Karmapa incarnations are known for their disinterest in worldly power, be it political, administrative or status associated with the title 'Karmapa' itself. This is considered to be one of the main characteristics that they all share in common.[1] The situation with the Sixteenth Karmapa, however, is more complicated. In Tibet, during the 1950s, he, in support of the Lhasa government, took part in the political negotiation with China with the hope to reach a peaceful resolution for Tibet's future. After arriving in exile, however, he decided to distance himself from the political agenda of the exile government, especially its cause of Tibetan independence, and insisted that Buddhist leaders should focus on religious matters only. The present section examines this topic by charting the change of his relationship with the Fourteenth Dalai Lama, Tenzin Gyatso (bsTan 'dzin rgya mtsho, 1935–), from Tibet pre-1959 to the diaspora.

While in Tibet, the Karmapa formed a close relationship with the Dalai Lama, on both formal and personal levels. Their first meeting took place in

Lhasa in 1941.² After a formal audience, the two also conferred in private in Norbulingka.³ In 1951, when the Dalai Lama returned from Dromo (Gro mo) to Lhasa, the Karmapa arrived from Tsurphu to welcome him.⁴ In 1953/1954, the Karmapa received Tantric empowerments from the Dalai Lama, through which they formed a spiritual bond.⁵ On his visit to Lhasa to attend the Kālacakra empowerment, the government offered him a grand reception, 'traveling under the "parasol of the Dharma", a dignified procession accompanied by great fanfare'.⁶ Such honour was reserved for only a handful of high-ranking lamas.⁷

As the political tension between China and Tibet accelerated in the 1950s, the relationship between the Karmapa and the Dalai Lama grew stronger. In 1954, at the invitation of the Chinese government, the Dalai Lama led a delegation of 400 Buddhist dignitaries and political officials to travel to Beijing. The Karmapa, as a key member of the delegation, attended several meetings and ceremonies.⁸ The purpose of the visit was to conduct peaceful negotiations with the Chinese government.⁹ The Karmapa, alongside the Dalai Lama, played a central role in the process.¹⁰ In the end, however, the trip turned out to be fruitless. On the way back, the Karmapa visited monasteries in Eastern Tibet as the Dalai Lama's representative and offered advice on both religious and political matters.¹¹ He gathered the leaders of the monasteries to welcome the Dalai Lama on his journey back from China in 1955. Later, the two met again in Lhasa.¹²

Back in Tsurphu, the Karmapa began to construct the Phuntsok Khyilpa (Phun tshogs 'khyil pa) hall for the Dalai Lama's visit in the coming year, 1956.¹³ The Dalai Lama's visit to Tsurphu is recorded in many accounts. It was the first time in history that a Dalai Lama visited a Karmapa in Tsurphu.¹⁴ The Karmapa received him with a grand procession and offerings. He led the Cham dance, performed the Black Crown Ceremony and introduced the Dalai Lama to a collection of rare holy objects. In return, the Dalai Lama conferred Avalokiteśvara empowerment and offered instructions on religious and political affairs. The Lhasa government made a large offering to the Tsurphu sangha.¹⁵ The Dalai Lama himself recalls his stay there in vivid detail:

> My two tutors were also there. . . . And of course both tutors were very close friends of the late Karmapa, particularly Trijang Rinpoche. They were always teasing each other. . . . Karma Rinpoche himself, you see, had this kind of jovial nature. A very nice person.¹⁶
>
> I remember very clearly the few days I spent there, a very happy memory, happy days, like a holiday.¹⁷
>
> He had a film projector and a generator, but the generator had broken down. So my driver . . . was able to repair the Karmapa's generator. The Karmapa was

very pleased! That night we were able to watch a film—a Hindi picture. . . . So through these things we became very close friends.[18]

These words convey the Dalai Lama's fondness for the Karmapa and their warm friendship. The Dalai Lama also recalls the Karmapa's visits to Lhasa for meetings commanded by the Chinese.[19] The two met frequently to exchange views on the political situation in Tibet.[20]

Later in 1956, the Lhasa government requested the Karmapa to travel to Chamdo (Chab mdo) with two government officials. This visit was intended to ease the tension between the Chinese army and local Tibetans. There, the Karmapa helped form a five-year truce. He then returned to Lhasa to report to the Dalai Lama.[21] Shamar gives a detailed account of the situation in Chamdo that paints a clear picture of the Karmapa's political engagement in China-Tibet relations. In 1951, the Chinese official (Wang cing min) led an offensive in Chamdo. After a short resistance, the Tibetan governor, Ngapö Ngawang Jigme (Nga phod Ngag dbang 'jigs med), surrendered. Wang summoned the local lords and officials of Eastern Tibet to proclaim socialist reforms. The Karmapa's brother, also Shamar's father, Trinley Namgyal (Phrin las rnam rgyal), criticised socialism at the assembly. In 1955, conflict sprung up between the Chinese army and a band of fighters from East Derge. This included a group headed by the Karmapa's nephew, Rari Tenam (Rwa ri bstan rnam). The Chinese government asked the Karmapa to go to Chamdo to resolve the conflict. The actions of his brother and nephew made him a target to the Chinese. Fearing that he would be captured, his brother Pönlop (dPon slob) and sister Yangchen (dByangs can) urged him to decline the request, but he went to Chamdo regardless.[22] In the course of the negotiation, he suggested to the Chinese: 'Since the people of Kham simply have no idea about the [current] affairs of the world, [you] will not be able to suddenly change the customs that have existed [here] for generations. For that reason, please build a good school first, and then introduce socialism through peaceful [measures].'[23] The Chinese official then asked the Karmapa to advise the areas where riots broke out.[24] These episodes highlight the Karmapa's role as a mediator in the political tension between China and Tibet.

In 1959, the Karmapa informed the Dalai Lama of his plan to leave Tibet.[25] They each took flight into exile separately. In India, they continued to strengthen their relationship. In a spiritual song that he composed in 1961, the Karmapa expresses admiration for the Dalai Lama, describing him as a central pillar of the entire teaching (*yongs rdzogs bstan pa'i srog shing*) and comparing him to the three Dharma Kings (*chos rgyal mes dbon rnam gsum de dang mtshungs par*).[26] The Dalai Lama helped the Karmapa restore the Shamar lineage. The Shamar incarnations had long been among the most influential tulkus in the Karma Kagyu school. This ended with the tenth incarnation, Mipham Chödrub Gyatso (Mi pham chos grub rgya mtsho, 1742–1792/1793). The Lhasa government banned his tulku lineage due to a political dispute between the Gelug and the Karma Kagyu.[27] In 1963, the Karmapa told the Dalai Lama that he had identified a Shamar reincarnation and sought his official confirmation.[28] The Dalai Lama approved of his choice: 'The examination conducted with the help of the Three Jewels revealed that Buddhism will benefit if the following son of Atub Pon is recognized as the reincarnation of Shamar Rinpoche.'[29] The endorsement brought the ban of the Shamar lineage that had lasted for centuries to an end. In 1964, the Dalai Lama himself conducted the haircutting ceremony for the Fourteenth Shamar, Mipham Chokyi Lodro (Mi pham chos kyi blo gros, 1952–2014); the Karmapa then enthroned him in Rumtek.[30]

Also in 1963, the Karmapa attended the Conference of all Tibetan Schools (*gangs ljongs ris med chos kyi tshogs 'du chen po*) chaired by the Dalai Lama in Dharamsala.[31] In a speech, he declared his wish that 'all Tibetans will be united together [in] harmony under the leadership of the great Dalai Lama whereby the celebration of freedom and independence [that is] the true victory [for] Tibet will soon take place, and [the Tibetans] will be able to enjoy the glory of the golden age of joy and happiness'.[32] This statement attests to his support for the Dalai Lama's leadership in exile. In the following years, the two paid formal visits to each other on several occasions. In 1967, the Karmapa met with the Dalai Lama in Dharamsala and studied with him.[33] During the 1970s, he received Tantric empowerment from the Dalai Lama[34] and conducted a longevity ceremony for him.[35] In 1981, the Dalai Lama inaugurated the monastic institute in the Karmapa's main seat in exile, Rumtek Monastery.[36] Meanwhile, the two continued to deepen their personal connection. Thrangu records a meeting in 1975 where they engaged in pleasant conversations, like two close friends.[37] In the Dalai Lama's own words: 'Whenever there was some big religious meeting, he always came. He was always invited. Then when he visited Ladakh or some nearby area he came to Dharamsala. . . . So we were like spiritual brothers which we remained until his death.'[38] The Dalai Lama also tells that when visiting Dharamsala, the Karmapa stayed at his mother's residence.[39] These words demonstrate their strong and enduring relationship.

Shamar, however, reports perceived tension between the Karmapa and the Dalai Lama that sprung from dissent between two political parties in the diaspora. In 1961, the Dalai Lama's second brother, Gyalo Thondup (rGyal lo don 'grub, 1927–), founded the 'United Party' (*gcig sgril tshogs pa*). This led to unease among many Tibetan lamas and nobles from Eastern Tibet who, in response, formed a rival party, the 'Thirteen Group' (*tsho khag bcu gsum*). The lamas of the Sakya, Nyingma and Kagyu schools, as Shamar claims, suspected that the Dalai Lama's two brothers aspired to give prominence to the Gelug school in the name of solidarity.[40] Shamar believes that the Karmapa supported the 'Thirteen Group' and favoured tradition over Gyalo Thondup's efforts of modernisation. This weakened the relationship between the Karmapa and the Dalai Lama.[41] McGranahan's study of these two parties accords with Shamar's account. Gyalo Thondup led the 'United Party' to implement socio-political reform with the purpose to unite Tibetans from different regions and schools. Yet, some viewed the party to prioritise the Lhasa system over the communities from Eastern Tibet. Thirteen settlement and monastery leaders, representing the Eastern Tibet system, launched the 'Thirteen Group' to oppose the 'United Party', Gyalo Thondup's reform and the Tibetan government-in-exile. The 'Thirteen Group' was, according to McGranahan, headed by the Karmapa.[42]

McGranahan and Shamar each interprets the tension between the two parties from a different angle. Shamar identifies sectarian rivalries as the primary issue; to him, the Karmapa supported the 'Thirteen Group' because he was a traditionalist. McGranahan shows that the Karmapa engaged in a movement that challenged the political policy of the exile government. Either way, the Karmapa's reported support for the 'Thirteen Group' appears to have affected his relationship with the Dalai Lama and the Tibetan government in Dharamsala.[43] Brown, however, holds a different view. He reports that the Karmapa refused to chair the 'Thirteen Group' so as to avoid confrontation with Dharamsala, though he did not support its cause of Tibetan independence either. That is to say, the Karmapa sought to stay clear of the conflict between the two parties.[44] The contradictions among the aforementioned accounts make it difficult to determine the Karmapa's attitude towards the two parties. Nonetheless, they all signal his dissociation from the exile government.

Brown's interview with the Dalai Lama clarifies the Karmapa's apolitical stance. The Dalai Lama explains that even though he supported non-sectarianism, with limited contact with other schools in Dharamsala, he faced suspicion. The 1962 conference[45] that brought together the representatives of all schools was misinterpreted as a scheme to consolidate the power of the Gelug school, which eventually overshadowed his relationship with the Karmapa.[46] The Dalai Lama recalls:

> On a personal level, still old friends; no problem. But as to the Tibetan community and the politics, a little bit of doubt, a little distance. . . . And later, I heard that in talking to some of his centres in Europe and America he [i.e., the Karmapa] said the Tibetan freedom struggle is politics, and that as spiritual practitioners they should not be involved. . . . Some people get the wrong impression, that this struggle is something political, a struggle for a few officials' benefit: the Tibetan government's benefit. But this struggle is necessary. It is Buddhadharma! . . . one Chinese friend . . . once told me that one of his close friends . . . had told him, 'The Dalai Lama is a politician; genuine lama is Karmapa.'

... So this is how wrong impressions are created. So Karmapa Rinpoche, I think perhaps he misled people a little bit, and that made me a little sad.[47]

This passage does not reveal whether the Dalai Lama and the Karmapa were involved in the conflict between the two parties. It, nonetheless, signals a certain degree of tension in their relationship. A key reason was their different points of view on Tibetan independence. The Dalai Lama believed it to be a necessary means to preserve the Dharma; the Karmapa dismissed it as a political matter. This changed the public perception of the two and their relationship. Furthermore, Shamar recounts a meeting in 1963 in which the Karmapa appealed to the Dalai Lama to appoint a secular ruler (*srid skyong*) to renounce political involvement and focus on teaching only.[48] This again points to the Karmapa's apolitical stance.

Despite the perceived tension with the Dalai Lama and his dissociation from exile politics, when the Karmapa died in 1981, the exile government showed its respect. It sent letters of condolence and dispatched representatives to receive his remains in Delhi and to attend the funeral ceremony in Rumtek. Its offices in Dharamsala were closed as Tibetans entered a period of mourning.[49] A member of its delegation to Rumtek, Juchen Thupten Namgyal, gives an emotional account of his attendance at the funeral with an unreserved expression of devotion.[50] This reflects the Karmapa's influence on the Tibetan diaspora overall.

5.2. CONNECTIONS WITH BHUTAN, SIKKIM AND INDIA

Throughout his life in exile, the Karmapa received crucial support from the royal families of Bhutan, Sikkim and the Government of India. Chapter 2 has brought to light the challenges facing Tibetans at the beginning of the diaspora. For the Karmapa, the existing lama-patron relationship with Bhutan and Sikkim, as well as his strong links with the Indian presidents and prime ministers, added an important advantage. This had a far-reaching impact on his activity, from his early resettlement leading up to the expansion phase. This chapter analyses this impact through three topics. First, it gives an overview of the historical ties between the Karmapa incarnations and Bhutan/Sikkim to provide context. The Sixteenth Karmapa built on this legacy and set out to strengthen his relationship with the royal families from as early as the 1940s. The remaining two topics discuss the main outcomes of his connections with Bhutan, Sikkim and India, including how they contributed to the expansion of the Karma Kagyu in the West.

5.2.1. Historical Connections with Bhutan and Sikkim

The links between the Karma Kagyu lineage and Bhutan goes back to the visit of the Fourth Shamar, Chödrak Yeshe (Chos grags ye shes, 1453–1524), to Bumthang in 1479. With the help of the lamas and chieftains there, he founded the first Karma Kagyu centre in Bhutan at Thangbi. The Fifth Shamar, Könchok Yenlak (dKon mchog yan lag, 1526–1583), visited Bhutan and founded several more centres.[51] The Tenth Karmapa, Chöying Dorje (Chos dbyings rdo rje, 1604–1674), is said to have initiated a connection with the ruling class of Bhutan through his prophecy of its founder, Shabdrung Ngawang Namgyal (Zhabs drung Ngag dbang rnam rgyal, 1594–1651). According to Shamar, the two met in Ralung; at that time, the Karmapa predicted that Ngawang Namgyal would gain influence in Bhutan. Soon after, conflict arose between the followers of Ngawang Namgyal and those of Pawo Tsuglag Gyatso (dPa' bo gtsug lag rgya mtsho, 1567–1633) who was the guru of the ruler of Tsang. This led to hostilities, which caused Ngawang Namgyal to flee to Bhutan. After arriving in Bhutan, he gradually assumed political power; this, Shamar believes to be the actualisation of the Karmapa's prophecy.[52] The events surrounding Ngawang Namgyal's flight to Bhutan and his rise to power there have been studied elsewhere.[53] Yet, none of the sources available to me mention his meeting with Chöying Dorje. The link between the two appears to be weak.

The relationship proper between the Karmapas and the royal family of Bhutan, as documented in historical records, began during the reign of the First King, Ugyen Wangchuck (O rgyan dbang phyug, 1862–1926). In 1904, on the occasion of the Younghusband expedition to Lhasa, Ugyen Wangchuck, then an influential governor in Bhutan, helped facilitate negotiations between the British and the Tibetans. This won him the trust of the British government which, in return, supported his appointment as the King of Bhutan in 1907.[54] Shamar tells that, en route to the peace talks, Ugyen Wangchuck saw the thangka of the Fifteenth Karmapa, Khakyap Dorje, in the Jokhang, which inspired his devotion and led him to send a messenger to Tsurphu with offerings for the Karmapa.[55] Again, no other source that I have consulted mentions this event. Some, however, allude to Ugyen Wangchuck's spiritual bond with Khakyap Dorje. According to Karma Phuntsho, when Ugyen Wangchuck's son died as an infant in 1903, the Karmapa consoled him and his wife; he predicted that they would soon have another son, which came to be the case two years later.[56] The two appeared to possess already a connection prior to the peace talks. When Khakyap Dorje died, Ugyen Wangchuck suffered in grief, even postponing the cremation of his queen who died around the same time.[57]

The relationship between the Sixteenth Karmapa and the Second King of Bhutan, Jigme Wangchuck ('Jigs med dbang phyug, 1905–1952), is recorded in more detail. It marks the highest point of influence that the Karma Kagyu ever held in Bhutan.⁵⁸ In 1944, the Karmapa went on pilgrimage in Bhutan at the invitation of Jigme Wangchuck. The king and Prince Jigme Dorji Wangchuck ('Jigs med rdo rje dbang phyug, 1928–1972) welcomed him with a grand procession.⁵⁹ They received empowerments from him and attended the Black Crown Ceremony.⁶⁰ The prince offered ten cars and 300,000 rupees.⁶¹ The two queens, Phuntsho Choden (Phun tshogs chos sgron) and Pema Dechen (Padma bde chen), invited the Karmapa to Tashi Choling (bKra shis chos gling) and Wangdu Choling (dBang 'dud chos gling), respectively. Princess Wangmo (dBang mo) invited him to Jampa Lhakhang (Byams pa lha khang);⁶² she helped fund the construction of his monastery Dargye Choling (Dar rgyas chos gling).⁶³ The king considered the Karmapa to be his root guru.⁶⁴ His sister, Ashi Konchok Wangmo (A zhe dgon mchog dbang mo), too became the Karmapa's disciple;⁶⁵ the Karmapa ordained her in 1946.⁶⁶

The relationship between the Karmapa incarnations and the royal family of Sikkim began with the Twelfth Karmapa, Changchub Dorje (Byang chub rdo rje, 1703–1732) and the Fourth King, Gyurmed Namgyal ('Gyur med rnam rgyal, 1707–1733). Shamar relates the story of their first encounter. Gyurmed Namgyal disguised himself as a beggar on a pilgrimage to Tibet. Changchub Dorje foresaw his visit to Tsurphu, and when they met, pointed out his true identity. The king was surprised and developed faith in Changchub Dorje. On his return, he founded the first Karma Kagyu monastery in Sikkim, Ralang Gompa (Ra lang dgon pa).⁶⁷ Tsultrim Gyatso (Tshul khrims rgya mtsho) maps the relationship between the successive Karmapas and kings of Sikkim. The Fourth King became the patron of the Twelfth Karmapa, following their meeting on the pilgrimage. He founded three Karma Kagyu monasteries in Sikkim: (1) Karma Rabtenling (Karma rab brtan gling) in Ralang in the south, (2) Karma Thubten Choling (Karma thub bstan chos 'khor gling) in Rumtek in the east and (3) Karma Tashi Chokhorling (Karma bkra shis chos 'khor gling) in Phodang in the west.⁶⁸ The Twelfth Karmapa is known to have consecrated all three directly from Tsurphu.

The Fourteenth Karmapa, Thekchok Dorje (Theg mchog rdo rje, 1798–1868), identified the Eighth King, Sidkeong Namgyal (Srid skyong rnam rgyal, 1819–1874), as the reincarnation of Situ Panchen's nephew Karma Rinchen Ngedön Tenzin (Karma rin chen nges don bstan 'dzin). Such identification strengthened the ties between the royal family and the Karma Kagyu school. The Karmapa conferred on Sidkeong Namgyal monastic vows and appointed him as the head of all Karma Kagyu monasteries in Sikkim. Now, the king was not only a patron but also a lineage holder. This brought the royal support for the Karma Kagyu to a new level. Thereafter, the Fifteenth Karmapa Khakyap Dorje identified the Tenth King, Sidkeong Tulku

Namgyal (Srid skyong sprul sku rnam rgyal, 1879–1914), as the reincarnation of the Eighth King,[69] thereby maintaining the close ties.

The Sixteenth Karmapa developed a close relationship with the Eleventh King of Sikkim, Tashi Namgyal (bKra shis rnam rgyal, 1893–1963). He paid regular visits to Gangtok in 1947, 1948, 1956 and 1957. The king offered a personal escort for his pilgrimage to India and Nepal and had him stay at the Royal Palace Monastery. In Gangtok, the Karmapa performed the Black Crown Ceremony.[70] In 1954, Prince Thondup Namgyal (Don grub rnam rgyal, 1923–1982) went to meet the Karmapa before he travelled to Beijing with the Dalai Lama.[71]

5.2.2. Flight and Resettlement

In 1959, the Karmapa took flight into exile. He led his party to cross the Tibet-Bhutan border. From that point on, the royal families of Bhutan and Sikkim and the Government of India coordinated their efforts to ensure his safety and proposed various places for his resettlement. Bhutan, at that time, was under the rule of the Third King, Jigme Dorji Wangchuck, who was close to the Karmapa. The king's aunt, Ashi Wangmo (A zhe dbang mo),[72] welcomed the Karmapa at the border and offered provisions. Then, at Kurjey Lhakhang (sKu rjes lha khang), Ashi Wangmo and the ministers welcomed him again on behalf of the king. The king asked his government to allow the Karmapa and his party to temporarily stay at Tashi Choling.[73] The Indian government intervened: since Bhutan shares a border with China, it was not safe for the Karmapa to stay there; hence, it offered him a residence in Punjab (India) instead. The Karmapa complied. En route to India, he met with the king and gave him his favourite horse as a token of gratitude. The king issued a document to confirm the transfer of ownership over the property of Tashi Choling to the Karmapa. On this property, the Karmapa was to build his foremost monastic seat in Bhutan. Ashi Wangmo accompanied the Karmapa to the border where he was greeted by the representatives of the Indian government and the King of Sikkim.[74] Later on, after the Karmapa settled down eventually in Rumtek (Sikkim), Ashi Wangmo went to work for him and provided financial aid.[75]

It was the Eleventh King of Sikkim, Tashi Namgyal, who sent a representative to join the Indian government official to meet the Karmapa at the Bhutan-India border. He asked the Indian government to allow the Karmapa to settle permanently in Sikkim, on account of the strength of the historical lama-patron relationship between the Karmapas and kings of Sikkim, and obtained its approval. The Karmapa then led his party to travel to Sikkim.[76] The king and prince asked him to choose a place to stay. For the purpose of reviving the Dharma, the Karmapa chose Rumtek.[77]

5.2.3. Building of Monasteries

The royal courts of Bhutan and Sikkim and the Indian government helped the Karmapa rebuild his monastic community in exile. In Bhutan, King Jigme Dorji Wangchuck continued to strengthen the relationship with the Karmapa. Each year between 1967 and 1970, the king invited the Karmapa to visit.[78] In 1967, the king and Queen Mother Phuntsho Choden gave the Karmapa Tashi Choling Dzong and a piece of land in Bumthang; they also pledged to cover the construction cost of a temple to be built there.[79] The Karmapa then erected a large monastery that accommodated over 300 monks.[80] The king also offered Land Rovers, jeeps and a truck to the Karmapa.[81] At the end-of-the-year ritual ceremony, the two queen mothers came to participate in the Karmapa's empowerment and teaching.[82] Over the years, the lama-patron relationship grew steadily. From 1968 to 1970, the king continued to invite the Karmapa to visit; the Karmapa received a total of 600,000 rupees in donations.[83] In 1971, the Karmapa sent Shamar and his secretary to attend the celebration of Prince Singye Wangchuck's (Seng ge dbang phyug, 1955–) new appointment as governor (*dpon slob*).[84] When the king died in 1972, the Karmapa travelled to Bhutan to conduct his funeral ritual.[85]

The Fourth King, Jigme Singye Wangchuck, also maintained a close connection with the Karmapa. In 1973, at his invitation, the Karmapa visited Thimphu and consecrated the *stūpa* of the late king. Like his father, Jigme Singye Wangchuck supported the construction of the Karmapa's Tashi Choling. In addition, Queen Mother Phuntsho Choden offered the temple Kanglung Sherubtse (Kang lung shes rab rtse).[86] In 1974, the Karmapa visited Bhutan for the king's royal coronation.[87] The king issued a Bhutanese diplomatic passport to the Karmapa; with this, the Karmapa was able to travel abroad.[88] It allowed him to visit the West very early on. The king continued to extend his patronage to the Karmapa: he funded the summer retreat in Rumtek, the construction of Tashi Choling, its monastic institute and a monastery for the Himalayan Buddhists in Calcutta; he also contributed to the printing of the Kangyur that the Karmapa oversaw.[89]

Both the royal family of Sikkim and the Government of India sponsored the construction of the Karmapa's monastic seat in exile, Rumtek Shedrub Chokhor Ling (Rum bteg bshad sgrub chos 'khor gling). To begin with, the Sikkimese king and prince supported the Karmapa's vision to re-establish the monastic community and decided to rebuild Rumtek.[90] They offered 74 acres of land near old Rumtek,[91] with exemption from tax.[92] In 1964, Thondup Namgyal laid the foundation. The Sikkimese government funded the initial period of construction; they built a road and supplied the monastery with electricity and water.[93] In 1963, when Tashi Namgyal died in a hospital in Calcutta, the Karmapa, visiting the city at that time, performed the ritual of consciousness transference (*'pho ba*) for him, and after returning to Gangtok, personally completed the funeral ceremony.[94] In 1965, the Karmapa attended the enthronement of the Twelfth King Palden Thondup Namgyal (dPal ldan Don grub rnam rgyal, 1923–1982).[95] In 1972, he visited the king in his Calcutta residence to warn him against a big obstacle to his political power and offer him a solution.[96] The Karmapa's warning and personal visit attest to his close relationship with the king.[97]

On the Indian side, the Karmapa built connections with President Radhakrishnan and Prime Minister Jawaharlal Nehru.[98] This helped him persuade the Indian government to provide support for Tibetan refugees.[99] The construction of new Rumtek would not have succeeded without their aid.[100] In 1961, the Karmapa met with Nehru in Delhi. Nehru released 400,000 rupees to fund the construction of Rumtek.[101] He also provided food and clothing and funded a dispensary there.[102] The Indian government then helped establish the Karmapa's institute in Delhi. In 1972, the Karmapa approached Prime Minister Indira Gandhi for the grant of land.[103] Eventually, in 1979, the government transferred a plot of land in South Delhi, Qutub Minar, near the remains of Ashoka Palace. Later that year, President Neelam Sanjiva Reddy joined the Karmapa to lay the foundation for the institute.[104]

Among all the monasteries that the Karmapa built in exile, Rumtek is of primary importance. As shown in the next chapter, in Rumtek, the Karmapa gathered the best teachers of his lineage, founded an institute and a retreat centre, and supervised the training of young tulkus and lamas as well as his Western disciples. In so doing, he created the fundamental infrastructure for the re-establishment of the monastic community and, more importantly, prepared necessary human resources for the expansion of his lineage to the West. Later, Part IV will show that the Karmapa's European disciple Freda Bedi whom he had trained in Rumtek made notable contributions to his activity in the West. The Karmapa himself, when touring Europe and North America, sent tulkus and lamas from Rumtek to build and manage monasteries, to hold the posts of resident teachers in the newly founded Dharma centres and to deliver teachings and train the first generation of Tibetan language translators. Many young tulkus, including his four primary disciples (i.e. Shamar, Situ, Jamgon Kongtrul and Gyaltsab) as well as Dzogchen Ponlop, Traleg Rinpoche and Chokyi Nyima, later became renowned Buddhist teachers in the West. These would not have been possible without the founding of Rumtek in the first place. As the expansion grew in scale, Rumtek served as the headquarters for the many Dharma centres that the Karmapa established worldwide.

The timing was also crucial here. Rumtek was built in the 1960s when other Tibetan Buddhist lineages were still struggling to survive in the refugee settlements in India. Rumtek was the first Tibetan monastery constructed for permanent use in the diaspora.[105] It was, from the early years, a very traditional monastery, constructed to high artistic standards; it appeared in many international magazines and became a major tourist attraction in Sikkim.[106] The construction would not have achieved such high standards without patronage from Sikkim and India. The royal families of Sikkim and Bhutan also helped Rumtek to become rather wealthy compared to other Tibetan monasteries.[107] In contrast, the majority of the Tibetan monasteries in early exile did not enjoy the same financial privilege. For example, the Sera Monastery, one of the three most prestigious monasteries of the Gelug school, was rebuilt in exile in 1970 in the Bylakuppe settlement in Mysore, South India; its assembly hall was erected in 1978,[108] twelve years after the construction of Rumtek was completed.

Unlike his counterparts in other schools, the Karmapa began his preservation efforts from outside the refugee settlements. Through his connections with Bhutan, Sikkim and India, he secured sufficient financial resources so that his activity would not be confined by the difficulties of resettlement that most Tibetans had to battle with in the early years of the diaspora. This certainly contributed to the global development of the Karma Kagyu school during the initial period of the transmission of Tibetan Buddhism to the West. The diplomatic passport that the Bhutanese king issued to the Karmapa, a rare privilege among exile lamas, also added an extra advantage. It allowed him to travel to the West with ease and with political prestige while most Tibetan lamas were travelling with refugee documents at that time. The Dalai Lama, for example, was only able to make his first visit to the United States in 1979 due to the sensitiveness of his political role in the diaspora.[109] By that time, the Karmapa had already conducted two extensive tours in the country, which largely raised the public profile of the Karma Kagyu. As shown later in Part IV, this advantage added to his appeal and attracted attention from governments, especially in the United States. It provided a platform for the Karmapa to introduce his tradition to mainstream society.

The Karmapa's close relationship with Bhutan, Sikkim and India endured till the end of his life. In 1979, when he was hospitalised in Delhi, Bhutanese princess Ashi Dekyi Yangdzom (A zhe bde skyid dbyangs 'dzoms) went to visit him.[110] In 1980, when his health severely deteriorated, the secretary to the Government of Sikkim immediately called upon an Indian military doctor to attend to him.[111] Both a helicopter and an Indian Air Force Dakota were arranged for his travel in India en route to Hong Kong for medical treatment.[112] Upon arrival in Hong Kong, the Indian High Commission helped secure a suite normally reserved for the British Colonial Governor of Hong Kong for his stay in Queen Mary Hospital.[113] After he died in the United States in 1981, Sikkimese government officials, members of the Bhutanese royal family and senior officials from the Government of India were among those who received his remains in Delhi. The Indian government arranged further transportation through Bagdogra and Libing (Sikkim) to Rumtek. Chief officers of the Indian army, representatives of the King of Bhutan and the Bhutanese government, and senior Sikkimese officials gathered to pay homage.[114] The governor of Sikkim offered condolences on behalf of the president and prime minister of India.[115] At a condolence ceremony attended by the chief minister, the governor read out the messages from Neelam Sanjiva Reddy and Indira Gandhi and announced plans to create a chair at the Sikkim Research Institute of Tibetology in commemoration of the Karmapa. Senior government officials, including the chief minister, chief judge, minister of finance and minister of education, delivered speeches.[116] All government offices and schools in Sikkim remained closed for a day to allow devotees to pay homage to the Karmapa. The government then instituted one week of mourning.[117] As the Karmapa's body was carried into Rumtek, the Sikkim Armed Police presented a guard of honour.[118] For the funeral ceremony, the Indian army set up tents near the monastery for shelter.[119] Among the 12,000 people attending the ceremony were delegations of the Indian government, the governor and chief minister of Sikkim and members of the royal families of Sikkim and Bhutan.[120] For the cremation ceremony, seventy soldiers from the Sikkimese Division of the Indian Army paid tribute with a twenty-one-gun salute.[121]

NOTES

1. Kagyu Office, "The Life of the Eighth Karmapa. Year Two. Day 4: Taking Harm as the Path and the Faults of Sectarianism and Bias," reported March 25, 2022, https://kagyuoffice.org/life-of-mikyo-dorje/#24; Kagyu Office, "Fifth Karmapa Deshin Shekpa"; Kagyu Office, "Karmapa Deshin Shekpa"; Karma nges don bstan rgyas, "rnam thar mdor bsdus"; 噶玛钨金, "让炯多杰," 38; 噶玛钨金, "德新谢巴," 60, 61; 噶玛善莲, "明成祖," 77.

2. Khra 'gu rin po che, *rgyal ba'i dbang po*, 343.12–343.14; bKra shis tshe ring, "'jig rten dbang phyug," 28.6; Brown, *Dance of 17 Lives*, 236; Zhanag Dzogpa Tenzin Namgyal, "Wondrous Activities," 32.

3. Terhune, *Karmapa*, 107.

4. Khra 'gu rin po che, *rgyal ba'i dbang po*, 349.15–349.18.

5. Khra 'gu rin po che, *rgyal ba'i dbang po*, 351.16–351.18, 352.2–352.4; bKra shis tshe ring, "'jig rten dbang phyug," 35.4–35.7; mKhas btsun bzang po, "rig pa'i rdo rje," 140.7–140.9; 'Jam dbyangs tshul khrims, "rig pa'i rdo rje," 236.11–236.12; Terhune, *Karmapa*, 106; Douglas and White, *Black Hat Lama*, 115; Kunsang and Schmidt, *Blazing Splendor*, 272–273; Brown, *Dance of 17 Lives*, 236; Finnegan, *Dharma King*, 40–41.

6. Kunsang and Schmidt, *Blazing Splendor*, 273.

7. Kunsang and Schmidt, *Blazing Splendor*, 273.

8. Khra 'gu rin po che, *rgyal ba'i dbang po*, 354.7–354.21; bKra shis tshe ring, "'jig rten dbang phyug," 35.10–35.12; mKhas btsun bzang po, "rig pa'i rdo rje,"

140.12–140.15; Lhundup Damchö, *Karmapa: 900 years*, 85; Finnegan, *Dharma King*, 11, 36–37; Terhune, *Karmapa*, 106; Jamgon Kongtrul Rinpoche, "XVI Gyalwa Karmapa," 11; Karma Thinley, "Rangjung Rigpe Dorje," 133; Douglas and White, *Black Hat Lama*, 115; Holmes, *Gyalwa Karmapa*, 26; Brown, *Dance of 17 Lives*, 42, 236; Tsering Namgyal Khortsa, "Sixteenth Karmapa," 80.

Tsering Namgyal Khortsa also reports that in 1950, the Karmapa participated in the negotiations with China on behalf of the Tibetan government (see Tsering Namgyal Khortsa, "Sixteenth Karmapa," 81).

9. Blo gros don yod, "rig pa'i rdo rje'i," 550.19–551.5.

10. Rin chen dpal bzang, "rig pa'i rdo rje," 272.15–272.23; Rum bteg, "rnam thar lo rgyus," 221.19–221.23; Karma rgyal mtshan, "dpal rgyal dbang karma pa na rim gyi mdzad rnam (4)," in *kaM tshang yab sras dang dpal spungs dgon pa'i lo rgyus ngo mtshar dad pa'i padma rgyas byed*, TBRC W27303. (khreng tu: si khron mi rigs dpe skrun khang, 1997), 71.9–71.13; Sherap Phuntsok, "Rangjung Rigpe Dorje," 173.

11. bKra shis tshe ring, "'jig rten dbang phyug," 35.13–35.16; 'Jam dbyangs tshul khrims, "rig pa'i rdo rje," 237.1–237.3; mKhas btsun bzang po, "rig pa'i rdo rje," 140.16–140.19; Douglas and White, *Black Hat Lama*, 115; Karma Thinley, "Rangjung Rigpe Dorje," 133; Kunsang and Aubèle, "Sixteenth Karmapa," 218; Tsering Namgyal Khortsa, "Sixteenth Karmapa," 80–81.

12. Khra 'gu rin po che, *rgyal ba'i dbang po*, 357.14–358.2; Douglas and White, *Black Hat Lama*, 115.

13. Khra 'gu rin po che, *rgyal ba'i dbang po*, 358.3–358.4; rDzogs chen dpon slob, "rig pa'i rdo rje," 283.5–283.6; bKra shis tshe ring, "'jig rten dbang phyug," 36.3–36.5; 'Jam dbyangs tshul khrims, "rig pa'i rdo rje," 237.6; mKhas btsun bzang po, "rig pa'i rdo rje," 141.1–141.2; Jamgon Kongtrul Rinpoche, "XVI Gyalwa Karmapa," 11.

The name of the building varies in other accounts: *Phun tshogs dga' khyil* (Kra shis tshe ring, "'jig rten dbang phyug," 36), and *Phun tshogs dga' 'khyil* (mKhas btsun bzang po, "rig pa'i rdo rje," 141; 'Jam dbyangs tshul khrims, "rig pa'i rdo rje," 237).

14. Finnegan, *Dharma King*, 40.

15. Khra 'gu rin po che, *rgyal ba'i dbang po*, 358.4–358.14; bKra shis tshe ring, "'jig rten dbang phyug," 36.3–36.17; Grags pa yongs 'dus, "bcu drug pa," 368.2–368.6; Blo gros don yod, "rig pa'i rdo rje'i," 551.8–551.16; 'Jam dbyangs tshul khrims, "rig pa'i rdo rje," 237.5–237.9; mKhas btsun bzang po, "rig pa'i rdo rje," 140.23–141.6; rDzogs chen dpon slob, "rig pa'i rdo rje," 283.7–283.10; Terhune, *Karmapa*, 107–108; Jamgon Kongtrul Rinpoche, "XVI Gyalwa Karmapa," 11; Karma Thinley, "Rangjung Rigpe Dorje," 133; Douglas and White, *Black Hat Lama*, 115; Lhundup Damchö, *Karmapa: 900 years*, 83; Finnegan, *Dharma King*, 40; Brown, *Dance of 17 Lives*, 236.

Terhune and Lhundup Damchö report the year of the Dalai Lama's visit to be 1955.

16. Terhune, *Karmapa*, 107.

17. Terhune, *Karmapa*, 108.

18. Brown, *Dance of 17 Lives*, 236.

19. Terhune, *Karmapa*, 108.

20. Kunsang and Aubèle, "Sixteenth Karmapa," 218.

21. bKra shis tshe ring, 36.17–37.7; Khra 'gu rin po che, *rgyal ba'i dbang po*, 358.15–358.21; 'Jam dbyangs tshul khrims, "rig pa'i rdo rje," 237.9–237.11; mKhas btsun bzang po, "rig pa'i rdo rje," 141.6–141.13; Grags pa yongs 'dus, "bcu drug pa," 368.7–368.13; Terhune, *Karmapa*, 108–109; Douglas and White, *Black Hat Lama*, 115–117; Karma Thinley, "Rangjung Rigpe Dorje," 133; Holmes, *Gyalwa Karmapa*, 26; Finnegan, *Dharma King*, 11.

According to Douglas and White, it was the Chinese who requested the Karmapa to visit Chamdo; there, he conferred empowerments and blessings to create stability.

Grags pa yongs 'dus points out that despite the Karmapa's visit, the circumstances did not improve.

22. Zhwa dmar, *sku tshe'i rnam thar*, 70.1–72.6.

23. *khams rigs rnams ni 'dzam gling gi gnas stangs mthong ba'i shes yon med mkhan sha stag yin tsang glo bur mi rabs nas yod pa'i goms gshis bsgyur thub kyin ma red | der brten slob grwa yag po btsugs te zhi 'jam thog nas spyi tshogs ring lugs ngo sprod gnang rogs gnang* (Zhwa dmar, sku tshe'i rnam thar, 72)

24. Zhwa dmar, *sku tshe'i rnam thar*, 72.12–73.3.

25. Jamgon Kongtrul Rinpoche, "XVI Gyalwa Karmapa," 13; Karma Thinley, "Rangjung Rigpe Dorje," 134; Holmes, *Gyalwa Karmapa*, 27; Kunsang and Aubèle, "Sixteenth Karmapa," 220; Dzogchen Ponlop, "Rangjung Rigpe Dorje," 292.

26. Rang byung rig pa'i rdo rje, "nyams dbyangs dgyes pa'i nga ro," in *rgyal dbang karma pa bcu drug pa chen po'i gsung 'bum 3*, ed. Jo sras bkra shis tshe ring (Dharamsala: Tshurphu Labrang; The Amnye Machen Institute, 2016), 10–11.

An English translation and commentary of the song in Martin, "*Music in the Sky*," 304.

27. For more information about the Shamar lineage, see Douglas and White, *Black Hat Lama*, 150; Terhune, *Karmapa*, 145–152; Brown, *Dance of 17 Lives*, 97–100.

28. Terhune, *Karmapa*, 117.

29. Terhune, *Karmapa*, 117.

30. Khra 'gu rin po che, *rgyal ba'i dbang po*, 368.1–368.6; Grags pa yongs 'dus, "bcu drug pa," 372.5–372.7; Brown, *Dance of 17 Lives*, 100; Finnegan, *Dharma King*, 84; Holmes, *Gyalwa Karmapa*, 29.

31. bKra shis tshe ring, "'jig rten dbang phyug," 39.14–39.17; Grags pa yongs 'dus, "bcu drug pa," 371.11–371.15; Terhune, *Karmapa*, 115; Finnegan, *Dharma King*, 51, 56–57.

Finnegan reports that the conference took place in Swarg Ashram and lasted for five days. Its main topic was the future of Tibetan Buddhism and the relationship between different lineages. The Dalai Lama and the Karmapa also held private meetings there.

32. *gong sa skyabs mgon chen po mchog gi dbu 'khrid 'og bod mi rigs yongs rdzogs mthun lam rdog rtsa gcig bsgril te | bod bden pa'i rgyal kha rang dbang rang btsan gyi dga' ston myur du 'char zhing | bde skyid rdzogs ldan gyi dpal la spyod thub bcas*

Rang byung rig pa'i rdo rje, "gangs ljongs ris med chos kyi tshogs chen thengs dang po'i skabs rgyal dbang karma pa rin po che'i gsungs bshad," in *rgyal dbang karma pa bcu drug pa chen po'i gsung 'bum 3*, ed. Jo sras bkra shis tshe ring (Dharamsala: Tshurphu Labrang; The Amnye Machen Institute, 2016), 17–18.

33. Khra 'gu rin po che, *rgyal ba'i dbang po*, 373.14–373.16; bKra shis tshe ring, "'jig rten dbang phyug," 40.14–40.15; Grags pa yongs 'dus, "bcu drug pa," 371.15–371.17; Terhune, *Karmapa*, 116.

Grags pa yongs 'dus gives the year 1963.

34. Finnegan, *Dharma King*, 121.

35. Grags pa yongs 'dus, "bcu drug pa," 376.9–376.13.

36. rDzogs chen dpon slob, "rig pa'i rdo rje," 287.4–287.6.

37. Khra 'gu rin po che, *rgyal ba'i dbang po*, 383.19–383.21.

38. Terhune, *Karmapa*, 115–116.

39. Brown, *Dance of 17 Lives*, 236.

40. Zhwa dmar, *sku tshe'i rnam thar*, 118.6–119.1.

41. Zhwa dmar, *sku tshe'i rnam thar*, 121.5–122.4.

42. Carole McGranahan, *Arrested Histories: Tibet, the CIA, and memories of a forgotten war* (Durham, NC: Duke University Press, 2010), 146–147.

43. Zhwa dmar, *sku tshe'i rnam thar*, 122.5–125.12, 126.15–127.2.

Zhwa dmar gives two examples to explain the tension between the Karmapa and the Tibetan government in Dharamsala that continued up to the late 1970s. Following the assassination of Gungthang Tsultrim (Gung thang tshul khrims), general secretary of the 'Thirteen Group', in 1978 (the year was 1977 in McGranahan, *Arrested Histories*, 260), some people believed that the Karmapa's life was in danger. Second, a Tibetan government official criticised the Karmapa in a newspaper in Nepal.

44. Brown, *Dance of 17 Lives*, 47–48.

45. This may refer to the Conference of All Tibetan Schools, though the year here is 1962, not 1963.

46. Brown, *Dance of 17 Lives*, 237.

47. Brown, *Dance of 17 Lives*, 237–238.

See also Levine, Introduction, xxvi.

48. Zhwa dmar, *sku tshe'i rnam thar*, 125.16–126.13.

49. Rum bteg, "dgongs rdzogs mjug mchod," 236.17–236.19, 237.15–237.20, 238.14–238.16, 241.17–242.1, 251.8–251.9; 'Ju chen thub bstan rnam rgyal, "rgyal dbang karma pa," 316.17–320.22; Shes bya, "bzod par dka' ba'i," 224.13–225.3; Shes bya, "bka' tshogs mchod 'bul grub ste phyir phebs," in *rgyal dbang karma pa bcu drug pa chen po'i gsung 'bum 1*, ed. Jo sras bkra shis tshe ring (Dharamsala: Tshurphu Labrang; The Amnye Machen Institute, 2016), 229.2–229.17; Shes bya, "dgongs rdzogs mchod sprin," in *rgyal dbang karma pa bcu drug pa chen po'i gsung 'bum 1*, ed. Jo sras bkra shis tshe ring (Dharamsala: Tshurphu Labrang; The Amnye Machen Institute, 2016), 231.7–231.8; Grags pa yongs 'dus, "bcu drug pa," 380.5–380.7.

50. 'Ju chen thub bstan rnam rgyal, "rgyal dbang karma pa," 315.3–326.4.

51. Karma Phuntsho, *The History of Bhutan* (India: Random House India, 2013), 186–187.

See also Zhwa dmar, *sku tshe'i rnam thar*, 88.3–88.4.

52. Zhwa dmar, *sku tshe'i rnam thar*, 88.4–89.2.

53. For example, Karma Phuntsho, *History of Bhutan*, 207, 212–254; Michael Aris, *Bhutan: The early history of a Himalayan kingdom* (Warminster: Aris & Phillips, 1979), 208–232; Michael Aris, *The Raven Crown: The origins of Buddhist monarchy in Bhutan* (London: Serindia Publications, 1994), 27; M. N Gulati, *Rediscovering Bhutan* (New Delhi: Manas Publications, 2003), 68.

54. Karma Phuntsho, *History of Bhutan*, 493–502; Aris, *Raven Crown*, 88–90; Shubhi Sood, *Bhutan, 100 Years of Wangchuck Vision* (Noida: S.D.S. Publishers, 2008), 61; Gulati, *Rediscovering Bhutan*, 122–127; V Coelho, *Sikkim and Bhutan* (New Delhi: Indian Council for Cultural Relations, 1971), 67.

55. Zhwa dmar, *sku tshe'i rnam thar*, 89.3–89.10.

56. Karma Phuntsho, *History of Bhutan*, 497.

57. Karma Phuntsho, *History of Bhutan*, 517, 530, 534.

58. Karma Phuntsho, *History of Bhutan*, 187.

59. Khra 'gu rin po che, *rgyal ba'i dbang po*, 345.1–345.4; 'Jam dbyangs tshul khrims, "rig pa'i rdo rje," 235.4–235.8; mKhas btsun bzang po, "rig pa'i rdo rje," 138.20–139.4; Zhwa dmar, *sku tshe'i rnam thar*, 66.5–66.12; Grags pa yongs 'dus, "bcu drug pa," 364.11–364.18; rDzogs chen dpon slob, "rig pa'i rdo rje," 282.11–282.18; Terhune, *Karmapa*, 101; Jamgon Kongtrul Rinpoche, "XVI Gyalwa Karmapa," 9; Douglas and White, *Black Hat Lama*, 113; Karma Thinley, "Rangjung Rigpe Dorje," 131; Kunsang and Aubèle, "Sixteenth Karmapa," 212; Lhundup Damchö, *Karmapa: 900 years*, 84; Finnegan, *Dharma King*, 34, 11.

60. Sherap Phuntsok, "Rangjung Rigpe Dorje," 172; Jamgon Kongtrul Rinpoche, "XVI Gyalwa Karmapa," 9; Karma Thinley, "Rangjung Rigpe Dorje," 131–132; Douglas and White, *Black Hat Lama*, 113; Kunsang and Aubèle, "Sixteenth Karmapa," 212.

61. Zhwa dmar, *sku tshe'i rnam thar*, 89.12–89.14.

62. Khra 'gu rin po che, *rgyal ba'i dbang po*, 345.1–345.9.

63. bKra shis tshe ring, "'jig rten dbang phyug," 38.12–38.14; 'Jam dbyangs tshul khrims, "rig pa'i rdo rje," 238.8–238.10; Terhune, *Karmapa*, 109; Douglas and White, *Black Hat Lama*, 117; Karma Thinley, "Rangjung Rigpe Dorje," 133.

In 'Jam dbyangs tshul khrims, the name of the monastery is Degye Choling (Dad rgyas chos gling).

Douglas and White and Karma Thinley each mentions a different monastery, built by Princess Azi/Azhi Wangmo: one in Kur Tod, North Bhutan, and the other in East Bhutan. However, they do not give the names of the monasteries.

64. Rum bteg, "rnam thar lo rgyus," 221.11–221.13; Karma rgyal mtshan, "rgyal dbang karma pa," 70.18–71.1.

65. Grags pa yongs 'dus, "bcu drug pa," 364.16–364.18; Aris, *Raven Crown*, 127.

66. Zhwa dmar, *sku tshe'i rnam thar*, 78.7–78.9.

'A zhe (dgon mchog) dbang mo' and 'dBang mo' possibly refer to the same person.

67. Zhwa dmar, *sku tshe'i rnam thar*, 83.11–84.9.

A similar, albeit less detailed, account in Coelho's Sikkimese history: Gyurmed Namgyal founded the first monastery of the Karmapa in Sikkim at Ralang in 1730; he met with the Ninth, not the Twelfth, Karmapa during a pilgrimage in Tibet

(Coelho, *Sikkim and Bhutan*, 6). Since the Twelfth Karmapa was Gyurmed Namgyal's contemporary, the reference to the Ninth Karmapa must be an error.

68. Tshul khrims rgya mtsho, "rig pa'i rdo rje," 39.7–39.13; Coelho, *Sikkim and Bhutan*, 6.

The link between the Fourth King and the Ninth Karmapa is a common error in the Tibetan sources. Many authors believe that Rumtek was founded by the Ninth Karmapa, Wangchuk Dorje. Tshul khrims rgya mtsho, however, maintains that Rumtek was founded by the Fourth King and consecrated by the Twelfth Karmapa. He points out the inaccuracy of the popular reference to the Ninth Karmapa: the Ninth Karmapa lived in the sixteenth century, prior to even the First King of Sikkim (See Tshul khrims rgya mtsho, "rig pa'i rdo rje," 39).

69. Tshul khrims rgya mtsho, "rig pa'i rdo rje," 39.7–40.4.

70. Khra 'gu rin po che, *rgyal ba'i dbang po*, 347.13–347.17, 359.9–359.11, 359.19–360.2; Grags pa yongs 'dus, "bcu drug pa," 366.8–366.10; rDzogs chen dpon slob, "rig pa'i rdo rje," 282.11–282.18; Tshurl khrims rgya mtsho, 2008, 40.5–40.14, 40.18–41.7; 'Jam dbyangs tshul khrims, "rig pa'i rdo rje," 237.14–237.15; mKhas btsun bzang po, "rig pa'i rdo rje," 141.17–141.18; bKra shis tshe ring, "'jig rten dbang phyug," 37.11–37.12; Terhune, *Karmapa*, 104, 109; Jamgon Kongtrul Rinpoche, "XVI Gyalwa Karmapa," 10, 12, 15; Karma Thinley, "Rangjung Rigpe Dorje," 132, 133; Douglas and White, *Black Hat Lama*, 114, 117; Kunsang and Aubèle, "Sixteenth Karmapa," 213, 219; Finnegan, *Dharma King*, 11, 39; Sherap Phuntsok, "Rangjung Rigpe Dorje," 173–174; Holmes, *Gyalwa Karmapa*, 26.

71. Khra 'gu rin po che, *rgyal ba'i dbang po*, 354.7–354.11; Tshurl khrims rgya mtsho, 2008, 40.15–40.17.

72. dGe legs bstan 'dzin, "'brug brgyud 'bras ljongs," 153.10, gives two possible names: A zhe chos dbang or A zhe dbang mo.

As mentioned earlier, the sister of the Second King, Ashi Konchok Wangmo (A zhe dgon mchog dbang mo), was the Karmapa's disciple. Both names, Ashi Chowang (A zhe chos dbang) and Ashi Wangmo (A zhe dbang mo), are likely to refer to the same person. To maintain consistency, I use the name Ashi Wangmo in my following discussion.

73. Tashi Choling was the summer palace built by the Second King for Queen Phuntsho Choden. See Karma Phuntsho, *History of Bhutan*, 540; Damchu Lhendup and Needrup Zangpo, *One Hundred Years of Development* (Thimphu: KMT Publishing House, 2014), 167.

74. dGe legs bstan 'dzin, "'brug brgyud 'bras ljongs," 153.8–153.12, 153.16–154.16, 155.16–156.21, 157.13–157.18.

See also Khra 'gu rin po che, *rgyal ba'i dbang po*, 362.7–362.10, 362.20–363.1, 363.2–363.4; rDzogs chen dpon slob, "rig pa'i rdo rje," 283.21–284.1, Zhwa dmar, *sku tshe'i rnam thar*, 78.10–78.12, Tshul khrims rgya mtsho, "rig pa'i rdo rje," 41.10–41.14, Terhune, *Karmapa*, 112; Douglas and White, *Black Hat Lama*, 118–119; Karma Thinley, "Rangjung Rigpe Dorje," 135; Holmes, *Gyalwa Karmapa*, 28; Kunsang and Aubèle, "Sixteenth Karmapa," 221; Damchu Lhendup and Needrup Zangpo, *One Hundred Years*, 167.

According to Khra 'gu, rDzogs chen dpon slob and Douglas and White, the princess who welcomed the Karmapa on his arrival in Bhutan was Tshul khrims dpal mo (Tsultrim Palmo). Khra 'gu and Douglas and White also report that this princess accompanied the Karmapa on his travel to Sikkim. Finnegan mentions a princess called Jetsun Tsulpal Chok, the daughter of the king, who requested the Karmapa to compose a text on refuge (See Finnegan, *Dharma King*, 130). They are likely to be the same person (Tsulpal as the abbreviation of Tshul khrims dpal mo).

Zhwa dmar mentions that the king offered 200,000 rupees to the Karmapa.

75. Zhwa dmar, *sku tshe'i rnam thar*, 78.12–78.14; Jamgon Kongtrul Rinpoche, "XVI Gyalwa Karmapa," 13.

76. Khra 'gu rin po che, *rgyal ba'i dbang po*, 363.4–363.10; Tshul khrims rgya mtsho, "rig pa'i rdo rje," 41.14–43.7; Grags pa yongs 'dus, "bcu drug pa," 369.14–370.2; rDzogs chen dpon slob, "rig pa'i rdo rje," 284.2–284.5; Terhune, *Karmapa*, 112; Karma Thinley, "Rangjung Rigpe Dorje," 135; Jamgon Kongtrul Rinpoche, "XVI Gyalwa Karmapa," 13–14; Douglas and White, *Black Hat Lama*, 118; Kunsang and Aubèle, "Sixteenth Karmapa," 221; Tsering Namgyal Khortsa, "Sixteenth Karmapa," 81.

77. Khra 'gu rin po che, *rgyal ba'i dbang po*, 363.12–364.2; rDzogs chen dpon slob, "rig pa'i rdo rje," 284.5–284.13; Grags pa yongs 'dus, "bcu drug pa," 370.2–370.4; Terhune, *Karmapa*, 112–113; Douglas and White, *Black Hat Lama*, 119; Karma Thinley, "Rangjung Rigpe Dorje," 135; Holmes, *Gyalwa Karmapa*, 28; Pardee, Skolnick and Swanson, *Sacred Prophecy*, 45; Kunsang and Aubèle, "Sixteenth Karmapa," 221; Lhundup Damchö, *Karmapa: 900 years*, 85; Brown, *Dance of 17 Lives*, 46; Dzogchen Ponlop, "Rangjung Rigpe Dorje," 292; *Recalling a Buddha*.

Two years before, when the Karmapa visited Gangtok, the monks from Rumtek Samten Chöling (Rum bteg bsam gtan chos gling) extended an invitation to him. He declined their invitation, but promised to go in the future. It is popularly believed that the Karmapa's response at the time was a sign of his foresight of future settlement in Rumtek in 1959. See Khra 'gu rin po che, *rgyal ba'i dbang po*, 360.2–360.6; Zhwa dmar, *sku tshe'i rnam thar*, 76.11–77.2, Tshul khrims rgya mtsho, "rig pa'i rdo rje," 41.7–41.9, mKhas btsun bzang po, "rig pa'i rdo rje," 141.23–142.2, bKra shis tshe ring, "'jig rten dbang phyug," 37.17–38.3, 'Jam dbyangs tshul khrims, "rig pa'i rdo rje," 238.2–238.3, 'Ju chen thub bstan rnam rgyal, "rgyal dbang karma pa," 325.19–325.22, Sherap Phuntsok, "Rangjung Rigpe Dorje," 174; Terhune, *Karmapa*, 109; Jamgon Kongtrul Rinpoche, "XVI Gyalwa Karmapa," 12; Karma Thinley, "Rangjung Rigpe Dorje," 134; Douglas and White, *Black Hat Lama*, 117; Holmes, *Gyalwa Karmapa*, 26–27; Kunsang and Aubèle, "Sixteenth Karmapa," 219; Brown, *Dance of 17 Lives*, 42; Ringu Tulku, "He Was Always Free," in *The Miraculous 16th Karmapa: Incredible Encounters with the Black Crown Buddha*, comp. Norma Levine (Arcidosso: Shang Shung Publications, 2013), 138; Dzogchen Ponlop, "Rangjung Rigpe Dorje," 292; Tsering Namgyal Khortsa, "Sixteenth Karmapa," 81.

78. In the study of Bhutanese history, Damchu Lhendup and Needrup Zangpo record the king's invitation to the Karmapa on three occasions (See Damchu Lhendup and Needrup Zangpo, *One Hundred Years*, 166–167).

The Karmapa's visits, at the invitation of the king, are mentioned briefly in the following *namthar* and English biographical accounts: rDzogs chen dpon slob, "rig pa'i rdo rje," 284.18–284.20; Jamgon Kongtrul Rinpoche, "XVI Gyalwa Karmapa," 15; Kunsang and Aubèle, "Sixteenth Karmapa," 223–224; Douglas and White, *Black Hat Lama*, 121.

79. Khra 'gu rin po che, *rgyal ba'i dbang po*, 374.10–374.13; Douglas and White, *Black Hat Lama*, 121; Holmes, *Gyalwa Karmapa*, 30.

Jamgon Kongtrul Rinpoche reports that the king also offered Kunga Rabten Dzong to the Karmapa, but he does not mention which year (See Jamgon Kongtrul Rinpoche, "XVI Gyalwa Karmapa," 15).

80. Jamgon Kongtrul Rinpoche, "XVI Gyalwa Karmapa," 15; Douglas and White, *Black Hat Lama*, 121.

81. Brown, *Dance of 17 Lives*, 49.

82. Khra 'gu rin po che, *rgyal ba'i dbang po*, 374.4, 374.19–374.21; Grags pa yongs 'dus, "bcu drug pa," 373.8–373.12; Douglas and White, *Black Hat Lama*, 120–121; Finnegan, *Dharma King*, 98–99.

A photograph that captures the two queen mothers' meeting with the Karmapa at Rumtek in 1978 (See Finnegan, *Dharma King*, 101) indicates a long-term relationship between them.

83. Zhwa dmar, *sku tshe'i rnam thar*, 89.14–89.16.

84. Khra 'gu rin po che, *rgyal ba'i dbang po*, 378.11–378.13.

85. Grags pa yongs 'dus, "bcu drug pa," 374.8–374.13 (The author mistakenly calls 'Jigs med rdo rje the Second King).

86. Khra 'gu rin po che, *rgyal ba'i dbang po*, 378.20–379.5; Grags pa yongs 'dus, "bcu drug pa," 374.14–375.2; bKra shis tshe ring, "'jig rten dbang phyug," 41.8–41.10.

87. Khra 'gu rin po che, *rgyal ba'i dbang po*, 380.4–380.5; Grags pa yongs 'dus, "bcu drug pa," 375.7–375.9; Finnegan, *Dharma King*, 100.

88. Khra 'gu rin po che, *rgyal ba'i dbang po*, 380.6–380.8; Ringu Tulku, "He Was Always Free," 140; MJ Bennett and Norma Levine, "Canada and the Three World Tours of His Holiness Karmapa," in *The Miraculous 16th Karmapa: Incredible Encounters with the Black Crown Buddha*, comp. Norma Levine (Arcidosso: Shang Shung Publications, 2013), 157.

According to Bennett and Levine, the royal family also issued a diplomatic passport to Jamgon Kongtrul and several national passports to the Karmapa's entourage.

89. Zhwa dmar, *sku tshe'i rnam thar*, 90.6–90.8; Rang byung rig pa'i rdo rje, "rang rnam bsdus pa," 66.4–66.7; Khra 'gu rin po che, *rgyal ba'i dbang po*, 379.3.

90. Khra 'gu rin po che, *rgyal ba'i dbang po*, 365.2–365.3, 366.17–366.19; Tshul khrims rgya mtsho, "rig pa'i rdo rje," 43.18–43.19, 44.18–44.20.

91. bKra shis tshe ring, "'jig rten dbang phyug," 39.8–39.10; rDzogs chen dpon slob, "rig pa'i rdo rje," 284.21–284.22; Tshul khrims rgya mtsho, "rig pa'i rdo rje," 44.23–45.1; Grags pa yongs 'dus, "bcu drug pa," 370.9–370.13; dGe legs bstan 'dzin, "'brug brgyud 'bras ljongs," 158.15–158.16; Terhune, *Karmapa*, 112–113; Jamgon Kongtrul Rinpoche, "XVI Gyalwa Karmapa," 14; Douglas and White, *Black Hat Lama*, 120; Karma Thinley, "Rangjung Rigpe Dorje," 136; Brown, *Dance of 17 Lives*, 46; Kunsang and Aubèle, "Sixteenth Karmapa," 221; Finnegan, *Dharma King*, 49; Tsering Namgyal Khortsa, "Sixteenth Karmapa," 81; *Recalling a Buddha*.

92. Khra 'gu rin po che, *rgyal ba'i dbang po*, 366.19–366.20; Kotwal, *God's Own Death*, 99; Finnegan, *Dharma King*, 48, 49.

93. Douglas and White, *Black Hat Lama*, 120; Karma Thinley, "Rangjung Rigpe Dorje," 136; Kunsang and Aubèle, "Sixteenth Karmapa," 222; Lhundup Damchö, *Karmapa: 900 years*, 84; Finnegan, *Dharma King*, 48, 49; Dzogchen Ponlop, "Rangjung Rigpe Dorje," 292; *Recalling a Buddha*; Tsering Namgyal Khortsa, "Sixteenth Karmapa," 81; Terhune, *Karmapa*, 114; Holmes, *Gyalwa Karmapa*, 29; Brown, *Dance of 17 Lives*, 46.

94. Grags pa yongs 'dus, "bcu drug pa," 371.18–372.5.

95. Grags pa yongs 'dus, "bcu drug pa," 372.8–372.10.

96. Zhwa dmar, *sku tshe'i rnam thar*, 47.15–52.1.

The Karmapa predicted a political obstacle that the king was to encounter. To remedy the foreseen situation, he advised the king to produce a certain type of Vajrapāṇi image. Shamar heard that the king assigned this task to his attendant who bought one from a Nepalese shop instead. Shamar believes that the king's failure to follow through the Karmapa's advice weakened his merit to reign over his country. Three years later, the king's reign came to an end.

97. For their close relationship, see also Finnegan, *Dharma King*, 128–129.

98. Zhwa dmar, *sku tshe'i rnam thar*, 79.3–79.6.

The Karmapa's meeting with Nehru in 1959/1960 is briefly mentioned in Karma Thinley, "Rangjung Rigpe Dorje," 135–136.

99. Rin chen dpal bzang, "rig pa'i rdo rje," 273.1–273.4; Rum bteg, "rnam thar lo rgyus," 222.1–222.2; Karma rgyal mtshan, "rgyal dbang karma pa," 71.13–71.15; Sherap Phuntsok, "Rangjung Rigpe Dorje," 174.

100. rDzogs chen dpon slob, "rig pa'i rdo rje," 285.7.

101. Zhwa dmar, *sku tshe'i rnam thar*, 86.4–86.9; Sherap Phuntsok, "Rangjung Rigpe Dorje," 174; Grags pa yongs 'dus, "bcu drug pa," 371.4–371.6; Douglas and White, *Black Hat Lama*, 119, 120; Karma Thinley, "Rangjung Rigpe Dorje," 136; Holmes, *Gyalwa Karmapa*, 28; Kunsang and Aubèle, "Sixteenth Karmapa," 222; Lhundup Damchö, *Karmapa: 900 years*, 85; Finnegan, *Dharma King*, 48, 49; Brown, *Dance of 17 Lives*, 46; Kotwal, *God's Own Death*, 99; Dzogchen Ponlop, "Rangjung Rigpe Dorje," 292; Tsering Namgyal Khortsa, "Sixteenth Karmapa," 81; *Recalling a Buddha*.

Holmes reports that the Indian government donated 1.4 million rupees.

102. Terhune, *Karmapa*, 114; Douglas and White, *Black Hat Lama*, 119, 120; Brown, *Dance of 17 Lives*, 46.

103. Zhwa dmar, *sku tshe'i rnam thar*, 110.1–110.5; Grags pa yongs 'dus, "bcu drug pa," 376.4–376.9; Jamgon Kongtrul Rinpoche, "XVI Gyalwa Karmapa," 17; Tsering Namgyal Khortsa, "Sixteenth Karmapa," 82.

According to Grags pa yongs 'dus, this took place in 1976.

104. Zhwa dmar, *sku tshe'i rnam thar*, 110.5–110.16; Grags pa yongs 'dus, "bcu drug pa," 378.10–379.2; Rin chen dpal bzang, "rig pa'i rdo rje," 273.15–273.20; Rum bteg, "rnam thar lo rgyus," 223.1–223.5; bKra shis tshe ring, "'jig rten dbang phyug," 42.12–42.14; Finnegan, *Dharma King*, 383, 404; Kotwal, *God's Own Death*, 99; Terhune, *Karmapa*, 120; Jamgon Kongtrul Rinpoche, "XVI Gyalwa Karmapa,"

18; Brown, *Dance of 17 Lives*, 87; Oberoi, "Dusum Khyenpa," 82; Dzogchen Ponlop, "Rangjung Rigpe Dorje," 293; Tsering Namgyal Khortsa, "Sixteenth Karmapa," 86.

According to Grags pa yongs 'dus, the land was granted in 1980.

The name of the institute in different accounts:

In Tibetan—Karma pa'i chos 'khor dbus (bKra shis tshe ring, "'jig rten dbang phyug," 42.)

In English—Karmapa Dharma Chakra Centre (Tashi Tsering, "Outer Biography," 16; Tashi Tsering, "A Biographical Sketch of the 16th Karmapa," *Tibetan Review* (August 1992): 17), Karmae Dharma Chakra Centre (Jamgon Kongtrul Rinpoche, "XVI Gyalwa Karmapa," 18) and the Kagyu International Buddhist Institute (Finnegan, *Dharma King*, 404).

Photographs of the meetings between President Neelam Sanjiva Reddy and the Karmapa on different occasions (Lhundup Damchö, *Karmapa: 900 years* 86; Finnegan, *Dharma King*, 116–117, 402–403) indicate their good relationship.

105. Finnegan, *Dharma King*, 48.

106. *Recalling a Buddha*.

107. Brown, *Dance of 17 Lives*, 48.

108. Sera Jey Monastic University, "Re-establishment at Bylakuppe," Published May 1, 2016, https://www.serajeymonastery.org/histroy/5-re-establishment-at-bylakuppe.

109. Tuttle, "Uniting Religion and Politics," 215.

110. Zhwa dmar, *sku tshe'i rnam thar*, 133.13–133.16.

111. Kotwal, *God's Own Death*, 64–66.

112. Kotwal, *God's Own Death*, 74–75, 80–83; Jamgon Kongtrul Rinpoche, "XVI Gyalwa Karmapa," 19.

113. Kotwal, *God's Own Death*, 83, 85–97, 251; Finnegan, *Dharma King*, 345.

See also Rum bteg, "dgongs rdzogs mjug mchod," 233.12–234.3; Grags pa yongs 'dus, "bcu drug pa," 379.7–379.10; Sherap Phuntsok, "Rangjung Rigpe Dorje," 175; Terhune, *Karmapa*, 121; Jamgon Kongtrul Rinpoche, "XVI Gyalwa Karmapa," 19.

114. Kotwal, *God's Own Death*, 232–250.

See also Rum bteg, "dgongs rdzogs mjug mchod," 237.4–237.20, 237.21–239.6; Shes bya, "bzod par dka' ba'i," 225.3–225.13; 'Ju chen thub bstan rnam rgyal, "rgyal dbang karma pa," 317.3–371.11; Kunsang and Aubèle, "Sixteenth Karmapa," 231; Bennett, "The Last Blessing," 397–398; Brown, *Dance of 17 Lives*, 82–83; Terhune, *Karmapa*, 125–126; *Recalling a Buddha*.

115. Rum bteg, "dgongs rdzogs mjug mchod," 235.12–236.10.

116. Rum bteg, "dgongs rdzogs mjug mchod," 252.9–253.22; Kotwal, *God's Own Death*, 250–253.

117. Rum bteg, "dgongs rdzogs mjug mchod," 236.14–236.16, 254.1–254.9; Kotwal, *God's Own Death*, 234.

118. Rum bteg, "dgongs rdzogs mjug mchod," 239.21–239.23; Kotwal, *God's Own Death*, 250.

119. Levine, *Love and Death*, 121–122; Nydahl 1992: 204.

120. Rum bteg, "dgongs rdzogs mjug mchod," 250.21–252.8; Grags pa yongs 'dus, "bcu drug pa," 380.3–380.7, 383.9–383.17; Kotwal, *God's Own Death*, 250; Brown, *Dance of 17 Lives*, 84; Levine, *Love and Death*, 122.

121. Rum bteg, "dgongs rdzogs mjug mchod," 249.13–249.17; Kotwal, *God's Own Death*, 39; Terhune, *Karmapa*, 130–131; Brown, *Dance of 17 Lives*, 84; Levine, *Love and Death*, 123; Levine, "Parinirvana of His Holiness," 385; Finnegan, *Dharma King*, 454; Tsering Namgyal Khortsa, "Sixteenth Karmapa," 86; *Recalling a Buddha*.

Chapter 6

Preservation Initiative

Since his time in Tibet, preservation had been at the core of the Karmapa's activity, as he summarises in his *rangnam*.[1] Shamar highlights particular historical circumstances. The emergence of the Ganden Phodrang, the rise to power of the Gelug school and the political intervention of the Mongols and the Chinese from the seventeenth century onwards had weakened the Kagyu school. To counter this, the Karmapa determined to revive the teaching of the Practice Lineage (*sgrub brgyud*).[2] In Tsurphu, he restored and expanded the existing buildings, constructed new shrines and produced statues, *stūpa*s, texts and other sacred objects.[3] He also carried out the same activity elsewhere in Central and Eastern Tibet.[4] He travelled across Tibet with a large entourage, known as the Great Encampment (*sgar chen*), to propagate the Dharma.[5]

    The Karmapa continued to perform the duty of a spiritual leader even when political turmoil began to manifest in Tibet during the 1950s. He gave teachings in Tsurphu.[6] He sheltered tulkus of different schools who fled from Eastern Tibet, including Situ, Sangye Nyenpa (Sangs rgyas mnyan pa), Dilgo Khyentse (Dil mgo mkhyen brtse) and Traleg Nyima Gyurme (Khra legs nyi ma 'gyur med), and arranged safe passage into exile for Situ, Jamgon Kongtrul, Sangye Nyenpa, Kalu Rinpoche, Tulku Urgyen and others.[7] Although his monks grew concerned about whether he planned to flee to India, he instructed them to build a monastic college in Tsurphu instead.[8] Despite that his officials at Tsurphu urged him to leave Tibet for his own safety, he decided to stay longer,[9] to be able to help the refugees.[10] Moreover, he reinstated the practice of his own lineage and restored Nyide (Nyi sde) monastery in Lhodrak (lHo brag);[11] there, he eased the worries of the monks about political tension with China.[12]

Eventually, in 1959, the Karmapa left Tibet with his lamas, monks and attendants, for the purpose of preserving the Dharma.¹³ They carried valuable statues, texts and ritual implements, and travelled for twenty-one days over the Himalayas.¹⁴ While travelling through Tibet, the Karmapa continued to conduct rituals, give teachings and visit pilgrimage sites.¹⁵ He led the party to cross the border into Bhutan where he started his life in exile.¹⁶ More than ever, he considered the preservation of the Dharma a top priority. When the King of Sikkim offered a place of residence in the royal palace, the Karmapa replied, with strong determination, that in order to revive the Dharma, he requested to settle in Rumtek Monastery instead.¹⁷ On 11 June 1959, the Karmapa arrived at Rumtek.¹⁸ Initially, his party faced very poor living conditions:

> Many of the Rumtek settlers started out living in tents but were unaccustomed to the environment. Weather conditions were moist in semitropical Sikkim, where it rained or was foggy for much of the year and had four solid months of heavy monsoon downpours. It was not the dry, crisp desert of the Tibetan plateau. Tibetan standards of cleanliness were more suited to the high desert, where bacteria do not proliferate. Bathing was not always *de rigueur*. Favourite foods such as meat and butter would not keep as well as they did at home. The drastically different climate, the trauma of war in Tibet, the loss of family and friends, and relocation in a strange place took its toll. There was much illness. Fevers, gastrointestinal problems, and the scourge of Tibetans, tuberculosis, were common afflictions. Facilities were nonexistent. The crumbling old Rumtek Monastery was only partially habitable.¹⁹

To render the situation more bearable, the Karmapa shared the possessions of his monastic household with his monks.²⁰ He also prepared temporary shelter and livelihood.²¹ His private secretary, Tenzin Namgyal, describes his leadership in these challenging circumstances: '[W]hen we escaped from Tibet we had so many difficulties such as illness, difficulties with the climate. We had no medicine, no doctors. But whenever there was a problem, His Holiness was the doctor, the guide. Always we were bringing him problems, and he would always have the answer. It is because of him that we survived.'²²

In his *rangnam*, the Karmapa recalls this period with a clear sense of purpose for the revival of the Dharma,²³ expressing single-pointed dedication to the benefit of others and renunciation of worldly concerns.²⁴ At the heart of his preservation efforts lie two important strategies. First is the re-establishment of the monastic community. This includes three measures: (1) building new Rumtek, (2) strengthening monastic discipline and (3) training the sangha. Second, he maintained non-sectarian accommodation, advocating cooperation between different schools.

6.1. RE-ESTABLISHMENT OF THE MONASTIC COMMUNITY

6.1.1. Building New Rumtek

In 1961, the Karmapa began to build new Rumtek which was to become his main seat in exile. He received crucial support from the Indian government and the royal family of Sikkim;[25] he himself also contributed to the cost.[26] The construction required substantial labour:

> Work on clearing the site began. . . . Monks and laymen pledged themselves to complete the clearing and preparatory work in the shortest possible time, working in both heat and cold. It took one hundred and eight men, working ten hours a day, some five hundred and forty days to clear and level the site. There were many casual labourers not included in this figure. . . . It took four years to complete the construction of the new centre. . . . One hundred and thirty disciples, including volunteers of various nationalities, worked together.[27]

The construction was completed in 1966.[28] The Karmapa and his monks moved into the new monastery on the Tibetan New Year.[29]

In new Rumtek, the Karmapa enshrined the sacred objects that he brought from Tibet.[30] He equipped the monastery with statues of the Buddha, lineage holders and Dharma protectors, murals, thangka paintings, musical instruments, Cham dance costumes and offering utensils. He sponsored artists, craftspeople and Tibetan opera performances. He founded a library and a printing house, and assembled the red-ink Derge Kangyur, the Narthang Kangyur and Tengyur, and over 1,000 volumes of texts belonging to the Kagyu and other schools.[31] Especially, the printing of the Derge Kangyur held particular importance to the preservation of Tibetan Buddhism in exile. On his arrival in Sikkim, the Karmapa had in his possession the first edition of the Derge Kangyur produced by Situ Panchen, Chökyi Jungne, who had offered it to the Thirteenth Karmapa, Dudul Dorje (bDud 'dul rdo rje, 1733–1797). He sent this edition to Delhi for printing; it became the first large Tibetan text printed in India using the photo-offset technique. The Karmapa then planned to print the Tengyur; this was completed by the time of his funeral in 1981.[32] Gene Smith helped with these projects and purchased copies for libraries in the United States.[33] The Karmapa himself distributed 500 copies of the Kangyur to monasteries of different schools in the Himalayan region[34] as well as Namgyal Institute of Tibetology in Sikkim.[35]

6.1.2. Strengthening Monastic Discipline

Several sources highlight the Karmapa's contribution to the consolidation of monastic discipline. This has three main aspects: propagation of monastic ordinations, revival of summer retreat and supervision of the monks' conduct. The Sixteenth Karmapa is generally held to be the most prolific bestower of novice and full ordination vows among the Karmapa incarnations in history.[36] The number of ordinations varies in different records. According to Lodrö Dönyö, he conferred monastic vows to nearly 10,000 lamas and tulkus.[37] Others speak of 3,000 plus up to many thousands.[38] The Karmapa himself observed monastic discipline strictly and trained his disciples accordingly. He clearly cherished the Vinaya: when he saw monks with loose conduct, he became very disappointed and sometimes shed tears.[39] Terhune reports: 'A good-natured man, he did have a temper, which was given full rein where erring monks were concerned.'[40] Ringu Tulku recalls that one time the Karmapa expressed a similar sentiment: 'I remember my parents telling him that in our family people would die very young when they were monks; what could they do for me to have long life? And he said, it doesn't matter if you die young as long as you are a good monk, that's better!'[41] This demonstrates the extent to which the Karmapa values monastic life.

The Karmapa initiated summer retreat at Rumtek in 1961, two years after his arrival in exile. The retreat followed the Tsurphu customs based on the 'Three Basic Rituals of the Vinaya' (*'dul ba gzhi gsum*).[42] The monastic household borrowed begging bowls for the sangha; all alms made to fully ordained monks were saved in the assembly hall.[43] This indicates the financial challenge at the time. Shamar reports that many Tibetan lamas teaching in exile hesitated to revive the Vinaya; the Karmapa's launch of summer retreat was an exception, and for them, timely encouragement.[44]

In new Rumtek, the Karmapa issued a code of conduct based on the Vinaya.[45] Lhundup Damchö describes a practice that served to sharpen the monks' awareness of monastic discipline:

> Each evening, the entire monastic assembly gathered for a detailed review of the personal conduct of each member. His Holiness himself presided over these nightly sessions, which were called *saldep*, meaning that guidance is given by reminding students of what they already know. For between one and two hours, everyone was not only permitted, but actively encouraged, to speak up about any infractions of monastic discipline they had committed themselves or observed others commit. The structure was entirely democratic, with ordinary monks fully authorized to point out any lapses they had witnessed even by the highest of lamas present. The system echoed the monastic training instituted by the Buddha himself, wherein the correction and confession of physical and verbal misdeeds was [sic] similarly conducted in open forum.[46]

Through this practice, the Karmapa created an open environment of scrutiny to safeguard the conduct of his monks. It proved to be effective: Rumtek developed a good reputation for discipline and won respect from local communities.[47]

6.1.3. Training the Sangha

Rumtek, in the early days, housed 150 monks. The Karmapa encouraged them to maintain rigour in both study and practice. They studied Buddhist texts and observed a strict schedule of daily rituals; they held confessional assembly for fully ordained monks (*nya stong gi gso sbyong*) and participated in sādhana *pūjā*s (*sgrub mchod*).[48] The Karmapa sought to bring together the different traditions of practice, especially the Tsurphu and Palpung systems.[49] He himself composed a history of refuge prayers and a new invocation ritual.[50] In 1960, he spent over a month conferring the grand empowerment and transmission of *The Treasury of Kagyu Mantras* (*bKa' brgyud sngags mdzod*) to fifteen lamas and tulkus, including his primary disciples, and 100 sangha members.[51] He also completed the empowerment and transmission of *The Treasury of Precious Instructions* (*gDams ngag mdzod*)[52] and the oral instruction of *The Eight Great Chariots of the Practice Lineage* (*sGrub brgyud shing rta brgyad*).[53] In 1964, he used a whole year to confer the instruction and transmission of the Ninth Karmapa's three Mahāmudrā treatises: *The Ocean of Definitive Meaning* (*Phyag chen nges don rgya mtsho*), *Pointing Out the Dharmakaya* (*Chos sku mdzub tshugs*) and *Dispelling the Darkness of Ignorance* (*Ma rig mun sel*).[54]

In new Rumtek, to ensure the quality of education for his disciples, the Karmapa summoned the best teachers of his lineage. He appointed Thrangu Rinpoche to be the abbot, Tenga Rinpoche as ritual master and Bokar Rinpoche the chief meditation master.[55] He founded a monastic college for twenty young tulkus and monks.[56] The new generation of disciples immersed itself in the study of scriptures and debate.[57] Throughout this period, the Karmapa continued to give teachings. In 1971, he conferred the empowerments and transmissions of *The Treasury of Extensive Teachings* (*rGya chen bka' mdzod*) and *Knowing One Liberates All* (*gCig shes kun grol*), the great empowerment of Kālacakra, the empowerment and instruction of Yongey Mingyur Dorje's Terma text of Dorje Drolö practice, as well as Mahāmudrā and the Six Yogas of Nāropā, which altogether lasted for three months.[58] During the summer retreat, he taught the texts on Mahāmudrā, the teachings of Gampopa, and so on.[59]

The Karmapa paid particular attention to the training of his four primary disciples, Shamar, Situ, Jamgon Kongtrul and Gyaltsab. With the hope that they would one day uphold the lineage teachings, he cared for them and kept them close since childhood, from Tibet into exile. In the Karma Kagyu school, the Karmapa's spiritual legacy is passed down from one incarnation to his close disciples, and then, from them onto the next incarnation. Once the disciples have died, the Karmapa will identify their reincarnations and become their teacher again. In this way, their teacher-disciple relationship is renewed across multiple lifetimes. The most prominent disciples of the Sixteenth Karmapa were the Twelfth Situ and the Third Jamgon Kongtrul whose predecessors were his main gurus.

The Eleventh Situ, Pema Wangchok Gyalpo (1886–1952), played a key role in the identification of the Sixteenth Karmapa. After the child was found, he, together with the Second Jamgon Kongtrul, Khyentse Özer (1902–1952), performed longevity rite and cleansing ritual.[60] In 1931, he enthroned the Karmapa at his monastery, Palpung,[61] and accompanied him to Tsurphu for the second enthronement.[62] He conferred on the Karmapa novice, bodhisattva and full ordination vows, as well as a large number of empowerments, transmissions and instructions, like filling the vase to the brim (*bum pa gang byo'i tshul du*).[63] In this way, the Karmapa progressed to the focal point of ultimate transmission (*don brgyud kyi rgyal sar phebs*)[64] and became a treasury of the instructions of the Tantra of meaning/ultimate transmission (*don rgyud/brgyud kyi gdams pa'i mdzod du gyur*).[65] Jamgon Kongtrul Khyentse Özer was the son and primary disciple of the Fifteenth Karmapa, Khakyap Dorje (1871–1922). He conferred important empowerments, transmissions and instructions on the Sixteenth Karmapa, like a father handing all his jewels to his son (*pha nor bu lag tu lhag med sprad pa*).[66] They exchanged spiritual songs,[67] and their minds became indivisible.[68] The Karmapa honoured him as the chief of his lineage.[69] The Karmapa's close relationship with Situ and Jamgon Kongtrul is encapsulated in the expression 'spiritual father and son' (*yab sras*).[70] After they both had died, the Karmapa identified their reincarnations and conducted their haircutting and enthronement rites.[71] He also identified the reincarnation of Gyaltsab and enthroned him,[72] but this is mentioned only briefly in the Karmapa's *namthar*. As for Shamar, the Karmapa asked the Dalai Lama to lift the ban on his reincarnation, and then formally enthroned him in Rumtek.[73]

The Karmapa brought his four primary disciples, along with other young tulkus, to Rumtek. There, he continued to care for them and oversee their education.[74] He trained them, in particular, in Mahāmudrā and the Six Yogas of Nāropā.[75] Dzogchen Ponlop recalls how the Karmapa met with the young tulkus on daily basis, dispensing advice and practising with them. He shared with them his vision to re-establish the lineage in exile and created an undisturbed spiritual environment in the monastery, free from politics.[76] In his *rangnam*, the Karmapa points out his purpose of training the young tulkus: to prepare them to propagate the Dharma worldwide.[77] To do so, he founded a monastic institute and a retreat centre at Rumtek with objectives that bring to the fore the clarity of his vision that sees study and practice as equally necessary means for training the sangha.[78]

The construction of the retreat centre, Yi'ong Samten Ling (Yid 'ong bsam gtan gling), began and was completed within the same year in 1978; thereafter, the Karmapa held the first three-year retreat for about twenty monks.[79] It was built on the mountainside at the back of Rumtek. Bokar Rinpoche served as retreat master.[80] Also in that year, the Karmapa began to build the monastic institute.[81] In 1980, he named it 'Karma Shri Nalanda Institute for Higher Buddhist Studies' (karma śrī nā landā'i ches mtho'i bshad grwa chen mo). He himself designed the building and its courses, even the textbooks. The Dalai Lama inaugurated the institute in 1981.[82] The system of monastic college in the Karma Kagyu school flourished under the leadership of the Seventh Karmapa, Chödrak Gyatso,[83] but was weakened as a result of the political turmoil during the time of the Tenth Karmapa, Chöying Dorje. The creation of the monastic institute in Rumtek marked a significant step towards the revival of this tradition.[84] Traleg Rinpoche considers the founding of both the retreat centre and the monastic institute to be a new phenomenon for the Tsurphu tradition. It was, in his words, 'in some way, quite radical'.[85] The Karmapa's resolve to strengthen his tradition in exile, in both scholarly study and spiritual practice, soon began to pay off. His four primary disciples, as well as Dzogchen Ponlop, Traleg Rinpoche and Chokyi Nyima, all became world-renowned Buddhist teachers.[86]

Apart from Rumtek, the Karmapa oversaw the construction of Tashi Choling (bKra shis chos gling) in Bhutan with patronage from the Bhutanese royal family. There, he also introduced summer retreat and instituted a monastic college.[87] Beyond Sikkim and Bhutan, the Karmapa restored and built monasteries and Dharma centres, including Buddhist colleges and retreat facilities, in India, Nepal, Southeast Asia, and later on, in Europe and North America.[88] By 1980, the number of the Dharma centres that he founded across the world had reached over 300.[89]

6.2. NON-SECTARIAN APPROACH

Non-sectarianism is a common approach shared by the Karmapa incarnations throughout history.[90] Following the tradition of his predecessors, the Sixteenth Karmapa made efforts to preserve the Dharma that reached well beyond his own lineage. He advocated a broad, unbiased stance towards all Tibetan Buddhist schools (grub mtha' ris med la gzigs pa'i spyan ras yangs).[91] Prior to exile, while travelling in Tibet, he visited monasteries of different schools.[92] In particular, he studied with the Dalai Lama, Khyentse Chökyi Lodrö, Shechen Kongtrul, Minling Chung Rinpoche and Tulku Urgyen Rinpoche.[93] He also transmitted Chokgyur Lingpa's Terma teaching to Minling Chung Rinpoche.[94] Furthermore, he helped identify reincarnate lamas of different schools,[95] and, as mentioned at the beginning of this chapter, offered shelter in Tsurphu to lamas who fled from Eastern Tibet regardless of affiliation.

The Karmapa continued to maintain such non-sectarian accommodation in exile. He characteristically referred to the Buddha's teaching as non-sectarian (*ris su ma chad pa*)[96] and those who promote division as the 'killers of the teaching' (*bstan pa'i lag dmar*).[97] At the First Conference of All Tibetan Schools (*gangs ljongs ris med chos kyi tshogs chen thengs dang po*), he articulated his vision:

> It is a splendid time to create new methods to thoroughly propagate the precious teaching of the Buddha, the excellent path to lasting happiness. . . . In Buddhist Tibet, from the three ancestral Dharma Kings up to the Fourteenth Dalai Lama, the lord of all non-sectarian teachings, [there has been] differentiation between four renowned schools with respect to [the way in which they] train disciples. [They all share] one single purpose: to obtain the very state of non-abiding nirvana, the lasting happiness. Thus, all Dharma practitioners have established steady and close friendships through peace. In India, within the Kagyu school, apart from a few lamas and tulkus of the Kamtsang, Dri-Tak ('Bri stag), Drukpa and Bashang ('Ba' shang) [who] managed to come, all the others stayed behind under the rule of Communist China. As a result, [it has become] difficult to revive the embers of the teaching. All practitioners have become concerned about such a significant decline. The enduring dissemination of the precious teaching of the Buddha in the future relies on the individuals . . . through cooperation, [I] have taken the great responsibility to uphold, preserve and disseminate this precious teaching of the Buddha.[98]

In this speech, the Karmapa emphasises the need for cooperation among different Tibetan schools. He stresses their common ground and warns of the difficulties in propagating the Dharma in exile. To him, non-sectarianism is a key strategy to revive Buddhism at such a critical juncture.

The Karmapa made practical efforts to strengthen the ties between different schools. He continued to turn to the Dalai Lama for teachings in Dharamsala.[99] Dilgo Khyentse and Chokling (mChog gling) Rinpoche attended his teachings in Rumtek along with many Kagyu lamas.[100] He distributed the Kangyur to the monasteries in Bhutan, India, Ladakh, Sikkim and Nepal regardless of their affiliation.[101] The leaders and senior teachers of other schools visited Rumtek on regular basis to consult with the Karmapa.[102] In 1971, the Karmapa discussed how best to revive the Himalayan Buddhist Society in Calcutta.[103] In 1975, he attended its conference in Darjeeling, to which the Dalai Lama and other Tibetan Buddhist leaders had been invited.[104] The conference was convened to support the development of Asian Dharma centres and the Himalayan Buddhist Society. Here, the Karmapa spoke of practical measures to preserve the Dharma.[105]

NOTES

1. *rgyal bstan 'dzin par nus pa'i skyes chen rnams la so byang sngags sogs kyi sdom pa dang | dbang lung khrid sogs 'chad spel | bstan gzhi gtsug lag khang gsar bzhengs | bshad sgrub kyi sde gsar 'dzugs sogs bod dang bod chen po'i ljongs su rgyal bstan ris su ma chad pa nyams pa slar gso dang mi nyams gong 'phel gyi bya ba mi dman tsam bgyis khul dang |* (Rang byung rig pa'i rdo rje, "rang rnam bsdus pa," 64.)

Translated into English in Appendix A (page 201 from '[I] teach and propagate the prātimokṣa' to 'and developing what had not').

2. Zhwa dmar, *sku tshe'i rnam thar*, 28.10–32.16.

See also Brown, *Dance of 17 Lives*, 35–36.

3. Rin chen dpal bzang, "rig pa'i rdo rje," 271.20–271.23; rDzogs chen dpon slob, "rig pa'i rdo rje," 282.3–282.4; Rum bteg, "rnam thar lo rgyus," 221.10–221.11; mKhas btsun bzang po, "rig pa'i rdo rje," 138.17–138.18, 139.23; Khra 'gu rin po che, *rgyal ba'i dbang po*, 346.7–346.9, 348.16; 'Jam dbyangs tshul khrims, "rig pa'i rdo rje," 235.3; Karma rgyal mtshan, "rgyal dbang karma pa," 70.17–70.18; Jamgon Kongtrul Rinpoche, "XVI Gyalwa Karmapa," 9; Karma Thinley, "Rangjung Rigpe Dorje," 131; Douglas and White, *Black Hat Lama*, 113; Holmes, *Gyalwa Karmapa*, 25, 28; Kunsang and Aubèle, "Sixteenth Karmapa," 212; Brown, *Dance of 17 Lives*, 41; Dzogchen Ponlop, "Rangjung Rigpe Dorje," 291.

4. Khra 'gu rin po che, *rgyal ba'i dbang po*, 361.6–361.7; Grags pa yongs 'dus, "bcu drug pa," 368.18–369.1; Rin chen dpal bzang, "rig pa'i rdo rje," 271.23–272.2.

5. The Great Encampment constituted an important aspect of the Sixteenth Karmapa's activity during his time in Tibet. For more detail, see Khra 'gu rin po che, *rgyal ba'i dbang po*.

Also called Karma Garchen (*karma sgar chen*), it is, according to Ogyen Trinley Dorje, a large, organised travelling encampment 'directly connected with the Karmapa and functioned as an administration for organizing the Karma Kagyu overall'. It is a distinctive method of the Karmapa incarnations for propagating the Dharma across Tibet. The Great Encampment emerged during the time of the Fourth Karmapa, Rolpe Dorje, reached its peak under the leadership of the Seventh Karmapa, Chödrak Gyatso, but was destroyed by Güshi Khan due to the political tragedy that befell the Tenth Karmapa, Chöying Dorje. It was well known for its strict codes of conduct on vegetarianism and prohibition of alcohol, elaborate Garchen Monlam ceremonies and the Karma Gadri (Gar-ri) style of painting. See Kagyu Office, "The Life of the Eighth Karmapa. Year One. Day 14: The Great Encampment during the Life of the 4th Karmapa Rölpai Dorje," reported March 8, 2021, https://kagyuoffice.org/life-of-mikyo-dorje/#14; Kagyu Office, "The Life of the Eighth Karmapa. Year One. Day 15: Rousing Bodhichitta and the Sacred Gandhola," reported March 10, 2021, https://kagyuoffice.org/life-of-mikyo-dorje/#15; Kagyu Office, "The Life of the Eighth Karmapa. Year One. Day 16: Vegetarianism in the Great Encampment and the Three-Fold Purity of Meat in the Vinaya," reported March 12, 2021, https://kagyuoffice.org/life-of-mikyo-dorje/#16; Kagyu Office, "The Life of the Eighth Karmapa. Year One. Day 19: Tibetan Art Forms: Menluk, Khyenluk and Gardri," reported March 16, 2021, https://kagyuoffice.org/life-of-mikyo-dorje/#19; Kagyu Office, "The

Life of the Eighth Karmapa. Year One. Day 20: Personal Reflections, More on Karma Gardri and Homage to the Gurus," reported March 17, 2021, https://kagyuoffice.org/life-of-mikyo-dorje/#20; Lhundup Damchö, *Karmapa: 900 years*, 78–79; 噶玛钨金, "若必多杰," 48; 噶玛钨金, "确札嘉措," 74, 76, 77; 噶玛钨金, "确映多杰," 24–25; 噶玛钨金, "米觉多杰," 86, 88; 噶玛善莲, "则拉岗," 73.

6. dGe legs bstan 'dzin, "'brug brgyud 'bras ljongs," 145.11–145.16.

7. Khra 'gu rin po che, *rgyal ba'i dbang po*, 360.19–361.2, 361.10–361.12; mKhas btsun bzang po, "rig pa'i rdo rje," 142.3–142.6, 142.15–142.17; 'Jam dbyangs tshul khrims, "rig pa'i rdo rje," 238.4–238.5; dGe legs bstan 'dzin, "'brug brgyud 'bras ljongs," 147.20–147.22; Jamgon Kongtrul Rinpoche, "XVI Gyalwa Karmapa," 12; Karma Thinley, "Rangjung Rigpe Dorje," 134; Douglas and White, *Black Hat Lama*, 117; Holmes, *Gyalwa Karmapa*, 27; Kunsang and Schmidt, *Blazing Splendor*, 319–322; Kunsang and Aubèle, "Sixteenth Karmapa," 216, 219; Brown, *Dance of 17 Lives*, 42, 45.

8. dGe legs bstan 'dzin, "'brug brgyud 'bras ljongs," 146.5–146.15.

9. Khra 'gu rin po che, *rgyal ba'i dbang po*, 361.2–361.5; Terhune, *Karmapa*, 110; Jamgon Kongtrul Rinpoche, "XVI Gyalwa Karmapa," 12–13; Karma Thinley, "Rangjung Rigpe Dorje," 134; Douglas and White, *Black Hat Lama*, 117; Kunsang and Aubèle, "Sixteenth Karmapa," 219.

10. Jamgon Kongtrul Rinpoche, "XVI Gyalwa Karmapa," 13; Karma Thinley, "Rangjung Rigpe Dorje," 134; Kunsang and Aubèle, "Sixteenth Karmapa," 219.

Kunsang and Aubèle report that the Karmapa helped thousands of Khampas who fled to Central Tibet.

11. bKra shis tshe ring, "'jig rten dbang phyug," 38.11–38.12; mKhas btsun bzang po, "rig pa'i rdo rje," 142.17–142.18; 'Jam dbyangs tshul khrims, "rig pa'i rdo rje," 238.4–238.5; Terhune, *Karmapa*, 109; Douglas and White, *Black Hat Lama*, 117.

12. Terhune, *Karmapa*, 110; Douglas and White, *Black Hat Lama*, 117.

13. Jamgon Kongtrul Rinpoche, "XVI Gyalwa Karmapa," 13; Karma Thinley, "Rangjung Rigpe Dorje," 134; Douglas and White, *Black Hat Lama*, 117–118.

14. Khra 'gu rin po che, *rgyal ba'i dbang po*, 361.17–361.21; Rang byung rig pa'i rdo rje, "rang rnam bsdus pa," 64.12–64.15; rDzogs chen dpon slob, "rig pa'i rdo rje," 283.15–283.21; dGe legs bstan 'dzin, "'brug brgyud 'bras ljongs," 146.18–148.12; Terhune, *Karmapa*, 111–112; Jamgon Kongtrul Rinpoche, "XVI Gyalwa Karmapa," 13; Karma Thinley, "Rangjung Rigpe Dorje," 134–135; Douglas and White, *Black Hat Lama*, 118; Holmes, *Gyalwa Karmapa*, 28; Kunsang and Aubèle, "Sixteenth Karmapa," 220; Lhundup Damchö, *Karmapa: 900 years*, 85; Brown, *Dance of 17 Lives*, 45; Dzogchen Ponlop, "Rangjung Rigpe Dorje," 292; Nydahl, *Entering the Diamond Way*, 73; *Modern Masters of Religion*.

The number of people travelling with the Karmapa varies in different accounts: 150 (Holmes, *Gyalwa Karmapa*, 28), 160 (Khra 'gu rin po che, *rgyal ba'i dbang po*, 361.17–361.18) and 200 (dGe legs bstan 'dzin, "'brug brgyud 'bras ljongs," 148.10; Terhune, *Karmapa*, 111).

According to Terhune, Jamgon Kongtrul and Karma Thinley, Dzogchen Ponlop, Shamar, Gyaltsab and Karma Thinley were among the Karmapa's entourage.

For detail about the Karmapa's escape route, see *Recalling a Buddha*.

15. dGe legs bstan 'dzin, "'brug brgyud 'bras ljongs," 148.17–153.5; Douglas and White, *Black Hat Lama*, 118; Karma Thinley, "Rangjung Rigpe Dorje," 135; Kunsang and Aubèle, "Sixteenth Karmapa," 220.

16. Karma Thinley, Holmes and Kunsang and Aubèle recount how the Karmapa led his party to cross the border just in time to avoid the Chinese army in close pursuit, hinting that the successful escape was due to his foresight through clairvoyance (see Karma Thinley, "Rangjung Rigpe Dorje," 135; Holmes, *Gyalwa Karmapa*, 28; Kunsang and Aubèle, "Sixteenth Karmapa," 221).

17. *rang re rnams 'og min thugs kyi 'khor lo dpal gyi stod lung mtshur phu gtsos sangs rgyas kyi bstan pa nyi ma shar ba lta bu de nyid yongs su bor nas gzhan yul du btsan byol 'byor ba 'di | rang mgo gang thon dang | tshe 'di'i bde skyid don gnyer tsam dang | g.yul 'khrug gi srog nyen tsam la brten btsan g.yol ma yin par bstan pa rtsa ba brlag shor ba de nyid kyi me ro slar gso gang thub dgos pa las gu yangs sos dal du bsdad thabs bral bas | bstan pa'i me ro slar gso'i gzhi'am | rtsa ba 'dzugs bskrun bya yul | rten 'brel dang dgos pa khyad par can gyis dbang gis sngon rgyal mchog dgu pas phyag btab gnang ba'i sa gnas rum bteg dgon du re zhig bzhugs gnas stabs bder gnang chog par gsungs |* (Khra 'gu rin po che, *rgyal ba'i dbang po*, 363–364.)

Translated into English in Appendix B (page 237–238 from 'After the Buddha's teaching [which used to be] like a shining sun' to 'that the Ninth Karmapa founded in the past').

Here again, the reference to the Ninth Karmapa is a common error in the literature.

18. Rang byung rig pa'i rdo rje, "rang rnam bsdus pa," 64.16; Khra 'gu rin po che, *rgyal ba'i dbang po*, 364.2.

This date is recorded in both sources as the fifth day of the fifth month of the pig year according to the Tibetan calendar.

19. Terhune, *Karmapa*, 113–114.

See also Douglas and White, *Black Hat Lama*, 119; Kunsang and Aubèle, "Sixteenth Karmapa," 221–222.

20. Khra 'gu rin po che, *rgyal ba'i dbang po*, 364.2–364.4; Jamgon Kongtrul Rinpoche, "XVI Gyalwa Karmapa," 14.

21. Rang byung rig pa'i rdo rje, "rang rnam bsdus pa," 64.18–65.1.

22. Brown, *Dance of 17 Lives*, 112.

23. *dal sdod skyid nyal bya rgyu'i dus skabs ma yin par | rgyal bstan slar gso bya rgyu'i las 'gan shin tu lci ba zhig rang gi 'gan du 'khri bar sems te |* (Rang byung rig pa'i rdo rje, "rang rnam bsdus pa," 64.)

Translated into English in Appendix A (page 201 from 'without time for happy leisure and rest' to 'to be [my] own responsibility').

24. *mdor na dkar po dge ba'i las la gzhan la re bcol dang | mi mang la zhal 'debs slong ba lta bu ma yin par | rang la gang yod ji 'byor gyi dngos po phangs med du dge rtsar btang ba yin cing | de'ang tshe 'di'i che thabs rnyed bkur grags 'dod sogs kyi rjes su 'jug pa ma yin par | gtso cher gzhan la phan na bsam pa'i re ba kho na'i sgo nas byas pa zhe gcig yin cing | gzhan phan kho na byung bsams pa'i re ba yod cing | da dung de gar rang gi bya ba mjug skyong rgyu tsam las 'jig rten na snyan grags can gyi mi'i grangs su 'jog pa phar zhog |* (Rang byung rig pa'i rdo rje, "rang rnam bsdus pa," 67.)

Translated into English in Appendix A (page 203 from 'In brief, neither entrusting others with' to 'among the famous people in the world').

25. See 5.2.3. Building of Monasteries.
26. Terhune, *Karmapa*, 114; Douglas and White, *Black Hat Lama*, 120.
27. Douglas and White, *Black Hat Lama*, 120.
    See also Lhundup Damchö, *Karmapa: 900 years*, 85; Finnegan, *Dharma King*, 48; Brown, *Dance of 17 Lives*, 46; *Recalling a Buddha*.
28. Khra 'gu rin po che, *rgyal ba'i dbang po*, 367.6–367.7, 370.12–370.17; rDzogs chen dpon slob, "rig pa'i rdo rje," 284.23–285.10; Zhwa dmar, *sku tshe'i rnam thar*, 86.9–86.10, 87.6–87.7; bKra shis tshe ring, "'jig rten dbang phyug," 39.8–39.14; Tshul khrims rgya mtsho, "rig pa'i rdo rje," 45.1–45.8; Grags pa yongs 'dus, "bcu drug pa," 370.12–370.13, 372.18–373.3; Rang byung rig pa'i rdo rje, "rang rnam bsdus pa," 65.6–65.8; Sherap Phuntsok, "Rangjung Rigpe Dorje," 174; Terhune, *Karmapa*, 114; Jamgon Kongtrul Rinpoche, "XVI Gyalwa Karmapa," 14.
    The period of construction is recorded slightly differently in some of these accounts. According to the Karmapa's *rangnam*, it is from the iron ox year (1961) to the fire horse year (1966) (Rang byung rig pa'i rdo rje, "rang rnam bsdus pa," 65.6–65.7).
29. Khra 'gu rin po che, *rgyal ba'i dbang po*, 370.17–370.19; Tshul khrims rgya mtsho, "rig pa'i rdo rje," 45.8–45.10; rDzogs chen dpon slob, "rig pa'i rdo rje," 285.11–285.13; Sherap Phuntsok, "Rangjung Rigpe Dorje," 174; Douglas and White, *Black Hat Lama*, 120; Holmes, *Gyalwa Karmapa*, 29; Brown, *Dance of 17 Lives*, 46.
30. Khra 'gu rin po che, *rgyal ba'i dbang po*, 370.14–370.17; Terhune, *Karmapa*, 114; Douglas and White, *Black Hat Lama*, 120; Holmes, *Gyalwa Karmapa*, 29; Dzogchen Ponlop, "Rangjung Rigpe Dorje," 292.
    Douglas and White, Finnegan and *Recalling a Buddha* include photographs of the sacred statues and relics that the Karmapa brought from Tsurphu and installed in new Rumtek (Douglas and White, *Black Hat Lama*, 134–142, Finnegan, *Dharma King*, 54–55; *Recalling a Buddha*).
31. Rang byung rig pa'i rdo rje, "rang rnam bsdus pa," 65.8–65.22; Khra 'gu rin po che, *rgyal ba'i dbang po*, 372.5–372.7, 372.10–372.17, 384.1–384.8; rDzogs chen dpon slob, "rig pa'i rdo rje," 286.1–286.4; Tshul khrims rgya mtsho, "rig pa'i rdo rje," 44.12–44.15; Grags pa yongs 'dus, "bcu drug pa," 374.5–374.7, 375.3–375.6; Rin chen dpal bzang, "rig pa'i rdo rje," 273.22; Jamgon Kongtrul Rinpoche, "XVI Gyalwa Karmapa," 15–16; Sherap Phuntsok, "Rangjung Rigpe Dorje," 175; Karma Thinley, "Rangjung Rigpe Dorje," 136; Douglas and White, *Black Hat Lama*, 121; Terhune, *Karmapa*, 119; Finnegan, *Dharma King*, 54, 62–63, 394–396, 389; Holmes, *Gyalwa Karmapa*, 31; Kunsang and Aubèle, "Sixteenth Karmapa," 223.
32. Interview with Gene Smith in *Recalling a Buddha*.
    Photographs of the ceremony to receive the printed copies of the Kangyur at Rumtek in *Recalling a Buddha*; Finnegan, *Dharma King*, 388–389.
33. Terhune, *Karmapa*, 119–120; Finnegan, *Dharma King*, 389.
34. Rum bteg, "rnam thar lo rgyus," 222.20–222.21, 223.6–223.7; Tshul khrims rgya mtsho, "rig pa'i rdo rje," 45.17–45.19; bKra shis tshe ring, "'jig rten dbang phyug," 43.3–43.7; Blo gros don yod, "rig pa'i rdo rje'i," 552.13–552.15; Rin chen dpal bzang, "rig pa'i rdo rje," 273.23–274.3; rDzogs chen dpon slob, "rig pa'i rdo rje," 286.5–286.10; Zhwa dmar, *sku tshe'i rnam thar*, 129.9–129.12; Karma rgyal mtshan 1997, 72.15–72.18; Terhune, *Karmapa*, 120; Jamgon Kongtrul Rinpoche,

"XVI Gyalwa Karmapa," 16; Karma Thinley, "Rangjung Rigpe Dorje," 136; Holmes, *Gyalwa Karmapa*, 31; Pardee, Skolnick and Swanson, *Sacred Prophecy*, 45; Kunsang and Aubèle, "Sixteenth Karmapa," 223; Brown, *Dance of 17 Lives*, 87; Ken Holmes, "The 16th Karmapa in Europe," in *The Miraculous 16th Karmapa: Incredible Encounters with the Black Crown Buddha*, comp. Norma Levine (Arcidosso: Shang Shung Publications, 2013), 286; Finnegan, *Dharma King*, 383; *Recalling a Buddha*.

35. Tshul khrims rgya mtsho, "rig pa'i rdo rje," 47.9–47.16.

36. Rum bteg, "rnam thar lo rgyus," 221.16–221.18; Karma rgyal mtshan, "rgyal dbang karma pa," 71.5–71.7; Rin chen dpal bzang, "rig pa'i rdo rje," 272.12–272.13; Pardee, Skolnick and Swanson, *Sacred Prophecy*, 45.

37. Blo gros don yod, "rig pa'i rdo rje'i," 549.19–550.7.

38. Grags pa yongs 'dus, "bcu drug pa," 383.17–383.18; Karma Thinley, "Rangjung Rigpe Dorje," 136; Holmes, *Gyalwa Karmapa*, 31.

39. Blo gros don yod, "rig pa'i rdo rje'i," 549.7–549.19.

40. Terhune, *Karmapa*, 119.

41. Brown, *Dance of 17 Lives*, 52.

42. Rang byung rig pa'i rdo rje, "rang rnam bsdus pa," 65.23–66.4.

See also Khra 'gu rin po che, *rgyal ba'i dbang po*, 366.16–366.17; Tshul khrims rgya mtsho, "rig pa'i rdo rje," 44.16–44.18, Douglas and White, *Black Hat Lama*, 119–120; Finnegan, *Dharma King*, 70.

43. Zhwa dmar, *sku tshe'i rnam thar*, 81.11–81.12, 81.16–82.1.

44. Zhwa dmar, *sku tshe'i rnam thar*, 82.1–82.5, 151.5–151.8.

45. Khra 'gu rin po che, *rgyal ba'i dbang po*, 370.20–371.1.

46. Lhundup Damchö, *Karmapa: 900 years*, 87.

47. Lhundup Damchö, *Karmapa: 900 years*, 87.

48. Khra 'gu rin po che, *rgyal ba'i dbang po*, 364.5–364.11; Tshul khrims rgya mtsho, "rig pa'i rdo rje," 43.12–43.18; Jamgon Kongtrul Rinpoche, "XVI Gyalwa Karmapa," 14; Holmes, *Gyalwa Karmapa*, 29.

Photographs of Rumtek rituals in Finnegan, *Dharma King*, 66–76.

According to Jamgon Kongtrul Rinpoche, the number of the sangha members (later on) exceeded 250.

49. Interview with Traleg Rinpoche in *Recalling a Buddha*.

50. Khra 'gu rin po che, *rgyal ba'i dbang po*, 364.11–364.13, 364.16–364.17.

According to Khra 'gu, the Karmapa composed the history of refuge prayers (*skyabs 'gro'i lo rgyus*) in 1959. He did so with the encouragement from the Bhutanese Princess, Tshul khrims dpal mo. Finnegan compiled an English translation of the text on refuge that the Karmapa composed in 1959 at the request of Princess Jetsun Tsulpal Chok (see Finnegan, *Dharma King*, 130–135). The Tibetan original is possibly the text mentioned in Khra 'gu's account.

51. Khra 'gu rin po che, *rgyal ba'i dbang po*, 365.16–366.2; Tshul khrims rgya mtsho, "rig pa'i rdo rje," 44.5–44.10; rDzogs chen dpon slob, "rig pa'i rdo rje," 284.13–284.18; Zhwa dmar, *sku tshe'i rnam thar*, 96.5–96.12; Grags pa yongs 'dus, "bcu drug pa," 370.5–370.7; Sherap Phuntsok, "Rangjung Rigpe Dorje," 175; Jamgon Kongtrul Rinpoche, "XVI Gyalwa Karmapa," 14, 15; Karma Thinley, "Rangjung Rigpe Dorje," 136; Kunsang and Schmidt, *Blazing Splendor*, 333.

52. Zhwa dmar, *sku tshe'i rnam thar*, 96.5–96.12; Grags pa yongs 'dus, "bcu drug pa," 370.5–370.7; Jamgon Kongtrul Rinpoche, "XVI Gyalwa Karmapa," 14; Kunsang and Schmidt, *Blazing Splendor*, 333.

53. Khra 'gu rin po che, *rgyal ba'i dbang po*, 366.2–366.4; Tshul khrims rgya mtsho, "rig pa'i rdo rje," 44.11–44.12; Karma Thinley, "Rangjung Rigpe Dorje," 136.

54. Zhwa dmar, *sku tshe'i rnam thar*, 96.12–97.10.

55. *Recalling a Buddha*; Sherap Phuntsok, "Rangjung Rigpe Dorje," 174; Surya Das, "Black Crown Lama," 5.

56. Zhwa dmar, *sku tshe'i rnam thar*, 87.9–87.16.

57. Khra 'gu rin po che, *rgyal ba'i dbang po*, 370.17–372.4; Tshul khrims rgya mtsho, "rig pa'i rdo rje," 45.8–45.17; rDzogs chen dpon slob, "rig pa'i rdo rje," 285.11–286.1; Blo gros don yod, "rig pa'i rdo rje'i," 552.15–553.4; Rang byung rig pa'i rdo rje, "rang rnam bsdus pa," 65.23–66.2; Sherap Phuntsok, "Rangjung Rigpe Dorje," 174–175; Kunsang and Aubèle, "Sixteenth Karmapa," 223; Brown, *Dance of 17 Lives*, 51; *The Lion's Roar*.

58. Khra 'gu rin po che, *rgyal ba'i dbang po*, 377.16–377.19; Zhwa dmar, *sku tshe'i rnam thar*, 97.10–97.13; Tshul khrims rgya mtsho, "rig pa'i rdo rje," 46.6–46.7; Grags pa yongs 'dus, "bcu drug pa," 373.18–374.5; Jamgon Kongtrul Rinpoche, "XVI Gyalwa Karmapa," 15; Douglas and White, *Black Hat Lama*, 121.

59. Zhwa dmar, *sku tshe'i rnam thar*, 97.13–98.3.

60. Khra 'gu rin po che, *rgyal ba'i dbang po*, 329.8–329.11; bKra shis tshe ring, "'jig rten dbang phyug," 27.1–27.3; 'Jam dbyangs tshul khrims, "rig pa'i rdo rje," 230.14–230.15; 'Ju chen thub bstan rnam rgyal, "rgyal dbang karma pa," 323.8–323.11; Blo gros don yod, "rig pa'i rdo rje'i," 546.1–546.5; Shes bya, "bzod par dka' ba'i," 226.18–226.20; rDzogs chen dpon slob, "rig pa'i rdo rje," 278.2–278.7; Sherap Phuntsok, "Rangjung Rigpe Dorje," 171; Terhune, *Karmapa*, 97, 98; Jamgon Kongtrul Rinpoche, "XVI Gyalwa Karmapa," 7; Douglas and White, *Black Hat Lama*, 109; Kunsang and Aubèle, "Sixteenth Karmapa," 205; Dzogchen Ponlop, "Rangjung Rigpe Dorje," 290.

61. Khra 'gu rin po che, *rgyal ba'i dbang po*, 330.9–331.4; bKra shis tshe ring, "'jig rten dbang phyug," 27.13–27.14; 'Ju chen thub bstan rnam rgyal, "rgyal dbang karma pa," 324.6–324.9; 'Jam dbyangs tshul khrims, "rig pa'i rdo rje," 231.10–231.12; Blo gros don yod, "rig pa'i rdo rje'i," 546.5–546.8; mKhas btsun bzang po, "rig pa'i rdo rje," 135.13–135.17; Shes bya, "bzod par dka' ba'i," 227.8–227.9; rDzogs chen dpon slob, "rig pa'i rdo rje," 278.11–278.13; Jamgon Kongtrul Rinpoche, "XVI Gyalwa Karmapa," 7; Douglas and White, *Black Hat Lama*, 109; Karma Thinley, "Rangjung Rigpe Dorje," 130; Holmes, *Gyalwa Karmapa*, 24; Kunsang and Aubèle, "Sixteenth Karmapa," 206; Lhundup Damchö, *Karmapa: 900 years*, 81; Brown, *Dance of 17 Lives*, 39; Levine, Introduction, xxii; Dzogchen Ponlop, "Rangjung Rigpe Dorje," 291.

62. Khra 'gu rin po che, *rgyal ba'i dbang po*, 331.12–331.14, 335.9–336.5; bKra shis tshe ring, "'jig rten dbang phyug," 29.1–29.3; 'Ju chen thub bstan rnam rgyal, "rgyal dbang karma pa," 324.13–324.19; 'Jam dbyangs tshul khrims, "rig pa'i rdo rje," 232.7–232.11; Tshul khrims rgya mtsho, "rig pa'i rdo rje," 38.1–38.6; Blo gros don yod, "rig pa'i rdo rje'i," 547.1–547.7; Karma rgyal mtshan, "rgyal dbang karma

pa," 70.2–70.7; mKhas btsun bzang po, "rig pa'i rdo rje," 136.13–136.21; Rum bteg, "rnam thar lo rgyus," 220.11–220.16; Shes bya, "bzod par dka' ba'i," 227.16–227.17; Rin chen dpal bzang, "rig pa'i rdo rje," 270.13–271.6; rDzogs chen dpon slob, "rig pa'i rdo rje," 279.22–280.6; Jamgon Kongtrul Rinpoche, "XVI Gyalwa Karmapa," 8; Douglas and White, *Black Hat Lama*, 110; Karma Thinley, "Rangjung Rigpe Dorje," 130; Holmes, *Gyalwa Karmapa*, 24; Pardee, Skolnick and Swanson, *Sacred Prophecy*, 45; Kunsang and Aubèle, "Sixteenth Karmapa," 207; Dzogchen Ponlop, "Rangjung Rigpe Dorje," 219.

63. Khra 'gu rin po che, *rgyal ba'i dbang po*, 336.11–336.13, 339.10–340.4, 346.1–346.5; Zhwa dmar, *sku tshe'i rnam thar*, 34.15–35.3, 35.8–35.11; bKra shis tshe ring, "'jig rten dbang phyug," 30.4–30.15, 33.16–34.12; Grags pa yongs 'dus, "bcu drug pa," 362.3–363.11, 365.1–365.18; Blo gros don yod, "rig pa'i rdo rje'i," 547.11–548.7, 549.3–549.6; mKhas btsun bzang po, "rig pa'i rdo rje," 138.3–138.4, 138.12–138.13, 139.5–139.15; Tshul khrims rgya mtsho, "rig pa'i rdo rje," 38.7–39.2; Rin chen dpal bzang, "rig pa'i rdo rje," 271.7–271.13; rDzogs chen dpon slob, "rig pa'i rdo rje," 280.11–280.13, 280.17–281.8; Rum bteg, "rnam thar lo rgyus," 220.18–221.9; 'Ju chen thub bstan rnam rgyal, "rgyal dbang karma pa," 325.4–325.9; 'Jam dbyangs tshul khrims, "rig pa'i rdo rje," 234.10, 235.9–235.10; Karma rgyal mtshan, "rgyal dbang karma pa," 70.9–70.13, 70.16–70.17; Shes bya, "bzod par dka' ba'i," 227.21–227.23; Rin chen dpal bzang, "rig pa'i rdo rje," 271.16–271.20; Sherap Phuntsok, "Rangjung Rigpe Dorje," 172; Terhune, *Karmapa*, 101, 104; Jamgon Kongtrul Rinpoche, "XVI Gyalwa Karmapa," 8–9, 9–10; Karma Thinley, "Rangjung Rigpe Dorje," 131, 132; Douglas and White, *Black Hat Lama*, 111, 113, 114; Karma Thinley, "Rangjung Rigpe Dorje," 129, 132; Holmes, *Gyalwa Karmapa*, 24, 25, 26; Pardee, Skolnick and Swanson, *Sacred Prophecy*, 45; Kunsang and Aubèle, "Sixteenth Karmapa," 205, 211, 212; Kunsang and Schmidt, *Blazing Splendor*, 190; Brown, *Dance of 17 Lives*, 40–41; Dzogchen Ponlop, "Rangjung Rigpe Dorje," 290; Nydahl, *Entering the Diamond Way*, 73.

64. Khra 'gu rin po che, *rgyal ba'i dbang po*, 340.5; rDzogs chen dpon slob, "rig pa'i rdo rje," 281.7–281.8.

65. bKra shis tshe ring, "'jig rten dbang phyug," 30.15–30.16; mKhas btsun bzang po, "rig pa'i rdo rje," 138.5.

66. Khra 'gu rin po che, *rgyal ba'i dbang po*, 348.16–349.4; Zhwa dmar, *sku tshe'i rnam thar*, 36.9–36.12, 37.8–38.2; Grags pa yongs 'dus, "bcu drug pa," 366.13–367.1; Blo gros don yod, "rig pa'i rdo rje'i," 550.13–550.17; rDzogs chen dpon slob, "rig pa'i rdo rje," 281.19–281.23; mKhas btsun bzang po, "rig pa'i rdo rje," 140.1–140.4; Tshul khrims rgya mtsho, "rig pa'i rdo rje," 38.7–39.2; Rin chen dpal bzang, "rig pa'i rdo rje," 271.7–271.13; Rum bteg, "rnam thar lo rgyus," 220.18–221.5; Karma rgyal mtshan, "rgyal dbang karma pa," 70.9–70.13; Sherap Phuntsok, "Rangjung Rigpe Dorje," 173; Jamgon Kongtrul Rinpoche, "XVI Gyalwa Karmapa," 10; Karma Thinley, "Rangjung Rigpe Dorje," 132; Douglas and White, *Black Hat Lama*, 114; Holmes, *Gyalwa Karmapa*, 24, 26; Kunsang and Aubèle, "Sixteenth Karmapa," 213; Kunsang and Schmidt, *Blazing Splendor*, 190; Dzogchen Ponlop, "Rangjung Rigpe Dorje," 291; Nydahl, *Entering the Diamond Way*, 73.

67. Khra 'gu rin po che, *rgyal ba'i dbang po*, 349.8–349.9; Zhwa dmar, *sku tshe'i rnam thar*, 38.3–42.10; Jamgon Kongtrul Rinpoche, "XVI Gyalwa Karmapa," 10–11; Karma Thinley, "Rangjung Rigpe Dorje," 132.

68. Khra 'gu rin po che, *rgyal ba'i dbang po*, 349.7.

69. Khra 'gu rin po che, *rgyal ba'i dbang po*, 349.5–349.7; Blo gros don yod, "rig pa'i rdo rje'i," 550.17–550.19; rDzogs chen dpon slob, "rig pa'i rdo rje," 281.23–282.1; mKhas btsun bzang po, "rig pa'i rdo rje," 140.4–140.5; Rum bteg, "rnam thar lo rgyus," 221.3–221.5.

70. Khra 'gu rin po che, *rgyal ba'i dbang po*, 339.10, 341.21–342.1, 349.10; mKhas btsun bzang po, "rig pa'i rdo rje," 139.7.

71. Khra 'gu rin po che, *rgyal ba'i dbang po*, 352.20–353.11,355.11–355.12, 356.12–357.2,364.18–364.21; bKra shis tshe ring, "'jig rten dbang phyug," 35.12–35.13, 35.16–36.2; Grags pa yongs 'dus, "bcu drug pa," 367.16–368.1; 'Jam dbyangs tshul khrims, "rig pa'i rdo rje," 237.3–237.4; mKhas btsun bzang po, "rig pa'i rdo rje," 140.20–140.21; rDzogs chen dpon slob, "rig pa'i rdo rje," 283.2–283.4; Terhune, *Karmapa*, 106–107; Jamgon Kongtrul Rinpoche, "XVI Gyalwa Karmapa," 11, 12; Karma Thinley, "Rangjung Rigpe Dorje," 133–135; Douglas and White, *Black Hat Lama*, 115; Holmes, *Gyalwa Karmapa*, 26; Brown, *Dance of 17 Lives*, 50, 51, 59–60; Finnegan, *Dharma King*, 26; Kunsang and Aubèle, "Sixteenth Karmapa," 218.

72. Khra 'gu rin po che, *rgyal ba'i dbang po*, 360.10–360.15, 360.17–360.18; bKra shis tshe ring, "'jig rten dbang phyug," 38.3–38.5; 'Jam dbyangs tshul khrims, "rig pa'i rdo rje," 238.5–238.6; mKhas btsun bzang po, "rig pa'i rdo rje," 142.6–142.7; Jamgon Kongtrul Rinpoche, "XVI Gyalwa Karmapa," 12; Karma Thinley, "Rangjung Rigpe Dorje," 134; Douglas and White, *Black Hat Lama*, 117; Holmes, *Gyalwa Karmapa*, 26.

73. See 5.1. Dissociation from the Exile Government.

74. Khra 'gu rin po che, *rgyal ba'i dbang po*, 378.18–378.19; Finnegan, *Dharma King*, 85; *Recalling a Buddha*.

75. Rin chen dpal bzang, "rig pa'i rdo rje," 274.11–275.4; Blo gros don yod, "rig pa'i rdo rje'i," 553.4–553.10; rDzogs chen dpon slob, "rig pa'i rdo rje," 287.16–287.21; Rum bteg, "rnam thar lo rgyus," 222.8–222.11; bKra shis tshe ring, "'jig rten dbang phyug," 43.2–43.3; Sherap Phuntsok, "Rangjung Rigpe Dorje," 175.

76. *Recalling a Buddha*.

77. *da bar bka' brgyud kyi skyes chen mchog sprul mtshan nyid dang ldan pa rnams dgung na phra stabs | dbang lung zab khrid sogs 'bogs rgyu dang mdo sngags gzhung chen khag la sbyangs pa mthar son gyis gdul bya skyong tub nges bgyid dgos pa dang | phyi yi bstan pa'i 'gan yang rkang len byed dgos pa sogs kyi las 'gan sna mang la brten | 'dzam gling yul gru kun tu 'khyam bzhin gnas bzhin pa* (Rang byung rig pa'i rdo rje, "rang rnam bsdus pa," 67–68.)

Translated into English in Appendix A (page 203–204 'until now' to 'will be travelling all over the world').

78. *bshad grwar bzhugs mkhan rnams kyang rnyed bkur grags 'dod sogs tshe 'di yi che thabs kyi rjes su 'brang ba ma yin par | bsam sbyor rnam par dag pas 'khor ba la yid dbyung zhing | dge tshul slong gi sdom pa rnam dag zhus pa zhe gcig dang | gzhan don rgyal sras spyod pa rlabs chen skyong thub pa'i slad | slob sbyong yang theg chen chos kyi bslab sbyang kho na gnang rgyu dang | de mtshungs sgrub sder bzhugs mkhan rnams kyang tshe 'di'i bya gzhag blo yis btang ste | zab lam phyag*

rgya chen po | *thabs zab mo nā ro chos drug gi nyams len tshul bzhin bgyid de* | *rim gnyis kyi gdeng dang ldan pa bka' brgyud gong ma rnams kyi rnam thar la rjes su slob thub pa dgos rgyu'i go sgrig byed bzhin pas mtshon* | (Rang byung rig pa'i rdo rje, "rang rnam bsdus pa," 66.)

Translated into English in Appendix A (page 203 from 'Those who reside in the institute' to 'confidence in the Two Stages').

79. Grags pa yongs 'dus, "bcu drug pa," 378.3–378.5; bKra shis tshe ring, "'jig rten dbang phyug," 42.9–42.12; Tshul khrims rgya mtsho, "rig pa'i rdo rje," 47.1–47.4; Rum bteg, "rnam thar lo rgyus," 222.2–222.4; Rin chen dpal bzang, "rig pa'i rdo rje," 273.4–273.6; Terhune, *Karmapa*, 118; Jamgon Kongtrul Rinpoche, "XVI Gyalwa Karmapa," 14; Kunsang and Aubèle, "Sixteenth Karmapa," 223; Finnegan, *Dharma King*, 383.

80. rDzogs chen dpon slob, "rig pa'i rdo rje," 286.20–286.23; Finnegan, *Dharma King*, 442.

A brief introduction of the retreat centre in *The Lion's Roar*.

81. Grags pa yongs 'dus, "bcu drug pa," 378.5–378.6; Jamgon Kongtrul Rinpoche, "XVI Gyalwa Karmapa," 14; Brown, *Dance of 17 Lives*, 87.

82. rDzogs chen dpon slob, "rig pa'i rdo rje," 286.23–287.6.

83. Chödrak Gyatso established the first monastic college in the Karma Kagyu lineage that combines the teachings of Mahāyāna and Vajrayāna in its curriculum, as well as several other important colleges that attracted students from China, India, Nepal and Mongolia (see 噶玛钨金, "确札嘉措," 76).

84. Interview with Dzogchen Ponlop in *Recalling a Buddha*.

85. *Recalling a Buddha*.

86. Interview with Gene Smith in *Recalling a Buddha*.

87. Khra 'gu rin po che, *rgyal ba'i dbang po*, 376.1–376.5, 376.8–376.14, 376.17–376.19, 378.19–378.20, 379.1–379.2, 379.20–380.1, 380.7–380.8, 383.2–383.5; Rin chen dpal bzang, "rig pa'i rdo rje," 273.6; Rang byung rig pa'i rdo rje, "rang rnam bsdus pa," 66.4–66.7; Grags pa yongs 'dus, "bcu drug pa," 373.13–373.17, 375.2–375.3; Sherap Phuntsok, "Rangjung Rigpe Dorje," 175; Jamgon Kongtrul Rinpoche, "XVI Gyalwa Karmapa," 15; Douglas and White, *Black Hat Lama*, 121.

88. Khra 'gu rin po che, *rgyal ba'i dbang po*, 373.7–373.13, 377.1–377.4, 377.19–377.21, 379.4–379.7, 379.19–379.20, 382.18–382.19, 383.2–383.5, 383.15–383.17; Rang byung rig pa'i rdo rje, "rang rnam bsdus pa," 66.7–66.11, 66.23–67.3, 67.1; Rin chen dpal bzang, "rig pa'i rdo rje," 273.7–273.12, 273.20–273.21; Rum bteg, "rnam thar lo rgyus," 221.18–221.19, 222.4–222.8, 223.5–223.6; Grags pa yongs 'dus, "bcu drug pa," 377.3–377.6, 378.7–378.10; rDzogs chen dpon slob, "rig pa'i rdo rje," 286.12–286.14, 287.7–287.11; Blo gros don yod, "rig pa'i rdo rje'i," 552.7–552.10; Zhwa dmar, *sku tshe'i rnam thar*, 60.11–61.4, 106.5–106.16; 'Ju chen thub bstan rnam rgyal, "rgyal dbang karma pa," 325.22–326.1; bKra shis tshe ring, "'jig rten dbang phyug," 43.1–43.2; Karma rgyal mtshan, "rgyal dbang karma pa," 71.7–71.9, 71.17–71.18, 71.1–71.2; Sherap Phuntsok, "Rangjung Rigpe Dorje," 175; Jamgon Kongtrul Rinpoche, "XVI Gyalwa Karmapa," 14–15, 17, 19; Douglas and White, *Black Hat Lama*, 121; Pardee, Skolnick and Swanson, *Sacred Prophecy*, 45–46.

146 Chapter 6

89. Rin chen dpal bzang, "rig pa'i rdo rje," 273.11–273.12; Rum bteg, "rnam thar lo rgyus," 222.7–222.8; Karma rgyal mtshan, "rgyal dbang karma pa," 72.1–72.2; Sherap Phuntsok, "Rangjung Rigpe Dorje," 175; Jamgon Kongtrul Rinpoche, "XVI Gyalwa Karmapa," 14; Kalu Rinpoche, *The Dharma: That illuminates all beings impartially like the light of the sun and the moon* (Albany: State University of New York Press, 1986), 11.

90. For example, the First to Fifth, Seventh, Eighth and Fourteenth incarnations. See Kagyu Office, "Faults of Sectarianism"; Kagyu Office, "4th Karmapa Rölpai Dorje"; Kagyu Office, "Fifth Karmapa Deshin Shekpa"; Kagyu Office, "Karmapa Deshin Shekpa"; 噶玛善莲, "明成祖," 77; 噶玛善莲, "六百年," 86; 噶玛钨金, "特秋多杰," 92–94; 噶玛钨金, "让炯多杰," 35; 噶玛钨金, "德新谢巴," 60, 61; 噶玛钨金, "确札嘉措," 73, 74.

91. Khra 'gu rin po che, *rgyal ba'i dbang po*, 335.9–335.10.

92. Khra 'gu rin po che, *rgyal ba'i dbang po*, 339.5–339.6, 356.1–356.3.

93. Khra 'gu rin po che, *rgyal ba'i dbang po*, 343.17–343.18, 351.16–351.18, 352.2–352.4, 360.18–360.19; bKra shis tshe ring, "'jig rten dbang phyug," 35.4–35.7, 38.6–38.8; rDzogs chen dpon slob, "rig pa'i rdo rje," 281.14–281.18; 'Jam dbyangs tshul khrims, "rig pa'i rdo rje," 236.11–236.12, 238.6–238.7; mKhas btsun bzang po, "rig pa'i rdo rje," 140.7–140.9, 142.7–142.9; Shes bya, "bzod par dka' ba'i," 227.19–227.21; Jamgon Kongtrul Rinpoche, "XVI Gyalwa Karmapa," 12; Karma Thinley, "Rangjung Rigpe Dorje," 131, 132, 134; Douglas and White, *Black Hat Lama*, 115, 117; Holmes, *Gyalwa Karmapa*, 25; Pardee, Skolnick and Swanson, *Sacred Prophecy*, 45; Kunsang and Schmidt, *Blazing Splendor*, 266–269, 272–273; Kunsang and Aubèle, "Sixteenth Karmapa," 217; Dzogchen Ponlop, "Rangjung Rigpe Dorje," 291; Brown, *Dance of 17 Lives*, 236; Terhune, *Karmapa*, 106; Finnegan, *Dharma King*, 40–41.

94. Khra 'gu rin po che, *rgyal ba'i dbang po*, 352.13–352.19; bKra shis tshe ring, "'jig rten dbang phyug," 35.7–35.9; Grags pa yongs 'dus, "bcu drug pa," 367.2–367.4; mKhas btsun bzang po, "rig pa'i rdo rje," 140.10–140.12; Jamgon Kongtrul Rinpoche, "XVI Gyalwa Karmapa," 11; Karma Thinley, "Rangjung Rigpe Dorje," 132–133; Douglas and White, *Black Hat Lama*, 115; Holmes, *Gyalwa Karmapa*, 26.

95. For example, the Karmapa identified the grandson of Dilgo Khyentse as the reincarnation of his three late teachers in one: Shechen Kongtrul, Shechen Rabjam and Shechen Gyaltsap. (See Kunsang and Aubèle, "Sixteenth Karmapa," 225–226, 304.)

96. Rang byung rig pa'i rdo rje, "rang rnam bsdus pa," 64.9–64.10, 66.10; Rang byung rig pa'i rdo rje, "gsungs bshad," 16.8.

97. Rang byung rig pa'i rdo rje, "rgyal dbang bcu drug pa rang byung rig pa'i rdo rje mchog gi bka' slob," in *rgyal dbang karma pa bcu drug pa chen po'i gsung 'bum 3*, ed. Jo sras bkra shis tshe ring (Dharamsala: Tshurphu Labrang; The Amnye Machen Institute, 2016), 20.14–20.15.

98. *gtan bde'i lam bzang rgyal bstan rin po che sgo kun nas dar rgyas spel gsum gyi thabs lam gsar du gtod pa'i dus skabs gzi brjid dang ldan pa zhig yin . . . bod chos ldan ljongs su | thog mar chos rgyal mes dbon rnam gsum nas | ris su ma chad pa'i bstan pa yongs kyi mnga' bdag gong sa skyabs mgon sku phreng bcu bzhi pa mchog*

gi bar gdul bya gang 'dul gyi ngor yongs su grags pa'i chos lugs kyi rnam dbye bzhir phye ba las 'bab don gtan du bde ba mi gnas pa'i myang 'das kyi go 'phang nyid 'thob bya'i dmigs yul gcig tu nges pa ltar | chos byed tshang mas thugs snang dkar 'jam yug gcig gis mthun 'brel dam zab gnang grub pa zhu rgyu | 'phags yul gyi phyogs su bka' brgyud kyi khongs | kam tshang | 'bri stag | 'brug pa | 'ba' shang sogs kyi bla sprul re gnyis phebs grub pa ma gtogs | gzhan rnams rgya dmar btsan 'og tu lus par brten bstan pa me ro slar yang gso thabs dka' ba lta bu'i nyams rgud ci che 'di la chos byed yin tshad kyis do snang skyabs 'dzin grub pa dang | ma 'ongs par rgyal bstan rin po che dar khyab yun gnas gang zag la rag las . . . phyar ba gru 'degs kyi sgo nas rgyal bstan rin po che 'di nyid 'dzin skyong spel gsum gyi thugs khul che bzhes grub pa (Rang byung rig pa'i rdo rje, "gsungs bshad," 16–17.)

    99. See 5.1. Dissociation from the Exile Government.

    100. Zhwa dmar, *sku tshe'i rnam thar*, 96.8, 97.7.

    101. See 6.1.1. Building New Rumtek.

    102. Interview with Achi Tsepal in *Recalling a Buddha*.

    103. Khra 'gu rin po che, *rgyal ba'i dbang po*, 378.16–378.17.

    104. bKra shis tshe ring, "'jig rten dbang phyug," 41.15–42.7; Lhundup Damchö, *Karmapa: 900 years*, 84; Finnegan, *Dharma King*, 120–121.

    105. Khra 'gu rin po che, *rgyal ba'i dbang po*, 383.17–383.19; Finnegan, *Dharma King*, 121.

Part IV

TRANSMISSION (II)

EXPANSION

The Karmapa's activity in the second phase of transmission directly led to the widespread development of the Karma Kagyu lineage in Europe and North America. This he achieved through two stages which are examined in detail in the last two chapters of this book. Chapter 7 focuses on the first stage. Four agents—Freda Bedi, Chögyam Trungpa, Akong Tulku and Kalu Rinpoche—prepared for the Karmapa's arrival in the West, each playing an important part in his tours. They adopted distinctively different approaches, ranging from the traditionalist to the innovative, which contributed to the diversity of the transmission. Such diversity, especially the trust the Karmapa placed in his early Western disciples, attests to his openness to adaptation. Chapter 8 investigates the second stage. It encompasses the Karmapa's three extensive Dharma tours to North America and Europe (1974–1975, 1976–1978 and 1980). On tour, the Karmapa formulated four key strategies to consolidate the development of his lineage. These strategies indicate both continuity with the preservation phase and change to adapt to new sociocultural environments. Particularly, his interfaith dialogue with the Catholic Church and engagement with the US government afforded him an opportunity to introduce Tibetan Buddhism to mainstream society.

Chapter 7

Preparing the Ground

7.1. FREDA BEDI

Freda Bedi (1911–1977) was the Karmapa's first Western disciple. She was instrumental in the early transmission of Tibetan Buddhism to the West, and in particular, the Karmapa's first tour in North America and Europe. Bedi was born in Derby, England, maiden name Freda Marie Houlston. She studied at the University of Oxford and, during that time, married Baba Pyare Lal Bedi. After graduation, she moved to India with her husband and joined him in the Indian Independence Movement. She became a political and social activist first in Lahore and later in Kashmir. In Lahore, she served as Gandhi's satyagrahi, practising non-violent resistance against the British imperial rule by voluntarily serving a prison sentence for three months.[1] In Kashmir, she formed a close friendship with Jawaharlal Nehru and his daughter Indira Gandhi.[2] After India achieved independence, she became a civil servant working in the Central Social Welfare Board under the Ministry of Education.[3]

Bedi's introduction to Buddhism began in Burma. In 1953, Nehru sent her on a six-month mission to Burma with the UN Social Services Planning Commission; there she learned meditation from a renowned Buddhist master U Titthila.[4] Then in 1956, on the occasion of the Buddha Jayanti, she met the Dalai Lama as the Indian government welcomed the Tibetan delegation in Delhi.[5] On a brief trip to Britain, she visited Buddhist centres in London and met with Christmas Humphreys, founder of the Buddhist Society.[6] These events served as a prelude to a new chapter in her life in which she found her spiritual path in Tibetan Buddhism.

In 1959, India was facing an influx of Tibetans fleeing into exile. Nehru appointed Freda Bedi as social welfare adviser on Tibetan refugees in the

Ministry of External Affairs.⁷ Bedi accepted this appointment with enthusiasm and a sense of commitment: 'I had a great wish to help them [the Tibetans] and I felt it with my particular background as a mother, social worker, and Buddhist.'⁸ She spent six months in the Tibetan refugee camps at Missamari and Buxa in West Bengal, working tirelessly for the Tibetans' resettlement.⁹ Through her connections with Nehru and Indira Gandhi, she ensured that the refugees receive immediate attention and direct support from the Indian government.¹⁰ She even persuaded Nehru to make a long trip to the Missamari camp to meet with the thousands of Tibetans there.¹¹ Her influence over the prime minister was crucial to the Indian government's handling of the Tibetan refugee situation. Because of her dedication to their welfare, the Tibetans addressed her with exceptional respect and gratitude, calling her 'Mummy'. Bedi herself recalls: 'Technically, I was Welfare Adviser to the Ministry, actually I was Mother to a camp full of soldiers, lamas, peasants and families.'¹² In 1960, she wrote an open letter to raise funds from the West for the Tibetans. This letter was reprinted in *The Middle Way*, the journal of the Buddhist Society in London, which led to the founding of the Tibetan Friendship Group.¹³ The group connected the curious and sympathetic Westerners with Tibetan monks and lamas in India with two primary goals: to render financial support to the Tibetans and to introduce Tibetan Buddhism to the West.¹⁴ For many Tibetan lamas, it initiated their first links with the West.

During her time in the refugee camps, Bedi had an opportunity to learn Tibetan Buddhism firsthand. In 1961, on a trip to Sikkim to help Tibetan refugees who just settled there, she met the Sixteenth Karmapa in Rumtek Monastery and became his first Western disciple.¹⁵ Her aspiration to preserve Tibetan Buddhism in exile grew stronger. At the start of the Tibetan diaspora, she already envisioned a future of Tibetan Buddhism spreading across the world: 'In the lamas we have inherited a tradition that dates back to the seventh century—spiritual richness we can only as yet partially realise. . . . I am sure the whole world will ultimately be enriched.'¹⁶ With this vision, she recognised the importance of the younger generation of Tibetan Buddhist leaders and teachers, especially the tulkus. To prepare them for this important task, she founded the Young Lamas' Home School to offer them a modern education alongside their traditional training.

The founding of the Young Lamas' Home School was visionary and significant. Because unlike other Buddhist countries in Asia, Tibet was never colonised by Western imperial powers. The process of modernisation and Buddhist reforms that largely influenced the modern development of Buddhism in other Asian countries never took place there. The Younghusband expedition at the start of the twentieth century introduced modernisation to Tibet, but its impact remained within the ruling class in Lhasa.¹⁷ The majority of Tibetan lamas and monks came into contact with modernity and the West for the first time only after they settled in exile. Their priority was to rebuild their tradition in the Indian subcontinent. Transmitting the Dharma to the West was, to many, unthinkable. The Young Lamas' Home School was therefore a crucial step towards the global proliferation of Tibetan Buddhism.

In 1961, the Young Lamas' Home School opened in Delhi and was relocated to Dalhousie soon afterwards. It received support from both Nehru and the Dalai Lama.[18] Enrolled there were young tulkus from all four schools of Tibetan Buddhism, aged seven to twenty-one.[19] The curriculum included a variety of subjects taught by Western volunteers, including English, French, German, Mathematics, Geography and History.[20] At the school, Bedi cared for the young tulkus with love and attentiveness. Ringu Tulku, who arrived there at the age of ten, recalls: '[Bedi was] a very kind and compassionate lady. Like a mother. We all used to call her Mummy.'[21] Frank Miller, a young Peace Corps volunteer visiting Dalhousie at the time, shares a similar observation: 'No one could visit the Dalhousie School and miss the reasons why she was known and loved as Mummy. The radiance of her warm, wry smile of Buddhist tolerance and love fitted the role of mundane and spiritual mother to all who approached her.'[22]

The modern education that the young tulkus received at the school enabled, and inspired, them to introduce Tibetan Buddhism to the West. These tulkus constituted the majority of the Tibetan lamas teaching in Europe and North America from the 1960s and 1970s.[23] Among them, four lamas contributed to the early transmission of the Karma Kagyu tradition. Chögyam Trungpa and Akong Tulku cofounded the first Tibetan Buddhist centre in Western Europe in 1967; they each made a remarkable contribution to the transmission of Tibetan Buddhism to North America and Europe, respectively. Chime Rinpoche[24] founded the first Tibetan Buddhist centre in England in 1973. Ato Rinpoche,[25] based in Cambridge, taught Buddhism privately. Chime Rinpoche's comment sheds light on the importance of the school to the transmission of Tibetan Buddhism to the West: 'Now looking back, I can see that all Tibetan Buddhism in the West was the result of her school. . . . We are all here through Sister Palmo [i.e., Freda Bedi]. All the Dharma coming to the West is rooted in Sister Palmo. . . . She is amazing.'[26] For Trungpa and Akong, Freda Bedi's support was particularly crucial. They met her upon their arrival at the Missamari refugee camp in 1960. She invited them to live in her home in Delhi and personally tutored them in the English language and culture.[27] She then placed both in the Young Lamas' Home School. At the school, she appointed Trungpa as principal and Akong as manager.[28] She recognised in Trungpa a marked potential for bringing Tibetan Buddhism to the West, and thus decided to help him receive a Western higher education. With her help, Trungpa obtained a Spalding scholarship to study at the University of Oxford.²⁹ With this arrangement, Trungpa and Akong journeyed together to Britain in 1963.

In 1966, the school transformed into a non-sectarian monastery.³⁰ In the same year, Freda Bedi arrived at Rumtek to receive novice ordination from the Karmapa, hence beginning her life as a Buddhist nun known as Sister Palmo.³¹ The Karmapa held Palmo in high esteem: he assigned a young nun to be her personal attendant, offered her a room to stay inside the monastery close to his own chamber and addressed her admiringly as 'Mummy.'³² Palmo studied and practised under his guidance and served as his secretary and adviser. The Karmapa, meanwhile, trained her to become a Buddhist teacher in her own right. He arranged for her to receive the nun's full ordination from the Chinese Buddhist tradition in Hong Kong, making her the first Western *bhikṣuṇī* in Tibetan Buddhism.³³ He also authorised her to confer Tantric initiations,³⁴ an exceptional privilege for any Western or female Buddhist teachers in the Tibetan tradition, even nowadays.

With the Karmapa's support, Sister Palmo began to travel overseas from the late 1960s. She propagated the Dharma in Southeast Asia, including Malaysia, Singapore and Thailand, and in South Africa.³⁵ Then, during and after the Karmapa's first tour to the West, she taught in Europe and North America.³⁶ Two aspects of her activity were of special significance to the transmission of Tibetan Buddhism at the time. First, she translated Tibetan texts into English to help Western practitioners break down language barriers in their study and practice.³⁷ Second, she transmitted a large number of Tantric initiations and instructions.³⁸ During these rituals, she read the Tibetan texts first, then the English translation.³⁹ For many American and British Buddhists, this meant that they were able to receive the transmission directly in their native language. Such was a rare advantage in the early years of Tibetan Buddhism in the West. A pioneer among Western Buddhist teachers, Palmo made a key contribution to the introduction of the Tibetan Tantric tradition, and in the process, facilitated the Karmapa's transmission of Tantric Buddhism on his world tours.

Sister Palmo was instrumental in initiating and organising the Karmapa's first tour to Europe and North America (1974–1975). The tour lasted for four and a half months and covered twelve different countries.⁴⁰ It was a monumental event in the initial period of transmission of Tibetan Buddhism to the West. From this tour, together with the following two that the Karmapa embarked on between 1976 and 1980, the Kagyu school reached an expansion unmatched by any other Tibetan school in the 1980s:⁴¹ over 300 Dharma centres spread across the world.⁴² By the early 1970s, Palmo's efforts on helping the young tulkus adapt to the modern world began to bear fruit: the four alumni from the Young Lamas' Home School, as mentioned earlier (Trungpa, Akong, Chime and Ato), paved the way for the Karmapa's activity in the West. The first stage in her vision of bringing Tibetan Buddhism to the West was completed. Next was for the Karmapa himself to arrive and teach. As his secretary and adviser, she encouraged him to travel to the West; she did so persistently for two years until he eventually agreed to go.[43] To prepare for the Karmapa's arrival, Palmo visited Britain in 1973 to meet with Akong and Chime, to deliver lectures and meditation instructions and to strengthen her networks with British Buddhists.[44] She also travelled to the European continent for a similar purpose.[45]

In November 1973, the Karmapa received an invitation from the Dharma Centre of Canada.[46] Formal preparations for the tour were underway. The plan was for him to visit the United States and Canada first, and then on to Europe.[47] In Rumtek, Palmo became the liaison between the Karmapa and the Dharma centres in Europe and North America.[48] She then travelled to the United States in 1974 to make further preparations.[49] There she met with Trungpa and visited his centres, and continued to deliver lectures, meditation instructions and Tantric teachings and initiations.[50] She introduced the Karmapa, the tradition of reincarnate lamas and Tibetan Buddhism to the public through interviews on newspaper, radio and television.[51] She built a relationship with Charles H. Percy,[52] a senator from Illinois, who consequently welcomed the Karmapa, both personally and on behalf of the US government, on all three of his tours to the United States. She also made the first contact with Native Americans, the Hopi community.[53] Through this contact, she initiated a meeting between its leader and the Karmapa, thereby creating an opportunity for him to engage in interfaith dialogue.

Sister Palmo accompanied the Karmapa throughout his tour in North America and Europe as the only Westerner in his entourage. She delivered public talks to prepare the audience and generate interest; she offered the introduction and explanation of rituals and teachings; she helped the Karmapa acclimate to Western culture, administered his schedules and arranged meetings and events.[54] She acted as a mentor to newcomers, offering guidance and sharing her own experience, and prepared those who were to take ordination vows from the Karmapa.[55] She also assisted the Karmapa with his interfaith efforts, including his meeting with Pope Paul VI in Rome[56] and his visit to Westminster Abbey in London where he was welcomed by Dean Edward Carpenter.[57] Through these activities, she bridged the gap between the Tibetan tradition and Western culture for the Karmapa's initial introduction to the West. In sum, Palmo's contribution to the Karmapa's activity in the West was both unique and significant. It started with a vision that Tibetan Buddhism would take root in the West. To achieve this vision, she exercised active agency in the cross-cultural exchange between Tibetan Buddhism and the West. She ranked among the first and most trusted Western disciples of the Karmapa and became an iconic figure in the global expansion of the Karma Kagyu lineage as an initiator, a facilitator and a communicator.

7.2. CHÖGYAM TRUNGPA

Chögyam Trungpa (1939–1987) was identified by the Karmapa as the Eleventh Trungpa of Surmang in the Karma Kagyu tradition. In 1959, he led a group of monks and laypersons to flee into exile, together with Akong Tulku. This turned into an arduous ten-month journey that ended with only fifteen survivors; almost 300 people died en route to India.[58] Upon arrival in India, Trungpa received support from Freda Bedi who placed him and Akong in the Young Lamas' Home School. In 1963, with the help of Bedi, his English tutor John Driver and the Tibet Society in Britain, he obtained a Spalding grant to study at the University of Oxford. The Karmapa advised him to propagate the Dharma in Britain and issued an official letter in support of his activity.[59]

In the same year, Trungpa travelled to England with Akong. At Oxford, he immersed himself in comparative religion and philosophy, yet with the ambition to 'teach and spread the Dharma'.[60] Four years later, Ananda Bodhi[61] transferred the trust deeds of Johnstone House in Scotland to him and Akong.[62] This they turned into 'Samye Ling Meditation Centre',[63] the first Tibetan Buddhist centre in Western Europe.[64] In its early years, the centre attracted several celebrities, including Leonard Cohen, David Bowie and R. D. Laing. However, in general, it developed rather haltingly. Its main followers came from the counterculture movement; their knowledge of Tibetan Buddhism was limited. Many dabbled in different Asian religions with no clear commitment to any particular tradition; only a few became Kagyu practitioners.[65] Trungpa was dissatisfied with the progress at Samye Ling, commenting that 'the scale of activity was small, and the people who did come to participate seemed to be slightly missing the point.'[66]

Ever since his arrival in India, Trungpa believed that Buddhism had the potential to flourish in the West. There, he met Westerners for the first time and held the opinion that to propagate the Dharma, he would need to study their language.[67] In 1968, the royal family of Bhutan invited him for a visit. As a part of his stay in Bhutan, he spent ten days in retreat at Taktsang where he developed a spiritual insight that became a prelude to the radical change in his approach to transmitting the Dharma. He decided to 'take daring steps' to tackle the issue of 'spiritual materialism'.[68] Back to Britain, he began to ponder how to devote himself more effectively to the dissemination of the

Dharma.[69] In 1969, a serious car accident left his left side paralysed. Shortly afterwards, he disrobed. In his own words:

> I realized that I could no longer attempt to preserve any privacy for myself, any special identity or legitimacy. I should not hide behind the robes of a monk, creating an impression of inscrutability which, for me, turned out to be only an obstacle. With a sense of further involving myself with the sangha, I determined to give up my monastic vows. More than ever I felt myself given over to serving the cause of Buddhism.[70]

To him, the decision to disrobe was a necessary step to fulfil his commitment to the Dharma. He then married his sixteen-year-old student Diana Pybus. This triggered much dissent among the students at Samye Ling.[71]

Trungpa's transmission strategy, from that point on, aimed to modernise Buddhism. This was in stark contrast to Akong's more traditionalist, progressive approach. As tension between the two increased, Akong sought arbitration from the Karmapa. According to Holmes:

> The XVIth Gyalwang Karmapa decided that although Trungpa Rinpoché may well act privately in the way he did, as a mahasiddha, it was not the right way to present the dharma in Europe and also not the way for an official Kagyu tulku to act in those circumstances, as it gave the wrong impression of the Kagyu lineage: a lineage that embraces the entire wealth of the Buddha's teachings, for the millions, and not solely the way of the 'crazy yogi', for the very few. Therefore, Trungpa Rinpoché was to be disinvested of his Kagyu status if he insisted on continuing in the same way and he could, until further notice, not be considered to be acting as a Kagyu tulku.[72]

The Karmapa clearly disapproved of Trungpa's approach.

In 1970, Trungpa left Samye Ling and moved to the United States. His autobiography does not mention the Karmapa's arbitration, but instead, explains his reason for leaving to be 'the meagre potential for genuine Buddhism in Britain at this time'.[73] His activity in the United States diverged further from the direction set out by the Karmapa and caused criticism and distrust from within the Tibetan circle. In 1973/1974, when conversing with the Hindu master Muktananda about teaching in the West, the Karmapa appeared to be disturbed about Trungpa's attempt to Westernise traditional teachings.[74] Many Tibetans expressed similar concerns; some condemned Trungpa as 'a maverick, a renegade' who had abandoned Buddhism and no longer taught the Dharma.[75] This signals Trungpa's isolation from his lineage and the Tibetan community at large.

Trungpa's activity in the United States was nonetheless very successful. He implemented his own vision of Buddhism with great impact, quickly gathering a large following. By the time of his arrival in 1970, he had published two books[76] that reached young Americans who were undergoing tremendous social change participating in the counterculture movement. The young hippies constituted the main adherents of Tibetan Buddhism and the core of Trungpa's community. To Trungpa, they 'still seemed to miss the point of Dharma, though not in the same way as in Britain, but in American free-thinking style.'[77] In response, Trungpa created two strategies, each featuring a particular stage of his activity in the United States.

Trungpa's first strategy consisted of two key components: adaptation and diversification. First, in adapting to American culture, he severed all ties with anything traditional or Tibetan; instead, he adopted a hippie lifestyle and experimented with unconventional teaching methods. He taught in fluent English and developed a warm and close relationship with his students, posing as their peer.[78] From very early on, he changed the themes of his teaching, veering from a traditional seminar on Gampopa's text to a programme called 'Work, Sex, and Money'.[79] In 1975, he founded the Nalanda Translation Committee. There he worked with a group of students to translate Tibetan texts into English so that his students could study and practise Buddhism in their own language.

To counteract his students' fascination with Tibetan Buddhism as something exotic, Trungpa introduced the Dharma in modern, Western terms. He presented Buddhism as 'an overall approach to life'[80] and invented a vocabulary aligned with psychology and poetry, free of metaphysical and philosophical jargon. For instance, he replaced the word 'enlightenment' with 'sanity', 'bewilderment' with 'neurosis'. This led him to describe the Buddhist path as 'a journey from neurosis to brilliant sanity'.[81] He taught meditation as a method to enable one to 'look directly into the nature of both wisdom and confusion'.[82] By creating the new terminology, he made his audience see the relevance of Buddhism to their everyday life. He devised a new mental health treatment, called 'Maitri Five Wisdoms', based on the concept of the Five Buddha Families in Tantric Buddhism. In the 'Mudra Space Awareness' programme, he introduced Tantric dance movements to the training of theatre performance. In this way, Tantric teachings became assimilated into American culture whereby attracting a broad range of audiences unfamiliar with Buddhism.[83]

Second, Trungpa interacted with different cultural traditions which came to be his main source of creativity. He borrowed elements from Theravāda Buddhism, Japanese Zen and English etiquette and blended Buddhist concepts with different forms of arts, including poetry, calligraphy, flower arranging, archery, theatre, film and photography. In 1974, he established the first Buddhist-inspired university in North America, Naropa Institute. The institute, in his own words, 'emphasizes the discipline of learning and the appreciation of our heritages of both the Orient and the Occident, grounded in meditation practice and commitment to personal development.'[84] To integrate different world traditions with modern culture, the institute recruited talent from a wide variety of backgrounds,[85] for example, poets Allen Ginsberg, Gary Snyder and Anne Waldman; anthropologist Gregory Bateson; physicist Jeremy Hayward; Harvard professor Ram Dass; musician John Cage; dancer Barbara Dilley; Buddhist scholar Herbert von Guenther and anthropologists/psychologists Joan Halifax and Stanislav Grof.[86]

Trungpa's efforts of adaptation and diversification produced positive results. They substantially increased his popularity as an innovative, unconventional Buddhist teacher who inspired a generation of young American Buddhists. His institution, Vajradhatu, founded in 1973, soon grew across North America and developed into a large organisation. Meanwhile, he did not step away from traditional methods completely. These he reserved for his most advanced students. After an initial introduction to 'crazy wisdom' and its sudden path,[87] he led them towards a more structured, progressive mode of training.[88] He guided students at the annual seminary to progress through the three *yāna*s that culminate in Atiyoga and Mahāmudrā.[89]

This first strategy features mainly in the first stage of Trungpa's activity in the United States, from 1970 to 1974.[90] The strategy for the second stage, beginning with the Karmapa's first visit in 1974, demonstrates, in comparison, a distinctively different character. Trungpa suddenly broke away from the hippie culture and began to introduce formalities to train his students in 'sacred outlook' (*dag snang*).[91] In preparation for the Karmapa's visit, he led his community through elaborate arrangements over a period of ten months:[92]

> It came as a shock to see their teacher work so intensely. He was quite capable at three o'clock in the morning of explaining in his soft voice how to iron the satin cloth used to cover the seat on which His Holiness would sit at Karma Dzong, the chief center in Boulder. It was the first time that most of his students had ever seen a traditional Tibetan throne, which Rinpoche insisted should be constructed in every city where the Karmapa would teach ... he toured every venue and would personally explain the significance of the particular decorations he wanted in each room where the Karmapa was going to give an initiation, meet people, and so on. Early on, he sent one of his students to Japan to buy the finest brocades for His Holiness's thrones and other uses. Then, once the brocades were received, he would meet with the seamstresses to discuss how to sew them and would personally visit them to see how the work was coming. He consulted with carpenters, painters, cooks, drivers, and others.[93]

Trungpa's attention to detail, high standard and full involvement reveal his determination to host the Karmapa in a lavish, traditional style. He also trained his students in social protocol and discipline:

Chögyam Trungpa encouraged his students, many of whom were rather disheveled at the time, to bone up on their Western etiquette, to work on their posture and polish their table manners, to press their best suit, or buy one, to find an elegant but modest dress, and to cut their hair and beards in some cases. At the same time, he gave intensive lessons in Tibetan culture and etiquette. He wanted his students to be as relaxed with and knowledgeable about the convention of making and serving Tibetan butter tea as they were with creating an English tea party or brewing and serving a good cup of coffee. To provide appropriate security and drivers for His Holiness, Rinpoche asked a group of his students to serve as guards. Their essential job was to create an appropriate environment to receive the Karmapa.[94]

The way Trungpa prepared for the Karmapa's first tour signals a radical change in his transmission strategy. While in the early years, he distanced himself from Tibetan culture and adopted a hippie lifestyle, now Trungpa began to encourage his students to conform to mainstream society and meet the expectations of the Tibetan tradition. As a result, he was able to receive the Karmapa in 1974 in such a grand manner that matched one that would suit a Chinese emperor.[95] He openly displayed devotion to the Karmapa, weeping upon meeting him and prostrating before him despite his disability,[96] which was possibly intended to show his American students how best to treat a teacher.[97]

The Karmapa visited Trungpa's Dharma centres in Arizona, California, Colorado, Massachusetts, Michigan, New Mexico, New York and Vermont. There, he performed the Black Crown Ceremony, bestowed empowerments and transmissions, conferred full ordination vows and conducted consecration rituals.[98] His first Black Crown Ceremony in New York attracted 3,000 attendees.[99] He met also with religious dignitaries, politicians, businessmen, artists and scholars.[100] Trungpa's students came to realise the significance of the Karmapa's extensive visit: 'What the Karmapa did for those of us who were students of Trungpa Rinpoche: it gave us this idea of the vastness of the tradition that he came from, so that it was not just us in this little community, our little world, but we were then joining this huge family of Tibetan Buddhist practitioners.'[101] To Trungpa's students, the Karmapa's visit deepened their understanding of the lineage and strengthened their connection to its teachings.

The Karmapa was impressed with Trungpa and his students. Trungpa himself recalls with satisfaction: 'In spite of a certain amount of uncertainty and clumsiness on the part of the students, His Holiness was extremely pleased with them and with what I had accomplished.'[102] The Karmapa told Trungpa's students that if they maintain the momentum, 'The Dharma will spread in America like wildfire on a mountain.'[103] This indicates his approval of Trungpa's approach. As a reward, he conferred on Trungpa the title 'Vajra Holder and Possessor of the Victory Banner of the Practice Lineage of the Karma Kagyü' (*rdo rje 'dzin pa karma sgrub brgyud bstan pa'i rgyal mtshan don brgyud 'chang ba*).[104] In so doing, he reinstalled Trungpa as a qualified, authentic lineage holder, marking a new era in Trungpa's activity in the West. For the first time since his departure from Samye Ling, Trungpa secured the Karmapa's approval.

Following the Karmapa's 1974 tour, Trungpa began to systematise the training of formality for his students through his introduction of the 'Shambhala Teachings'. These teachings derive from his spiritual visions of the Kingdom of Shambhala.[105] They draw on this mythical kingdom as the model for an 'enlightened society' in modern times. Trungpa explained the Shambhala Training Programme[106] as follows:

> Shambhala Training is designed and developed on the basis of training and discipline, uplifting and civilizing ourselves. . . . How we can actually be a decent, dignified, and awake human being. How to conduct ourselves properly in this society without laying trips on others or ourselves. . . . So the idea is quite a practical one in the sense that we should learn how to conduct ourselves properly to what is known as the Great Eastern Sun vision, which is the notion of perpetually looking ahead, forward.[107]

The Shambhala Training constituted a discipline of conduct that transformed Trungpa's interaction with students into a ritualised practice with a strong emphasis on formality and hierarchy. Before then, Trungpa dressed casually as a 'jolly fellow' indulging in the hippie culture; from this point on, he 'manifested as a king, a completely regal presence.'[108] Thus trained, Trungpa's community continued to organise the following tours of the Karmapa in a grand manner:

> The elegance and splendour so exquisitely created with loving devotion by Chögyam Trungpa and the Vajradhatu organisation, was carried throughout all three tours in 1974, 1977, and 1980. There were grand receptions with lavish displays, such as at the Park Plaza hotel in New York where the entire top floor was booked for the occasion; sumptuous and regal venues for the Black Crown, like the world-famous Lincoln Centre; palatial mansions where His Holiness was hosted by people who were rulers in their own realms. The 16th Karmapa was welcomed like a Universal Monarch at the centre of this magnificent mandala.[109]

Through these lavish arrangements, Trungpa and his American students demonstrated to the West the religious prestige of the Karmapa.

The Karmapa's trust and confidence in Trungpa continued to grow. In 1976, during a television interview, he says that he feels encouraged by Trungpa's activity; it inspired him to establish a monastic seat in the United States. He recommends Trungpa's centres to the viewers who are interested in learning more about Buddhism and the Kagyu teachings.[110] In another interview when visiting New York in 1980, he tells that he is impressed by the discipline of Trungpa's students at Dharmadhatu.[111] Furthermore, he announced his support for the appointment of Trungpa's regent, Ösel Tendzin.[112] In *The Rain of Wisdoms*,[113] he praised Trungpa as the sun that radiates the precious Kagyu teachings all over the world (*bka' brgyud kyi bstan pa rin po che 'dzam gling rgyal khab yongs la nyi ma ltar gsal bar byed pa*).[114]

The dramatic change in Trungpa's transmission strategies between 1970 and 1980 may have been strategic after all. It is possible that Trungpa severed ties with tradition to seek freedom to experiment with novel ideas and methods with a particular purpose in mind: to communicate effectively with his American students the majority of whom came from the counterculture generation. He acted as their peer in order to guide them through a transformation so that they would eventually embrace tradition and, at the same time, appreciate their own culture again and re-enter mainstream society. Ultimately, he prepared his students for the formal transmission of the lineage from the Karmapa on tour.

7.3. AKONG TULKU

Akong Tulku (1940–2013) was identified by the Karmapa as the Second Akong of Dolma Lhakang Monastery in Eastern Tibet.[115] In 1959, he joined Trungpa to take flight into exile. Upon arrival in India, he and Trungpa received support from Freda Bedi who placed both in the Young Lamas' Home School. In 1963, he accompanied Trungpa to Britain. Prior to his departure, the Karmapa asked him to teach Tibetan medicine in the West.[116] In Oxford, while Trungpa was studying, Akong worked as a hospital porter to cover their living expense. In 1967, the two cofounded Samye Ling in Scotland. Three years later, Trungpa left for the United States to further his own vision of the Dharma. Akong stayed on and gradually developed Samye Ling into a traditional Tibetan Buddhist monastery with affiliated Dharma centres across Europe and in Africa. Over the years, he invited Buddhist teachers from different Tibetan schools as well as the Theravāda and Zen traditions to teach at Samye Ling; he worked with psychiatrists to develop a new therapy treatment based on Buddhist practice;[117] he also continued to practise Tibetan medicine[118] and deeply engaged in humanitarian activities.[119] In 2011, the British Home Secretary awarded Akong the '60 years, 6 people' accolade to honour the contribution that he, as a former refugee, had made to the country.[120]

Akong's approach to the transmission of Tibetan Buddhism was traditionalist and progressive in nature. He did not wish to adapt Buddhist doctrines and practices to Western culture. The Karmapa and senior lamas in the Kagyu school supported his stance, as Holmes reports:

> This tradition-based orientation was to be confirmed again and again, first by Kalu Rinpoché, during his 1970 visits, then by the Karmapa during his 1974 and 1977 visits, later by the Tai Situpa and Khenchen Thrangu Rinpoché, throughout the 1980s and 1990s and subsequently by all our visiting teachers. . . . Akong Rinpoché had made the correct choice . . . for Europe, at least.[121]

Akong laid out his vision through three main objectives for Samye Ling: 'to preserve and protect Tibetan culture and religion', 'to promote the buddhadharma' and 'in particular, to preserve and promote the teachings of the Kagyu lineage and especially those of the Karma Kamtsang line.'[122] With preservation as the central focus of his activity, he considered lineage identity a top priority.

Akong strove to protect tradition which he emphasised in his training of students. He invited Karma Kagyu lineage holders to give Tantric teachings at Samye Ling. To build a Buddhist college there, he sought advice from the Karmapa, Kalu Rinpoche and Thrangu Rinpoche on the choice of texts to teach; he invited Tsultrim Gyamtso and Thrangu to teach in the college; he also sent his students, Ken and Katia Holmes, to study and translate Tibetan texts into English.[123] To introduce the tradition of long retreat, he consulted the Karmapa and visited Kalu's retreat centre in France. He spent three years preparing his students for the retreat, and then in 1984 launched the first retreat programme at Samye Ling, introducing, for the first time, the long retreat of the Karma Kagyu tradition to the West.[124] Furthermore, Akong attached great importance to the gradual path that progresses through the three *yānas*. At Samye Ling, he instigated a ten-year training programme. The students must spend the first four years studying traditional texts. These include Tibetan texts Gampopa's *Ornament of Precious Liberation* (*Dwags po thar rgyan*), Mipham Rinpoche's *Entering the Ways of the Wise* (*mKhas pa'i mtshul la 'jug pa'i sgo*) and Jamgön Kongtrül Lodrö Thayé's *Torch of Certainty* (*Nges don sgron me*), as well as classical Indian texts, such as Śāntideva's *Entering the Way of the Bodhisattva*[125] (*Bodhisattvacaryāvatāra*) and Asaṅga's *Mahāyāna Uttaratantra Shastra* (*Ratnagotravibhāga Mahāyānottaratantra Śāstra*). The students then would practise in retreat for the next four years. This is followed by two more years of study on post-retreat texts, in particular, the Third Karmapa's *Profound Inner Meaning* (*Zab mo nang don*) and the Hevajra commentary.[126]

Akong developed Samye Ling into a traditional Tibetan Buddhist monastery. He did so in a cautious and gradual manner for long-term impact. Initially, he was reluctant to assume the role of a Buddhist teacher, but instead, acted as an administrator of the fledgling community there.[127] It was only when the Karmapa granted him the honorary title *Dharmacharya* during his visit in 1974 that Akong took up the leadership of Samye Ling as its abbot.[128] Still, before the Karmapa's second visit to Europe in 1977, ten years after Samye Ling was founded, he was, as Holmes recalls, 'very, very unsure of the future of Tibetan Buddhism in the UK and the West.'[129] This began to change after he witnessed a positive public response to the Karmapa's visit and personally received his advice. He then launched the Samye Project, a construction plan for a traditional temple, libraries, lecture rooms and museums in Samye Ling.[130] At the centre of the Samye Project was the construction of the Main Temple which he spent ten years, from 1978 to 1988, completing.[131]

Akong played an important role in the Karmapa's two tours in Europe (1974–1975 and 1977–1978). In 1974, the Karmapa arrived in Britain after completing an extensive visit to North America. His following itinerary included Denmark, France, Germany, Italy, Netherlands, Norway, Sweden and Switzerland.[132] Prior to the Karmapa's arrival, Akong emphasised to his students the significance of this visit and led them through elaborate preparations.[133] The Karmapa spent three weeks at Samye Ling where he conferred refuge, vows, empowerments and teachings. He performed the Black Crown Ceremony three times in a village nearby, Eskdalemuir, and once in Edinburgh.[134] During that time, Holmes noticed a close bond between the Karmapa and Akong.[135] After Samye Ling, the Karmapa travelled to London.[136] Then, in Birmingham, Manchester and Essex, he performed again the Black Crown Ceremony.[137] Thereafter, Akong accompanied him to France and Italy. In France, he helped the Dharma centre in Paris to prepare for the Karmapa's arrival and arranged his visit to Dordogne where Bernard Benson had recently donated land. In Italy, he attended the Karmapa's private audience with Pope Paul VI.[138]

The Karmapa's second tour in Europe lasted for seven months, from June 1977 to January 1978.[139] Akong organised the entire tour,[140] preparing the Karmapa's stays in over twenty destinations in Austria, Belgium, Britain, Denmark, France, Germany, Netherlands, Norway, Sweden and Switzerland.[141] Organising the Karmapa's tour in Europe was, in many ways, more challenging than in the United States. By the time the Karmapa conducted his first US tour in 1974, Trungpa had already established a large institution with Dharma centres that spread across the country. He could draw on these to organise the tour. In comparison, Akong's Samye Ling was a traditional Dharma centre with a moderate number of followers; its influence had yet to reach the Continent. It was during the Karmapa's tour that his students began to open new Samye Ling branches in other European countries: one in Brussels (Belgium) and one in Barcelona (Spain).[142] Even so, Akong's resources remained limited; he was only able to marshal a small team to work with him for the tour. To make the Karmapa's travels across Europe easier and more cost-effective, he converted a second-hand bus.[143] The exterior of the bus was painted in maroon colour, bearing the Karmapa's emblem.[144]

Akong assisted the Karmapa in the creation of his European monastic seat. At the start of the tour, he arranged to meet with Benson to discuss the acquisition of land in Dordogne where the monastery was to be built.[145] Later on, the Karmapa returned to Dordogne to consecrate the new centre, Dhagpo Kagyu Ling.[146] He also arranged for the Karmapa to meet with political and Christian leaders.[147] In addition, he personally stepped in to protect the Karmapa. Holmes reports several instances where the Karmapa faced hostility. In one such threat, Akong intervened himself:

> [A] psychotic person broke into the Karmapa's company, smoking a cigarette. It was frightening yet fearlessly Rinpoché tackled him, removed the cigarette and extinguished it by grinding it into his own hand and then escorted the person out of the room. The same man turned up again later, in Scotland, where it took five policemen and three police doctor's injections to subdue him. Akong Rinpoché was fearless and did not hesitate for one moment to put his own life on the line to protect His Holiness.[148]

In the United States, Trungpa had trained a group of students to serve as the Karmapa's guards; Akong, lacking in resources, took on this task himself, at least here.

The Karmapa set out to consolidate the traditional training of his European devotees. He called on Khenpo Tsultrim Gyamtso from Rumtek to teach on the tour, so that he himself could focus on the conferral of refuge, bodhisattva vows and empowerments.[149] He instructed Akong's disciples, Ken and Katia Holmes, to study the Tibetan language with Tsultrim Gyamtso[150] and asked Katia to serve as his interpreter in Belgium.[151] At Akong's request, he allowed Tsultrim Gyamtso to continue to teach in Dordogne after his departure. This led to the launch of a six-month intensive course, studying Gampopa's *Ornament of Precious Liberation* and Asaṅga's *Mahāyāna Uttaratantra Shastra*. The students in this course translated the two texts into English; many of them were to become Tibetan language translators and interpreters.[152]

Holmes recalls two instances that shed light further on Akong's indispensable role in the Karmapa's transmission of the lineage. First, Akong grew concerned about Ole Nydahl, the Karmapa's European disciple who had opened a few Dharma centres in Scandinavia and begun to teach the Dharma in Europe with the Karmapa's consent.[153] He expressed his concern to Holmes on several occasions: 'He [Nydahl] will be very helpful for beginners but if it goes to his head and he tries to do more, it could be dangerous.'[154] Jamgon Kongtrul too was worried: he made similar remarks to Holmes and expressed sadness and disapproval.[155] When the Karmapa was invited to propagate the Dharma in southern Africa, he sent Nydahl to give elementary teachings. Nydahl, however, used this opportunity to fashion himself as the 'Representative of the Karmapa in Africa'. The Karmapa rebutted this appropriation of rank and appointed Akong as his official representative in Africa.[156] Second, Akong led the preparation of the monastery in Dordogne for the Karmapa's visit. Having noticed that the two resident Tibetan lamas, Lama Gendun Rinpoché and the Karmapa's nephew Jigme-la, lacked focus and leadership:

> [Akong] Rinpoché set to work with extreme diligence, not shying from any physical task, much to the surprise of the community who had seen their resident Tibetans as brilliant examples of inactivity, physically. The catalytic effect of Rinpoché's industry awakened an enthusiasm in the group and they joined in more and more. Further, Rinpoché started giving talks to make it clearer how significant the Karmapa's visit would be and how everything had to be done to make it a success. A new dynamic emerged and the centre ended up ready for His Holiness.[157]

With Akong's organisation and assistance, the Karmapa's tour in Europe became successful. Towards the end of the tour, in December 1977, at the request of Akong's students, the Karmapa composed a long-life prayer for him:[158]

> Spreading everywhere the sublime activity of the lineage that transmits realisation of absolute truth, and wearing the armour of pure intention rooted in bodhicitta, you care for beings and look after them. You clearly manifest the teachings of the realisation tradition, fully matured within you. May the truth of your aspirations endure forever.
> Holding and upholding the teaching of the practice lineage of the four transmissions and following the profound example of the extraordinary lives of the great masters of our tradition, you nurture beings. Through the power of the truth of your former good deeds, aspirations and prayers, may forever shine this sun whose lights illuminate the teachings of the Victorious One.
> Working with inexhaustible clarity of intelligence in an infinity of places, you manifest all sorts of extraordinary skills and qualities in order to conquer the thick darkness of ignorance which obscures the essential nature of beings. We pray that this buddha-emanation which gives us certainty of our own buddha-nature may live long among us.[159]

This prayer expresses in full the Karmapa's confidence in Akong and acknowledgement of his achievements in the West.

7.4. KALU RINPOCHE

Kalu Rinpoche (1905–1989) was identified by several eminent lamas[160] as the reincarnation of the activity of Jamgön Kongtrül Lodrö Thayé. Due to his father's intervention, however, he was never enthroned. He received the title of Khenpo (*mkhan po*) at the age of eleven and entered his first three-year retreat at sixteen. Two years after completing the retreat, he began a fifteen-year-long solitary practice. Thereafter, at Situ's request, Kalu began to establish and supervise retreat centres.[161] The Bhutanese Princess, Ashe Wangmo,[162] became a devoted student. She requested the Karmapa to appoint Kalu as abbot of Jangchub Choling Monastery; the Karmapa agreed and sent him to Bhutan in 1957.[163] Kalu then founded retreat centres in Dalhusy,[164] Tso Pema and Madhya Pradesh.[165] In 1966, he settled in Samdrup Darjayling Monastery in Sonada.[166] Retreat was a focal theme throughout Kalu's life, not only in the Himalayas but also later in the West. Between 1971 and 1982, he travelled abroad five times to Europe, North America and Asia where he established over seventy Dharma centres and twenty retreat locations.[167] His students remember him for his optimism, humour, warmth, openness and communication skills.[168] The Dalai Lama praised Kalu: '[O]f all the lamas working to spread the Dharma throughout the world, there was none whose activity and kindness were greater than that of [Kalu] Rinpoche.'[169]

Kalu was one of the earliest Tibetan lamas in exile to attract Western students. He was among the few who advocated the propagation of Tibetan Buddhism in the West. On account of his contact with Westerners in India, he believed that 'Tibetan Buddhism was more universal than just Tibetan and that Westerners could also find a spiritual nourishment within it.'[170] As early as 1970, in consultation with the Karmapa, he sent his close disciple Lama Gyaltsen on an exploratory visit to Europe and the United States.[171] At that time, most Tibetans in India had little knowledge of the West:

> Tibetans had a blurred idea of the West. For them, because it was so far away, it was almost a mythical land from which no one returned. To go there was to disappear. When people close to Lama Gyaltsen knew he was getting ready for this great journey, they were astonished. What strange reason could persuade him to undertake such a crazy adventure? He simply replied that the only reason for his departure was the request made by Kalu Rinpoche and the Karmapa.[172]

This was the time when many Tibetans were still not ready to embrace the idea of disseminating the Dharma in the West.

Gyaltsen's trip proved to be fruitful. His observation in the United States gives positive indications:

> He, especially, had begun to understand the Western paradox: a material comfort, unbelievable to an Easterner, accompanied by a strong inner discomfort. Many of his new friends had no religion, but he felt their need for something although their search was largely undefined. . . . He particularly insisted on the notion that, according to Buddhism, all beings possess the seed of Buddhahood, the potential of becoming awakened, an idea that often provoked certain interest.[173]

This observation signals a potential opportunity for Tibetans to establish their Buddhist tradition in the West. On his return to India, Gyaltsen shared his findings with the Karmapa: to propagate the Dharma in the West, they needed a lama with spiritual accomplishment, not a scholar.[174] The Karmapa followed his advice: 'If Kalu Rinpoche can go to the West, he will certainly accomplish much benefit. He is a real bodhisattva and his realization is very great.'[175] Nonetheless, other lamas were sceptical, because, unlike Trungpa and Akong, Kalu was neither young nor well informed about Western culture. Still, Kalu himself remained optimistic.[176] In 1971, in response to his Western disciples' request, he began his first visit to the West; he toured Italy and France, then the United States and Canada.[177] Especially, from his visits to the United States, he gained more confidence in transmitting Buddhism to the West: the country offered, as he discovered, 'personal freedom for one to practice the religion of one's choice and for religions to establish themselves, even though they may be very new to this country.'[178]

Kalu showed interest in Christianity, which helped him understand Western culture. He was among the first Tibetan lamas to participate in the interfaith dialogue in the West. Prior to his travel to Europe, he had already read about Christianity and expressed a wish to meet with its priests; this, however, baffled many Tibetans.[179] On his first world tour in 1971, he visited Jerusalem and met with Pope Paul VI in Rome, the first meeting between a pope and a Tibetan lama. He spoke to the pope about Eastern Tibet and declared his intention to benefit all beings.[180] Paul VI's response, as Gyaltsen recalls: 'Nowadays, there are wars and great difficulties on the planet earth; this is because people do not keep the vows and commitments they have made. From that, there is misfortune and suffering in this world. I beg you to pray for people to respect their vows and commitments in order for harmony to reign throughout the world.'[181] The pope appeared to have invited Kalu to join forces for a common goal—the harmony of the world. This meeting marks the beginning of Kalu's friendship with mainstream religion in the West. It laid the foundation for the Karmapa's meeting with Paul VI four years later.

Kalu believed that the pope had encouraged him to propagate the Dharma.[182] When confronted by a Frenchman who claimed that the dissemination of

Buddhism in France, a country with a large Christian population, would be impossible, Kalu replied:

> I, myself, have met with the Pope and felt great joy at this meeting. I have a great esteem for Christians, and I believe that they also would appreciate Buddhist teachings. . . . Christianity and Buddhism have the same goal, which is to help all beings. . . . Both traditions share in preventing beings from falling into inferior worlds and in guiding beings towards liberation. They can understand each other, and I hope my teaching will be beneficial.[183]

Here, Kalu presents Buddhism as a tradition that shares core values with Christianity. To him, the Christian values of faith, love and morality would help Buddhism establish itself in the West.[184] He held the opinion that all religions share the same goal; Tibetan Buddhism constituted only one of many traditions and it would not suit all.[185] This realistic, perhaps also diplomatic, approach allowed him to neutralise hostility in the early years of his activity in the West.

Kalu's transmission strategy consisted of two principal components. First is his appointment of Tibetan lamas as resident teachers. He hand-picked over thirty Tibetan lamas from India and placed them in the Dharma centres that he had founded on his tours.[186] He explains:

> In sending resident teachers to centers, I considered the fact that these people have been involved in the practice and study of dharma from a very early age, that they have spent their lives trying to practice and to understand as much as they can, and that they have all done the three-year, three-month retreat program of training in meditation and study which qualifies them as a teacher.[187]

Kalu views a lifetime immersion in Buddhist teaching and practice as an essential factor that qualifies one to teach Buddhism. Yet, the Tibetan lamas had to adapt to new sociocultural environments for this arrangement to be effective; most of them lacked confidence in teaching Westerners. Kalu, aware of this challenge, took care to maintain close contact with the resident teachers.[188]

Second, Kalu relied on traditional teaching methods. He praised Trungpa for his creative adaptation of Buddhism to American culture.[189] Nonetheless, the situation for himself was different: unlike Trungpa who lived in the United States, Kalu was only able to teach Buddhism to the Western audience for short periods on his tours. Therefore, he was convinced that he needed to present the teachings in their original form: 'if I were going to accomplish anything, I would have to teach the Dharma in a traditional way, without combining it with any other viewpoints.'[190] He introduced basic

Buddhist concepts, conferred refuge, lay precepts and bodhisattva vows, and taught Tantric practice. He emphasised lineage identity in his teachings: 'Although in each of the four schools of Tibetan Buddhism there are lineages leading to complete enlightenment, and although there is no difference at that ultimate level between the schools, I felt very strongly that it was important to maintain the identity of the Kagyü lineage.'[191] Accordingly, he introduced the Kagyu preliminary practice (*sngon 'gro*), and taught the life stories of the lineage founders—Marpa, Milarepa and Gampopa.[192] He focused on the gradual path that progresses through the three *yāna*s. At the final stage of his activity in the West, in 1982, he conferred the Kālacakra empowerment in New York to over 1,000 people to prepare for the Mahāmudrā transmission.[193]

Kalu's most remarkable contribution to the transmission of Tibetan Buddhism to the West was his introduction of three-year retreat. Retreat was at the centre of his spiritual life. Many Western students flocked to him mainly because of their interest in his experience of solitary practice in the mountains in Tibet. He had built and managed many retreat centres in both Tibet and the Indian subcontinent. When visiting Europe and North America, he launched the first three-year retreat programmes for Western practitioners. In the Tantric tradition, long retreat is of particular significance to the practitioner's spiritual development. Kalu's retreat programmes allowed the Tantric tradition to flourish in the West. To begin with, he selected students based on the level of their traditional training: these students would have completed the preliminary practice several times and attained a reasonable proficiency in the Tibetan language. In 1976, he built retreat facilities in France and started the first three-year retreat there. This inspired more people to apply for the next programme. Soon afterwards, Kalu instituted retreat centres in Sweden, Canada and the United States.[194]

Kalu's transmission of Tibetan Buddhism through a traditionalist approach laid important groundwork for the Karmapa's activity in the West. Prior to his first tour, the Karmapa sent Kalu to Europe. Holmes recalls Kalu's arrival at Samye Ling in vivid detail:

> In 1974, he [Kalu] arrived accompanied by a large monastic party of over a dozen, including five Bhutanese lamas, fresh out of three-year retreat. They were fully-equipped with ritual and musical instruments, huge smiles and much enthusiasm: a very powerful dharma team indeed. They arrived on the day of a full moon. That night, sitting on the front steps of Samye Ling, they played the long *radong* horns and oboe-like *jaling* well into the clear, still night, letting the very typical, unique Tibetan sounds resound along a European valley for the first time ever.[195]

At Samye Ling, Kalu conferred vows, teachings and initiations daily for an entire month. This visit became a milestone in the development of Tibetan Buddhism in Europe.[196] Kalu's intensive transmission of tradition set in motion a crucial period of transition at Samye Ling. It helped bring to an end the influence of the hippie culture within the community and marked the beginning of its transformation into a traditional Tibetan Buddhist centre. His visit there also attracted newcomers and prepared a larger audience for the Karmapa.[197] Especially, since Tantric ritual was an essential element of the Karmapa's tours, Kalu's dissemination of Tantric Buddhism prepared for its reception.

NOTES

1. Levine, *Freda Bedi*, 13–14, 95; Vicki Mackenzie, *The Revolutionary Life of Freda Bedi: British feminist, Indian nationalist, Buddhist nun* (Boulder, CO: Shambhala, 2017), 45; Andrew Whitehead, *The Lives of Freda: The Political, Spiritual and Personal Journeys of Freda Bedi* (India: Speaking Tiger Books, 2019), Kindle, 111, 113; Kabir Bedi, "Karmapa and the Gelongma," in *The Miraculous 16th Karmapa: Incredible encounters with the Black Crown Buddha*, comp. Norma Levine (Arcidosso: Shang Shung Publications), 74; Brown, *Dance of 17 Lives*, 61.

2. Levine, *Freda Bedi*, 14, 134, 154, 159; Mackenzie, *Freda Bedi*, 59–60, 86; Whitehead, *Lives of Freda*, 11, 201.

3. Levine, *Freda Bedi*, 116; Mackenzie, *Freda Bedi*, 79; Whitehead, *Lives of Freda*, 195, 200, 201.

4. Levine, *Freda Bedi*, 116, 204; Mackenzie, *Freda Bedi*, 80; Whitehead, *Lives of Freda*, 193; Bedi, "Karmapa and the Gelongma," 74.

5. Levine, *Freda Bedi*, 205; Whitehead, *Lives of Freda*, 204.

6. Whitehead, *Lives of Freda*, 204.

7. Levine, *Freda Bedi*, 14, 134; Mackenzie, *Freda Bedi*, 89; Whitehead, *Lives of Freda*, 206–207; Bedi, "Karmapa and the Gelongma," 74.

8. Levine, *Freda Bedi*, 205.

9. Levine, *Freda Bedi*, 205; Mackenzie, *Freda Bedi*, 89, 90; Whitehead, *Lives of Freda*, 206–207, 212–213.

10. Whitehead, *Lives of Freda*, 210–211, 213, 214, 215–216.

11. Whitehead, *Lives of Freda*, 214–215.

12. An excerpt from Freda Bedi's letter to her friend Muriel Lewis in Levine, *Freda Bedi*, 135; Mackenzie, *Freda Bedi*, 91; Whitehead, *Lives of Freda*, 206.

13. Levine, *Freda Bedi*, 137; Whitehead, *Lives of Freda*, 223.

14. Levine, *Freda Bedi*, 137–138.

15. Levine, *Freda Bedi*, 170–175; Mackenzie, *Freda Bedi*, 94–95; Whitehead, *Lives of Freda*, 218–219; Bedi, "Karmapa and the Gelongma," 74.

16. Whitehead, *Lives of Freda*, 221–222.
See also Levine, *Freda Bedi*, 141.

17. See 2.1.1. Western Imagination.

18. Levine, *Freda Bedi*, 150, 206; Mackenzie, *Freda Bedi*, 101; Whitehead, *Lives of Freda*, 231; Bedi, "Karmapa and the Gelongma," 74.

19. Whitehead, *Lives of Freda*, 227–228; Brown, *Dance of 17 Lives*, 62.

20. Levine, *Freda Bedi*, 150–152, 157; Mackenzie, *Freda Bedi*, 114; Whitehead, *Lives of Freda*, 231, 233, 257.

21. Whitehead, *Lives of Freda*, 233.

22. Levine, *Freda Bedi*, 146.

23. Levine, *Freda Bedi*, 216–217; Mackenzie, *Freda Bedi*, 102.

24. Chime Rinpoche (1941–) is a reincarnate lama in the Karma Kagyu school and a disciple of the Sixteenth Karmapa. He received his monastic education in Benchen Monastery in the Kham region of Tibet. In 1959, he fled to India, then in 1965, travelled to the UK and joined Trungpa and Akong in Oxford. In 1973, he founded his own centre, Kham House, later renamed as Marpa House, in England. Different from Trungpa and Akong, he has kept a rather low profile throughout his teaching career. The most detailed account of his life available to me is an interview in *The Telegraph*: Mick Brown, "David Bowie's Buddhist Master: 'David rang me up and said I have a very big problem'," *The Telegraph*, May 22, 2016, https://www.telegraph.co.uk/men/thinking-man/david-bowies-buddhist-david-rang-me-up-and-said-i-have-a-very-bi/#.

25. Ato Rinpoche (1933–) is a reincarnate lama in the Karma Kagyu school and a disciple/attendant of the Sixteenth Karmapa. He received his monastic education in Nezang Monastery in the Kham region of Tibet. In 1959, he fled to India. The Karmapa appointed him as the representative of the Kagyu school in the Religious Office of the Tibetan government-in-exile. In 1967, he moved to Cambridge, England. A brief account of his biography in Ato Rinpoche, "Biography," accessed July 3, 2018, https://www.atorinpoche.com/biography.

26. Levine, *Freda Bedi*, 158.

27. Levine, *Freda Bedi*, 147; Bedi, "Karmapa and the Gelongma," 74.

28. Mackenzie, *Freda Bedi*, 108–109; Whitehead, *Lives of Freda*, 259; Holmes, "16th Karmapa in Europe," 282; Brown, *Dance of 17 Lives*, 62.

29. Levine, *Freda Bedi*, 148–149; Mackenzie, *Freda Bedi*, 122; Whitehead, *Lives of Freda*, 259; Holmes, "16th Karmapa in Europe," 282; Brown, *Dance of 17 Lives*, 62.

30. Levine, *Freda Bedi*, 152; Whitehead, *Lives of Freda*, 270.

31. Levine, *Freda Bedi*, 14, 184–189; Mackenzie, *Freda Bedi*, 138; Whitehead, *Lives of Freda*, 274; Bedi, "Karmapa and the Gelongma," 73; Brown, *Dance of 17 Lives*, 62; Finnegan, *Dharma King*, 60, 61.

The Karmapa conferred the name: Karma Tsultrim Kechog Palmo.

The year when the Karmapa ordained Bedi differs in two accounts: 1963 (see Bedi, "Karmapa and the Gelongma," 73), and 1964 (see Brown, *Dance of 17 Lives*, 62).

32. Levine, *Freda Bedi*, 236–237, 272; Mackenzie, *Freda Bedi*, 139; Whitehead, *Lives of Freda*, 275, 280.

33. Levine, *Freda Bedi*, 189; Mackenzie, *Freda Bedi*, 139–142; Whitehead, *Lives of Freda*, 286–288; Bedi, "Karmapa and the Gelongma," 73; Finnegan, *Dharma King*, 60.

34. Levine, *Freda Bedi*, 246, 296; Mackenzie, *Freda Bedi*, 149–150; Whitehead, *Lives of Freda*, 284.
35. Levine, *Freda Bedi*, 307–309; Mackenzie, *Freda Bedi*, 148–149; Whitehead, *Lives of Freda*, 284–286; Bedi, "Karmapa and the Gelongma," 75.
36. Levine, *Freda Bedi*, 280, 290–303; Mackenzie, *Freda Bedi*, 163–167; Whitehead, *Lives of Freda*, 297; Bedi, "Karmapa and the Gelongma," 75.
37. Levine, *Freda Bedi*, 253–254, 294; Mackenzie, *Freda Bedi*, 155; Whitehead, *Lives of Freda*, 283–284.
38. Levine, *Freda Bedi*, 291, 296–299; Mackenzie, *Freda Bedi*, 149–150, 163–165.
39. Mackenzie, *Freda Bedi*, 165.
40. Whitehead, *Lives of Freda*, 294.
41. As Baumann observes, the Kagyu school marked the largest scale of expansion of Tibetan Buddhism in the 1980s, followed by the Gelug, Nyingma and Sakya. See Martin Baumann, "Creating a European Path to Nirvana: Historical and contemporary developments of Buddhism in Europe," Journal of Contemporary Religion 10, no. 1 (1995), quoted in Robert Bluck, British Buddhism: Teachings, practice and development (London and New York: Routledge, 2006), 19.
42. See 6.1.3. Training the Sangha.
43. Levine, *Freda Bedi*, 217; Mackenzie, *Freda Bedi*, 156–157; Whitehead, *Lives of Freda*, 289.
44. Whitehead, *Lives of Freda*, 289–290.
45. Whitehead, *Lives of Freda*, 290.
46. Levine, *Freda Bedi*, 241–242.
47. Whitehead, *Lives of Freda*, 290–291.
48. Levine, *Freda Bedi*, 243; Mackenzie, *Freda Bedi*, 158; Whitehead, *Lives of Freda*, 293–294.
49. Whitehead, *Lives of Freda*, 290–291.
50. Levine, *Freda Bedi*, 244, 247, 249.
51. Levine, *Freda Bedi*, 252; Whitehead, *Lives of Freda*, 291.
52. Levine, *Freda Bedi*, 251, 253.
53. Levine, *Freda Bedi*, 249–251, 254; Whitehead, *Lives of Freda*, 291; Bedi, "Karmapa and the Gelongma," 75.
54. Levine, *Freda Bedi*, 265–266, 274, 289; Mackenzie, *Freda Bedi*, 159.
55. Levine, *Freda Bedi*, 267, 269–271, 273, 276, 278; Holmes, "Akong Tulku Rinpoche's Role," 77.
56. Levine, *Freda Bedi*, 282–284; Finnegan, *Dharma King*, 308; Mackenzie, *Freda Bedi*, 166.
57. Levine, *Freda Bedi*, 274–275.
58. Their journey into exile is recorded in detail in Chögyam Trungpa, *Born in Tibet*, 4th ed. (Boston & London: Shambhala, 2000); *Akong: A remarkable life*, DVD, directed by Chico Dall'Inha (London: Awareness Media Productions, 2017). See also Chöje Lama Yeshe Losal Rinpoche, "The Early Life of Chöje Akong Tulku Rinpoche," in *Only the Impossible is Worth Doing: Recollections of the supreme life*

and activity of Chöje Akong Tulku Rinpoche, eds. Gelong Thubten and Gelong Trinley (Dzalendra Publishing; Rokpa Trust, 2020), 16–17.

59. Zhwa dmar, *sku tshe'i rnam thar*, 100.5–100.9; Chögyam Trungpa, "Epilogue," in *Born in Tibet* (Boston & London: Shambhala, 2000), 251–252; Ken Holmes, "The Journey West," 2014, http://www.akong.eu/journeywest.htm; Holmes, "16th Karmapa in Europe," 282–283; *Recalling a Buddha*.

60. Chögyam Trungpa, "Epilogue," 252.

61. Ananda Bodhi (George Leslie Dawson), a Canadian Buddhist teacher first trained in the Burmese tradition, was identified by the Karmapa to be the reincarnation of Ju Mipham Namgyal Rinpoche of the Nyingma school. The Karmapa enthroned him and gave him the name 'Karma Tenzin Dorje Namgyal Rinpoche'. Since then, he was known as Namgyal Rinpoche. He founded the Dharma Centre of Canada and invited the Karmapa to visit. As briefly mentioned in 7.1. Freda Bedi, it was from this invitation that the Karmapa's plan for his first tour to North America began to unfold. For more detail, see Bennett and Levine, "Three World Tours," 158–161; Holmes, "16th Karmapa in Europe," 283; Levine, *Freda Bedi*, 242–243, 268; Khra 'gu rin po che, *rgyal ba'i dbang po*, 377.21–378.3, 382.1–382.3; Finnegan, *Dharma King*, 196.

62. Ken Holmes, "The Finding and Founding of Samye Ling," 2014, http://www.akong.eu/sl_early.htm; Holmes, "16th Karmapa in Europe," 283.

63. Chögyam Trungpa, "Epilogue," 252.

64. There are three centres of the Tibetan Buddhist tradition founded in the West prior to Samye Ling: the Kalmykian Kalachakra Temple of Saint Petersburg (Russia, 1915), a temple founded by Kalmykian refugees in Belgrade (Serbia, 1929) and the Lamaist Buddhist Center in New Jersey (United States, 1958) (see Holmes, "Samye Ling").

Samye Ling is now renamed as Kagyu Samye Ling, Tibetan Buddhist Monastery and Centre for World Peace and Health (see Kagyu Samye Ling, "Home," accessed February 13, 2015, http://www.samyeling.org).

65. Holmes, "16th Karmapa in Europe," 283.

66. Chögyam Trungpa, "Epilogue," 252–253.

67. Chögyam Trungpa, "Epilogue," 251.

68. Chögyam Trungpa, "Epilogue," 253–254.

69. Chögyam Trungpa, "Epilogue," 253–254.

70. Chögyam Trungpa, "Epilogue," 254–255.

71. Chögyam Trungpa, "Epilogue," 255.

72. Ken Holmes, "A Defining Moment: The disagreement between Trungpa Rinpoché and Akong Rinpoché concerning how the teachings should be given in Samyé Ling," 2014, http://akong.eu/AR_CTR.htm.

73. Chögyam Trungpa, "Epilogue," 256.

74. Didi Contractor, "The Meeting of Mahasiddhas," in *The Miraculous 16th Karmapa: Incredible Encounters with the Black Crown Buddha*, comp. Norma Levine (Arcidosso: Shang Shung Publications, 2013), 92, 94–95; Finnegan, *Dharma King*, 96–97.

75. Fabrice Midal, *Chögyam Trungpa: His life and vision* (Boston, New York: Shambhala Publications, 2004), 301.

76. *Born in Tibet* published in 1966 and *Meditation in Action* published in 1969.
77. Chögyam Trungpa, "Epilogue," 256.
78. Webster, "Naropa Institute," 15.
79. Midal, *Chögyam Trungpa*, 16.
80. Gratton-Fabbri, "At Play in Paradox," 229.
81. Judith L Lief, "Transforming Psychology: The development of Maitri Space Awareness practice," in *Recalling Chogyam Trungpa*, ed. Fabrice Midal (Boston: Shambhala Publications, 2005), 275.
82. Lief, "Transforming Psychology," 275.
83. Gratton-Fabbri, "At Play in Paradox," 274–275. For more detail on "Maitri Five Wisdoms" and "Mudra Space Awareness," see Midal, *Chögyam Trungpa*; Pierre Jacerme, "Maitri Space Awareness: The need for place," in *Recalling Chögyam Trungpa*, ed. Fabrice Midal (Boston and New York: Shambhala Publications, 2005), 111–138; Lief, "Transforming Psychology"; Lee Worley, "The Space Between: The theater legacy of Chögyam Trungpa," in *Recalling Chögyam Trungpa*, ed. Fabrice Midal (Boston and New York: Shambhala Publications, 2005), 289–304.
84. Chögyam Trungpa, "Epilogue," 261.
85. Reed Bye, "The Founding Vision of Naropa University," in *Recalling Chögyam Trungpa*, ed. Fabrice Midal (Boston and New York: Shambhala Publications, 2005), 144, 147.
86. Gratton-Fabbri, "At Play in Paradox," 228–229.
87. For more detail on this teaching, see Chögyam Trungpa and Sherab Chödzin, *Crazy Wisdom* (Boston and London: Shambhala, 1991).
88. Midal, *Chögyam Trungpa*, 121.
89. Midal, *Chögyam Trungpa*, 122–144.
90. Some aspects of the strategy were carried on beyond this period, for example, the Nalanda Translation Committee founded in 1975.
91. Midal, *Chögyam Trungpa*, 295, 302.
92. Terhune, *Karmapa*, 67; Finnegan, *Dharma King*, 160–165, 198.
93. Midal, *Chögyam Trungpa*, 297.
   See also Brown, *Dance of 17 Lives*, 70; Roth and Levine, "USA Introduction," 151.
   Video recordings of the preparation in *Recalling a Buddha*.
94. Midal, *Chögyam Trungpa*, 298.
   See also Brown, *Dance of 17 Lives*, 70.
95. Terhune, *Karmapa*, 65.
96. Midal, *Chögyam Trungpa*, 299–300.
97. *Recalling a Buddha*.
98. Khra 'gu rin po che, *rgyal ba'i dbang po*, 380.14–381.12; bKra shis tshe ring, "'jig rten dbang phyug," 41.10–41.15; Grags pa yongs 'dus, "bcu drug pa," 375.10–375.15; Terhune, *Karmapa*, 118; Roth and Levine, "USA Introduction," 152; Levine, *Freda Bedi*, 256–264; *The Lion's Roar*.
99. Roth and Levine, "USA Introduction," 152; Levine, *Freda Bedi*, 256.
100. Midal, *Chögyam Trungpa*, 296; Roth and Levine, "USA Introduction," 154–155; Tsering Namgyal Khortsa, "Sixteenth Karmapa," 83.

101. Interview with Derek Kolleeny in *Modern Masters of Religion*.
102. Chögyam Trungpa, "Epilogue," 261.
103. Terhune, *Karmapa*, 67.
104. English: Midal, *Chögyam Trungpa*, 302; Tibetan: Rang byung rig pa'i rdo rje, "shing stag 1974 zla 8 tshes 13 'khod zur mang drung pa rin po cher rdo rje 'dzin pa karma sgrub brgyud bstan pa'i rgyal mtshan don brgyud 'chang ba'i mtshan gnas stsal ba'i bka' shog," in *rgyal dbang karma pa bcu drug pa chen po'i gsung 'bum 3*, ed. Jo sras bkra shis tshe ring (Dharamsala: Tshurphu Labrang; The Amnye Machen Institute, 2016), 84.1–84.16.
105. Midal, *Chögyam Trungpa*, 218–221.
106. For more detail on this programme, see Chögyam Trungpa and C. R. Gimian, *Shambhala: the sacred path of the warrior* (Boulder, CO: Shambhala, 1984).
107. Midal, *Chögyam Trungpa*, 235.
108. Midal, *Chögyam Trungpa*, 494.
109. Roth and Levine, "USA Introduction," 155.
110. Interview with the Sixteenth Karmapa on the American television programme "Vermont Report" (December 1976) in *Recalling a Buddha*.
111. Peck, Devorah, and the Kagyu Video Project, "Wish Fulfilling Gem, An Interview with H.H. the 16th Gyalwa Karmapa," *The Meridian Trust* video, 48:16, 1983. https://meridian-trust.org/video/wish-fulfilling-gem-an-interview-with-h-h-the-16th-gyalwa-karmapa_dldv000167/.
112. Rang byung rig pa'i rdo rje, "me 'brug 1976 zla 12 tshes 8 'khod zur mang drung pa rin po che'i zhal slob 'od gsal bstan 'dzin drung pa rin po che'i rgyal tshab tu bskos bzhag rgyab gnyer gyi bka' shog," in *rgyal dbang karma pa bcu drug pa chen po'i gsung 'bum 3*, ed. Jo sras bkra shis tshe ring (Dharamsala: Tshurphu Labrang; The Amnye Machen Institute, 2016), 89.1–89.8.
113. The Nālandā Translation Committee, trans. *The Rain of Wisdom: The essence of the ocean of true meaning* (Boulder and London: Shambhala, 1980).
114. Rang byung rig pa'i rdo rje, "zur mang drung pa rin po che'i chos tshogs nas bka' brgyud mgur mtsho dbyin bsgyur deb la che brjod," in *rgyal dbang karma pa bcu drug pa chen po'i gsung 'bum 3*, ed. Jo sras bkra shis tshe ring (Dharamsala: Tshurphu Labrang; The Amnye Machen Institute, 2016), 49.1–49.11.

For the English translation of the Karmapa's words, see The Nālandā Translation Committee, "*Rain of Wisdom*."

115. Ken Holmes, "Biographical Background," 2014, http://akong.eu/biobackground.htm.

For more detail on Akong's time at Dolma Lhakang, see Yeshe Losal Rinpoche, "Early Life," 11–16; *Akong: A remarkable life*.

116. Katia Holmes, "Pioneer of Tibetan Medicine in Europe," in *Only the Impossible is Worth Doing: Recollections of the supreme life and activity of Chöje Akong Tulku Rinpoche*, eds. Gelong Thubten and Gelong Trinley (Dzalendra Publishing; Rokpa Trust, 2020), 248; Holmes, "The Journey West."

Akong was renowned for his expertise in Tibetan Traditional Medicine. For more detail, see Holmes, "Pioneer of Tibetan Medicine."

117. Tara Rokpa Therapy, "History," accessed March 24, 2015, http://www.tara-rokpa.org/therapy/about/history/index.php. For more detail, see Gelong Thubten, and Gelong Trinley, eds., *Only the Impossible is Worth Doing: Recollections of the supreme life and activity of Chöje Akong Tulku Rinpoche* (Dzalendra Publishing; Rokpa Trust, 2020), 292–330.

118. Akong was a pioneer in the introduction of Tibetan Traditional Medicine to Europe. For more detail, see Holmes, "Pioneer of Tibetan Medicine."

119. Akong oversaw a large number of humanitarian projects through his charity ROKPA International. For more detail, see Lea Wyler, "ROKPA of Dr Akong Rinpoche," in *Only the Impossible is Worth Doing: Recollections of the supreme life and activity of Chöje Akong Tulku Rinpoche*, eds. Gelong Thubten and Gelong Trinley (Dzalendra Publishing; Rokpa Trust, 2020), 333–415; Lea Wyler, "Changing Ourselves—Changing the World," in *Only the Impossible is Worth Doing: Recollections of the supreme life and activity of Chöje Akong Tulku Rinpoche*, eds. Gelong Thubten and Gelong Trinley (Dzalendra Publishing; Rokpa Trust, 2020), 421–426; Vivienne Kernohan, "ROKPA in Zimbabwe," in *Only the Impossible is Worth Doing: Recollections of the supreme life and activity of Chöje Akong Tulku Rinpoche*, eds. Gelong Thubten and Gelong Trinley (Dzalendra Publishing; Rokpa Trust, 2020), 416–420.

120. Kagyu Samye Ling, "Choje Akong Tulku Rinpoche," accessed March 12, 2015, http://www.samyeling.org/about/dr-choje-akong-tulku-rinpoche/; Holmes, "The Journey West."

121. Ken Holmes, "A Defining Moment: The disagreement between Trungpa Rinpoché and Akong Rinpoché concerning how the teachings should be given in Samyé Ling: continued . . .," 2014, http://akong.eu/AR_CTR_2.htm.

122. Ken Holmes, "Akong Rinpoché and Samye Ling. Part 4: His 'Aims & Objects'," 2014, http://akong.eu/SL_4.htm.

See also Dharmacharya Kenneth Holmes, "Chöje Akong Tulku Rinpoche's Role in Bringing Dharma to the World," in *Only the Impossible is Worth Doing: Recollections of the supreme life and activity of Chöje Akong Tulku Rinpoche*, eds. Gelong Thubten and Gelong Trinley (Dzalendra Publishing; Rokpa Trust, 2020), 68–69.

123. Ken Holmes, "Akong Rinpoché Establishing Buddha-Dharma. Part Nine: Dharma teachings . . . beginning the task," 2014, http://akong.eu/teachings_1.htm; Holmes, "Akong Tulku Rinpoche's Role," 89.

124. Lama Zangmo, "Reflections on Retreat," in *Only the Impossible is Worth Doing: Recollections of the supreme life and activity of Chöje Akong Tulku Rinpoche*, eds. Gelong Thubten and Gelong Trinley (Dzalendra Publishing; Rokpa Trust, 2020), 132–133; Holmes, "Akong Tulku Rinpoche's Role," 103–105; Ken Holmes, "Akong Rinpoché Establishing Buddha-Dharma. Part Eleven: A study programme," 2014, http://akong.eu/teachings_3.htm.

125. That is, *A Guide to the Bodhisattva's Way of Life* mentioned in 1.1. Overview of Life-Writing in Tibetan Buddhism.

126. Holmes, "Part Eleven"; Holmes, "Akong Tulku Rinpoche's Role," 92.

Holmes ascribes *Profound Inner Meaning* to the Ninth Karmapa. This may be an error, or he may refer to a different text, but he does not give its Tibetan name.

127. Vin Harris, "A New Samye—Getting Started," in *Only the Impossible is Worth Doing: Recollections of the supreme life and activity of Chöje Akong Tulku Rinpoche*, eds. Gelong Thubten and Gelong Trinley (Dzalendra Publishing; Rokpa Trust, 2020), 36, 41; John Maxwell, "The Arrival of Akong Rinpoche in the West," in *Only the Impossible is Worth Doing: Recollections of the supreme life and activity of Chöje Akong Tulku Rinpoche*, eds. Gelong Thubten and Gelong Trinley (Dzalendra Publishing; Rokpa Trust, 2020), 30; *Akong: A remarkable life*.

128. Maxwell, "Arrival of Akong Rinpoche," 32.

129. Ken Holmes, "Akong Rinpoché Establishing Buddha-Dharma. Part Two: An initial hesitation," 2014, http://www.akong.eu/dharma_2.htm.

See also Holmes, "Akong Tulku Rinpoche's Role," 70.

130. Ken Holmes, "Akong Rinpoché Establishing Buddha-Dharma. Part Eight: The Samye Project," 2014, http://akong.eu/dharma_8.htm; Holmes, "Akong Tulku Rinpoche's Role," 70.

131. Holmes, "An Initial Hesitation."

For detail about the Samye Project, especially the building of the Main Temple, see *Akong: A remarkable life*; Harris, "A New Samye," 35–60.

132. Khra 'gu rin po che, *rgyal ba'i dbang po*, 382.11–382.20; Grags pa yongs 'dus, "bcu drug pa," 375.15–375.18, 376.1–376.3; Levine, *Freda Bedi*, 274–284; Finnegan, *Dharma King*, 275.

133. Holmes, "Transformed and Saved," 360.

134. Ken Holmes, "The Special Connection with the XVIth Gyalwang Karmapa: 3. Rinpoché's Role in the 1974 Visit to Europe of the Gyalwang Karmapa," 2014, http://www.akong.eu/k16_3.htm.

See also Khra 'gu rin po che, *rgyal ba'i dbang po*, 382.5–382.10; Holmes, *Gyalwa Karmapa*, 30; Holmes, "16th Karmapa in Europe," 286–287; Holmes, "Akong Tulku Rinpoche's Role," 77–78.

135. Holmes, "1974 Visit"; Holmes, "Akong Tulku Rinpoche's Role," 78.

136. Khra 'gu rin po che, *rgyal ba'i dbang po*, 382.5–382.10; Holmes, *Gyalwa Karmapa*, 30; Holmes, "16th Karmapa in Europe," 287; Finnegan, *Dharma King*, 280–281.

137. Brown, *Dance of 17 Lives*, 65.

138. Holmes, "1974 Visit"; Ken Holmes, "The Special Connection with the XVIth Gyalwang Karmapa: 5. Rinpoché's Role in the 1977 Visit to Europe of the Gyalwang Karmapa: Part two . . . the actual tour," 2014, http://www.akong.eu/k16_5.htm.

See also Khra 'gu rin po che, *rgyal ba'i dbang po*, 382.20–383.2; Holmes, *Gyalwa Karmapa*, 30–31; Jamgon Kongtrul Rinpoche, "XVI Gyalwa Karmapa," 16; Holmes, "Akong Tulku Rinpoche's Role," 78; Holmes, "Pioneer of Tibetan Medicine" 287; Nydahl, *Riding the Tiger*, 49, 50–51; Finnegan, *Dharma King*, 308.

139. Ken Holmes, "The Special Connection with the XVIth Gyalwang Karmapa: 4. Rinpoché's Role in the 1977 Visit to Europe of the Gyalwang Karmapa: Part one . . . Preparations," 2014, http://www.akong.eu/k16_4.htm; Holmes, "Akong Tulku Rinpoche's Role," 78.

140. Holmes, "1974 Visit"; Holmes, "Actual Tour"; Holmes, "16th Karmapa in Europe," 287; Ken Holmes, "Memories of the Buddha Karmapa," in *The Miraculous*

16th Karmapa: Incredible Encounters with the Black Crown Buddha, comp. Norma Levine (Arcidosso: Shang Shung Publications, 2013), 289.

141. Holmes, "Part One . . . Preparations"; Holmes, "Actual Tour."

See also Holmes, "Akong Tulku Rinpoche's Role," 78; Kunsang and Aubèle, "Sixteenth Karmapa," 229; Brown, *Dance of 17 Lives*, 72; Nydahl, *Riding the Tiger*, 110–134; Finnegan, *Dharma King*, 275.

142. Ken Holmes, "The Special Connection with the XVIth Gyalwang Karmapa: 7. Rinpoché's Role in the 1977 Visit to Europe of the Gyalwang Karmapa: Part four . . . founding the first Samye Dzongs and launching Khenpo Tsultrim," 2014, http://www.akong.eu/k16_7.htm; Finnegan, *Dharma King*, 311; Carlo Luyckx, "Akong Rinpoche's Activity in Belgium," in *Only the Impossible is Worth Doing: Recollections of the supreme life and activity of Chöje Akong Tulku Rinpoche*, eds. Gelong Thubten and Gelong Trinley (Dzalendra Publishing; Rokpa Trust, 2020), 167–170; Lama Tsondru, "The Origins of Dharma in Spain," in *Only the Impossible is Worth Doing: Recollections of the supreme life and activity of Chöje Akong Tulku Rinpoche*, eds. Gelong Thubten and Gelong Trinley (Dzalendra Publishing; Rokpa Trust, 2020), 183–184.

143. Holmes, "Part One . . . Preparations"; Holmes, "Akong Tulku Rinpoche's Role," 78–79; Finnegan, *Dharma King*, 284–285.

144. Holmes, "Transformed and Saved," 364.

Photographs of the bus in Finnegan, *Dharma King*, 285; Holmes, "Part One . . . Preparations".

145. Holmes, "Actual Tour"; Holmes, "Akong Tulku Rinpoche's Role," 79.

146. Ken Holmes, "The Special Connection with the XVIth Gyalwang Karmapa: 6. Rinpoché's Role in the 1977 Visit to Europe of the Gyalwang Karmapa: Part three . . . reflections on Rinpoché's qualities," 2014, http://www.akong.eu/k16_6.htm; Holmes, "Akong Tulku Rinpoche's Role," 82; Holmes, "16th Karmapa in Europe," 287; Holmes, "Buddha Karmapa," 302–303; Finnegan, *Dharma King*, 321–326.

The detail of this event varies in different accounts:

Holmes reports that almost 1,000 people attended the event; Lhundup Damchö tells of 800 attendees for the event which included empowerments and the Black Crown Ceremony and lasted for twelve days.

147. Holmes, "Reflections on Rinpoché's Qualities"; Holmes, "Akong Tulku Rinpoche's Role," 82; Holmes, "Buddha Karmapa," 292, 296.

148. Holmes, "Reflections on Rinpoché's Qualities."

See also Holmes, "Akong Tulku Rinpoche's Role," 81.

149. Holmes, "Actual Tour."

150. Holmes, "Actual Tour"; Holmes, "Akong Tulku Rinpoche's Role," 80; Holmes, "Buddha Karmapa," 291; Willems, "Under Karmapa's Black Crown," 356; Holmes, "Transformed and Saved," 364.

151. Holmes, "First Samye Dzongs"; Holmes, "Transformed and Saved," 365–366.

152. Holmes, "First Samye Dzongs"; Holmes, "Akong Tulku Rinpoche's Role," 90.

153. Ole Nydahl (1941–), a member of the counterculture movement, was among the Karmapa's earliest Western disciples. He assisted the Karmapa on his two tours in Europe, but, in the process, developed, what many consider to be, a personality cult.

As a result, he was criticised as a controversial figure within the Karma Kagyu lineage and beyond. For more detail, see Burkhard Scherer, "Trans-European Adaptations in the Diamond Way: Negotiating public opinions on homosexuality in Russia and in the U.K.," *Online—Heidelberg Journal of Religions on the Internet* 6 (2014), 103–125; Burkhard Scherer, "Conversion, Devotion, and (Trans-)Mission: Understanding Ole Nydahl," in *Buddhists: Understanding Buddhism Through the Lives of Practitioners*, ed. Todd Lewis (West Sussex: John Wiley & Sons, Ltd., 2014), 96–106; Tenpel, "Propaganda: The making of the holy lama Ole Nydahl," *Buddhism Controversy Blog*, June 30, 2014, https://buddhism-controversy-blog.com/2014/06/30/propaganda-the-making-of-the-holy-lama-ole-nydahl/; Holmes, "First Samye Dzongs"; Brown, *Dance of 17 Lives*, 209–210.

154. Holmes, "Part One . . . Preparations."
155. Holmes, "Part One . . . Preparations."
156. Holmes, "First Samye Dzongs"; Holmes, "Buddha Karmapa," 301.
157. Holmes, "Part One . . . Preparations."
   See also Holmes, "Akong Tulku Rinpoche's Role," 79.
158. Ken Holmes, "The Special Connection with the XVIth Gyalwang Karmapa. A Long-Life Prayer (Shapten) for Akong Rinpoché," 2014, http://www.akong.eu/shapten.htm.
159. Holmes, "Long-Life Prayer."
   The English translation was produced by Ken and Katia Holmes with the help of Khenpo Tsultrim Gyamtso.
160. Palpung Situ Rinpoche, Dzokchen Kongtrul Rinpoche, Sechen Kongtrul and Kado Situ. See Lama Gyaltsen, "Lama Gyaltsen's Memories," in *Excellent Buddhism: An exemplary life*, Kalu Rinpoche, trans. Christiane Buchet (San Francisco, CA: ClearPoint Press, 1995), 21.
161. Ngawang Zangpo, Introduction, 32–34; Gyaltsen, "Lama Gyaltsen's Memories," 21–30; Holmes, "16th Karmapa in Europe," 285.
162. That is, Ashi Wangmo as mentioned in 5.2.2. Flight and Resettlement.
163. Bokar Rinpoche, "The Events of Kalu Rinpoche's Life," in *Excellent Buddhism: An exemplary life*, Kalu Rinpoche (San Francisco, CA: ClearPoint Press, 1995), 32, 46.
164. This may refer to Dalhousie.
165. Gyaltsen, "Lama Gyaltsen's Memories," 32–33.
166. Bokar Rinpoche, "Kalu Rinpoche's Life," 47.
167. Bokar Rinpoche, "Kalu Rinpoche's Life," 48.
168. Ngawang Zangpo, Introduction, 34.
169. Bokar Rinpoche, Lama Gyaltsen, and Khenpo Lodro Donyo, "Kalu Rinpoche's Last Moments," in *Excellent Buddhism: An exemplary life*, Kalu Rinpoche (San Francisco, CA: ClearPoint Press, 1995), 54.
170. Gyaltsen, "Lama Gyaltsen's Memories," 36.
171. Gyaltsen, "Lama Gyaltsen's Memories," 33–34.
172. Gyaltsen, "Lama Gyaltsen's Memories," 33–34.
173. Gyaltsen, "Lama Gyaltsen's Memories," 34.
174. Gyaltsen, "Lama Gyaltsen's Memories," 35.

175. Gyaltsen, "Lama Gyaltsen's Memories," 35.
176. Gyaltsen, "Lama Gyaltsen's Memories," 35–36.
177. Gyaltsen, "Lama Gyaltsen's Memories," 36.
178. Kalu Rinpoche, *The Foundations of Tibetan Buddhism: The gem ornament of manifold oral instructions which benefits each and everyone accordingly* (Ithaca, NY: Snow Lion Publications, 1999), 175.
179. Gyaltsen, "Lama Gyaltsen's Memories," 39–40.
180. Gyaltsen, "Lama Gyaltsen's Memories," 36, 38, 40.
181. Gyaltsen, "Lama Gyaltsen's Memories," 38.
182. Gyaltsen, "Lama Gyaltsen's Memories," 38–39.
183. Gyaltsen, "Lama Gyaltsen's Memories," 36–37.
184. Kalu Rinpoche, *Excellent Buddhism: An exemplary life* (San Francisco, CA: ClearPoint Press, 1995), 75.
185. Ngawang Zangpo, Introduction, 35–36.
186. Bokar Rinpoche, "Kalu Rinpoche's Life," 48.
187. Kalu Rinpoche, *Foundations of Tibetan Buddhism*, 180.
188. Kalu Rinpoche, *Foundations of Tibetan Buddhism*, 176.
189. Kalu Rinpoche, *Dharma: That Illuminates*, 7.
190. Kalu Rinpoche, *Dharma: That Illuminates*, 7.
191. Kalu Rinpoche, *Dharma: That Illuminates*, 10.
192. Holmes, "16th Karmapa in Europe," 285–286.
193. Kalu Rinpoche, *Dharma: That Illuminates*, 8–11; Bokar Rinpoche, "Kalu Rinpoche's Life," 47–48; Kagyu Droden Kunchab, "The Kalachakra in America," accessed August 26, 2018, http://www.kdk.org/lama-lodu-bio-20.html.
194. Rick Fields, *How the Swans Came to the Lake: A narrative history of Buddhism in America*, 3rd ed. (Boston, Mass.: Shambhala Publications Inc., 1992), 335.
195. Holmes, "16th Karmapa in Europe," 284–285.
    See also Holmes, "Akong Tulku Rinpoche's Role," 71.
196. Holmes, "Akong Tulku Rinpoche's Role," 71; Luyckx, "Rinpoche's Activity in Belgium," 164.
197. Holmes, "Akong Tulku Rinpoche's Role," 71.

Chapter 8

Strategies on Tour

The Karmapa was convinced that the transmission of Tibetan Buddhism to the West would be successful. He himself stated: 'Westerners are not more or less suited to practice Buddhism.'[1] When giving a public talk at the University of Colorado, he told the audience: 'I have confidence that you all are capable of experiencing this fruition of buddhahood.'[2] He pointed out that the purpose of his tours was to help people establish a connection with the Dharma so that they were able to make progress on the spiritual path:

> Because we are in a fortunate time, America, Canada, Europe and the whole world receive the light of the Buddha's compassion. People now want to practice and it gives them much joy. But in order to do the practice, you have to meet with the right situation and this meeting itself is the extraordinary blessing of the Dharma. Once having received this wonderful teaching, it is the responsibility of the Dharma practitioner to pass the teachings on to those who are ready for them.[3]

Here, the Karmapa entrusts his Western students with the transmission of the lineage into the future. Accordingly, he conferred monastic vows, encouraged Western nuns of the Tibetan tradition to receive full ordination and ensured that his students had the opportunity to study Buddhism, translate texts and practise in retreat.[4] Meanwhile, being aware of the challenges in the cross-cultural exchange between the West and Tibet, he understood the need for adaptation:

> If you consider Eastern and Western religions, you can see that the faith in religion can be the same even though the religions themselves are different. If you consider philosophy, however, you will see that there is a difference. In Western countries, therefore, teachers must speak according to Western thought patterns

so that the seed of Dharma can fully enter into the experience of Western people. This is the way in which the lamas speak.[5]

For tradition to truly take root in the West, the Karmapa developed four main strategies for his tours to Europe and North America. These included: (1) prioritisation of Tantric rituals, (2) founding of monasteries and Dharma centres, (3) friendship with other Buddhist traditions and different religions and (4) engagement with governments and politicians. These strategies reflect both continuity with the preservation phase and change in order to adapt to the new sociocultural context. They shaped the transformation of Tibetan Buddhism in its initial period of transmission to the West.

8.1. PRIORITISATION OF TANTRIC RITUALS

The Karmapa rarely delivered verbal discourse but focused instead on Tantric rituals, especially his signature Black Crown Ceremony. This is clearly in contrast to his extensive transmissions at Rumtek Monastery in early exile.[6] There are three possible reasons: (1) different type of audience, (2) lack of qualified interpreters/translators and (3) spiritual attribute of the Karmapa, namely 'teaching by being'.

First, the lengthy transmissions that the Karmapa imparted at Rumtek were principally intended for young tulkus and lamas, his primary disciples in particular. The purpose was to train the younger generation of lineage holders, which was crucial to the preservation of tradition. The audience therefore largely consisted of monastics with lifelong immersion in Buddhist study and practice. In the West, during the 1970s when Tibetan Buddhism was still a new arrival, the potential audience for the Karmapa was comprised of newcomers and early-stage practitioners. Compared to the lamas and monks gathered at Rumtek, these Westerners not only were spiritually less mature but also came from very different sociocultural backgrounds. Chapter 2 has shown that many participated in the counterculture, new religious and New Age movements with little grounding in the culture or history of Tibetan Buddhism.[7] Consequently, the Karmapa would have to choose a suitable form of transmission for his new audience.

Ritual, in this context, has a special advantage over verbal discourse: it engages the audience more directly, through symbols and gestures, with an immediate effect on an individual at the experiential level. Especially, the Black Crown Ceremony, as demonstrated in Chapter 4,[8] requires no prior Buddhist knowledge for the attendees. Through ritual, the Karmapa 'created strong Dharma connections with the large assemblies' which 'drew in new disciples seeking a spiritual path'.[9] It was thus an effective means to create the foundation for his introduction of tradition and to increase the scale of development from an early stage. Hence the Black Crown Ceremony can be considered a key reason for the success of the Karmapa's tours in Europe and North America. The ceremony was advertised as a public event, and the Karmapa performed it very frequently, even two to three times per day, to thousands of people. His television interview in the United States in 1976 also began with a ritual that he led with a group of Tibetan monks on stage.[10] Through Tantric rituals, the Karmapa offered Westerners access to the Tantric tradition of Tibetan Buddhism. This also facilitated the reception of his traditional spiritual image examined in Part II.

Second, during the time of the Karmapa's tours, in the 1970s, translators or interpreters for Tibetan Buddhist teachings were few in number and lacked experience. Ringu Tulku holds the opinion that had there been more translators at that time, the Karmapa would have given more teachings.[11] Holmes reports that the Karmapa's translator Achi, a young Tibetan educated in a Catholic school in India, possessed little knowledge of Tibetan Buddhism. This made it difficult for the Karmapa's teachings to be conveyed accurately to the audience.[12] Under such circumstances, verbal discourse was yet to be a reliable means of transmission. The Karmapa tried to resolve this issue by sending Khenpo Tsultrim Gyamtso from Rumtek to train Tibetan language translators in Europe during and after his second tour there.[13] Meanwhile, he may have decided to work within the constraint by prioritising ritual instead. However, he did not make this decision merely out of convenience. When speaking to his Western students, he made it clear that the Tantric path should be practised with caution:

> Tantra is the shortest path—very direct—and it carries on the teachings pointedly, exactly. Anything that [is] direct has danger within it. As flying a plane is more direct than a car or train, if there is a crash on the plane the fatalities are worse. Buddhism deals with shedding the protective ego and neurotic patterns, and that is a dangerous prospect.[14]

Third, the Karmapa's emphasis on ritual can be linked to his spiritual attribute: 'teaching by being'. He was known for giving instructions through 'physical gestures' and 'mere presence'.[15] Ösel Tendzin recalls: 'Just seeing him made us happy . . . in a simple way; a simple gesture made you feel like there was a very definite goodness in the world.'[16] Traleg Rinpoche asserts: 'I'm sure everyone who met him would say to you that he taught from simply being Karmapa, and we all learnt tremendous amount from being with him.'[17] Holmes believes that the Karmapa taught by 'directly manifesting enlightened qualities and spiritual activity of a buddha'.[18] This, according to him, is related to the Karmapa's spiritual attribute of liberation through sight, hearing, touch or memory.[19] Chapter 4 has shown that during the liberation-through-seeing Black Crown Ceremony, various wondrous visions arose in the minds of the Western audience; some even recognised the nature of mind.[20] Since 'teaching by being' constituted a distinctive aspect of the Karmapa's activity, it became the most significant, and attractive, element of his tours in the West. According to tradition, no one else in the lineage, except for the Karmapa incarnations, holds the authority to perform the Black Crown Ceremony. By giving priority to this ritual, the Karmapa offered Westerners a special, direct experience of his spirituality.

8.2. FOUNDING OF MONASTERIES AND DHARMA CENTRES

The Karmapa founded monasteries and Dharma centres in North America and Europe throughout his tours. This became the most tangible outcome of his activity in the West. He received donations of land from devotees in New York, Yukon (Canada), Hantum (Netherlands) and Dordogne (France).[21] Particularly, he sent lamas and monks to build his American and European monastic seats in the United States and France, respectively.[22] Following his 1974 tour to the United States, he drew up a plan for the construction of a monastery there. He appointed his personal attendant Tenzin Chönyi to oversee the administration and Bardor Tulku to supervise the construction.[23] On his 1977 visit, with a donation from Chia Theng Shen,[24] he purchased land for the monastery which he named Karma Triyana Dharmachakra (KTD). He assigned Khenpo Karthar to be its abbot; he instructed him to create a library to store the Tibetan texts that he had given to the monastery and to build a retreat centre to train disciples in the three-year retreat of the Karma Kagyu tradition.[25] In 1980, he produced a blueprint for the monastery and consecrated the land on which the shrine was to be built.[26] This monastery, together with its affiliated centres, named as Karma Thegsum Choling, was under the direct guidance of the Karmapa himself.[27] In France, he received a donation of land from Bernard Benson in 1974 and created his European seat there on his second visit in 1977.[28] Furthermore, in 1980, his American students Hanne and Maurice Strong offered 200 acres of land in Southern Colorado for the construction of a monastery, retreat centre and Tibetan medical facility.[29] To coordinate the construction and management of the monasteries and Dharma centres, the Karmapa founded Karma Kagyu Trusts.[30] In 1981, in response to the requests from the Dharma centres around the world, he opened the Kagyu International Headquarters/Office at Rumtek.[31]

To ensure the sustainable development of the monasteries and Dharma centres, he sent lamas to the West to serve as resident teachers.[32] To these lamas, he set the standard of conduct using his own experience as an example. In 1976, prior to his second world tour, he addressed the lamas and monks at

Rumtek on how best to teach students and propagate the Dharma in foreign countries. He emphasised the need to examine each student's mind, renounce worldly aspirations and strengthen one's own commitment to benefit others.[33] In his own words:

> I and the elderly lama (the Sixteenth Karmapa [himself] and Kalu Rinpoche) have toured the world more than once. [Our] goal is certainly not to make money; it is for nothing else but the benefit of sentient beings. What we call the sublime Dharma is aimed solely at taming the confused sentient beings. Therefore, [if] you consider it to be the guru's command, going because [you] have to go, [I] think it will be difficult [for you] to accomplish [any] benefit for the teaching and beings. [You] must be fearless and develop courage. Never meddle in worldly pursuits. Being a Dharma practitioner, abandon [any] attachment to sensory enjoyments, involvement in profit-making activities, in brief, activities in conflict with the Dharma. [You should, instead, carry out your activity] based on the deeds of an authentic practitioner, thereby benefiting others. If [you] do so, [your] students will gather like streams gathering into an ocean.[34]

In this speech, the Karmapa cautions against indulgence in worldly pursuits. He does not stop at the theoretical level but shares his personal experience from the world tour as a point of reference for others. His advice centres around the traditional teachings of renunciation and *bodhicitta*, but it is also relevant to the time. By the mid-1970s, Tibetan Buddhism had only begun to establish a footing in the West. As the leader of the lineage, the Karmapa stressed the importance of these teachings to help the lamas and monks sharpen motivation and strengthen discipline so that they were able to uphold the same vision and standard when they themselves participated in the transmission of the lineage to the West.

The Karmapa's strategy proved to be successful. After completing his third tour in 1980, he told Kalu Rinpoche that the number of overseas Dharma centres had reached approximately 320.[35] By the early 1980s, most Dharma centres in Europe and the United States belonged to the Karma Kagyu school.[36] This strategy can be seen as a continuation of the preservation phase but with a very different orientation. In the early exile, the Karmapa concentrated on rebuilding the monastic community in the Indian subcontinent; founding monasteries was its focal point. In the expansion phase here, he did not establish monasteries and Dharma centres to promote monasticism; this would not be realistic in the West. Instead, he intended to provide his Western disciples, mostly lay practitioners, with necessary training facilities for the long-term growth of their community.

Through television interviews during his visits to the United States, he declared his purpose for creating monasteries and Dharma centres as to make the teachings as available as possible to the Americans. He emphasises, in particular, the importance of the guru-disciple relationship[37] and the gradual path in which one makes progress step by step.[38] Both signal his traditionalist approach. He explains that by building centres and sending Tibetan lamas to teach, he hopes to help students integrate the Dharma into their everyday life. The students should, in turn, exert themselves in their training with discipline and a strong sense of responsibility so that they are able to set good examples for generations to come. The centres that are under the guidance of different Kagyu teachers should not develop competitiveness against each other, but rather work together to create a sacred atmosphere for the transmission to take place properly.[39] The Karmapa's advice here points to a sustainable transmission, on both individual and organisational levels. He himself also helped committed students further their spiritual progress by offering them direct, in-person guidance.[40] This strengthened their personal connection with the lineage; many became Buddhist teachers and leaders of their communities, contributing to the continued development of the tradition in the West.

8.3. FRIENDSHIP WITH OTHER BUDDHIST TRADITIONS AND DIFFERENT RELIGIONS

The Karmapa consolidated the existing connection with other Tibetan schools and, at the same time, built new relationships with other Buddhist traditions and different religions. This can be understood as a continuation of his non-sectarian approach in Tibet and the early exile.[41] Yet, the focus here is different. In the preservation phase when he endeavoured to rebuild his lineage in the Indian subcontinent, he advocated close cooperation between different Tibetan schools to tackle the challenge that they all faced in exile. Non-sectarianism at that time was crucial for all schools to secure a supportive environment for their revival. The Karmapa's top priority, however, was to preserve the Karma Kagyu lineage. He concentrated on the re-establishment of the monastic community by building new Rumtek, strengthening monastic discipline and training his sangha.

Moving on to the expansion phase, the Karmapa's priority shifted. When touring Europe and North America, he extended his non-sectarian efforts to include the Theravāda and Zen traditions as well as other religions. Such shift was propelled by a different set of dynamics. The sociocultural and religious environments in Europe and North America differed significantly from Tibet and the Indian subcontinent. The rise of the counterculture movement allowed Asian religions to establish a presence. Nonetheless, to the interested and curious Westerners, Tibetan Buddhism was just one of several options to be tested for their spiritual value. Various lineages of

Tibetan Buddhism, together with the Theravāda, Zen Buddhism and Hinduism, coexisted in close proximity within a host culture shaped by Christian values and secular discourse. Within this context, friendly contact with other Buddhist traditions became a practical means for survival and growth. Nonsectarianism provided an ever more relevant and necessary orientation to achieve expansion.

The Karmapa was ready to adapt to the new situation. The focus on lineage preservation in the early exile was replaced with a more accommodating approach. Spiritual tolerance came to be a central theme of his tours in the West. In a television interview during his visit to the United States in 1976, he tells that the different schools of Tibetan Buddhism share the same essence in their teachings.[42] In California, he visited the Dharma centres of the Sakya and Nyingma schools and met with Sakya lamas Dezhung Rinpoche and Thartse Rinpoche, Nyingma lamas Dudjom Rinpoche and Tarthang Tulku, as well as Zen teachers Maezumi Roshi and Richard Baker, and the Vietnamese Zen patriarch for North America Thich Thien-An.[43] In New York, he met with Chinese masters Venerables Minchih, abbot of the Da-Jue Temple in New York and chairman of the Buddhist Association of the United States; Chanyun, founding abbot of the Lian-Yin Temple in Taiwan; and Richang, the head of the Fu-Chih Foundation in Taiwan.[44] In London, he taught at Sogyal Rinpoche's Nyingma centre[45] and paid visits to the Thai and Sri Lankan Buddhist centres.[46] In Europe, he also met with Theravāda and Zen teachers, especially Taizen Deshimaru.[47]

The Karmapa also established links with other religions and spiritual traditions. In the United States, he visited the Ashram of Baba Muktananda for a discussion of Buddhist and Hindu Tantra.[48] He met with native peoples, such as the Hopi in the United States and the Blackfoot in Canada.[49] He also attended an interfaith conference in Washington.[50] In Rome, he had a private audience with Pope Paul VI, accompanied by Akong Tulku, Sister Palmo (Freda Bedi) and Namkhai Norbu.[51] At this meeting, he proposed to promote harmony between world religions.[52] The pope, in turn, 'praised the Karmapa for fostering the "spiritual as well as moral values of humanity"' and addressed him as 'Your Holiness'.[53] They exchanged gifts, including medallions, books and a Buddha statue, with 'genuine warmth and mutual respect'.[54] Freda Bedi recalls that the pope invited the Karmapa to return to Rome for a longer stay.[55] The Karmapa also met with the Roman Catholic archbishop of Westminster, the dean of Westminster Abbey[56] and the leader of the ecumenical Christian Center of Dialogue in Denmark.[57] Through these meetings, he contributed to the interfaith dialogue on a global level. His connection with the Catholic Church, in particular, allowed him to introduce Tibetan Buddhism to mainstream culture in the West.

8.4. ENGAGEMENT WITH GOVERNMENTS AND POLITICIANS

The Karmapa engaged with governments and politicians, especially while on tour in the United States. Since early exile, he had distanced himself from the Tibetan cause to ensure that his vision to revive the Dharma was free from politics.[58] Due to his strong connections with the royal courts of Bhutan and Sikkim and the Government of India, he was able to gain access to financial resources to support his preservation initiative.[59] In the West, he maintained his apolitical stance. When meeting with the press, he emphasised his pure religious intention and expressed disinterest in politics.[60] Still, his tours attracted political attention. His Bhutanese diplomatic passport conferred privilege, as did his position as a recognised religious leader. In the 1970s, the situation with the Tibetan diaspora was seen as politically sensitive in the United States; the Dalai Lama was only able to visit there for the first time in 1979.[61] This would have made the Karmapa, travelling with the official status of a Bhutanese diplomat instead of a Tibetan refugee, possibly the highest-ranking, most influential leader of Tibetan Buddhism that the country, and its government, had ever received.

Before the Karmapa's first tour in 1974, Freda Bedi had already formed a friendship with Senator Charles H. Percy who consequently extended a warm welcome to the Karmapa on all his tours in the United States.[62] Chögyam Trungpa built on the connection with Percy to bring the Karmapa to mainstream society. Following the Karmapa's first visit, Senator Percy wrote in a letter to Trungpa:

> America's roots are firmly planted in the soil of religious freedom. . . . Certainly, His Holiness the Gyalwa Karmapa experienced this element of the American spirit during his visit to the United States in 1974. . . . We seek to be at peace with all the people of the world . . . we are a tolerant and understanding people. We carefully guard religious freedom as one of our most treasured national principles.[63]

To Percy, the Karmapa's visit attests to America's commitment to religious freedom. This reflects the US government's effort to integrate the visits of high-profile religious figures into its own political narrative. The senator's letter was included in the book *Empowerment* that Trungpa produced to celebrate the Karmapa's first tour. This book begins with the following statement: 'This volume is dedicated to the United States of America on the occasion of its Bicentennial, in honor of the warmth and openness with which the United States has received the wisdom and insights of diverse traditions throughout its unique history.'[64] In the foreword, Trungpa expresses his gratitude for the hospitality that the country extended to the Karmapa.[65] He also declares that through the Dharma, his American students who had rejected their own culture came to appreciate America again.⁶⁶ In this way, he placed the Karmapa's visit within the context of a mutually beneficial relationship. He drew on the political discourse of religious freedom to introduce the Karmapa to the American people. Once endorsed by the government, Tibetan Buddhism that the Karmapa represented ceased to be merely a foreign arrival, but instead, became integrated into American values.

The US government's interest in the Karmapa continued to grow in his following two tours. The Karmapa, in response, actively engaged with it. Between 1976 and 1977, in Washington, D.C., Senator Percy invited the Karmapa to his own mansion; the Karmapa attended a reception in Capitol Hill with over ninety senators and congressmen.⁶⁷ In Los Angeles, the mayor and police department, along with other dignitaries, welcomed him.⁶⁸ In 1980, upon his arrival in Washington, D.C., the US government issued a letter of welcome. Percy invited him to a Congress luncheon at the Capitol Building; the Karmapa delivered a speech on the Dharma and world peace.⁶⁹ Again, as Percy's guest, at the Senate Foreign Relations Committee breakfast, he joined a discussion on world affairs and world peace.⁷⁰ At KTD, the Karmapa's main seat in the United States, Percy served as an honorary member of the first Board of Advisers.⁷¹ In Los Angeles, the Karmapa met with Mayor Tom Bradley; his arrival was featured on three television channels.⁷² In New York, Mayor Ed Koch welcomed him to the city; his letter of invitation states: 'New Yorkers revere the ancient precepts of the Kagyu order of Buddhism and honor your holy presence here as a distinguished visitor to our city.'⁷³

The Karmapa received similar honours in Canada. In 1974, the lieutenant governor of British Columbia welcomed him at Government House.⁷⁴ In 1977, the mayor of Montreal, Jean Drapeau, received him with the highest protocol.⁷⁵ These high-level receptions give one a good sense of the esteem in which the Karmapa was held in North America. They offered him a platform to introduce his tradition, and Tibetan Buddhism as a whole, to mainstream society.

NOTES

1. Finnegan, *Dharma King*, 420.
2. Finnegan, *Dharma King*, 380.
3. Finnegan, *Dharma King*, 380.
4. Finnegan, *Dharma King*, 420.
5. Finnegan, *Dharma King*, 380.
6. See 6.1.3. Training the Sangha.
7. See 2.2. Introduction of Buddhism.
8. See 4.1. Black Crown Ceremony.

9. Lhundup Damchö, *Karmapa: 900 Years*, 87–89.
10. Interview with the Sixteenth Karmapa on the American television programme 'Vermont Report' (December 1976) in *Recalling a Buddha*.
11. Ringu Tulku, "He Was Always Free," 138.
12. Holmes, "First Samye Dzongs."
13. See 7.3. Akong Tulku.
14. Finnegan, *Dharma King*, 249.
15. Ogyen Trinley Dorje, Foreword to *Dharma King: The life of the 16th Gyalwang Karmapa in images*, by Damchö D Finnegan (New York: KTD Publications; Himachal Pradesh: Altruism Press, 2014), 6.
16. *The Lion's Roar*.
17. *Recalling a Buddha*.
18. Holmes, "16th Karmapa in Europe," 286.
19. Holmes, "16th Karmapa in Europe," 286–287.
20. See 4.1. Black Crown Ceremony.
21. Finnegan, *Dharma King*, 322, 312–313.
22. Khra 'gu rin po che, *rgyal ba'i dbang po*, 383.2–383.5, 383.15–383.17; Zhwa dmar, *sku tshe'i rnam thar*, 106.5–106.14.
23. Roth and Levine, "USA Introduction," 153; Finnegan, *Dharma King*, 422.
24. Chia Theng Shen (沈家楨 1913–1997), chairman and chief executive of the American Steamship Company, was the Karmapa's foremost patron in the United States. Several accounts report his donation of land for the construction of the Karmapa's main seat in North America. Shen also sponsored his printing projects, provided accommodation for his visits and later funded his medical treatment. For more detail, see Khra 'gu rin po che, *rgyal ba'i dbang po*, 380.18–380.20, 381.21–382.1; Jamgon Kongtrul Rinpoche, "XVI Gyalwa Karmapa," 16; Finnegan, *Dharma King*, 139, 422; Lama Karma Drodül, *Amrita of Eloquence: A biography of Khenpo Karthar Rinpoche*, trans. Lama Yeshe Gyamtso (New York: KTD Publications, 2008), 88–89; Roth and Levine, "USA Introduction," 153; Sharon Mumbie, "Dharma In My Bones," in *The Miraculous 16th Karmapa: Incredible encounters with the Black Crown Buddha*, comp. Norma Levine (Arcidosso: Shang Shung Publications, 2013), 242; Kotwal, *God's Own Death*, 257; Nydahl, *Riding the Tiger*, 90, 94.
25. Lama Karma Drodül, *Amrita of Eloquence*, 145–146; Finnegan, *Dharma King*, 422; Kunsang and Aubèle, "Sixteenth Karmapa," 228.
26. Lhundup Damchö, *Karmapa: 900 Years*, 90, 92; Finnegan, *Dharma King*, 422–424; Roth and Levine, "USA Introduction," 155; *The Lion's Roar*.
27. Devorah Peck and the Kagyu Video Project, "Wish Fulfilling Gem." See also Finnegan, *Dharma King*, 422.
28. See 7.3. Akong Tulku.
29. Roth and Levine, "USA Introduction," 155–156.
30. Jamgon Kongtrul Rinpoche, "XVI Gyalwa Karmapa," 16.
31. Terhune, *Karmapa*, 131–132; MJ Bennett, "The Picnic," in *The Miraculous 16th Karmapa: Incredible Encounters with the Black Crown Buddha*, comp. Norma Levine (Arcidosso: Shang Shung Publications, 2013), 107.

"bKa' brgyud 'dzam gling dbus rgyun las khang" (See Rum bteg, "rnam thar lo rgyus," 223.23) and "rGyal yongs bka' brgyud dbus rgyun las khungs" (See Rum bteg, "dgongs rdzogs mjug mchod," 257.17) may both refer to this organisation.

32. For example, in 1978, he sent thirty lamas from India to the Dharma centres overseas. See Jamgon Kongtrul Rinpoche, "XVI Gyalwa Karmapa," 17.

33. Rang byung rig pa'i rdo rje, "mchog gi bka' slob," 22–23.

34. *nga rang bla rgan gnyis (rgyal dbang karma pa bcu drug pa mchog dang | ka lu rin po che |) gyis 'dzam gling skor thengs phyed gnyis tsam red song | de dngul e thob kyi don min | sems can gyi don ma gtogs rtsa ba nas med | dam pa'i chos zhes bya ba de sems can rmongs pa 'dul phyir kho na yin stabs | khyed rang tsho'i bsam par bla ma'i bka' red | 'gro rgyu 'gro dgos | bstan 'gro'i don 'grub pa dka' mo red bsam ste | dpa' mi zhum zhing | sems stobs bskyed dgos | srid kyi cha la byus gtogs rtsa ba nas mi dgos | chos pa yin tshe 'dod yon la chags zhen | tshong khe gtong len sogs mdor na chos min gyi spyod lam spangs te chos pa rnam dag gi las lam la gzhi bzung nas gzhan don byas na | rgya mtsho la chu phran 'dus pa ltar | gdul bya 'dus te yong gi red |* (Rang byung rig pa'i rdo rje, "mchog gi bka' slob," 22.)

35. Kalu Rinpoche, *Dharma: That Illuminates*, 11.

36. Brown, *Dance of 17 Lives*, 102.

37. Interview with the Sixteenth Karmapa on the American television programme 'Vermont Report' (December 1976) in *Recalling a Buddha*; Devorah Peck and the Kagyu Video Project, "Wish Fulfilling Gem."

38. Interview with the Sixteenth Karmapa on the American television programme 'Vermont Report' (December 1976) in *Recalling a Buddha*.

39. Devorah Peck and the Kagyu Video Project, "Wish Fulfilling Gem."

40. Lhundup Damchö, *Karmapa: 900 Years*, 87–89.

41. See 6.2. Non-Sectarian Approach.

42. Interview with the Sixteenth Karmapa on the American television programme 'Vermont Report' (December 1976) in *Recalling a Buddha*.

43. Khra 'gu rin po che, *rgyal ba'i dbang po*, 381.17–381.19; Finnegan, *Dharma King*, 186, 250, 251, 441; Roth and Levine, "USA Introduction," 152; *Recalling a Buddha*.

44. Finnegan, *Dharma King*, 250.

45. Finnegan, *Dharma King*, 278–279.

46. Khra 'gu rin po che, *rgyal ba'i dbang po*, 382.9–382.11; Lhundup Damchö, *Karmapa: 900 Years*, 88.

47. Holmes, "Buddha Karmapa," 296–297; Nydahl, *Riding the Tiger*, 47, 124; Finnegan, *Dharma King*, 316.

48. Finnegan, *Dharma King*, 156; Contractor, "Meeting of Mahasiddhas," 92.

The Karmapa had already formed a friendship with Muktananda back in India. See Contractor, "Meeting of Mahasiddhas," 88–93; Finnegan, *Dharma King*, 96–97.

49. Roth, "Iron Bird Flies," 181–184; Bennett and Levine, "Three World Tours," 163; Finnegan, *Dharma King*, 137, 262–263.

50. Finnegan, *Dharma King*, 428.

51. Khra 'gu rin po che, *rgyal ba'i dbang po*, 382.19–382.20; Grags pa yongs 'dus, "bcu drug pa," 375.18–376.1; Zhwa dmar, *sku tshe'i rnam thar*, 114.9–114.10;

Jamgon Kongtrul Rinpoche, "XVI Gyalwa Karmapa," 16; Kunsang and Aubèle, "Sixteenth Karmapa," 228; Lhundup Damchö, *Karmapa: 900 Years*, 87, 88, 89; Finnegan, *Dharma King*, 308–309; Dzogchen Ponlop, "Rangjung Rigpe Dorje," 293; Nydahl, *Riding the Tiger*, 48; Holmes, "16th Karmapa in Europe," 287; Holmes, "Buddha Karmapa," 296; Holmes, "1974 Visit"; Levine, *Freda Bedi*, 282–284; *Recalling a Buddha*.

52. Jamgon Kongtrul Rinpoche, "XVI Gyalwa Karmapa," 16.
53. Finnegan, *Dharma King*, 309.
54. Finnegan, *Dharma King*, 309.
55. Levine, *Freda Bedi*, 284.
56. Holmes, "Buddha Karmapa," 296; Levine, *Freda Bedi*, 274–275.
57. Nydahl, *Riding the Tiger*, 120.
58. See 5.1. Dissociation from the Exile Government.
59. See 5.2. Connections with Bhutan, Sikkim and India.
60. Finnegan, *Dharma King*, 216.

A news article, titled "A Tibetan view of church-state politics: Head lama, in Hub on tour, puts stress on 'spirituality'," published in *Boston Globe*, records the Karmapa's view (See *Recalling a Buddha*).

61. See 5.2.3. Building of Monasteries.
62. See 7.1. Freda Bedi.
63. Charles H Percy, "Dear Rinpoche," in *Empowerment: The visit of His Holiness the 16th Gyalwa Karmapa to the United States* (Boulder, CO: Vajradhatu Publications, 1976).
64. *Empowerment: The visit of His Holiness the 16th Gyalwa Karmapa to the United States* (Boulder, CO: Vajradhatu Publications, 1976).
65. *Empowerment*.
66. *Empowerment*.
67. Roth and Levine, "USA Introduction," 155; Finnegan, *Dharma King*, 254–255, 429; Tsering Namgyal Khortsa, "Sixteenth Karmapa," 84.
68. John Welwood, "Discovering Buddha Nature in Disneyland," in *The Miraculous 16th Karmapa: Incredible Encounters with the Black Crown Buddha*, comp. Norma Levine (Arcidosso: Shang Shung Publications, 2013), 265; *Recalling a Buddha*.
69. Jamgon Kongtrul Rinpoche, "XVI Gyalwa Karmapa," 18; Lhundup Damchö, *Karmapa: 900 Years*, 90; Finnegan, *Dharma King*, 428.
70. *Recalling a Buddha*.
71. Roth and Levine, "USA Introduction," 155.
72. Finnegan, *Dharma King*, 428.
73. Finnegan, *Dharma King*, 429.
    This meeting is also recorded in *Recalling a Buddha*.
74. Bennett and Levine, "Three World Tours," 160; Levine, *Freda Bedi*, 266.
75. Bennett and Levine, "Three World Tours," 163; Finnegan, *Dharma King*, 266.

Conclusion

This book examines the life of the Sixteenth Karmapa, Rangjung Rigpe Dorje, with a particular focus on his transmission of Tibetan Buddhism in exile. It is an application of the critique of anti-Orientalism intended to introduce balance to the existing scholarship that privileges reception over transmission agency. Here, Tibetan agency takes centre stage, and the transmission is presented as a cross-cultural phenomenon that involves the active participation of both the receiver and the transmitter. The study draws on data collected from written accounts, collections of photographs, recordings of interviews and documentaries in Tibetan and English language. These sources contain historical evidence as well as collective and individual memories from the Karmapa's disciples.

The Karmapa's transmission strategies emphasised continuity with tradition with some openness to adaptation. They proved to be effective. On the one hand, his Western disciples perceive him as a 'Dharma King', a manifestation of the Sixth Buddha of Fortunate Aeon Siṃha and Bodhisattva Avalokiteśvara, who possessed miraculous powers, including the abilities to predict his own rebirth and to liberate others upon sight. Such perception is developed through a combination of Western disciples' conformity with tradition and their personal experience. On the other hand, the Karma Kagyu had, by the 1980s, reached an expansion unmatched by any other Tibetan school: over 300 Kagyu centres spread across the world; most Dharma centres in Europe and the United States belonged to the school. The Karmapa's traditionalist approach and his success on the global scale challenge the widely held assumption that the transmission is primarily a matter of Westernisation.

To understand the Karmapa's strategies and his success, the study seeks to answer two questions: (1) How did the Karmapa achieve the fast and widespread development of his tradition? (2) What were his main contributions to the preservation of Tibetan Buddhism and its transmission to the West? This has led to an in-depth investigation into the Karmapa's role as the transmitter in two important phases of his activity in exile: preservation and expansion. Each phase required specific strategies and resources. In the preservation phase, the Karmapa prioritised the restoration of the monastic community. His dissociation from the exile government allowed him to concentrate on religious matters. His connections with the royal courts of Bhutan and Sikkim and the Government of India guaranteed safety for his flight and access to financial resources during his resettlement. They offered him a special advantage: to carry out his activity beyond the confines of the refugee settlements where most Tibetan Buddhist lineages rebuilt themselves at a much slower pace. He was thus able to establish his main seat in exile, Rumtek Monastery, as early as the mid-1960s. Rumtek became the first Tibetan monastery constructed for permanent use in the diaspora, built to high artistic standards. There he undertook his preservation initiative with notable impact. He was among the first Tibetan lamas in exile to revive the tradition of summer retreat. Due to his efforts to strengthen monastic discipline, the Rumtek sangha developed a good reputation and won respect from local communities. He assembled a high-quality teaching force, created training facilities and supervised the training of young lamas and tulkus as well as his Western disciples.

The Karmapa's activity in Rumtek had a far-reaching impact on the expansion phase and beyond. The most significant example is his training of Freda Bedi to become a Buddhist teacher in her own right. Bedi then played an instrumental role in his activity in the West. On tour in Europe and North America, he sent lamas and tulkus from Rumtek to build and manage monasteries, to hold the posts of resident teachers in Dharma centres and to deliver teachings and train Tibetan language translators. This helped him quickly scale up the expansion. Rumtek also served as the headquarters for the Dharma centres that he founded in the West. Over the years, his four primary disciples and other tulkus, such as Dzogchen Ponlop, Traleg Rinpoche and Chokyi Nyima, became world-renowned Buddhist teachers. Furthermore, the Karmapa travelled to the West not as a political refugee, but as a prestigious guest to local governments, thanks to his Bhutanese diplomatic passport issued by the King of Bhutan. This added to his appeal, giving him an opportunity to introduce Tibetan Buddhism to mainstream society.

In the preservation phase, the Karmapa contributed, in two ways, to the preservation and transmission of Tibetan Buddhism. First, in training young tulkus, lamas and Western disciples in Rumtek, he built human resources from the early years to ensure sustainable development of his lineage into the future. Second, he printed the Kangyur, Tengyur and other important Buddhist texts. The Derge Kangyur project marked the beginning of the photo-offset printing of large Tibetan texts in exile. Copies of the Derge Kangyur were distributed to monasteries of different schools in the Himalayas as well as libraries in the United States to support academic research.

The second phase, expansion, consisted of a more ambitious undertaking. It began in 1963 when the Karmapa sent two young tulkus, Chögyam Trungpa and Akong Tulku, to Britain. Transmitting the Dharma to the West was, in many ways, a challenging task. On the one hand, new concepts and phenomena, such as 'Modernist Buddhism', 'Post-modernist Buddhism' and the counterculture, new religious and New Age movements, created a favourable environment for Buddhism to establish a footing in the West. On the other hand, the manner in which Buddhism established itself there differs considerably from Tibet and the Himalayan region. In pre-modern Tibet, Buddhism became a widespread religion on account of patronage and support from the royal courts and local governments. In the West, there was some government support, but it usually fell into two categories: academic research and refugee policy. Tibet and Tibetan Buddhism were rather foreign to mainstream society. Therefore, the Karmapa had to develop new strategies to achieve expansion. This he did in two stages. First, he sent four agents, Freda Bedi, Chögyam Trungpa, Akong Tulku and Kalu Rinpoche, to prepare the ground. Second, on tour in the West, he formulated four strategies to consolidate the development of his lineage. In both stages, he maintained a traditionalist approach but also demonstrated openness to adaptation.

The four agents each made a unique contribution to the early transmission of Tibetan Buddhism to the West. Their approaches ranged from the traditionalist to the innovative. Both Akong Tulku and Kalu Rinpoche were traditionalists. Akong was initially uncertain about the future of Tibetan Buddhism in the West; however, encouraged by the Karmapa, he developed Samye Ling into a full-scale Tibetan Buddhist monastery. He was instrumental in the Karmapa's two extensive tours in Europe. Kalu, through his decade-long work in North America and Europe, from 1971 to 1982, introduced the Kagyu teachings in their most traditional form and founded the first retreat centres in the West. In so doing, he prepared the ground for the Karmapa's transmission of tradition. Bedi was the Karmapa's first Western disciple. She founded the Young Lamas' Home School in India which trained the first generation of Tibetan lamas to teach in the West, including Trungpa and Akong. She served as the Karmapa's secretary and adviser in Rumtek, encouraged him to travel to the West and organised his first tour to North America and Europe. As the only Westerner in his entourage, she helped bridge the gap between the Tibetan tradition and Western culture, which was crucial to the transmission at a time when Tibetan Buddhism was still a new phenomenon. Both Kalu and Bedi contributed to the propagation of Tantric ritual in the West which, in turn, facilitated the Karmapa's transmission of Tantric Buddhism on his tours.

Chögyam Trungpa was the most versatile and innovative of the four agents. Soon after his arrival in the United States in 1970, he attracted a large following that mainly consisted of young people associated with the counterculture movement. Initially, he severed all ties with tradition and adopted a hippie lifestyle. He propagated Buddhist teachings through two strategies: adaptation and diversification. Nonetheless, in preparation for the Karmapa's first visit in 1974, he began to train his students in formality and ritual hierarchy. As a result, his American students received the Karmapa in a grand style and a dignified manner. The change in his approach may have been strategic after all. He established communication with the counterculture generation for the purpose of guiding them to re-enter mainstream society and preparing them for the Karmapa's transmission of tradition.

In this first stage of the expansion phase, the Karmapa contributed to the transmission of Tibetan Buddhism through the diversity of transmission strategies from his four agents. These agents came from very different backgrounds: Akong and Trungpa belonged to the younger generation of Tibetan tulkus; Kalu represented a much older generation; Bedi, an Oxford graduate, political activist and social worker, encountered Tibetan Buddhism through her work on the Tibetan resettlement for the Indian government. Through different approaches, their activities shaped the early transmission of Tibetan Buddhism in dynamic ways. Such diversity and the trust that the Karmapa placed in his agents, particularly his Western disciples, attest to his openness to adaptation.

In the second stage, the Karmapa created four strategies while on tour in Europe and North America: (1) prioritisation of Tantric rituals, (2) founding of monasteries and Dharma centres, (3) friendship with other Buddhist traditions and different religions and (4) engagement with governments and politicians. The first two concern the transmission of the Dharma proper; the last two are connected to a broader religious and political context. They feature both continuity with the preservation phase and change to adapt to new sociocultural environments.

By prioritising ritual over verbal discourse, the Karmapa was able to connect with his audience more directly with less reliance on language translation. It offered Westerners an opportunity to experience, what tradition believes to be, his remarkable spiritual attribute, 'teaching by being'. Through the Black Crown Ceremony, he reached a large number of newcomers, which certainly contributed to the swift development of the tradition. He founded monasteries and Dharma centres to provide practitioners with training facilities and resources. It proved to be the most tangible outcome of his activity in the West which ensured sustainable growth for his Western community. He developed a more accommodating approach to address the challenge of transmitting Buddhism in host cultures shaped by Christian values and secular discourse. This was achieved by extending his non-sectarian efforts to include other Buddhist traditions and different religions and participating in interfaith dialogue. A friendship with the Catholic Church helped his tradition gain acceptance into mainstream culture. His interaction with governments and politicians bore a similar effect: it offered him a platform to introduce his tradition to mainstream society.

In this second stage of the expansion phase, the Karmapa made four key contributions to the transmission of Tibetan Buddhism. First, his propagation of Tantric ritual enabled a widespread transmission of Tantric Buddhism. Second, his efforts to build monasteries and Dharma centres scaled up the spread of Tibetan Buddhism. Third, his training of Western practitioners and Buddhist teachers, carried on from the preservation phase, created necessary human resources for the sustainable development of Tibetan Buddhism in the West. Fourth, his interfaith dialogue with Christianity and interaction with Western governments brought Tibetan Buddhism to mainstream society.

Appendix A

Rangjung Rigpe Dorje's Rangnam—*a Brief Autobiography*

[p.64] I have carried the crown of the name, Buddha Karmapa.[1] Born [as] someone without Dharma, [I was] bestowed onto [my] head the very weighty crown of the name, the glorious Karmapa, at the age of eight, according to the signs with physical appearance and the meaning of the prophecies [given by] the lamas in the past. Since then, up to the age of thirty-six [1959], [I] studied with many good teachers. [I] teach and propagate the *prātimokṣa*, bodhisattva and Tantric vows as well as empowerments, transmissions and instructions to the great masters who can uphold the Buddha's teaching. [I] build anew the foundation of the teaching—temples, and establish Buddhist institutes and retreat centres. [Thereby,] in Tibet itself and greater Tibet, [for] the non-sectarian teaching of the Buddha, [I] did merely a lowly person's work which was restoring what had declined and developing what had not.

When I was thirty-six years old [1959], Tibet completely lost [its] true religious and political independence. As the critical time was about to come, I [led] the great masters who are holders of the Kagyu teachings [to take flight into exile], carrying together the sacred representations of the enlightened body, speech and mind [of the Buddha]. On the journey, gradually, [we] arrived at the special place in the hidden land Sikkim, Rumtek Samten Chöling (Rum bteg bsam gtan chos gling), on the fifth day of the fifth month of the pig year [11 June 1959]. From then on, without time for happy leisure and rest, [I] consider the very weighty task of reviving the Buddha's teaching to be [my] own responsibility. [p.65] [I] arranged temporary livelihood and shelter for the sangha. On the land of this monastic seat of the Kagyu [school], Shedrub Chokhor Ling, [which is] the holy place of the activity [of] the glorious Akaniṣṭha, [I] finished establishing a monastic community. At that time, good signs of illusory kind emerged, including my own experience and dream, that a very good foundation of the teaching was arising in many a country in the world, east and west. Hence, the work was starting from the iron ox year [1961]; [by] the beginning of the fire horse year [1966], [the construction of] the shrine halls [which are] the foundation [of the teaching] and the living quarters of the sangha were both completed successfully. [As for] the representation of the enlightened body inside [the shrines], [I have produced] one thousand buddha statues, made from medicine and clay and fully gilded, murals of the 'Six Ornaments and Two Supreme Ones', the 'Sixteen Elders', the 'Seven Buddhas',[2] as well as the 'Golden Garland of the Kagyu'. [I have] created from copper and gold statues of the 'Golden Garland of the Kagyu, Buddhas of the Three Times' and the 'Three Siddhas from Kham'. Regarding the representation of the enlightened speech, [I] assemble the Derge red-ink [edition] of the Kangyur, the Narthang edition of the Kangyur and Tengyur, and over one thousand volumes of the teachings of the Buddha [preserved] in different schools, mainly the four senior and eight junior lineages of the Kagyu. [I] make the new block print edition of the precious Kangyur of the Buddha, based on the Derge red-ink edition, as well as approximately fifteen volumes of block print of the exclusive, profound instructions of the Kagyu [school], the *maṇḍala* sādhana of the Tantra section, and the detailed commentaries on the Sūtra and Tantra. Through the help of Chia Theng Shen who lives in the United States, [I] have completed the printing of forty-plus volumes of commentaries and detailed commentaries on the profound instructions of the Kagyu [school], the Sūtra and Tantra, science, annals of the royal lineage and religious history, as well as the teachings of renowned Indian *paṇḍita*s and *siddha*s, 500 copies for each volume [using the method of] xerography. [p.66] [I] have put in place the assembly of intensive group sādhana practice, sādhana *pūjā*s, and *pūjā*s scheduled on auspicious days, according to the flawless tradition of Tsurphu in Tölung, the monastic seat of the heart of Akaniṣṭha, by whatever means necessary [to ensure that] the old tradition is uncorrupted, like in the monastic seat Tsurphu. Each year, [I organise] the assembly of summer retreat through the authentic application of the 'Three Basic Rituals of the Vinaya'. Meanwhile, on account of [my] steady lama-patron relationship with successive Kings of Bhutan, [I] have successfully constructed new shrine halls, [which are] the foundation [of the teaching], and living quarters of the sangha in Tashi Choling of Bumthang, Bhutan for the founding of the great advanced institute of the Kagyu [school]. Likewise, in Nepal, I have constructed mainly a great number of monasteries [to propagate] the teaching, and have helped create the best possible conditions. As a result, now in Nepal, [I] have established many new monastic communities. Moreover, [I] have also built, for some time, the foundation of the precious non-sectarian teaching of the Buddha across India, Nepal, Sikkim and Bhutan. This year, on the holy day that celebrates the return of the Buddha from heaven, [I] will establish a great advanced Buddhist institute and a retreat centre as part of this monastic seat of the activity of Akaniṣṭha. Those who reside in the institute will not chase worldly pride, such as material gain and honour, and ambition for fame. With pure thoughts and conduct, [they] will be weary of samsara, and have taken solely the pure novice and full ordination vows. To be able to sustain the powerful practice of the bodhisattva for the benefit of others, [they] will also train single-pointedly in the Mahāyāna. In the same way, once [they] have renounced worldly affairs, those who reside in the retreat centre practise properly the profound path, Mahāmudrā, and the profound means, the Six Dharmas of Nāropā. [The retreat centre] is organised as necessary so that [they] will be able to follow the examples of the Kagyu forefathers with confidence in the Two Stages. In brief, [I] create new Dharma communities, [including] temples [which are] the foundation [of the teaching], [p.67] living quarters of the sangha, as well as institutes and retreat centres in each and every country and region in the world, east and west. At least, [I] have founded Dharma centres for men and women with the hope and aspiration that [I would] be able to place in [their] minds even the slightest seed of the Dharma in addition to [their] mundane pursuits. In brief, neither entrusting others with [the task of performing] virtuous activity nor soliciting for donations from the public, [I] have given whatever material wealth I possess without hesitation, as the root of virtue. Also, without pursuing worldly pride, i.e., material gain and honour, and ambition for fame, importantly, [I] acted wholly on account of nothing but the hope that [I] will benefit others. [I] have hoped that the true benefit for others has arisen. Even now, all that is left is to continue with the remainder of my [own] activity. There is no question [of me] positioning [myself] among the famous people in the world. Although [I] thought carefully through the Dharma, [I] do not consider [myself] as belonging to the middle kind of practitioners; nor do I have confidence in myself. However, due to the blessing of the name of the [Kagyu] forefathers, whatever kind of Dharma activity [I] have undertaken is never left unfinished. Nonetheless, as [told in their] life stories, the Kagyu forefathers lived [the life of] the son of mountains, donned the clothes made from mist, and endured the loss of food, clothing and speech. In one life one body, [they] achieved the state of unified Vajradhāra. As outer signs, [at the time of death,] the sky was filled naturally with all kinds of rainbow clouds and rainfalls of flowers. For the benefit of the disciples, [they] illustrated the radiance of rejoicing in the five wisdoms, leaving behind five coloured relics. From the illusory body of a dirty beggar, [they] departed in a rainbow body with only hair and fingernails to remain. [I] strongly believe that, still in my lifetime, there have been plenty of people [who achieved high levels of realisation] just like that. I have thus, since childhood, aspired to become one like them, and always exert myself in the practice of the 'Three Solitudes'. Yet, until now, since the exalted Kagyu masters, the supreme reincarnations endowed with natural signs, are at a young age, [p.68] [I] have given [them] empowerments, transmissions and profound instructions. With [this] and the best knowledge in the great texts of the Sūtra and Tantra, [they] will be able to nurture [their own] disciples. [This is what I] must certainly do. Since [they will carry out] many kinds of tasks, including the need to specialise in teaching [the Dharma] abroad, [they] will be travelling all over the world. This is my situation.

I request that [this text] be translated into English in the highest quality, [and] then dispatched specially as soon as possible. Best wishes.

NOTES

1. This is the only *rangnam* text of the Sixteenth Karmapa that has been published so far, compiled by Jose Tashi Tsering (Jo sras bkra shis tshe ring) in Volume 1 of the *Collected Works of the Sixteenth Karmapa* (*rgyal dbang karma pa bcu drug pa chen po'i gsung 'bum 1*). Therein, the Karmapa outlines his contribution to the preservation of Tibetan Buddhism, particularly his achievements in exile. The text is not dated, but its content gives a clue: the Karmapa mentions his plan to build a Buddhist institute and a retreat centre at Rumtek Monastery in that very year. This, according to other sources (referenced in 6.1.3. Training the Sangha), is 1978. By that time, the Karmapa had travelled twice to North America and Europe and achieved notable success in propagating Tibetan Buddhism in exile. Three years later, he died in the United States. Hence, he wrote this text at the peak of his transmission of Tibetan Buddhism in exile; its content reveals his personal reflection on his own life and activity. At the end of the text, the Karmapa specially requests that the text be translated into English. However, I have not been able to find any English translation; it is unclear whether this *rangnam* has ever been translated and distributed at all. The text itself has only come to light since the publication of the *Collected Works* (*gsung 'bum*) in 2016.

2. *Rab* in *sangs rgyas rab bdun* in this text may be a typographical error or variant spelling of *rabs*.

Appendix B

Rangjung Rigpe Dorje's Namthar, *Composed by Thrangu Rinpoche— The Life Story of the Victorious One, the Great Sixteenth [Karmapa]*

[p.321] [Summary of the chapters:]

[Chapter 1:] First, how the succession of [his previous] lives came about, in relation to the great prophecies [in] the Sūtra and Tantra, and the way [he] took rebirth;[1]

[Chapter 2:] Then, the great masters identified [him to be the Karmapa incarnation], and offered throne offerings [for his] enthronement in each of the Kagyu monastic seats;

[Chapter 3:] How [he] conducted [his] studies in the presence of [his] teachers, beginning with writing and reading, and up to [the practice of] Mahāmudrā and the Six Dharmas of Nāropā;

[Chapter 4:] In order to increase the accumulation of merits, [he] went on pilgrimages and made offerings in the south [of Tibet], the holy land India and the snow mountains;

[Chapter 5:] For the sake of the teaching and the welfare of beings, [he] travelled to various regions of India, China and Tibet;

[Chapter 6:] To revive the embers of the teaching, [he] became a refugee in India, and then established anew the great monastic seat Shedrub Chokhor Ling (bShad sgrub chos 'khor gling);

[Chapter 7:] Through the lama-patron relationship in India, Nepal, Sikkim and Bhutan, [he] founded new monastic seats that uphold [the tradition of] the teaching and practice;

[Chapter 8:] [He] maintained [his] enlightened activity by travelling to Western countries to spread the precious teaching of the Buddha.

[p.322] This is the life story of the glorious lord of the Victorious Ones, the Karmapa Rangjung Rigpe Dorje, up to [when he] reached the age of fifty-two:

Om swasti
By remembering you, the torment of samsara is dispelled
With [your] renowned virtuous deeds [which] perfectly fulfil all wishes
The life story of a buddha pervades the world
[I] shall pay homage to [you,] the assembly of the Wish-fulfilling Jewels

On the surface of the mirror of your [all-]knowing wisdom
The appearance of the profound and vast wisdoms of true nature and multiplicity
Arises [as] unobscured, completely pure, and has become perfected
The lord of the Victorious Ones, Rigpe Dorje, please bestow auspiciousness

In this land of snow mountains, [Tibet, you are] the best of men
Whose reputation as the Karmapa is uninterrupted
Likewise, in tens of hundreds of millions Jambu Continents
[You are] the unique manifestation of the inconceivable wisdom

In accordance with everything that is to be known
Is the inexhaustible ocean of wondrous enlightened activity
If not even shown by the minds of the noble ones
How is it to be experienced by the minds of ordinary beings?

Like the label of a priceless jewel
[p.323] Hearing [which] will definitely be meaningful and without distortion
[This] little tale will elucidate
The manner [in which] the life story of a holy being [unfolds]

Now I am writing down briefly the life story of Rangjung Rigpe Dorje, the sixteenth successor from [within] the lineage of Karmapa incarnations, the glorious lord of the Victorious Ones, the embodiment of the enlightened activity of all buddhas. Unifying the enlightened activity of all buddhas in general, [the Karmapa] transforms whoever [he] trains in an inconceivable way [like] a miraculous play. Since [it is] even beyond the very nature of things taught by the bodhisattvas [who have] achieved the *bhūmi*s as well as the sphere of what can be known, how is someone like me, a lowly ordinary being, able to produce even the slightest courage that is required [to tell the story of his life]? Nonetheless, like spectacles that delight the faithful, within the perception of ordinary disciples, [I] shall begin with the method that follows the manner in which [he] protected the teaching and the vast benefit of beings and demonstrated the display of extraordinary miracles for the purpose of taming the untamed. [I] have arranged the topics to be discussed, ordering [them] into eight chapters.

Chapter 1: First, how the succession of [the previous] lives [of the Karmapa] came about, in relation to the great prophecies [in] the Sūtra and Tantra, and the way [he] took rebirth

Furthermore, from the magnificent voice of the supreme teacher Śākyamuni Buddha scattered the flowers of prophecy as follows:

In the *Samādhirāja Sūtra*:
Two thousand years after my passing
The teaching will appear in the country of the red-faced [people]
[They] will become the disciples of Avalokiteśvara
At the time when the teaching declines there

[p.324] Bodhisattva Siṃhanāda
Will appear, known as the Karmapa

[Here, the Buddha] prophesied the emanation of Bodhisattva Siṃhanāda [who] will become enlightened as the Sixth Buddha of Fortunate Aeon in future.
Also, the *Tantra of the Blazing, Wrathful Meteorite*[2] says:

In the completely pure *maṇḍala*
[The one] who embodies the buddhas of the ten directions
In order to show the accomplishment in this life
The renowned one called the Karmapa will emerge

[This text] prophesied [the Karmapa's] true form which is the embodiment of the buddhas of the three times. Moreover, the second buddha [of] Uḍḍiyāna[3] [gave the prophecy]:

Protecting the enlightened activity of Avalokiteśvara
Düsum Khyenpa will emerge in [a place] known as Tsurphu
Wearing the Black Hat, the crown of the buddha families, [which is] the sign of empowerment
[He] guides countless beings in each moment

[This verse] prophesied [the Karmapa's] monastic seat and crown. Furthermore:

Translator Gyalwa Chokyang, listen to me
In the semi-circular palace, the emanation of enlightened speech
Twenty-one [of] your reincarnations will appear in future
[p.325] [You are] the emanation of Avalokiteśvara, the one who knows all the three times

[This verse] prophesied [the Karmapa] appearing in twenty-one reincarnations. In particular, regarding the modality of giving prophecy specifically [about] the Great Sixteenth [Karmapa], the Terma prophecy of Orgyen Chokgyur Dechen Lingpa says:

The names [of those] that must [come] after the nirvana of Thekchok [Dorje]
Dewe Dagnyi (bDe ba'i bdag nyid),[4] Rigpe Dorje
Ogyen Trinley,[5] Samten,[6] and so on, will emerge.

According to what the prophecies have thoroughly praised, regarding the beginning of the story about [his] previous lives, [the Karmapa] offered mendicant rags gathered from heaps of rubbish to the Tathāgata, Arhat, fully enlightened Buddha Ngaro Nyenpa (Nga ro snyan pa), and then generated supreme *bodhicitta* for the first time. In future, [he] will be reborn as Devaputra Legpakye (Legs pa skyes) in Tuṣita heaven as the crown prince of the Fifth Buddha of Fortunate Aeon. Then, [he] will gaze at Jambu Continent with four observations, and be born in a city called Metoklha (Me tog lha), as the son of King Sengetak (Seng ge stag) and Queen Gawe Ngaro (dGa' ba'i nga ro). [He] will turn the holy Wheel of the Dharma for 70,000 years, once [he] has been truly perfected and become a buddha called Siṃhanāda, the Sixth Buddha of Fortunate Aeon. [During the time between generating *bodhicitta* and achieving buddhahood, he] endeavours to [undertake] the vast deeds of a bodhisattva. Furthermore, [in the period when] the teaching of Buddha Śākyamuni [prevailed], in Riwo Tala,[7] [the Karmapa] was the very embodiment of compassion, Avalokiteśvara. In the noble land India, [he was born in the form of] many *paṇḍita*s and *siddha*s, including the masters Saraha and Nāgabodhi. In the land of snow, Tibet, [he was born in the form of] many scholars and *siddha*s, such as Translator Gyalwa Chokyang, [Geshe] Potowa Rinchen Sal and Sharawa.

[p.326] [The Karmapa] was also born as great benefactors of the teaching, such as the Dharma protector, King Songtsen Gampo. Thereby, [he] benefited greatly the teaching and beings. Most notably, [he] appeared in the succession of reincarnations, beginning with the master Düsum Khyenpa, and up to the lord of the Victorious Ones, Khakyap Dorje. All [those who] see, hear, remember [or] touch [him] are free from the suffering of lower rebirth in samsara, and [he] establishes [them] in the state of higher rebirth and liberation.

Yet again, [he] considers [himself] as refuge, protector, and friend of those who lived in the degenerate age. Particularly, in Tibet, when the teaching of the Buddha was being subdued, [he] was reborn [as the Sixteenth Karmapa], donning the hardened armour of *bodhicitta* to revive the embers of the teaching. First, regarding the method of giving prophecy, again generally, the Karmapa is the earliest of all Tibetan tulkus. All the Tibetan scholars and *siddha*s agree [on this]. When these great noble [Karmapa incarnations] are being identified, [the method] is not merely divination or requested prophecy [from others]. There is the tradition of passing down the scroll of text that bestows the prophecy after the previous incarnation sees for certain, with the wisdom of knowing what is to arise, the circumstances [in which his future reincarnation is to be born], such as the place and time [of birth]. After the very [scroll of text] is fetched, with effort, the true supreme reincarnation will definitely be found. With the clear vision [into] the future, the supreme Buddha the Great Fifteenth [Karmapa] issued the seal of secrecy [on] the testament which [he] bestowed as the prophecy, [and] gave [it] to the learned gelong Jampal Tsultrim. According to this [prophecy]:

[In] the eastern direction from here, [on] the bank of the golden river
In a part of the region seized by the brave archer
On the lap of the poised majestic lion
[p.327] On the mountain of glory, adorned with A and Thub
In the house of earth [belonging to] the family of virtuous overlords
[I] see a dwelling place in the womb of a worldly *ḍākinī*
[I will be] born on a full moon day of ox or mouse year[8]
From the realm of Samantabhadra, the all-encompassing atiyoga
The great lamp of wisdom unifying appearance and awareness
Called Rangjung Khyabdak Rigpe Dorje

According to the meaning of the prophecy, [the Karmapa was born] in the eastern direction of the great monastic seat [in] Tsurphu Valley, in the territory of Derge [of] the Kham region. [On] the bank of the golden river, the gently flowing famous Drilung ('Bri klung), at the time of the arrival [of] the accomplished one, King Gesar of Ling, the landscape [of] Dankhok (mDan khog) was ruled by Tsazhang Danma Changdra (Tsha zhang mDan ma byang khra) who attained mastery in archery. It was near the temple Langthang Changchub Drolma (gLang thang byang chub sgrol ma), [which is] one of the four border temples built by Dharma King Songtsen Gampo. [The Karmapa] was born in a family called Athub (A thub) which was the virtuous family of overlords enthroned in front of the King of Derge. [His] father Tsewang Phuntsok (Tshe dbang phun tshogs) enjoyed the status of the son of the great Dharma King of Derge; [his] mother Kalsang Chödrön (sKal bzang chos sgron) was a worldly *ḍākinī* in human form. [He] was the seventh sibling of [their] eight children, four sons and four daughters, born on the fifteenth day of the sixth month of the wood male mouse year of the fifteenth cycle, 1924. Moreover, as [he] stayed in [his] mother's womb, the sound of uttering the *mani* mantra was clearly heard. On the fourteenth day of the sixth month, he disappeared from [his mother's] womb. As a result, [his] parents inevitably grew anxious. [p.328] [Yet] again, [he returned to] stay in [his] mother's womb. [He] displayed wondrous miracles as such. At first, even when [he] was staying in [his mother's] womb, the fifth supreme reincarnation of Dzogchen Thubten Chökyi Dorje (rDzogs chen Thub bstan chos kyi rdo rje) identified [him] as a bodhisattva reincarnation. He prophesied that [his] place of birth was not to be in a layman's house; [he] must be born by the pure and remote Senge Namdzong (Seng ge rnam rdzong). Accordingly, [the Karmapa] was born in that very place; [this is also] in accord with [the line in] the testament of the previous Karmapa: 'On the lap of the poised majestic lion'. [At] the time of [his] birth, incredible, miraculous good signs arose: all [those present] perceived the sound of all kinds of divine music and pleasant songs from the sky and in between; white rays of light permeated the sleeping tent; there, the water in the water jug and offering water turned into milk.

When [he] was above four, five years of age, through play [the Karmapa] would hit an egg on the ground from the highest floor [of his] family palace, [and the egg] would not break. Moreover, [he] tied up the rim [of] a porcelain cup that pours yogurt. Today, [these objects associated with] the wondrous miracles [that he] demonstrated are still seen in the chest of treasures of the Athub family.

Chapter 2: The great masters identified [him to be the Karmapa reincarnation], and offered throne offerings [for his] enthronement in each of the Kagyu monastic seats

On the occasion of granting recognition, Situ Pema Wangchok Gyalpo saw in his dream the lord of the Victorious Ones, Khakyap Dorje, sitting above the bedroom of the Athub family where [he] would take birth, with [his] hands crossed [holding] vajra and bell, [and his] legs crossed in vajra [posture]. The testament of the late Karmapa [i.e., Khakyap Dorje] was [composed] in numerical code [in place of letters]. Although others were not able to know [the meaning of this testament], through thorough examination, Palpung Khyentrul Rinpoche made [his] decision. After [he and Situ] gave the same consent, [the child was] clearly identified [as the Karmapa reincarnation]. [p.329] Previously, since the testament was [kept] very secret and holy, minor obstacles arose when the appeal was made to the [Lhasa] government. As a result, the enthronement [of the Karmapa reincarnation] to the golden throne had to be delayed briefly. Nonetheless, in the end, wisdom Dharma protectors accomplished [their] activity in time, whereby [the reincarnation's] true nature came to be manifest. Hence, all obstacles and interruptions diminished by themselves. When the appeal was made to the Great Thirteenth Dalai Lama, he agreed with the above-mentioned identification. Then came [his] reply [that] the reincarnation was indisputable; [he] granted a genuine recognition. In the year of iron male horse of the sixteenth cycle [1930], when [the Karmapa] was seven years old, Maitreya Situ Rinpoche and Jamgon Kongtrul Rinpoche both came specially, first conferring [on him] longevity empowerment for the sake of his long life, performing cleansing ritual, and giving [him] robes, a name, as well as layman's vows.

On the twenty-seventh day of the first month of the iron sheep[9] year [1931], Palpung Khyentrul Rinpoche, together with [the Karmapa's] attendant from Tsurphu, firstly offered the black hat through cleansing ceremony, [whereby they] opened a variety of profound gateways to auspicious interdependence. Thereafter, [the Karmapa] granted [them] an audience. On the twenty-ninth day, Sangye Nyenpa (Sangs rgyas mnyan pa) Rinpoche had an audience [with the Karmapa].

On the first day of the second month, [the Karmapa] rode to Palpung, and stayed at Danam Gyaling (mDan rnam rgyal gling). The sangha of that monastery faithfully requested an audience [with him], and offered the *maṇḍala* and representations [of the enlightened body, speech and mind of the Buddha]. Then, the Ling (gLing) family [held] a welcoming reception and had an audience with him. The Derge government officials rode to welcome [him] first in Zipa Wata So (Zis pha wa ta so), and then again in Mokda (rMog mda). On the journey, gradually, [he] arrived at Lhundrub Teng (lHun grub steng), the capital of Derge. [He] gave audiences and blessings to the government officials headed by the Dharma King of Derge, Tsewang Düdul (Tshe dbang bdud 'dul), and Queen of Nangchen, [p.330] Yudrön (g.Yu sgron), as well as the public. On the journey, at the invitation of Kunsang Tse (Kun bzang rtse) from Jangra (lCang ra) Palace, [he visited there and] granted an audience. Then, in Tsezuldo (rTse zul mdo), Alo Paljor (A lo dpal 'byor) monastery welcomed [him], and in Gönje (mGon lce), [he] granted an audience to the sangha. In Gosela (mGo se la), over 600 monks and lay people rode to welcome [him], headed by the sangha of Palpung. In a region called Shidrema (gZhi khre ma), [he] opened anew the gateway to [auspicious] interdependence from the past: in that auspicious, excellent place, Kenting Tai Situ Maitreya Pema Wangchok Gyalpo arrived specially [to welcome him], and exchanged khata [with him].

Thereafter, on the eighth day of the second month, in the great monastic seat, Palpung Thubten Chökhor Ling (dPal spungs thub bstan chos 'khor gling), an extensive arrangement of welcoming procession [with] incense was made. Water was sprinkled in all places inside and outside [of the monastery]. Continuous offerings of canopies and banners were joined together. The scent of purifying smoke and incense wafted along like clouds. From the midst [of all this], [the Karmapa] was invited into the great assembly hall, hence requested to sit on the high throne supported by fearless lions. Meanwhile, the supreme refuge Situ Rinpoche offered [to the Karmapa] the *maṇḍala* and representations [of the enlightened body, speech and mind], as well as long-life prayer. Later, on the twelfth day, in the great palace of Yiga Chödzin (Yid dga' chos 'dzin), among the assembly of the profound and vast [ceremony that] enthroned [the Karmapa] on the throne supported by lions, those proficient in the scriptures of the Sūtra and Tantra took the lead through the offering of the Dharma, [giving] elaborate explanations on the Tantra and great scriptures [of the Mahāyāna]. Then, the lamas, tulkus and monastic communities from different schools of the Chamdo region, devout patrons, together with kings and ministers, especially the lamas, tulkus and sangha who were undoubtedly the lineage holders of the Kamtsang[10] [tradition], as well as all those [belonged to] the Kagyu school [p.331] presented a vast arrangement of throne offerings. In addition, [they] articulated [their devotion] through the prayer: as long as samsara has not been emptied, [may you ever] remain and turn the Wheel of the profound and vast holy Dharma. [The Karmapa, in turn,] opened a hundred gateways to [his enlightened] activity [by which] great benefit for the teaching and beings was to arise.

Next, in general, [the Karmapa] abides naturally [in] all primordial qualities. And yet, to show ordinary disciples that it is necessary to achieve all temporary and ultimate qualities [by] relying on the perseverance and wisdom of each individual, [he] began to train in writing and reading, at first in the presence of the master Tashi Tsering (bKra shis tshe ring). On the first day of Saga Dawa month, [he] went to preside over the assembly of the Great Compassionate One Śrī Guhyasamāja. On the fifteenth day, [he] granted empowerments and audiences. On the twenty-second day of that month, to be enthroned on the high Dharma throne in the temple of Tsurphu Valley, the holy place of the heart of Akaniṣṭha that had become the sole source of teachings of the Practice Lineage, [the Karmapa] departed from Palpung together with Situ Rinpoche and Palpung Khyentrul Rinpoche. The sangha of Palpung went to see [them] off. On the journey, gradually, [the Karmapa] visited monasteries, including Tertön (gTer ston) monastery, Kyabche (sKyabs che) monastery, and Gyune (rGyun ne) monastery, and granted audiences. The 'middle monastic seat' [i.e., Karma Monastery][11] welcomed [him] and invited him [to visit]. However, since [he] arrived [only for] a short stay, [he] did not accept [their invitation].

Thereafter, [the Karmapa] visited in turn Drungram (Drung ram) monastery, Labo (Bla bo) monastery, Do (rDo) monastery. A few [of those who] served the King of Nangchen rendered service [to him] throughout many stations on the way. [He then] arrived at Ganden (dGa' ldan) monastery, Zurmang Namgyal Tse (Zur mang rnam rgyal rtse), Chokling (mChog gling) monastery, and Goche (Go che) monastery. [p.332] [He also] visited Tra'ug Nedo (Khra 'ug gNas mdo) among other places. [Those encountered him] coincidently [on his] many journeys approached [him] for an audience. Upon [his] arrival in Kyodrak (sKyo brag), [he received] the invitation from Nangchen. The assistant of the disciplinary officer, Chözang (Chos bzang), [came] first from the welcoming reception [organised by] the administration of Tsurphu Great Encampment, and requested an audience [with the Karmapa].

Next, as [the Karmapa] travelled gradually, the leading prince of Nangchen welcomed [him]; [he] then visited the capital city of Nangchen. Along the way, the monastic communities in general as well as the lamas and tulkus from the 'middle monastic seat' in particular went specially to meet [him]. Then, [he] travelled past Palkha Dermo (dPal kha lder mo) monastery and arrived at Dilyag (Dil yag) monastery. [There, he] granted audiences to the lamas, tulkus and sangha headed by two tulkus, Datrul (Zla sprul) and Saju (Sa bcu). [While] in Gina (sGi rna) monastery, the monastic household and administration of Tsurphu Great Encampment [arranged] an elaborate welcoming reception and [set up] monks' tent quarters orderly, with [the Karmapa's] tent [known as] Tsephel Kundü (Tshe 'phel kun 'dus) put up in the middle. Inside [his tent], the treasurer of the Great Encampment among others invited [him] and offered the *maṇḍala* and representations [of the enlightened body, speech and mind]. The Karmapa was also pleased, seeing those who welcomed [him] as old acquaintances. Furthermore, [he] granted audiences accordingly [to] lamas, tulkus and monastic communities, [as well as] local devotees of both high and low status [who] came to see [him] from across Tibet. On the thirteenth day, when [he] performed for the first time the donning of the liberation-through-seeing Black Crown, rainbow clouds gathered in the sky and rain of flowers fell. [Through] incredible miracles [like this], [he] demonstrated the beginning of [his] life's journey to establish all beings on lasting happiness.

Thereafter, as Palpung Khyentse Rinpoche was about to return to [his own] monastic seat, [the Karmapa] granted him an audience and gave [his] permission. On the fifteenth day, the lamas and monks from the welcoming party of the Great Encampment participated in the confessional assembly of fully ordained monks. From Trongpa, on the journey, gradually, [the Karmapa] arrived at Nagchu (Nag chu). Nagchu Dzong requested [him to perform] the donning of the precious liberation-through-seeing Black Crown. Next, as [he] resumed [his] journey, on the nineteenth day of the seventh month, [p.333] [he] arrived in front of the Nyenchen Tanglha, and offered extensive presents as well as a white divine yak [to the mountain god Tanglha]. [The yak] went straight from the encampment to Tanglha's temple as if led by someone. Miraculous sign arose [showing] that [Tanglha] actually received the presents. On the twentieth day, Bodhisattva Jamgon Rinpoche and his retinue travelled to Palpung from Central Tibet and met [with the Karmapa], by which a host of auspicious connections became fully manifest. In Lathok Latse (La thog la rtse), the administration of Tsurphu Great Encampment, as well as the monastic household of Chögong Gyaltsab (Chos gong rGyal tshab), presented [to the Karmapa] the first welcoming reception. Then, in Yakchukha (Yag chu kha), the monastics and lay people from Yangchen (Yangs chen) monastery and Golo (rGo lo) monastery requested an audience [with him].

Next, in Pichukha (Spis chu kha), at the second welcoming reception [held] by the monastic household and administration [of] Tsurphu Great Encampment, the primary disciple of the previous Karmapa, Jampa Rinpoche, together with the representative of Chögong's monastic household, went to meet [the Karmapa]. On the fourth day of the eighth month, [while the Karmapa arrived] at the upper part of Tsurphu, Chögong Gyaltsab Rinpoche, Nenang Pawo Rinpoche, the monastic household of Tsurphu Great Encampment, and the sangha of Chögong and Nenang all rode to welcome [him]. Thus, the good sign that brought together brilliant light of auspicious interdependence arose for the first time.

Then, on the fifth day when a hundred gateways manifested naturally as the result of interdependence between the outer and inner auspiciousness according to astrology, [the Karmapa] arrived at the monastic seat in Tsurphu valley, [which is] a great monastic seat, the holy place of the heart of Akaniṣṭha. First, the monastic household and administration [held] a welcoming reception in the garden Samdrub Ling (bSam 'grub gling). [Beginning] from [the banner] called 'The Five Buddha Families', the assembly [that formed like] a garland of jewels was holding aloft victory banners that were victorious over all hostile regions, five-coloured hanging brocade and different types of flags. [The assembly] welcomed [the Karmapa] with limitless special offerings of gods and humans. [These include] all kinds of music [played from] wind, string and percussion instruments, parasols of peacock feathers, as well as six types of auspicious long-life substances and the Cham dance [led] by supreme lions connected to the past. [p.334] [The Karmapa] stepped into Tashi Khangsar (bKra shis khang gsar), the middle room of the temple in Tsurphu valley, the place where successive Karmapas, the glorious lords of the Victorious Ones, had blessed and stayed, the holy place of the heart of Akaniṣṭha, the *maṇḍala* of glorious Cakrasaṃvara. Immediately [after he arrived], the entire assembly there offered [to him] the *maṇḍala*, the representations [of the enlightened body, speech and mind], together with a ritual for long life. After that, one day in the ninth month, [he] rode to Lhasa and received a hair-cutting ceremony in front of the Thirteenth Dalai Lama. On this occasion, the great Dalai Lama had a clear vision that [the Karmapa] was wearing a crown inseparable [from his] head, even though [the Karmapa] did not put on [his material] crown at all. The senior council minister from Mön (Mon) who was present said to [the Karmapa's] father: 'Today the precious supreme tulku did not take off [his] hat'. [The Karmapa] actually showed the miracle of the crown of self-manifesting wisdom being inseparable [from him]. At that time, especially for [the Karmapa's] enthronement on the golden throne of successive [Karmapas], the lord of the Victorious Ones, the great Dalai Lama granted the name, Thubten Rigdrol Yeshe (Thub bstan rig grol ye shes), and composed a long-life prayer titled 'The Excellent Vase of the Nectar of Immortality'. In [this prayer, the Dalai Lama] writes:

The foundation or root of all the qualities of learnedness is the three trainings
Especially, [for] as long as [you] live, the discipline received in the presence of the preceptor and master
The meaning of the four divisions of the Vinaya, the samayas and vows
May you protect [them] as [you would protect your own] eyes, following the example of the elder monk Mahākāśyapa

Moreover, according to the permissions issued by [his] lama and yidam as well as the prophecies, the previous Karmapa sought help from a consort of the path for the purpose of examining the hindrances[12] and faults of subtle channels and energies in [his] practice. [It] appears that [the Dalai Lama] is expressing [his] disapproval [of the previous Karmapa's decision to have a consort]. However, [this] is not the case. [p.335] The great bodhisattva [i.e., the Dalai Lama] granted a prophecy which contains a true speech and clear vision of the future that this very Karmapa [i.e., the Sixteenth], the lord of the Victorious Ones, would share a similar quality with the perfectly liberated monk Mahākāśyapa. [This] vision has indeed come to be true. [The Dalai Lama] also [says]:

[For those who have] wrong views[13] [and thus] become blind [in their] own tradition
May you clearly manifest [as] a guide [leading them towards] the well-mapped path to liberation

And:

Whatever pure life stories of the Kagyu [masters] there are
May you be able to thoroughly carry through the examples of [your] predecessors

In general, the lord of the Victorious Ones, [the Karmapa, had] a broad, unbiased stance among all [Tibetan Buddhist] schools. Particularly, [he] held very dearly the unique view, meditation and conduct of [his] own tradition. [He] put [them] into practice, striving for the mere purpose that the meaning of the teaching would remain for long without decline. When meeting [the Sixteenth Karmapa, the author of the verses, i.e., the Dalai Lama] was speaking the true supplication and words of good wishes. [This] has made [me feel] moved [with] goosebumps out of great devotion to the author [i.e., the Dalai Lama]. In the eleventh month, [the Karmapa] returned to [his] monastic seat. On a very auspicious special day according to astrology, [he] received an elaborate enthronement ceremony on the throne of fearless lions in the temple of [the Karmapa] incarnations in Tsurphu valley. The great holy masters Maitreya Tai Situ Pema Wangchok Gyalpo, the refuge and protector Drukchen Mipham Chökyi Wangpo ('Brug chen Mi pham chos kyi dbang po), Gyaltsab Drakpa Gyatso (rGyal tshab Grags pa rgya mtsho), and Pawo Tsuglag Mawa (dPa' bo gTsug lag smra ba) scattered the flowers of auspicious words of power. Those who were proficient in scriptures and reasoning spoke about the life stories of buddhas and bodhisattvas, [p.336] the system of grounds and paths, the five perfections [the ceremony was] endowed with, and *maṇḍala* [offering]. All beings, [humans] and gods alike, headed by the monasteries that belonged to the four senior and eight junior lineages of the Kagyu, [presented] gifts to show [their] gratitude for [the Karmapa's] endeavour in the service that brought joy to many. [In this way, they] opened a hundred gateways of [auspicious] interdependence, [so that the Karmapa's] lotus feet would [remain] firm for numerous kalpas as vast as the ocean.

Chapter 3: How [the Karmapa] conducted [his] studies in the presence of [his] teachers, beginning with writing and reading, and up to [the practice of] Mahāmudrā and the Six Dharmas of Nāropā.

For four years since then, [the Karmapa] demonstrated [his enlightened activity] by means of engaging in study and contemplation in front of the great teacher Bo Gangkar Rinpoche. At that time, [he] told Gangkar Rinpoche many miraculous stories of [his] previous lives that [he] recalled. Then, at the age of twelve, on the third day of the twelfth month of the wood pig year [1935], [he] rode to Eastern Tibet with the purpose of studying the essential instructions of the profound Dharma in general, and the extraordinary Six Dharmas of Nāropā as well as Mahāmudrā in particular, with great holy masters, mainly the lord of refuge Maitreya Situ Rinpoche, [who trained him] in the manner of filling the vase to the brim. On the eighth day, [he] arrived at Yangchen Chiso (Yangs can spyi so). A spring that had never existed before appeared afresh. As [he] went in the hot spring of Tadzi (rTa rdzi), even though it was wintertime, many snakes were coming [towards him]; [he] was playing [with them] around [his] neck and on [his] lap. On the twenty-ninth day, [he] arrived at the foot of Tanglha's mountain, and then went to the temple. At that time, the very white divine yak that [he] offered [to Tanglha] in the iron sheep year [1931] emerged from the Tanglha mountain valley and [went] directly towards the encampment with a joyful look, roaring and waving [its] tail; [it] then disappeared. All [those present] witnessed [this], hence were amazed. After that, in Umatang (dBu ma thang), [his] younger brother Ponlop Rinpoche came from Dzogchen (rDzogs chen) monastery to welcome [him] [p.337] and celebrate [his arrival]. Meanwhile, the monastic household and administration of the Great Encampment also [created] an auspicious interdependence; [the Karmapa] granted audience [to each of them] individually. Then, since the devotees along [his] journeys, including Nagchu (Nag chu), appealed in person, [he] fulfilled [their] wishes through the donning of the precious liberation-through-seeing Black Crown as well as empowerments. In the fire mouse year [1936] when [he] was thirteen years of age, [he] went to a place called Tsobur (mTsho 'bur) on the border of the upper part of Trongpa ('Brong pa). There was a small river there. Since [it was] winter, [it] became frozen. When the Karmapa went on [its] surface, [he] left [his] footprint. Later, even after the frozen [surface] melted, [his] footprint appeared clearly on the surface of the river. [He] showed an unusual display of miracles like [this].

Thereafter, again, when [the Karmapa] arrived at Latsang (Bla tshang) monastery, [his] porcelain cup bounced from the top of the table and hit the floor heavily, and yet did not break. Then, on the fifth day of the third month, [he] arrived at Gina. There, [he] bestowed blessings by touching the head of [each of those in] the retinue of the welcoming parties headed [by] the steward of the monastic household of Palpung, as well as the staff and petty officials [at] Nangchen station.[14] After that, [he] arrived at the upper and middle parts of Ripa (Ri pa), and granted empowerments, the donning of the precious Black Crown and a cleansing ceremony for monasteries. On this occasion, since the Kazakh army advanced [on the area], the King of Derge and the King of Nangchen came together to request [the Karmapa] to examine [the situation]. [The Karmapa] uttered prayers of the common teachings and the ritual of Dorje Drolö to repulse [the invading] army. When lighting the fire of exorcism in the fire ceremony, all [those present] saw a large mass of fire moving towards the eastern direction [for as far as] many days' journey.

Next, [the Karmapa] travelled to the lower part of Ripa, Tongnag Lachung (sTong nag bla chung) and Lachen (Bla chen) monastery. In Lachen monastery, as [he] was uttering consecration and purification [ritual with] a clear mind, relics emerged from the blessed barley [which are] now kept among the sacred objects of the Great Encampment. After that, [he] visited Tsangsar Gönpo (Tshangs gsar mgon po) monastery, [p.338] Nam (gNam) monastery, Karchung (dKar chung) monastery, and granted empowerments, the Black Crown [Ceremony], consecration and cleansing rituals [for] sacred objects; thereby, [he] largely protected the benefit of beings. Then, [he] arrived at Tana (rTa rna) monastery, and stayed in the chamber of *mahāsiddha* Yerpa Yeshe Tseg (Yer pa ye shes brtsegs). When staying in Ripa Mema (Ri pa smad ma) monastery, a pet with one ear that had been offered [to him] left [its] hoof print clearly on a rock.

Thereafter, while protecting the benefit of beings, [the Karmapa travelled] past Gechag (Gad chags) monastery and arrived at Dzongo Ritrö (rDzong mgo ri khrod). Since water was very scarce there and [the residents] had to carry [water] from far away, Lama Samten Gyatso requested [the Karmapa to give blessings so that a source of] water would appear. For this reason, [the Karmapa] had a bath; then a drizzle fell and a rainbow tent of light arose. Later, a new spring appeared [flowing] constantly from the very spot where [he] had the bath. After that, on the journey, gradually, [he] reached Dilyag monastery. At that time, all [those present] saw [him] riding the pet with one ear, and through a miracle, coming to the top of the tent rope on his tent, passing in circles, and then coming down.

Next, at the invitation of the King of Nangchen, [the Karmapa] travelled to his palace. [There, he] bestowed longevity empowerment. Since [his trip] coincided with [that of] Khyentrul Rinpoche [who was] on [his] way to Central Tibet, [the Karmapa] received in front of him the empowerments of the [Karma] Pakshi guru sādhana [that came from] the pure vision of Yongey Mingyur Dorje[15] and White Tara from Atiśa's tradition. Then, [he] visited Japa (Ja pa) monastery. At that time, [there was] a Tsen spirit, Chāgyal Metri (Phyā rgyal me tri), in the mountain at the back of the monastery, whom the previous Karmapa, Thekchok Dorje, commanded to uphold samaya and installed as a guest god. For this reason, [the Karmapa] offered [to this god] a pet—a red Tsen horse. [The horse] went to the top of the mountain as if led by someone, which clearly showed that [it] was taken [by the god]. Then, on the first day of the eighth month, [the Karmapa] visited the 'middle monastic seat' Karma Monastery, after which [he] was requested to sit on top of [the throne] known as 'the Karmapa's red throne' that the successive Karmapas of the past used to be seated on; [he] was then enthroned [there]. [p.339] Karme

Khantrul (Karma'i mkhan sprul) offered a religious discussion on the life stories of successive Karmapa incarnations, together with the *maṇḍala* and three representations [of the enlightened body, speech and mind]. On this occasion, some statues of the Kagyu Golden Garland took off [their] hats [as a sign of greeting to the Karmapa]. [This] reveals unimpededly [his] real characteristic of a holy master. Situ Rinpoche also rode to welcome [the Karmapa as he] left [Karma] monastery and headed to [Situ's monastic seat].

Thereafter, [the Karmapa travelled] past Lhatog (lHa thog) and visited monasteries of different schools in general, and the Kagyu monastic seats in particular, including Kyabje (sKyabs rje) monastery and Drungram. [There, he] largely benefited beings. [He then travelled] past Kamtogdru (sKam thog gru) and stayed in Alo Tsesum Do (A lo rtse sum mdo). He granted audiences to the king and ministers of Derge. On the fifth day of the tenth month of the fire mouse year [1936], at the age of thirteen, [he] was received at the front of the procession of the welcoming party from Palpung Thubten Chökhor Ling with plenty of necessary offerings. The spiritual father and son [i.e., Situ and the Karmapa] arrived together; [the Karmapa] spent [his] time day and night listening and contemplating the sections of scriptures about Buddhist and non-Buddhist knowledge as well as the Tantra section that is vast like the ocean. [When the Karmapa was] fifteen years old, in the tiger year [1938], on the sixth day of the first half of the [first] lunar month [which was] the festival celebrating the great miracles displayed by the Buddha, Situ Rinpoche Karma Shedrub Chokyi Senge Ngedön Tenpe Gyaltsen assumed the roles of both preceptor and master to bestow [on the Karmapa] firstly the layman's vows and then the novice vows in front of Situ Chökyi Jungne's *stūpa*, Chökhor Tashi Gomang (Chos 'khor bkra shis sgo mang). [He also] offered [to the Karmapa] the name, Palden Rangjung Rigpe Yeshe Lungtog Chökyi Nyima Trinley Dönkun Drubpe De (dPal ldan rang byung rig pa'i ye shes lung rtogs chos kyi nyi ma phrin las don kun grub pa'i sde).

Furthermore, on the ninth day, [the Karmapa] received altogether the two bodhisattva vows which originated from two traditions, Vast Conduct and Profound View. Then, [he] was given the name Changchub Sempa Lodrö Shiwe Nyingpo Shanphen Chökyi Dawa (Byang chub sems dpa' blo gros zhi ba'i snying po gzhan phan chos kyi zla ba). [p.340] Moreover, [he] studied the Golden Dharma of Marpa of Lhodrak compiled together in *The Treasury of Kagyu Mantras*, and the essential instructions of the Eight Great Chariots of the Practice Lineage abbreviated in *The Treasury of Precious Instructions*, including the empowerments that ripen, instructions that liberate, and the supporting reading transmission. [He] also received the great empowerment of glorious Kālacakra. In brief, [the Karmapa] received [these teachings from Situ who taught him] in the manner of filling the vase to the brim, thereby arriving at the focal point of ultimate lineage.

Thereafter, [since] the King of Lhatog died, [the Karmapa] rode there. On the journey, [he] reached Troru (Khro ru) and Dzigar ('Dzi sgar), [and] identified the reincarnation of Chogtrul (mChog sprul). On the way back, [he] visited the monastic seats, including Dzodzi (mDzo rdzi), Gyune, Kyabje and Drungram, protecting the benefit of beings by taming them in whatever means necessary. After that, he returned to Palpung. On the third day of the ninth month of the earth tiger year [1938], the spiritual father and son [i.e., Situ and the Karmapa] rode together towards the direction of Lithang. On the way, Dzongsar (rDzong gsar) monastery headed by Khyentse Rinpoche rode to welcome [them] and invited [them to his monastery]. During the donning of the precious liberation-through-seeing Black Crown, Khyentse Rinpoche Chökyi Lodrö perceived directly [the Karmapa in] the form of Düsum Khyenpa; the Black Crown also rose about one cubit high from [the Karmapa's] head. During that period, [the Karmapa] visited the sacred objects inside Dzongsar monastery.

Next, on the journey, gradually, [the Karmapa] arrived at Pangphug (sPangs phug) monastery in Lithang. When visiting the statue of Düsum Khyenpa which had spoken before, by having a conversation [with each other], the spiritual father and son, the Karmapa and Situ Rinpoche, each left a footprint on top of the stone [placed at] the base of the right and left pillars in the shrine. In addition, during [their] circumambulation, [the Karmapa's] dog also left [its] claw prints [on a rock], and [his] horse left [its] hoof prints[16] in the stable. The two supreme refuges [i.e., Situ and the Karmapa] again each left a footprint on the path of circumambulation. [p.341] When [they] went to circumambulate a lake, all [those present] heard the pleasant sound of conch and trumpet coming from inside the lake [as if announcing their arrival]. [They] also left many footprints on the lakeshore. In this way, [they] accomplished [miracles that] could actually be seen by ordinary people. [The Karmapa] made tea offerings and gave alms in the monastery. After that, [he] arrived at Drukshi ('Brug zhi) monastery, and performed empowerments, cleansing and consecration rituals. There, two villages, Muti (rMu ti) and Jagphu (lCags phu), lost eighty-four lives due to ten-year-long nasty fights of all kinds [between them] out of hatred [accumulated] from the past. The heads [of the two villages] each paid an individual visit to [the Karmapa who, in turn,] established [them both] on the path of happiness through the generosity of fearless protection.

There, [the Karmapa's] teacher Karma Tsering died, showing a miraculous sign that [his body] remained in meditation without decay for about two days. During that time, [the Karmapa] gave a teaching on the practice of the two accumulations and performed a perfect cremation ceremony. Afterwards, [he travelled to] Dzago (rDza sgo) monastery, Chagtreng Lhago Tsotö (Phyag phreng lha go mtsho stod) monastery, Bangra (Bang ra) monastery, [where he] fulfilled [people's] wishes. When visiting Pangphug, [he] appeared to be jumping and running near the shrine where there was the statue of Düsum Khyenpa which had spoken before; [in doing so, he] left seven footprints [which were discovered] later.

Next, on the twelfth day of the third month, as [the Karmapa] travelled towards Palpung, [he] arrived at Lithang Gönchen (Li thang dgon chen). There, the messenger of the Chinese government or the secretary of the Chinese leader came to ask [him] to go to China. However, considering that there would be little benefit to either the teaching or the practitioners other than merely the arrogance of politics, [he] sent back the messenger with an explanation that [he] did not manage to go in person due to the weather conditions. On the sixth day of the fifth month, [he] arrived at Palpung.

Thereafter, [the Karmapa] received the empowerment and transmission of the *Compendium of Sadhanas*, and studied the texts in stages in front of Khyentrul Rinpoche. Then, on the fifteenth day of the ninth month of the iron dragon year [1940], [he] rode to the monastic seat Tsurphu in Central Tibet. [p.342] When Situ Rinpoche and Khyentse Rinpoche both saw [him] off, the spiritual fathers and son shed tears, unbearable to be apart, and exchanged khatas.

Next, [the Karmapa continued] to travel gradually. On the eighth day of the tenth month, [he] was reunited with [his] parents and younger brother, the master Ponlop Rinpoche, at [his] birthplace in Dankhok. Then, [he] visited the Kagyu monastic seats, including Danam Gyeling (mDan rnam rgyas gling), Drutse Drung ('Bru tshe bhrung) monastery, Dranthang (Dran thang) monastery and Shagön (Zhwa mgon) monastery. Nyenpa Rinpoche went to welcome him to visit Benchen Samdrub Chöling (Ban chen bsam 'grub chos gling). In the protector's temple, the horse in the statue of the protector Shingkyong (Zhing skyong) that Nyenpa Rinpoche newly constructed neighed. As a result, [the Karmapa] created a new ransom ritual 'thread-cross of fulfilment' of Shingkyong. [He] watched the Cham dance of [Padmasambhava on] the tenth day. Then, [he] reached Thrangu monastery and watched the Cham dance of longevity sādhana, and so on. On his way to Damkar ('Dam dkar) monastery, [he visited] Mani from China, and consecrated the prayer wheel installed with 100 million *mani* mantras that Traleg Rinpoche newly constructed.

Thereafter, [the Karmapa travelled] past Damkar, Thrangu, Benchen, La'o (Bla'o) and Dütsitil (bDud rtsi mthil), and arrived at Namgyaltse (rNam rgyal rtse). There, the [two groups] Tse (rTse) and Ling (gLing) had disputes for many years and [committed] bad deeds of killing and bloodshed for a long time. [The Karmapa] mediated the hostility [between them] and united [their] monasteries. As a result, from then on, [they held] no bad feelings [for each other], just like a waxing moon free from clouds. [The Karmapa then] performed a hair-cutting ceremony for the supreme reincarnation of Trungpa, Chökyi Gyatso.

Next, [the Karmapa travelled] past the monastic seat of the great Tertön Chokgyur Lingpa, Tsike Norbu Sumdo (rTsi rke nor bu gsum mdo), and then arrived at Karma Monastery. There, for the duration of about fifteen days, [he] bestowed extensive teachings of the empowerments that ripen and instructions that liberate on the devotees. Later, [he] fulfilled the wishes of the devotees in the capital city of Nangchen, as well as Palkha Dermo monastery and Dilyag monastery. Then, [he] visited Gina monastery. [p.343] On the fifteenth day of the sixth month, [he] arrived at the front of Anye Dringye (A mye 'bring rgyas) of Damshung ('Dam gzhung). There, [he] performed the sādhana prayers, including the ransom ritual 'thread-cross of fulfilment'[17] [of] the eight classes of gods and spirits. In general, the local god had made offerings to successive Karmapa incarnations with every extraordinary object made by non-humans. This time, again, [he] offered [to the Karmapa] a flawless, precious and magnificent Dzi stone. Then, on the journey, gradually, [as the Karmapa travelled to] a place called Olung ('O lung) on the twentieth day of the sixth month, [his] mother died. Feeling [great] sadness, [he] performed Phowa and cremation ceremony [for her].

Thereafter, [the Karmapa travelled] past Bartha (Bar mtha') and Nagchu while sustaining the enlightened activity of taming beings in whatever means necessary. On the tenth day of the ninth month, [he] arrived at the great monastic seat in Tsurphu valley. The lamas and monastic officials of the monasteries and the monastic community headed by Pawo Rinpoche and Gyaltsab Rinpoche presented a lavish welcoming reception. [He] stayed there afterwards.

Next, on the fifteenth day of the tenth month, [the Karmapa] went to Lhasa to [have his] first audience [with] the fourteenth reincarnation of the All-Knowing Dalai Lama. In accord with the genuine custom of [their] predecessors, all the activities of their audience were completed successfully. Then, [he] returned to [his] own monastic seat and studied the scriptures. [He] studied the section of Chokgyur Lingpa's Terma teaching in front of Surmang Tentrul (Zur mang bstan sprul) Rinpoche; [he then] studied the parts of the teaching [of which Surmang Tentrul] did not have the transmission in the presence of Lama Samten Gyatso. [He] received reading transmissions from the supreme reincarnation Urgyen Rinpoche. On the twenty-sixth day of the first month of the water horse year [1942], as the construction of the new palace began, the gold offered by non-humans was discovered; [it appeared] spontaneously from within a wall. The construction of the many special interior and exterior sacred objects lasted until the water sheep year [1943].

[p.344] *Chapter 4: In order to increase the accumulation of merits, [the Karmapa] went on pilgrimages and made offerings in the south [of Tibet], the holy land India and the snow mountains*

On the fourth day of the second month of the wood monkey year [1944], [the Karmapa] travelled to the south. First, in Shongpa Lhachu (gZhong pa lha chu),[18] [he] performed 100 Tantric feasts through the mind sādhana. Then, at Atiśa's throne in Nyethang (sNye thang), [he] uttered Atiśa's sādhana of offering to the lama.[19] After that, in the snow mountain Thökar (Thod dkar),[20] [he] received from the Great Translator[21] [the teaching of] Pacification, Chöd and Nyingthig empowerments and transmissions. Next, [he] travelled to Samye. In Yushalkhang (g.Yu zhal khang), Kharag Yongdzin (Kha rag yongs 'dzin) Rinpoche offered [him] a long-life ritual in connection with the repelling practice, the invocation of *ḍākinī*s. [The Karmapa] performed 100 Tantric feasts of the mind sādhana and made extensive offerings. In Hepo (Has po) mountain,[22] [he] made smoke offering to the local gods of the world in general as well as Tibet, and asked [them] for protection. Then, [he] visited the site of the central monastic seat of Phagmo Drupa, Kuntu Zangpö NagTrö (Kun tu bzang po'i nags khrod), and [performed] vast offerings of Tantric feasts. In Zangri Khamar (Zangs ri kha dmar),[23] [he conducted] 100 Tantric feasts of Chöd. In Tradruk (Khra 'brug), [he performed] the ritual of the 'Four *Maṇḍala*s of Tara'. In Ne'u Dongtse (sNe'u gdong rtse), [he offered] tea and alms. In Yarlung Sheldrak (Yar lung shel brag), [he performed] 100 Tantric feasts of Padmasambhava. In Rechungphuk (Ras chung phug), [he offered] tea and alms. In Chongye Riwo Dechen ('Chong rgyas ri bo bde chen), [he offered] tea and alms to over 1,000 members of the sangha.

Thereafter, in Lhodrak, [the Karmapa performed] 100 Tantric feasts of Padmasambhava at Nawojog (sNa bo cog), Dranpa Chagdor (Bran pa phyag rdor) and Lhodrak temple.[24] [He] visited the sacred objects in Lhodrak Kharchu (lHo brag mkhar chu)[25] as well as Lhamo Jagphur (lHa mo lcags phur).[26] In Palgyi Phukring (dPal gyi phug ring), [he performed] 100 Tantric feasts. Then, in Lhodrak Nyide (lHo brag nyi lde) monastery, [he] visited the sacred objects and [offered] tea and alms to the monks. [He then] visited Sekhar Guthok (Sras mkhar dgu thog) [i.e., the nine-story tower built by Milarepa], and uttered the guru sādhana of Marpa, Milarepa and Gampopa. [He] went to Lhodro Bolung (lHo gro bo lung). When uttering the guru sādhana of Marpa, [he had] the vision of the three forefathers, and prayed [to them] with intense devotion. [He then] arrived at Tagnya Lungten Phuk (sTag gnya' lung bstan phug).[27] [He] made extensive offerings of Tantric feasts in connection with the guru sādhana of Milarepa. [p.345] At the invitation of the Second King of Bhutan, Jigme Wangchuck, [he travelled] past a retreat place from Karchung in Mön and arrived in Bhutan. [He] made offerings by performing 100 Tantric feasts at Zhabjethang (Zhabs rje thang) and Thangkhabir (Thang kha sbir). The King and Prince of Bhutan, together with servants, rode to welcome [him] with a lavish procession; [then, he] stayed in the temple which had the body imprint of Padmasambhava.

Next, at the invitations issued individually by the Queens, Phuntsho Choden and Pema Dechen, [the Karmapa] visited Tashi Choling and Wangdu Choling respectively, and gave empowerments that ripen and instructions that liberate to whoever to be tamed. Then, Princess Wangmo invited [him] to Jampa Lhakhang; [there, he] made extensive offerings. [He] consecrated the *stūpa* of Benchen Khenpo (Ban chen Khenpo). [He also] stayed in Bumthang for a long time. For the many thousands of devotees, [he] fulfilled [their] wishes individually through empowerments and the Black Crown [ceremony]. [He] bestowed on the King of Bhutan the torma empowerments of Marpa, Milarepa and Gampopa, as well as Protector [Mahākāla] and Kīlaya. [He] showed miraculous deeds. For example, when he offered khata to the Padmasambhava statue that was two-story high in Kurjey Lhakhang, the statue took [the khata] directly to the circle of hair between the two eyebrows.

Thereafter, on the fifteenth day of the fifth month, [the Karmapa] travelled to Tibet. At that time, the King, ministers and servants shed tears out of sadness [due to] devotion. Especially, the king himself sobbed out loud with unbearable sorrow for being separated from the Karmapa. [The Karmapa] said that [it] was a sign that [they] would not meet again. Then, [he offered] tea and alms to the sangha of Lhalung (lHa lung) monastery. [He] visited the sacred objects outside and inside Guru Lhakhang. After that, on the journey, gradually, he and his retinue arrived at [his] own holy monastic seat on the fifteenth day of the sixth month. [p.346] On the eleventh day of the ninth month of the wood rooster year [1945], Maitreya Situ Rinpoche visited [the Karmapa's] monastic seat. In the tenth month, [the Karmapa] received the empowerments and transmissions of the *Treasury of Extensive Teachings* and *Knowing One Liberates All*. Then, in the fire male dog year [1946], when [he] was over twenty-three years of age, [he] received full ordination vows through jñāpti-caturtha-karman in the presence of Maitreya Situ Pema Wangchok Gyalpo on the fifteenth day of the first month celebrating the Buddha's display of miracles. Thereby the life story of a venerable monk among many great masters who were the holders of the teaching filled the world.

Next, starting from the beginning of the fire pig year [1947], [the Karmapa] produced new types of offering utensils and statues and carried out all sorts of repairs. For the sangha, [he] put into practice the visual transmission and established a new examination of the discipline of pure conduct. [He] also looked after Situ Rinpoche and his retinue [on their] ride to Eastern Tibet. Then, on the fifteenth day of the fourth month, [he] travelled to Western

Tibet [on] a pilgrimage in the great snow mountain, Mount Kailash, and the holy land India. Passing through the north, including Gade (dGa' bde), [he] protected the benefit of beings in each and every village. [He] visited Bukar ('Bu dkar) and Mandong (sMan ldong) monastery. At the beginning of the ninth month, [he] visited the white Vairocana statue in Tradun (sKra bdun) and made abundant offerings of Tantric feasts.

Thereafter, [the Karmapa travelled] past the border of Nepal, Mustang. On the first day of the eleventh month, [he] arrived at Pokra (sPogs ra). The sacred object of the Great Encampment, a sword ([which caused] the gathering of Mongolian butchers [to be] torn and burned)[28] got lost. [He] carried out an investigation for about seventeenth days, and yet [the sword] was not found. Later, a fire [burned down] that place[29] [which caused] fear. However, an old woman who used to serve [the Karmapa] was not harmed at all. On the twenty-third day, [the Karmapa] arrived at Lumbinī, the birthplace of our Buddha, and made abundant offerings. Then, [he] travelled to Nepal. In front of the three *stūpa*s, [he] made offerings that were profound and extensive in connection with the Tantra section. [p.347] In the holy caves, Asura and Yangleshö, [he] made offerings by performing 100 Tantric feasts of Padmasambhava. During this time, along [his journey through] the north of Nepal, such as Nyeshang (sNye shangs), [he performed the donning of] the precious liberation-through-seeing Black Crown and empowerments to over 10,000 people, fulfilling the wishes of each and every one [of them] accordingly.

Next, [the Karmapa] arrived at Vārānasī, the site where the Buddha turned the Wheel of Dharma. [He] made offerings as plentiful as the ocean of clouds by performing the offering rituals of Neju (gNas bcu) as well as the Buddha and his eight close disciples. Then, [he] arrived at Bodhgayā in India, the place where the 1,002 buddhas of Fortunate Aeon manifest enlightenment. In front of the Mahābodhi *stūpa* and the Bodhi tree, [he] made profound and extensive offerings, and did many circumambulations. [He] made aspirations as well as possible: [May] the times of disease, famine and war do not arise in the world; [may] the precious teaching of the Buddha spread, flourish, and remain for long!

Furthermore, [the Karmapa] visited the Cool Grove charnel ground and the meditation cave of Shabari [where he] made offerings as abundant as possible. On that occasion, the three Karma Kagyu monasteries in Sikkim [sent their] invitation. Hence, on the third day of the first month of the earth mouse year [1948], [he travelled] to Gangtok in Sikkim via Calcutta. [He] met with the King of Sikkim, Tashi Namgyal, [and] fulfilled the wishes of all [by performing] empowerments and the [ceremony of] the precious Black Crown for the king, ministers, monasteries and the public. Then, [he] reached Bodhgayā again, after which [he] travelled to Tso Pema. The lotuses surrounding the lake had not emerged in that year, [and yet,] as soon as the Karmapa arrived to circumambulate the lake, they emerged as if to welcome [him]. [He] offered khata and made abundant offerings, including Tantric feasts and the thousand-fold offering.

Next, along the journey via Khunu (Khu nu), [the Karmapa] made people grateful [by performing] appropriate[30] empowerments that ripen and instructions that liberate. [p.348] [He] returned to the front of Mount Kailash.[31] In Driraphuk ('Bri ra phug), [he] performed the offering of Tantric feasts and uttered the ritual of Tara at Drolma (sGrol ma)[32] above. The lake called Kapāla (Ka Pā la) was solidly frozen due to contamination in the past. At that time, [as the Karmapa arrived there], the surface [of the lake] melted. [He] visited thoroughly the [holy] places, including Dzutrul Phuk (rDzu 'phrul phug), Gyangdrak Phuk (rGyang grags phug) monastery and Trügo (Khrus sgo), and [made] offerings of tea and alms to the whole sangha there. After completing many circumambulations, [he travelled] to Drakyar (Brag skyar) via Trongpa Sengtö ('Brong pa seng stod). [He] restored old representations of [the enlightened] body, speech and mind and produced new [ones] in the monastery. [Then, he] visited the places in that direction at the invitation of [local] devotees, fulfilling the wishes of each individual accordingly. [He] visited Gegye (dGe rgyas) monastery, and successfully fulfilled [people's] wishes [through] the donning of the precious Black Crown, cleansing ceremony, consecration, and so on. Again, [he] visited, gradually, Bukar monastery and Mandong (sMan sdong), satisfying the people along the journey through teachings and material wealth. [Then], [he] bestowed teachings [according to people's] wishes in Galo (rGa lo) and Yangchen (Yangs can). On the seventeenth day of the eleventh month, with an elaborate arrangement of welcoming reception [held] by the monastic household at home, [he] arrived at [his] own seat, Tsurphu.

In the earth ox year [1949], [the Karmapa] constructed anew Dargye Chöling (Dar rgyas chos gling) grove.[33] Bodhisattva Jamgon, the glorious Khyentse Özer, travelled specially to Tsurphu. [The Karmapa] requested [him] to grant the empowerment of the *Treasury of Precious Termas*. Then, in the fifth month, [Khyentse Özer] accomplished the prayers that overcome difficulties. Hence, on the twenty-seventh day of the sixth month, [he] began [the empowerment on] a very auspicious day according to astrology. According to the approach of the Great Fifteenth Karmapa, [they] successfully completed the study of the empowerments that ripen, instructions that liberate, and supporting reading transmissions of the *Treasury of Precious Termas* on the twenty-fourth day of the sixth month of the iron tiger year [1950]. [p.349] Moreover, [the Karmapa] spent time studying the vast section of the extraordinary profound Dharma, including *Mahāmudrā, the Ocean of Certainty* and *The Profound Path, the Six Dharmas of Nāropā* [which Khyentse Özer] entrusted [him] with. Especially, like a father handing all his jewels to his son, [Khyentse Özer] offered [the Karmapa] the essential instructions of ultimate transmission. [The Karmapa] also installed [Khyentse Özer] as the chief of [his] own lineage and asked [him] to abide in the Golden Garland of the precious lineage of the Kagyu. Since [their] minds became one, the wisdom of the lama and the disciple came to be inseparable. Jamgon Rinpoche also uttered a song of realisation that clearly reveals the Karmapa's level of spiritual attainment. In the iron hare year [1951], Vajradhāra Jamgon Rinpoche and his retinue travelled to Palpung of Derge in the east. [Prior to Jamgon's] departure, the spiritual father and son exchanged khata, unable to bear to be apart. [Then, the Karmapa] rewarded the reincarnation of Palpung Khyentrul Rinpoche on the Dharma throne.[34]

Chapter 5: In order to spread the teaching and increase the welfare of beings, [the Karmapa] travelled to various regions of India, China and Tibet

To welcome the great All-Knowing Dalai Lama on [his] journey from Dromo (Gro mo) to Lhasa, [the Karmapa] departed from [his] monastic seat on the twenty-seventh day of the sixth month. On the eighth day of the seventh month, [the Karmapa] met with the Dalai Lama in Zechökhor Yangtse (Zas chos 'khor yang rtse) and laid out an orderly arrangement of abundant offerings. [Since] the officials and monastic assembly of the monastery appealed in person, [the Karmapa] bestowed [on them] the donning of the precious Black Crown and empowerments. [He] offered tea and alms to the general gathering [of the sangha]. [Then, he] returned to [his] monastic seat. After that, on the ninth day of the tenth month, [he] travelled to Nyemo (sNye mo) at the invitation of the [local] community. [p.350] [He] visited, in stages, Lhabu (lHa bu) monastery, Pakar (Pa dkar) monastery and Nyemo Gyedo (sNye mo sgye mdo) monastery, and bestowed appropriate empowerments and the donning of the Black Crown [according to people's] wishes. [He] made elaborate offerings of tea and gifts to the sangha.

Thereafter, the old Japa monastery and the leaders and people of Markyang Dzong (Mar rkyang rdzong) invited [the Karmapa]; hence, [he] visited [there]. When [the Karmapa was] performing the precious liberation-through-seeing Black Crown [Ceremony] and giving public blessings to the leaders and people[35] of that region, Drupön Tenzin (sGrub dpon bstan 'dzin) Rinpoche saw in [his] pure vision [that] Jomo Gangkar (Jo mo gangs dkar)[36] came to receive the blessings [in the form of] a beautiful woman carrying a ceremonial arrow in [her] hand. Some farmers in that region [suffered] severe hardships every year as a result of the damage [caused] by flooding. Although all [of them] built dams accordingly on the side of the field, due to the flood from the main flow of the river, [they] were helpless, unable [to avoid damage]. In that circumstance, [they] asked the Karmapa for protection. Hence, [he] gave

[them] blessed barley grains in large quantity, and told [them] kindly that if [they] were to sow these very grains in the soils where there were dangers of flood, [they] would have no such dangers [anymore]. [They] followed [his advice]. Therefore, in summer, when the river swelled,[37] it changed course, as the people wished, [flowing] towards a region called Nyemoru (sNye mo ru) where there was no field. [This shows the Karmapa's] great kindness [to the people].

Next, [the Karmapa] fulfilled the wishes of the people along [his] journey, including Chöde (Chos sde) monastery and Chuzang (Chu bzang) monastery. On the twenty-second day of the eleventh month, [he] arrived at [his] monastic seat. To repulse serious smallpox that had lasted for an entire year, [he] performed subjugation, burning and casting through [the ritual of] Kīlaya, a Terma revealed by Ratna Lingpa (Ratna gling pa); thereby [he] made the epidemic die out. On the sixth day of the second month of the water dragon year [1952], Gyaltsab Rinpoche Drakpa Gyatso died. [The Karmapa] conducted the funeral ritual [for him]. Then, the thirteen communities and the new Bartha community of Namru (gNam ru) invited [him to visit]. [p.351] [He] rode [there] in the fifth month, and satisfied [the people's needs] in each region through the Dharma appropriate [for them], including empowerments, cleansing ceremonies, consecrations, the donning of the precious liberation-through-seeing [Black Crown], the smoke offerings and Patö (dPa' bstod) of Dralha (dGra lha), as well as Tsope Chirim (Tsho pa'i spyi rim).[38] [He] visited Shawadrak (Shwa ba brag), Zarmo (Zar mo) monastery and Karchung monastery. While staying in Karchung monastery, [he] spit on the surface of a wall. [Someone] wrapped up [the spittle] in paper and kept [it] as an object of faith, from which over 1,000 relics emerged. [It is] now kept among the [sacred] objects of the Great Encampment. During this time, the supreme refuge Situ Rinpoche died on the twenty-fifth day of the eighth month. Hence, [the Karmapa] made elaborate offerings with deep sorrow.

Thereafter, [the Karmapa] fulfilled the wishes of [the people in] the regions, including Dolpa (Dol pa) and Namru. [He] visited Dziri ('Dzi ri) monastery and other places. On the seventeenth day of the eighth month, [he] arrived at [his] own seat. On the third day of the third month of the water snake year [1953], [he] travelled to Nakar (sNa dkar) in [his] own area. [He] fulfilled [people's] wishes accordingly [through] the consecration of sacred places at the mountain peak where a local god [resided], assembling gods and demons [to receive] samaya, cleansing ceremony [for] the mountain, cleansing ceremony [for] the valley, as well as empowerments and the donning of the precious Black Crown. Later, [he] reached Dargye Chöling grove. On the twenty-eighth day of the fourth month, for the purpose of receiving the great empowerment of Yamāntaka in the presence of the great All-Knowing Dalai Lama, [the Karmapa] stayed in Kunde Ling (Kun bde gling) in Lhasa. Then, in front of the Jowo Buddha statue, [he] made profound and extensive offerings, including 1,000-fold offerings and 100 Tantric feasts. [He] met with the great All-Knowing Dalai Lama. On this occasion, [he] heard the unbearable news that Jamgon Rinpoche died. Missing him deeply, [he] conducted the funeral ritual [for Jamgon] as profoundly as possible. [p.352] Furthermore, [he] visited all the holy places in Lhasa, including Jokpori (Cog po ri), making abundant offerings. At the beginning of the eighth month, as [the Dalai Lama] began to give the great empowerment of Yamāntaka, [the Karmapa] came to receive [it]. Like [their] successive predecessors in the past, [the Karmapa's] connection with the great Dalai Lama through the Dharma came to be firm and profound.

[The Karmapa] met with the two tutors of the Dalai Lama. Completing all the ceremonies successfully, [he] left on the twenty-fifth day of the eighth month. As Nenang (gNas nang) monastery, led by Pawo Choktrul (dPa' bo mchog sprul) Rinpoche, [held] the welcoming reception in a very profound manner, [the Karmapa] arrived there. [He] performed empowerments, the donning of the precious Black Crown, cleansing ceremonies and consecrations. As an auspicious interdependence, [he] watched the play of Ache Lhamo (A ce lha mo) with great celebration. On the first day of the ninth month, [he] arrived at [his] monastic seat. In general, travelling or staying in [his] monastic seat, [he] undoubtedly strove for the enlightened activity to purely develop the treasure of the teaching [in] whatever [way] suitable [for the beings].

Thereafter, Mindrolling Chung (sMin grol gling gCung) Rinpoche requested the empowerment and transmission of Chokgyur Lingpa's Terma teaching from the Karmapa. Accordingly, in connection with the new year celebration of the wood horse year [1954], [the Karmapa] began the empowerment and transmission. In the fourth month, [he] presided over the 'Seven Profound Dharmas of Vajra Kīlaya'. [He] completed [the empowerment and transmission], marking the end with the ritual to receive the *siddhi*. In the fifth month, since [he] performed the Tantric feast of the medicine sādhana through the 'Eight Classes of Sādhanas of the Nyingma Kama and Terma traditions', [he] began [to teach] the sādhana and completed [the teaching], at Chung Rinpoche's request.

During this period, the treasurer of the mountain hermitage above Palpung, Yönten (Yon tan),[39] [together with his] servant, came to meet [the Karmapa] and requested [him] to identify the reincarnation of the late [Jamgon Kongtrul]. In response, [the Karmapa wrote] a divination letter:

[p.353] On the left side of Jowo Śākyamuni
A family of a wealthy householder [whose] door faces the south
The number of people [living there] is endowed with an auspicious mark[40]
The sound of the name Padma reveals wisdom[41]

The child was born in the wood horse year
The emanation of Vairocana Jamgon Lama
Whose reincarnation becomes evidently unmistaken

Due to the change in circumstances, the original divination letter [that contains] these words cannot be found. Yet, this letter was composed according to the memory of the previous Jamgon's attendant.

Furthermore, Trongsar Behu Drakpa Namgyal ('Brong gsar be hu Grags pa rnam rgyal) made repeated requests to [the Karmapa] in person, saying that since there was no qualified lama or tulku to lead the monastery that he built anew, the Karmapa should appoint one worthy of [being revered] as the refuge of this life and beyond. [The Karmapa] replied: 'In general, the emanations of [the enlightened] body, speech and mind of a holy master are incredible. Hence, [I shall] identify a reincarnation of Palpung Khyentse of Derge in the east. If [you] enthrone him as the chief of your monastery, it will be of great benefit to the teaching and beings.' [The Karmapa's] divination letter is as follows:

Straight [from] Central Tibet in the upper part of the west
Within the distance of two days' journey at a high speed
[p.354] A family of a householder with little wealth [whose] door faces the east
The father's name is Ngagi Wangchuk Gönpo (Ngag gi dbang phyug mgon po)
The mother's name is Aya Tāra Chökyi Drön (A ya tā ra chos kyi sgron)
The child of the couple was born in the dog year
[His] family lineage is pure and [he is endowed] with the true nature of a holy [person]
Undoubtedly certain [that he is] the emanation of Khyentse Wangpo (mKhyen brtse dbang po)

Accordingly, the reincarnation was correctly found. During this period, the Chinese government [issued] an order inviting the high lamas and officials of Tibet, headed by the great All-Knowing refuge and protector, the Dalai Lama, [to visit China]. Hence, on the thirteenth day of the fifth month, [the Karmapa] departed from [his] own monastic seat for Lhasa. The Prince of Sikkim, Lama Thondup Namgyal, went specially to meet [him].

Next, on the fifteenth day, [the Karmapa] set off together with the lamas and officials of Tibet. On the journey, gradually, [they travelled] past Drikung ('Bri gung), Kongpo (Kong po) and other places. Po'o Tongjuk Dzong (sPo'o stong 'jug rdzong) welcomed [the party] with high lamas and noblemen, made living arrangements and hosted an elaborate banquet. Then, [the Karmapa] gave teachings widely to the lamas and monks in Dateng (Zla steng) monastery and Yuru (g.Yu ru) monastery. In Chamdo, the treasurer of Palpung, Lama Chokga (Cog ga), requested [the Karmapa] to put an end to the dispute over the reincarnation of Situ Rinpoche. Thereafter, [the party travelled] past Dartsedo (Dar rtse mdo) and arrived in Chengdu. The Dalai Lama, the Karmapa and others headed to Beijing by plane. The Chinese government presented a grand welcoming reception. [The Karmapa] stayed in a place called Beijing Phande (Phan bde). [He] spent his time, day and night, on activities, such as meeting government officials and sharing opinions at ceremonies. At that time, [p.355] a person called Wan Mantru'u (Wan man phru'u) was specially assigned as [the Karmapa's] Chinese secretary. [One day,] when [he] went to visit [the Karmapa, he] did not see him on the seat; instead, [he] saw sunlight shining [on the seat]. Then, [he] came out of the living room and asked [the Karmapa's] attendant Jinpa (sByin pa) where the Karmapa had gone. Jinpa explained that [the Karmapa] did not go anywhere at all; [he] was staying in the living room. Hence, [Wan Mantru'u] returned to the living room to see [the Karmapa]. [This] time, [he] saw the Karmapa sitting on the seat; there was no window whatsoever that [would allow] sunlight to shine through to the seat. [He] was very surprised. Generally speaking, he was a true believer of communism. Yet, thereafter, [he] developed faith in the Dharma and Dharma practitioners as well as genuine devotion to the supreme refuge [i.e., the Karmapa].

Thereafter, Bo Gangkar Rinpoche visited [the Karmapa] frequently and had Dharma discussions [with him]. On the twenty-second day of the ninth month, [the Karmapa] issued the divination letter for [the reincarnation of] Situ Rinpoche that contains clear explanations and a sketch of [his] birthplace. Gangkar Rinpoche dictated the letter and sent a messenger to Palpung (by the time the divination letter arrives, [it] must be inserted here). Then, [the Karmapa] visited Tianjin, Nanjing, Wuxi and Hangzhou among other places. During that time, [he] also performed empowerments for a few Chinese monks. After that, [he] departed for Tibet. The leader of Gyarong Trichu (rGya rong Khri bcu) of Yakngar (G.yag rngar) sent an earnest invitation [to the Karmapa] from Gyarong (rGya rong); yet [the Karmapa] did not manage to go. On the twenty-ninth day of the twelfth month, [the Karmapa] arrived at Dartsedo. On the new year day of the wood sheep year [1955], Trijang (Khri byang) Rinpoche and Chung (gCung) Rinpoche exchanged khatas [with the Karmapa] as [a new year] greeting. As Trijang Rinpoche was leaving for Lithang, [the Karmapa] granted [him] a departure audience. [He also] prophesied the lifespan of Gangkar Rinpoche [which] later turned out to be true. [While] in Minyak (Mi nyag), [he] bestowed monastic vows to an assembly of over 100 [monks] from Ganden.

[p.356] Next, at the invitation of the wealthy [patrons] in Hor Athub (Hor a thub) and Taso Lakar (rTa so la dkar), [the Karmapa visited] the monasteries of different schools, including Drakgo (Brag mgo), Kardze (dKar mdzes) and

Dargye (Dar rgyas). [He] visited Bangan (Ban rgan) monastery; [there, he] offered tea and alms to the monks, and performed cleansing and consecration ceremonies [for] the sacred objects. [He] granted [the monastery] a large amount of silver [offered to him by] devotees from the monastery for the purpose of [setting up] an endowment fund for [the construction of] the representations of the enlightened body, speech and mind. Then, [he] travelled to Yilung (Yid lhung) and Gönchen (dGon chen).[42] [He] gave teachings to a public audience of over 10,000 people, headed by the aristocrats of Derge. At the invitation of the treasurer of Palpung, Lama Chokga (Cog ga), [the Karmapa] visited Palpung monastery, received by a lavish procession upon [his] arrival. On this occasion, feeling disturbed as the reincarnation of Situ Rinpoche was yet to be found, [he] gave careful advice that while it was necessary to find for definite the genuine reincarnation of the late Situ Rinpoche, [there was] no need to be overwhelmed by intense desire whatsoever. For the sake of the reincarnation of Situ Rinpoche, [the Karmapa] uttered the protector sādhanā [for] seven days in the protector's temple. Then again, with the insight of prophetic wisdom, [he composed] a clear and detailed divination letter [that revealed] the essential characteristics of the place and family [where the reincarnation was born]; [this he] explained [in a way that was] easy to understand. Then, [he] specially sent a search party. As a result, the reincarnation was found for certain. [He] sent immediately [his] nephew Samtrul (bSam sprul) and Drubpön Tenzin Rinpoche to offer cleansing ceremony [to the reincarnation]. One day in the [same] month, the lamas and monks of Palpung, the lamas and tulkus of the Karma Kagyu monasteries gathered in that area, as well as the people from the regions in that area, over 10,000 [in total], welcomed [the reincarnation]. The sangha welcomed [him] once again with numerous special offerings. Then, [they] invited the precious supreme reincarnation to [enter] the Yiga Chödzin shrine hall. In front of the precious liberation-through-seeing Maitreya Buddha [statue] in the main shrine, the Karmapa conducted a hair-cutting ceremony [for the reincarnation]. Again, on another day of the month, [the reincarnation] was installed on the golden throne. [p.357] The great Dharma King of Derge also attended the ceremony, making lavish throne offerings. The ceremony then concluded successfully. During that period, all the lamas and tulkus from Eastern Tibet [gathered] at the ceremony went to see [the Karmapa] and had audiences [with him]. Furthermore, the political change at that time was becoming [as dramatic] as a display of lightning. [The Karmapa] instructed [them] in clear detail and [in a way that was] easy to understand: [they should] avoid unfavourable conditions and establish favourable conditions [with skilful] method and wisdom so that obstacles to the teaching of the Buddha would not arise because of the political change. Then, within a fairly short time, the teaching flourished, unharmed by the change in circumstances.

Thereafter, [the Karmapa] gave grand blessings in Tsandra,[43] Palpung Khyentrul Rinpoche's retreat centre, and Chödruk (Chos drug) retreat centre. [He] bestowed on the supreme reincarnation of Situ Rinpoche the bodhisattva vows from two traditions, the empowerments of the nine deities of the red Avalokiteśvara in the Karma Kagyu tradition and Chokgyur Lingpa's mind sādhana 'Wish-fulfilling Jewels', as well as the special initiation and torma empowerment of the glorious wisdom protector, the two-armed Mahākāla. [He] gave full ordination vows to over 300 lamas, tulkus and monks from the monasteries in Eastern Tibet who gathered there. Then, since [this visit] coincided with the Dalai Lama's journey to Tsezurdo (rTse zur mdo), [the Karmapa] invited [him], gathering the leaders of all the monasteries in Eastern Tibet, making grand preparations for [his] arrival and inviting [him] to confer teachings. The Dalai Lama continued to travel to Chamdo. The Karmapa stayed on in that region. With loving-kindness and compassion, [he] bestowed the teachings [that were] like the nectar of [his] heart and essential instructions on [the practice of] the profound, virtuous holy Dharma in this [life] and all [future lives] to the lamas, tulkus and monastic officials of various [ranks] from the monasteries headed by Palpung, as well as the noblemen of Derge. After that, [he travelled] past Chamdo, and arrived in Lhasa on the fourteenth day of the fifth month. [p.358] [He] made grand offerings in Potala [Palace] and the temples of Trulnang ('Phrul snang). After bidding farewell to the Dalai Lama, [he] reached [his] monastic seat, Tsurphu, on the eighteenth day.

Next, at the beginning of the seventh month, [the Karmapa] restored [his] palace and finished building the new Phuntsok Khyilpa (Phun tshogs 'khyil pa).[44] In the fire monkey year [1956], according to the old tradition, the Dalai Lama travelled to [his] own place of residence; [the Karmapa] sent an invitation request [to the Dalai Lama], and made preparations for [his visit to Tsurphu]. On the fifth day of the sixth month, the Dalai Lama departed from Lhasa. In Tashigang (bKra shis sgang), the Karmapa greeted [him] with khata. Later, [the Dalai Lama] was received with a [welcoming] procession as well as elaborate [offerings] including music. [He] stayed in the living quarters, Phuntsok Khyilpa. The Tibetan government made abundant offerings of tea and alms to the sangha. [The Dalai Lama] watched the grand Cham dance of [Padmasambhava on] the tenth day, bestowed the empowerment of Avalokiteśvara to the monks and lay people headed by the Karmapa, and offered broad instructions on both the Dharma and worldly affairs. [He] visited the sacred objects of the Great Encampment. In addition, [the Karmapa] performed the donning of the precious liberation-through-seeing Black Crown. On the thirteenth day, after bidding farewell to [the Karmapa, the Dalai Lama] returned [to Lhasa].

Thereafter, on the twentieth day of the seventh month, the messenger of the [Lhasa] government arrived. Hence, [the Karmapa] travelled to Lhasa.[45]

Even though all [his] entourage led by the treasurer of the Great Encampment requested [the government's] permission [to relieve the Karmapa of this duty, to him,] there was no other way but to go [there] in person. Thus, [he travelled] past Kongpo and arrived at Chamdo on the twenty-ninth day. [He] visited a place called Uyön (dBu yon) Society every day and tried his best to offer strategies for the teaching and the welfare of beings through peace. Countless people from Eastern Tibet went to see [him] day and night; [he gave] them blessings and [made] profound and vast aspirations for them. Then, [he] returned to Lhasa, bid farewell [to the Dalai Lama] in Norbulingkha, [p.359], and visited the holy sites, mainly the wish-fulfilling jewel the Jowo Buddha, making profound and extensive offerings. On the twenty-fifth day of the eighth month, [he] arrived at [his] own monastic seat.

Soon afterwards, [the Karmapa had] the idea of going on pilgrimage to India. Hence, [he] left [his] own monastic seat on the twenty-ninth day of the ninth month. Based on an invitation [to the Karmapa] sent in the past, Chögön (Chos mgon) Rinpoche hosted a welcoming reception; [the Karmapa] arrived at Dechenchö (bDe chen chos) monastery. [He] carried out a wide [range of activities], including empowerments and the donning of the Black Crown [which were] suitable [to the audience], as well as offerings of tea and alms to the sangha of the monastery, cleansing and consecration rituals for the sacred objects inside and outside [the monastery], and offerings of Tantric feasts. After that, [he] left [there]. Along [his] journey, [he] satisfied [the needs of] the people through the Dharma and material wealth. Then, on the twenty-third day of the tenth month, [he] arrived in Gangtok; the King of Sikkim and [his] ministers welcomed [him]. Then, [he] satisfied [the needs of] the devotees through empowerments and the donning of the precious Black Crown, according to [their] own wishes. Then, [he travelled] past Siliguri; in both Vulture Peak Mountain and Bodhgayā, [he] made grand offerings. [He] met with Dzongsar Khyentse Rinpoche [who] was staying [there]. After that, [he made] offerings in Vārāṇasī. [He then] surveyed the city of Bheta. Afterwards, [he arrived] in front of the three *stūpa*s in Nepal [where he] made profound and extensive offerings of Tantric feasts, the 'Ocean of the Tantra Section', as well as perfumed robes. [He] satisfied [the needs of] the devotees present there through the empowerments that ripen and instructions that liberate.

Next, [the Karmapa travelled] past Lucknow and [arrived at] the meditation caves, Ellora and Ajanta. [There, he] performed offerings of Tantric feasts and prostrations. Then, on the journey, gradually, [he] arrived at Dorjeling (rDo rje gling). In Dotsuk (rDo btsug) monastery, [he] carried out a wide [range of activities], including empowerments, the Black Crown [Ceremony], consecration and cleansing rituals. On the third day of the second month of the fire rooster year [1957, he] visited Gangtok again and met with the King of Sikkim.

[p.360] Thereafter, Photang (Pho tang) monastery invited [the Karmapa] to visit. [There, he] fulfilled [the people's] wishes through the Dharma [they] longed for, including empowerments and the Black Crown [Ceremony]. Then, [he] reached Gangtok. The gathering of monks from Rumtek Samten Chöling (Rum bteg bsam gtan chos gling) too invited [him]. At that time, [he] said: 'I shall come later'. Thus, the monks [thought that] if [he] was unable to come in person when [he] was nearby then, [they would have] no chance of inviting [him] once he had gone [back] to Tibet. For that reason, [they] insisted that [he should] come this time. [The Karmapa] said: 'I shall take my time to come later'; [by saying so], he was making a prophecy for the future. Then, [he travelled] past Dromo and protected the benefit of beings in each Kagyu monastery, [including also] Dungkar (Dung dkar). On the ninth day of the third month, [he] reached [his] own monastic seat.

Immediately [upon his arrival, the Karmapa began to] produce the precious liberation-through-taste Black Pills. At the request of the officials from the monastic household of Chögong, [he composed] the divination letter [for] the identification of the supreme reincarnation of Gyaltsab Rinpoche as follows:

From this monastery, within two days' journey at a high speed to the upper part of an area in the west
The householder with average wealth [whose] door faces the east
The father's name is Lodrö (Blo gros) [and] the mother's name is Drolma (sGrol ma)
The child was born in the wood horse year

According to what is clearly said [in this letter], the genuine [reincarnation] was found for certain. On the sixteenth day of the sixth month, [the reincarnation] received a hair-cutting ceremony [from the Karmapa]. On the twenty-second day, an auspicious day according to astrology, [his] enthronement ceremony was completed in a grand manner with throne offerings. In the earth dog year [1958], [the Karmapa] received the transmission of the 'Seven Treasuries of Longchenpa' from Shechen Kongtrul Rinpoche. During this time, Eastern Tibet [encountered] very significant change in circumstances. As a result, Maitreya Situ Rinpoche and [his] retinue reached the monastic seat Tsurphu of Akaniṣṭha on the nineteenth day of the fourth month. Furthermore, [p.361] [the Karmapa] looked after the many lamas and tulkus who arrived [at Tsurphu from Eastern Tibet], including Sangye Nyenpa Rinpoche, Dilgo Khyentse (Dil mgo mkhyen brtse) and Traleg Nyima Gyurme (Khra legs nyi ma 'gyur med), with kindness and excellent hospitality. As the change in circumstances escalated, the officials [of Tsurphu], including the treasurer of the Great Encampment, earnestly requested [the Karmapa] to handle [his] duty carefully, i.e., to move to somewhere else. However, [the Karmapa] said: 'When it is time, I shall go'. He [conducted] the protector [Mahākāla] *pūjā*, Ratna Lingpa's repelling ritual of Kīlaya and the war-repelling ritual of Dhṛtarāṣṭra. According to the prophecy of the Tertön Rahtro (Raḥ khro), [he] built three *stūpa*s that tame the demons and consecrated [them]. Due to the blessings of these *pūjā*s which were satisfactory and pure, [the Karmapa] was able to travel safely on [his] escape [from Tibet into exile]. At that time, Shechen Kongtrul Rinpoche was arrested and taken to an unknown place. As soon as [he] heard [about this, the Karmapa] conducted a funeral ritual [for him]. Then, [he] specially sent Situ Rinpoche and [his] retinue to Bhutan, and the lamas and tulkus, including Nyenpa Rinpoche, temporarily to Nyide monastery in Lhodrak.

Chapter 6: To revive the embers of the teaching, [the Karmapa] became a refugee in the holy land India, and then established anew the great monastic seat Shedrub Chokhor Ling with shrines and sacred objects

In the earth pig year [1959], [the Karmapa] made many predictions and decided to go to India. On the fourth day of the second month of the earth pig year, [he] summoned 160 lamas, monks and attendants, and gathered [items] of the highest possible value, including the priceless sacred objects of the deities of the successive Karmapas, the [representations of] the enlightened body, speech and mind [from which] the brilliance of blessings radiates, and the extremely important offering utensils. Carrying [these items] together, [they] left in a rush.

[p.362] During this time, [when reaching] the iron bridge [over] the Tsangpo River, [the Karmapa's party] crossed over safely, in spite of the severe turmoil of war. Then, Sharpa Chöje (Shar pa chos rje)[46] made a request that his son Tenzin Kyabje (bsTan 'dzin skyabs rje) would be able to travel to India and Bhutan together with [the Karmapa]. Because of that, [the Karmapa] made a prophecy that [his son's] name [which was] very good [would] open the gateways to auspicious interdependence. Afterwards, as [people] suffered from the change in circumstances, [the Karmapa] gave them protection and made aspirations as best as [he could]. [He] arrived at Sekhar and Nyide monastery in Lhodrak. [He] made abundant offerings with the best aspirations for people [who faced] the suffering of danger to life during wartime. Then, [he] crossed the border between Bhutan and Tibet. On the twenty-sixth day, [he] arrived at Zhabjethang (Zhabs rjes thang). Princess Tsultrim Palmo (Tshul khrims dpal mo) congratulated the Karmapa and [his] retinue for [their] success of safe arrival, offering [them] perfect presents. [He then] travelled to Kujeythang (sKu rjes thang) [where he] met with Situ Rinpoche and Khyentse Rinpoche. After that, [he made] grand offerings of

Tantric feasts in Kurjey Lhakhang and Jampa Lhakhang. Once again, [he] made vast aspirations that [he would] be able to revive the embers of the Buddha's teaching in free countries. [He] satisfied [the needs of] the gathering of devotees in that area through empowerments and teachings.

Thereafter, [the Karmapa] visited Tashi Choling. [He] granted monastic vows and full ordination vows to seventy monks from Kurtö Dargye Chöling (sKur stod dar rgyas chos gling) in Bhutan. On the fifth day of the fourth month, [he] travelled to India through [the help of] the Bhutanese government. At this time, [he] left for Sikkim together with Maitreya Situ Rinpoche and Princess Tsultrim Palmo. [He] granted audiences to eighty members of the sangha from Trongsar (Krong gsar). Along the journey, [he] satisfied [the needs of] the people through the Dharma and material wealth. Then, [he] met with the King of Bhutan, Jigme Dorji, in a place called Khasa Drakchu (Kha sa brag chu) in the vicinity of the capital city Thimphu. [p.363] Furthermore, the monastic assembly of Punakha (Pu na kha) and the Bhutanese people showed great respect [to him]. Then, through the Bhutanese government, [he] had a discussion with the Indian government. As a result, [it was] decided that [he should take up] residence in Dharamsala in the region of the Indian state Himachal [Pradesh]. Accordingly, [he] travelled gradually across Bhutan. At the entry of Baksa (sBag sa) region, the representative of the government of Sikkim Densapa Tashi Dradül (gDan sa pa bKra shis dgra 'dul) and the representative of the Indian government Adrukbhabu (A brug bha bu) went together specially to meet [the Karmapa]. In consideration of the sacred and pure commitment [in] the lama-patron [relationship] through successive generations, beginning from the Ninth Karmapa Wangchuk Dorje up to the present Dharma King Tashi Namgyal, [they] invited the Karmapa and [his] entire retinue [to settle] in Sikkim, which the Indian government fully accepted. Accordingly, on account of the connection through the Dharma from the past and [his] clear vision into the future, [the Karmapa] decided to go there. On the twenty-fifth day of the fourth month of the earth pig year [1959], [he] arrived in Gangtok [where] the Karma Kagyu monasteries in Sikkim held a welcoming reception [for him]. Through countless venerations and praises, the Dharma King and Prince of Sikkim, together with ministers and attendants, promised that [the Karmapa] was allowed to even take up residence [in] whichever of the many places at [his] disposal, primarily the Taktse (sTag rtse) palace. Nonetheless, the Karmapa said: 'After the Buddha's teaching [which used to be] like a shining sun was completely cast aside [in Tibet], mainly [in] the magnificent Tsurphu in Tölung (sTod lung) [which is] the wheel of the heart[47] of Akaniṣṭha, we became refugees in a different country. [We did so] not to be able to just take care of ourselves, nor to merely strive for the happiness of this life, nor to only avoid losing our lives in war. [We] must revive as best as [we] can the embers of the very root of the teaching that has been destroyed. Hence, it is not possible [for us] to be at ease [and] live leisurely. For this reason, [our] task [is to] establish the foundation or basis upon which [we can] revive the embers of the teaching. On account of the [auspicious] connection and [this] special purpose, [p.364] simply allow [us] to take up residence temporarily at Rumtek monastery, the place that the Ninth Karmapa founded in the past.' On the fifth day of the fifth month [11 June 1959], [the Karmapa] arrived at Rumtek monastery. At that time, although the Karmapa, as well as [his] attendants, monks and lay people, did not have enough places to stay or very good living conditions, [the Karmapa] shared[48] [with them] whatever [his] monastic household had in [its] possession. With regards to the [practice] arrangements in accordance with the Dharma, the 150 lamas, tulkus and members of the sangha [performed] the ritual of 'the Four *Maṇḍala*s of Tara' every morning; in the afternoon, [they practised] the propitiation ritual of the Dharma protectors of [their] own tradition. On the fifteenth and the thirtieth day [of each month, they held] confessional assembly of fully ordained monks; on the eighth, tenth and twenty-fifth day, [they performed] sādhana *pūjā*s of Cakrasaṃvara, Vajravārāhī and red Avalokiteśvara. During the intervals, Drubpön Tenzin Rinpoche taught the commentaries of the texts, *The Jewel Ornament of Liberation* and *The Bodhisattvacharyāvatāra*, as well as the oral instructions of the profound path, the Six Dharmas of Nāropā, for senior lamas and monks. [The Karmapa] spent [his] time on Dharma activities. Particularly, encouraged by Princess of Bhutan, Tsultrim Palmo, he composed the history of refuge prayers.

On the seventh day of the sixth month, [the Karmapa] heard about the death of Dorlop (rDor slob) Rinpoche Özer Wangchuk ('Od zer dbang phyug) from Tashi Choling in Bhutan. [He then] immediately made aspirations and offerings [for him]. Moreover, at this time, [he] composed a new invocation ritual, titled 'The Assembly of the Golden Garlands, the Practice Lineage of the Past', which [he] placed in the prayer ever since.

Thereafter, the reincarnation of Jamgon Rinpoche, together with [his] parents, came specially [to meet the Karmapa]. On an auspicious day according to astrology, [the Karmapa] conducted hair-cutting ceremony [for him], offered [him] robes, and granted the empowerments of Karma Pakshi guru sādhana, the red Avalokiteśvara and the White Tara from Atiśa's tradition. [p.365] Then, since the monks did not have robes because of the recent change in circumstances, [he] acquired new [robes] which [he] provided each and every one [of them] with.

Next, Prince Palden Thondup Namgyal (dPal ldan don grub rnam rgyal) paid a visit to [the Karmapa]; [he] decided to build a new monastery [to propagate] the teaching. On the eighth day of the eleventh month [which was] very auspicious according to astrology, [the Karmapa] measured [the land] of the local nāga, asked for [permission to use] the land, and performed smoke offering. [He] offered the prince a Padmasambhava statue of good quality made in Shali in India as an award. Then, on the twenty-third day, [he] travelled specially to Kagön Rabling (Ka dgon rab gling) at [its] invitation, and presided over the year-end Mahākāla *pūjā*. In that area, [local traditions] like Bön were performing animal sacrifice. [The Karmapa] bestowed blessings, [telling the local people that] the killings [that they committed] up to then were unnecessary; [it was] satisfactory [to make offerings] through the burning of red food and a genuine propitiation ritual in the protector's temple. As a result, from then on, in that area, offerings through killing were no longer needed. [The Karmapa] returned to [his own] Dharma centre. Afterwards, his elder sister in Bhutan died; [he] made offerings and dedications to the lamas and tulkus of different schools; the sangha assembly of [his] Dharma centre made grand offerings individually [through] the Duntsik (bDun tshig) [ritual]. Later, on the fifteenth day of the twelfth month, [he] travelled specially on pilgrimage to India. [He] visited Bodhgayā and Vārānasī, making lavish offerings and fulfilling the wishes of the devotees [who] gathered there. [Then, he] returned to [his] monastic seat. Starting from the third day of the fifth month of the iron mouse year [1960], [he taught] the great [text] *The Treasury of Kagyu Mantras* that put together the precious Tantra section that Marpa brought [back from India] to fifteen lamas and tulkus, including the four supreme reincarnations,[49] Sangye Nyenpa, Traleg Rinpoche, Dilgo Khyentse, and over 100 members of the sangha as well as many Dharma practitioners in Sikkim. [He] taught every day without break, regardless of hardships. In this way, [the teaching] was fully completed on the fourth day of the sixth month, [p.366] [which was] the auspicious day [celebrating] the Buddha's turning of the Wheel of Dharma, with a thanks-giving offering of Tantric feasts [at the end]. Then, beginning [from] the eleventh day of the sixth month, [he] completed with great kindness the empowerments that ripen, instructions that liberate, and supporting reading transmission of the oral instruction of the Eight Great Chariots of the Practice Lineage.

At that time, the usual [type of] books, such as treatises, cycles of arts and sciences, and the Tantra section of secret mantras, were extremely rare. [The Karmapa] considered the foundation of the teaching to solely depend on scriptures. Hence, [he] established a new worksite to publish the wood [block print of] many [books], including *The Jewel Ornament of Liberation, The Words of My Perfect Teacher*, the root text and commentary of *The Profound Inner Meaning, Hevajra Mulatantra Raja* and *Uttaratantra, The Bodhisattvacharyāvatāra*, the root text of *Guhyagarbha*, the protector prayers Dangwa Namsek (*sDang ba rnam sreg*) and Minub Tengye (*Mi nub bstan rgyas*). [He] produced a new statue of the Golden Garland of the Kagyu, one cubit in size, and summoned lamas and monks, including the teachers and disciples belonging to [his] own [tradition]. In this way, [he] began to revive the embers of the teaching.

Thereafter, in the iron ox year [1961], the Karmapa also held the summer retreat [for] the sangha regularly in accord with the teaching in the Vinaya texts. [This is] clearly [predicted] in the Terma prophecy of Orgyen Chokgyur Dechen Lingpa; [it occurred] at the right timing as a result of [the Karmapa's] deep love for the sangha which upholds purely the application of the Vinaya. During that time, the holy Dharma King Tashi Namgyal and Prince Palden Thondup Namgyal reached an agreement [with the Karmapa on] establishing anew the monastic community. [They] donated a free area of land with complete exemption from tax. In the water tiger year [1962], a very big war broke out in the regions of Ladakh and Bomdila. Hence, all kinds [of people] from Kalimpong, Darjeeling and Gangtok were seeking refuge [elsewhere]. [p.367] At that time, however, through [his] clear vision into the future, the Karmapa not only stayed [with his] mind completely at ease but also gave an appropriate command to those who sought divination regarding the change in circumstances, [reassuring them] that there was no danger. [He] spent three weeks [practising] the war-repelling ritual of Dorje Drolö. On the twenty-first day of the ninth month, Nyenpa Rinpoche died. On the tenth day of the tenth month, [the Karmapa's] younger brother Ponlop Rinpoche died. Hence, [the Karmapa] conducted grand offerings and funeral rituals [for them]. On the twenty-second day of the eleventh month, [he] began to build a new monastery [to propagate] the teaching. The monks and laymen, officials and common people, worked hard [on] the construction, regardless of the hardships of rain and heat. During this time, [it was] solely the Karmapa's compassion [that made it] possible [for the construction] to proceed smoothly without [any] faults, such as [damage] caused by landslides or [incidents of people] falling from the top of the scaffolding.

At this time, [the Karmapa's] pet, a peacock, escaped into the mountains. A [bird] that looked like a raven chased [it] and brought [it back] into the peacock nest. [When his] small birds flew into the sky, [the Karmapa] gave a signal [with his] hand, then [they all] returned. During the early years of [his] life, [he had] a dog called Yidruk (g.Yi phrug) [that] would not eat meat on the fifteenth and thirtieth day [of each month]; if [people] forgot the dates, [they] would certainly say, 'Today probably falls on the fifteenth or the thirtieth day of the month; Yidruk is not eating meat', which was miraculous. During [his] lifetime in general, [the Karmapa] liked small birds very much; when they died, [they] were able to abide in Thukdam [for] one, two, or three days. Even though they were animals, [the ones of] lower rebirth, by the power of the aspiration and *bodhicitta* of the great bodhisattva, [they] became [his] disciples, and then entered the completely pure path of liberation and the all-knowing [wisdom]. This was our real experience.

[p.368] Next, in the wood dragon year [1964], although the supreme reincarnation of the All-Seeing Shamar Rinpoche was not allowed to be installed [on] the golden throne in recent years [as] decreed by the [Lhasa] government, [the Dalai Lama] advised that it was necessary to arrange enthronement [for Shamar] and decided to restore [his] status primarily by installing [him] on the golden throne. Then, on the third day of the third month, [Shamar] departed for Dharamsala together with Tobga (sTobs dga') to receive a hair-cutting ceremony in front of the great Dalai Lama according to the traditional customs.

Thereafter, [the Karmapa composed] the divination letter for the refuge and protector, Drukchen ('Brug chen) Rinpoche, as follows:

The thunder of the enlightened activity of the buddhas [in] the three times
The protector whose prestige is beyond the boundaries of the sky
The moon of his manifestation in this life
Is seen in this way, through the signs, such as the place of birth
In a specific part of Kuli of the country, the holy land India
The flow of the lunar realm [is] the unchanging bliss and emptiness
Playing in the navel of the consort [who has] the wisdom of the three empowerments
With the innate fruit, the six elements [that] smile
[He] enters the womb in the perfect pure family

[The Karmapa] also granted the Drubgo (bsGrub sgo) ritual. Furthermore, [he composed] the divination letter for Yongdzin (Yongs 'dzin) Rinpoche [from] Dechenchö (bDe chen chos) monastery as follows:

From Ewaṃ, the dharmatā of the foundation of co-emergence
The moon that rises [in] the unobstructed *nāda maṇḍala*
[p.369]
In a part of the region that stored the two benefits of primordial purity
The voice that will lift the victory banner of the means of appearance
The name by the water-born lotus of the wisdom of emptiness
The miracle of transformation, the play of the son [who is] the supreme reincarnation
Born [in] the year [that is] the beginning of the twelve signs
Thinking without hesitation with the sign of [a] holy person
The light that rises in the solidified self-appearing space
[He] is the true reincarnation of the holy one

[The Karmapa] also [granted] the Drubgo ritual. Moreover, according to the divination letter [that he composed] for Dzigar Choktrul ('Dzi sgar mchog sprul) Rinpoche:

In the special field of the guru [in] the south
In a part of the excellent region known as Pa (sPa)
The supreme means is called Lodrö (Blo gros) and the wisdom is called Tsomo (mTsho mo)
The child of the householder with average wealth was born in the ox year
Rising in the appearance of solidified illusion

[The Karmapa] also bestowed the ritual, including the 100-syllable [mantra that] eliminates obstacles. Furthermore, [he composed] the divination letter [for] the reincarnation of Sangye Nyenpa:

The only glorious [master] of the teaching, Mahāsiddha Virupa
Accomplished the Danma (mDan ma) emanation intentionally for the sake of beings
The dance manifesting the embodiment of supreme enlightened activity
[p.370]
The field of Dharma [in] the southern region [in] the eastern direction from here
The place of the *siddha* the *mahāguru* of Paro
The householder with little wealth [of] a pure family lineage
In the style of the father's name similar to the friend of the sun [i.e., Śākyamuni]
[And] the mother's name with [the word] Chö (chos)
The child [who is] the very true supreme reincarnation [was born] in the dragon year
The manifestation of enlightened activity [is] the glory of the brilliant teaching of the Practice [Lineage]
[He] upholds the lineage [which is] the jewel garland of ultimate transmission
And aspires to ripen and liberate those who are to be tamed in all places

[The Karmapa] also bestowed a ritual. Clearly in accord with the divination letters, all the supreme reincarnations were found for certain. On the thirteenth day of the fourth month, [the Karmapa] installed the supreme reincarnation of the All-Seeing Shamar on the golden throne. Then, most of the construction work of the new monastery [for] the teaching was finished; at the end of the fire snake year [1965], [the construction of] the shrine hall, as well as the living quarters of the sangha in the surrounding area, was completed successfully. [The Karmapa] placed in the shrine the representations of the enlightened body, speech and mind [which contain] brilliant blessings. [These he] brought from Tibet through hardships [that he] treated with contempt. [Now he] made [them into] an unequalled, excellent field of merit for all gods and humans. Then, on the first day of the first month, with the [auspicious] interdependence [of] the New Year, the Karmapa and his primary disciples led the sangha to move into the new monastic seat.

Since then, the members of the sangha strictly followed the Buddhist code of conduct established according to the Vinaya texts. [p.371] [The Karmapa] organised appropriately [for them] monthly sādhana *pūjā*s and *pūjā*s scheduled on specific days:

The first month: the seven-day sādhana, the 'Union of Means and Wisdom';[50]
The second month: the seven-day rituals, the 'Four *Maṇḍala*s of Tara' and Tseringma;
In the third month: the seven-day sādhana *pūjā* of Vajravārāhī;
The fourth month: 'The Eight Sections' on the tenth day according to the old tradition, and Tertön Chokgyur Lingpa's intensive group sādhana practice of Kīlaya, [performed] by turns, [with] elaborate Cham dance. [These] were not merely performances; rather, [they were] practised through the three pure stages [i.e., preparation, main part and conclusion] accordingly;
The fifth month: the seven-day [practice of] Cakrasaṃvara;
The sixth month: the Ganachakra of Pacification and Chöd;
The summer retreat:[51] [the monks] spent [their] time discussing the Dharma, including the teaching and study of treatises, arts and sciences, and the Tantra section; the Karmapa and his primary disciples led the sangha, devoting all [their] time to Dharma talks and speech, based on the education level and proof of training of each member.
In the eighth month: 'the Ocean of Songs of the Kagyu' and regular liturgical texts;
In the ninth month: the red Avalokiteśvara and Karma Lingpa's [Terma cycle of] 'The Hundred Peaceful and Wrathful Deities';
In the tenth month: 'The Great Gate to Enlightenment of Vairocana';
The eleventh month: the seven-day torma propitiation of the four-armed Mahākāla;
The twelfth month: the seven-day torma offering of the two-armed Mahākāla with elaborate Cham dance;
The fifteenth and thirtieth day of each month: confessional assembly of fully ordained monks;
The tenth and twenty-fifth days[52]
Yearly sādhana *pūjā*s [performed] uninterruptedly.

A group of four fully ordained monks [practised] in the great protector's temple. [The Karmapa] founded new protector temples of Dorje Drolö and Tseringma, and continuously made [the protectors] satisfied without interruption, so as to benefit the teaching and the happiness of beings in general, and particularly the teaching and politics [of] Tibet. Regularly, the Karmapa's primary disciples as well as young lamas and tulkus persistently studied the treatises of arts and sciences, the Sūtras and Tantras, [engaging in] explanation, examination [p.372] and debate. All members of the sangha, senior and young, [learned to] write and read, memorise the twelve rituals of the Tantra section, draw lines and [make] coloured sand [for the creation of *maṇḍalas*], make tormas and torma decorations, and play melodies and music. [In this way, the Karmapa] created the dominant condition for the foundation of the essence of the teaching, the Twelve Divisions of the Buddhist Canon and the Three-fold Training, to be established.

Furthermore, [regarding] the representation of the enlightened body, [there were] 1,000 Buddha statues, one cubit and twelve fingers high, filled [according to] the standard. [The Karmapa] consecrated [them so that] the wisdom beings truly dissolved [within], thereby [they became] great objects of offering. [He then] offered golden robes to [the statues]. He and his primary disciples made statues[53] with their own hands; all [those] gathered there saw relics that emerged from each statue. Therefore, [these statues] were endowed with great blessings.

[Regarding] the representation of the enlightened speech, the library [preserved] the Derge red-ink edition of the precious Kangyur, the commentary [collection] of the high-quality Narthang edition of Tengyur, and the teachings of different schools, including *The Treasury of Precious Termas*. [The Karmapa] founded a printing house to restore the teaching by constantly making woodblock prints. Similarly, [there were] thangkas of the Three Roots of the Ocean of the Tantra section, including the Kagyu Golden Garland, yidams and Dharma protectors, [and] all sorts of new and old instruments, including exquisite offerings and Cham dance costumes made from various kinds of fine garments, as well as well-fitted masks of peaceful and wrathful deities, dresses for Cham dance, black hats, and symbolic instruments, together with new and old offering utensils of fine quality made from gold and silver. In brief, [the Karmapa] set anew a worthy example of both the representations [of the enlightened body, speech and mind] and the building [of a monastery], accomplished in [people's] immediate perception.

Chapter 7: Through the lama-patron relationship in India, Nepal, Sikkim, and Bhutan, [the Karmapa] founded new monastic seats that uphold [the tradition of] the teaching and practice

In the fire sheep year [1967], [p.373] on the twelfth day of the fifth month, at the invitation of the people of Ladakh, [the Karmapa] departed from [his] monastic seat Rumtek. [He travelled] past Delhi and Chandigarh, and arrived at Leh, the capital city of Ladakh, on the seventeenth day. [He] met with Prince Bakula (Ba ku la) Rinpoche, Ladakh Togdan (rTogs ldan) Rinpoche among others, and satisfied [the needs of] all the people in Leh through the donning of the precious Black Crown, empowerments and teachings.

Thereafter, on the journey, gradually, [the Karmapa visited] Himitaktsang (Hi mi stag tshang) monastery, Yungdrung (g.Yung drung) monastery and Trektse (Khregs rtse) monastery. [He] made meaningful connections with the local people of Ladakh in general and the Tibetan refugees through the teachings [according to] the wishes of each individual. As [he] gradually [travelled] across the north of Ladakh, Drupön Dechen Tsewang (sGrub dpon bde chen tshe dbang) Rinpoche came to meet [him]. Hence, [the Karmapa] entrusted [him with the task of] building new monastic seats of the Kagyu [school there]. As a result, later [Drubpön Dechen Tsewang] built two monasteries and one nunnery; both the representations [of the enlightened body, speech and mind] and the buildings were complete, whereby [he] certainly had accomplished [his task] for the teaching. Similarly, Lama Chime Dorje ('Chi med rdo rje) also fulfilled [the Karmapa's] command that [he] must build monasteries in Leh of Ladakh, and founded monasteries with complete representations [of the enlightened body, speech and mind] and buildings.

Next, on the twenty-first day, [the Karmapa] travelled from Ladakh, past Chandigarh, [and arrived] in Dharamsala [where he] visited the great Dalai Lama and [his] two tutors. After that, [he] reached Birshi (sBir gzhis) and Mount Kailash. On the first day of the seventh month, [he] bestowed novice vows to two tulkus and thirteen monks in Khamtrul's (Khams sprul) private residence. Then, [he] accomplished some important [tasks] for the teaching in Delhi, [whereby] fulfilling the purpose of the trip. Afterwards, [he travelled] past Calcutta and visited Lama Kalu's retreat centre in Sonada of Darjeeling and Chatral Sangye Dorje's (Bya bral sangs rgyas rdo rje) Longchen Nyinthig retreat centre. [There, he] made the aspirations that bring down blessings, [praying] that the retreat centre would develop further, and the experience and realisation of the practitioners resident there would increase; [p.374] [he] also performed consecration. Then, in Sonada, [he] bestowed novice vows to over ten members of the sangha headed by Kyabgon Drukchen Rinpoche and Traleg Kyabgon (Khra legs skyabs mgon). On the twenty-fourth day, [he] arrived at [his] own monastic seat. Later, at the invitation of the great King of Bhutan and the [Bhutanese] government, [he] journeyed south on the tenth day of the eighth month. [He reached] Tashi Choling in the capital city, and conducted long-life practice in strict retreat for a week in Samdrup (bSam 'grub) cave of Paro Taktsang (sPa gro stag tshang).

Thereafter, [the Karmapa] went on pilgrimage in Kyichu (sKyid chu), and performed consecration in both new and old temples. In view of the decline of the Buddha's teaching, the great King of Bhutan [developed] a strong intention to revive the embers of the teaching, aimed at solely the happiness of beings. Therefore, the King of Bhutan Jigme Dorji and Queen Mother

Phuntsho Choden together offered [the Karmapa] two estates in full, [a piece of land in] Bumthang and Tashi Choling Dzong. [They] also planned to cover the construction cost of the new temple gradually. [The Karmapa then] returned to [his] monastic seat.

At that time, Khamtrul Rinpoche came to visit [the Karmapa] and requested [him] to identify the reincarnation of Dechö Chögön (bDe chos Chos mgon). [The Karmapa] composed the divination letter immediately, as follows:

On the side of the river of Elephant Treasure that flows fast
The name of supreme means is Gönpo (mGon po) and the name of wisdom is Padma
A child [was born in] the sheep year

During the year-end torma offering,[54] [the Karmapa] bestowed empowerments and teachings on the two Queen Mothers, Phuntsho Choden and Pema Dechen, who specially came from Bhutan, [whereby] fulfilling [their] wishes. On the first day of the second month of the earth monkey year [1968], [p.375] [he] installed the seventh reincarnation of [his] nephew, Ponlop Rinpoche, on the golden throne. [He] identified this reincarnation [even] before the mother Lekshe Drolma (Legs bshad sgrol ma) was pregnant. [He] said, in a way that [his] treasurer Damchö Yongdu (Dam chos yongs 'du) and the tea servers could understand, that the reincarnation of Ponlop Rinpoche would be in Lekshe's body. [The reincarnation] was born as [the Karmapa prophesied]. Still, to cut through doubts, [the parents] requested the great Dalai Lama to also conduct divination; [the Dalai Lama's reply] came, [confirming that the child] was the genuine [reincarnation]. Moreover, when Yapa Sönam Gyatso (Ya pa bsod nams rgya mtsho) and [his] wife Semo Zimlak (Sras mo 'zim lags) came to meet [him, the Karmapa told that [Semo Zimlak] was pregnant with the reincarnation of Zurmang Gharwang. Previously, while in Tibet, [the Karmapa] also [wrote] the divination letter for the reincarnation of Traleg Nyima Gyurme from Ga Thrangu (sGa Khra 'gu) monastery. The letter was dated on the nineteenth day of the fifth month of the wood horse year [1954] [when the Karmapa] gave [it to the monastery]. [He] said that [it should be kept in] secrecy until the tenth day of the first month of the new year; once the letter had been opened after that [day], [they] must search [for the reincarnation]. Accordingly, [they] opened [the letter] and read [it] at the right time. The divination [letter] reads as follows: the reincarnation of Traleg Nyima Gyurme [is in] the western direction from the monastery, within [the journey of] three stations [travelled by] a good horse; the householder [has] low to average wealth; the name of the father is Lodrö (Blo gros) and the name of the mother is Padma; their child was born in the sheep year. [The letter] also [tells] the ritual [to be done for the reincarnation]. As [they] searched [for the reincarnation] according to [the Karmapa's letter, the reincarnation] was found for definite, without any doubt, like placing the jewel into [one's] own hand: [the child] was born on the eighth day of the first month of the wood sheep year [1955];[55] [his] parents, age and year sign, and signs at the time of birth [were all in accord with the letter]. It shows that [there is] no choice but to recognise [the Karmapa as] a real buddha with the higher perception [of reality] without obstruction.

Furthermore, there are many accounts of [the Karmapa] maintaining the activity of identifying [the reincarnations of] great masters of different schools. However, since the original documents of the divination letters were left behind in Tibet, [I] am not able to write down the details here, for which I ask for [your] forgiveness. From the twenty-second day of the sixth month, [p.376] [the Karmapa] granted the transmission of the Indian texts on Mahāmudrā to the high tulkus and the sangha in general. Once again, at the invitation of the King of Bhutan and [his] ministers, [the Karmapa] journeyed south. [He] specially visited Thimphu and Paro. At the border temple Kyichu Lhakhang, [he] stayed in retreat practising White Tara. [He] arranged timber and other [materials] for the construction of [his] new monastic seat, Tashi Choling. [He also] made perfect offerings, including tea and alms, to the sangha in Paro and Thimphu. [He] reached [his] own monastic seat afterwards. Then, [he] made brief visits to Calcutta and Delhi, and brought genuine devotees to spiritual maturity through teachings and empowerments. Beginning from the nineteenth day of the fourth month of the earth rooster year [1969], as the building of Tashi Choling of Bumthang was about to start, [the Karmapa], for the purpose of initiating the first summer retreat, specially assigned [the task of] commencing the construction of the monastery to thirty lamas and monks, including Riwar Bakyö (Ri bar bag yod) Rinpoche, [together with the Karmapa's] treasurer Damchö Yongdu as the leader. [He] appointed a [retreat] master,[56] and instructed [others to make] profound and vast aspirations that the teaching would spread and flourish in future. Three months later, the Karmapa and his primary disciples also paid a brief visit to Thimphu to meet the Dharma King, and then travelled to the construction site of the monastery in Bumthang. At the invitation of [his] nephew Tobga and Princess Ashi Chokyi (A zhe chos skyid), [the Karmapa] visited Wangdu Choling. [He] identified the supreme reincarnation of Namkhai Nyingpo (Nam mkha'i snying po) of Lhodrak and made grand offerings in Kurjey Lhakhang. Then, [he] returned to Tashi Choling. To tame the land for the construction of the new shrine, [he] performed the seven-day ritual of Cakrasaṃvara with sand *maṇḍala*. [He] then [performed] the ritual of the 'Prosperity of Mahākālī', after which [he] returned to Rumtek. [He] visited Nepal at the invitation of the Kagyu monasteries there. [He paid homage to]

Swayambhunath Stūpa and [p.377] consecrated the temple newly founded by Dazang Choktrul (Zla bzang mchog sprul) Rinpoche. Moreover, the Swayambhunath Stūpa was offered to him; with the motivation [that the teaching would] spread and flourish in future, [he] commanded that Saju Rinpoche must stay there and oversee [the *stūpa*]. [He] also assigned [Saju] the mission of building Kirti (Kir rti) monastery. At the invitation of Lama Drubseng (sGrub seng) and the Tibetan community from Pokhara, [he] visited [there] briefly, fulfilling [people's] wishes through empowerments and the donning of the Black Crown. [He] advised Lama Drubseng on the administration and development of the monastery. [He] returned to [his] own monastic seat Rumtek via Nepal. [As] Dilgo Khyentse Rinpoche appealed in person, [the Karmapa] identified the reincarnation of Shechen Rabjam and installed [him] on the Dharma throne on the thirteenth day of the first month of the iron dog year [1970].

During this time, [the Karmapa had made] the majority of the villages in Sikkim abolish the custom of animal sacrifice and take the oath that [they] would never do it again from then on. He composed a dedication prayer of red smoke offering to the local gods and non-humans and gave [his] blessing to replace [animal sacrifice]. Thereby, animal sacrifice was no longer needed. On the fifteenth day of the fourth month of the iron pig year [1971], [the Karmapa] granted full ordination vows to the All-Seeing Shamar Rinpoche. On the nineteenth day of the fifth month of the iron pig year [1971], [he] kindly bestowed the complete empowerments and transmissions of *The Treasury of Extensive Teachings* and *Knowing One Liberates All* compiled by the Ninth Karmapa on all the lamas and monks headed by high tulkus as well as many lamas and monks in exile [who were] present, including Ayang (Aḥ yang) tulku. On this occasion, [he] entrusted Ayang Rinpoche with the task to build Kagyu monasteries in the Tibetan settlement in Mysore. [He] kindly granted empowerments and teachings to 100 devotees from Canada. [p.378] [He] bestowed on a fully ordained monk called Ananda Bodhi the vows of individual liberation in the Mahāyāna tradition. By the power of [his] aspirations in the past, [Ananda Bodhi] brought immense benefit to the teaching. [The Karmapa] enthroned [the reincarnation of] Drungram Gyaltrul (Drung ram rgyal sprul) Rinpoche [whom he had] previously identified in Nepal. A leader of a Dharma centre in the Philippines came to meet [the Karmapa] in person; [he] had previously been a disciple of the great master Bo Gangkar Rinpoche. [The Karmapa] kindly granted [him] many empowerments and transmissions at [his] request, including Cakrasaṃvara, Hevajra and Mahamaya. As the Karmapa reached the age of forty-nine [which is considered] an obstacle year, twenty lamas and monks of the lineage of the Yongey Tulku,[57] Tertön Mingyur Dorje, [performed] the torma propitiation of Dorje Drolö [for him, during which time good] signs appeared. Ten lamas and monks headed by

Bakyö Rinpoche carried out [the practice of] the Trochu Dugdong (Khro bcu dug gdong) propitiation of Yamāntaka. Moreover, all the other monasteries also completed the outer and inner rituals [for the Karmapa]. [The Karmapa] specially sent the All-Seeing Shamar Rinpoche and [his] treasurer as [his] representatives to [attend] the official celebration of the Prince of Bhutan Singye Wangchuck's new appointment as Governor; the trip came to be successful. Then, during wintertime, to remain in good health, [he] visited most of the holy places in India, performing offerings of Tantric feasts and [making] grand offerings in each place.

Thereafter, [the Karmapa] spoke about the restoration and founding of the temples of the Himalayan Buddhist Society in Calcutta. [Then, he] returned to [his] monastic seat Rumtek. On the fifteenth day of the first month of the water ox year [1973], [he] bestowed full ordination vows on Maitreya Situ Rinpoche, Jamgon Rinpoche, and Gyaltsab Rinpoche. After that, [he] continued with the work of constructing Tashi Choling. At the invitation of the Fourth King of Bhutan, Jigme Singye Wangchuck, [the Karmapa] visited Thimphu. [p.379] [He] consecrated the *stūpa* built for the funeral ritual of the late King of Bhutan. [He] travelled to Tashi Choling; seventy members of the sangha promised [to enter] summer [retreat]. Furthermore, the King of Bhutan also provided help and support as much as he could for the construction of the monastery. [The Karmapa] identified and enthroned the [reincarnation of] Zurtrul (Zur sprul) from Thrangu monastery. [He] specially sent twelve lamas and monks headed by Traleg Kyabgon for the administration of the temple Kanglung Sherubtse (Kang lung shes rab rtse) offered by the Queen Mother Phuntsho Choden; [he] also advised [them] to do whatever was the best for the purpose of the teaching.

Next, on the way back, [the Karmapa] happened to be invited [by Kalu Rinpoche] specially to consecrate a *stūpa* newly built by him, as well as [his] retreat centre and temple. Pleased with Kalu Rinpoche's great *bodhicitta* and perfect accomplishment, [the Karmapa] bestowed teachings and blessings on Rinpoche's foreign disciples who were present there, [and] offered a longevity ritual for [his] long life specially [for] the purpose of the teaching. Then, [he] travelled to [his] own monastic seat. Trongpa Khyentse ('Brong pa mkhyen brtse) Rinpoche visited [him] to request empowerments and essential instructions. As most of the empowerments and transmissions were completed, [the Karmapa] also advised [Trongpa Khyentse] not to be discouraged [from generating] the very profound *bodhicitta* [for] the purpose of the teaching. [The Karmapa] sent [him back] to [his] own monastic seat in order [for him] to develop [his] local monastery. [He] created all the favourable conditions for the production of new statues of Mahākāla, Mahākālī and Vajrasadhu in the protector's temple of the newly constructed Rumtek monastery. Later, [he also] kindly filled and consecrated [them]. [He] oversaw the administration of the Karma Kagyu monastery in Pokra (sPog ra) and provided necessities, hats and costumes of Cham dance, all by himself, thereby giving whatever [support] suitable [for the development of the monastery]. Then, in the wood tiger year [1974], with the intention to build a new monastic college in Tashi Choling, [he] drew up a register of procedure for organising the schedules of grades and classes, [p.380] and particularly for printing pecha [i.e., textbooks]. On the fifteenth day of the first month, the Karmapa and his primary disciples bestowed monastic vows on [the reincarnation of his] nephew Ponlop Rinpoche, Nyenpa Rinpoche and Drupön Rinpoche.

Thereafter, from the fifteenth day of the fourth month [onwards, the Karmapa] paid a brief visit [to Bhutan to attend] the enthronement of the Fourth King of Bhutan. [He] opened new gateways to [auspicious] interdependence for the official celebration of the [Bhutanese] government. Then, he and his disciples also applied for passports in order to travel abroad. [He] visited Tashi Choling again, hence completing its [opening] ceremony, after which [he] travelled to [his] monastic seat Rumtek.

Chapter 8: [The Karmapa] maintained [his] enlightened activity by travelling to Western countries to spread the precious teaching of the Buddha

The time [predicted in] the Terma prophecy of the great Tertön Chokgyur Lingpa had come: on the twenty-fifth day of the seventh month, [the Karmapa] began [his] journey to Europe and the United States in the West. [He travelled] past London and arrived in New York of the United States [where the local] Dharma centres [organised] a welcoming reception [for him]. In the assembly hall of the Dharma centre Dharmadhatu newly founded by [Chögyam] Trungpa Rinpoche, [he] performed the donning of the precious Black Crown, the empowerment of Tara and the transmission of the 'Homage to the Twenty-One Taras'. In addition, [he] kindly granted the empowerment of the guru sādhana of Mahāsiddha Karma Pakshi to 100-plus [practitioners who] had completed the 400,000 preliminary practices. A person known as Mr Shen[58] took the responsibility of printing pecha [textbooks] for the new monastic college to be founded [by the Karmapa]. [The Karmapa] visited the Dharma centre in Colorado at [its] invitation. [There,] over 500 people had an audience with him. Later, [he] granted the empowerment of the guru sādhana of [Karma] Pakshi to fifty worthy students, both men and women. [He] visited the meditation centre named 'Tail of the Tiger'. [p.381] [There, he] uttered the 'Aspiration Prayer for the Spread of the Teaching' and the 'Aspiration Prayer of Mahāmudrā', with profound and vast aspirations that the teaching would spread and flourish; obstacles and mistakes would not arise [in] the meditators; [thereby] perfect *samādhi* would have arisen in [their] mind, and [they] would have obtained for definite the final fruition, the state of the unification of the two *kāya*s. [He] gifted [the centre] with a Buddha statue and a thangka of the two-armed Mahākāla as the main representation [of the enlightened body of the Buddha] of that [centre]. [He] recited the offering and invocation prayers of the Dharma protectors. [He then] visited the Dharma centre in Boulder named Karma Dzong and granted the transmission of 'The Prayer of Mahāmudrā'. Later, [he] bestowed the initiation of the Dharma protector, the two-armed Mahākāla, to 200 disciples headed by Trungpa Rinpoche. [He] granted full ordination vows to a Western[59] novice monk [and] performed the donning of the precious Black Crown to 800 devotees [who were] members of the centre.

Furthermore, [the Karmapa] bestowed the empowerment of the guru sādhana of [Karma] Pakshi on 200 disciples of Trungpa who practised *śamatha* meditation, [and] consecrated the houses of the meditation centres. Then, [he] also granted audiences and formed connections [with people] through the teaching in the Dharma centre called Dorje Khyung Dzong. After that, [he] visited three Indian reservations in the United States. There, a bad harvest was [expected] to occur soon due to the lack of rainfall. Hence, [the local people] asked the Karmapa for help. Starting that evening, very heavy rain fell. Thus, unusual faith in the Dharma was growing inevitably [among] the local people. Then, [the Karmapa] specially visited the Dharma centres of the Kagyu, Sakya and Nyingma [schools] in California, thereby fulfilling [people's] wishes [by forming] connections through the teaching, [including] empowerments and transmissions. [He] arrived at the city Vancouver in Canada afterwards. [He] visited Kalu Rinpoche's Dharma centre, granted empowerments and transmissions, and formed connections [with people] through the teaching. [After that, he] reached Toronto. Later, [as] Mr Shen requested [him] to build a new monastery, [the Karmapa] discussed [this with him]. [p.382] [He] performed the donning of the precious Black Crown in Namgyal Rinpoche's Dharma centre as well as a Dharma centre of the Nyingma [school]. [He] conducted the insertion of dhāraṇī and cleansing ritual for Namgyal Rinpoche's newly built *stūpa*. Furthermore, with profound and vast aspirations for meditation centres, [he] visited Karma Thinley's Dharma centre Kampo Gangra and granted the empowerment of Green Tara. Then, [travelling] by plane, [he] arrived at Samye Ling in Scotland to the north of England. In the assembly hall, [he] performed the donning of the precious Black Crown and the initiation of the guru sādhana of Milarepa. After that, [he] satisfied [the needs of] the devotees there headed by the master Akong Rinpoche through empowerments and teachings. Later, [he] visited London. In Tulku Chime's Dharma centre, [he] granted a Buddha statue and pecha [texts]. Similarly, [he] visited the Buddhist Dharma centres of Thailand and Sri Lanka. [Later, travelling] by plane, [he] toured Norway, Sweden, Denmark, Netherlands and Belgium, performing in each place the donning of the precious Black Crown and the empowerments necessary to tame beings, including Milarepa, Avalokiteśvara and Mañjuśrī, in front of faithful disciples. [He] formed connections [with people] through the teaching, bringing [those who had not entered the path of the Dharma] into the Dharma and [helping] those who had begun [to travel on] the path to liberation develop experience and realisation in [their] minds. [In this way, he] created immeasurable benefit [for] the beings by whatever means suitable [to them]. In France, [he] visited the Dharma centre of the Kagyu [school], Ösel Ling, and the Dharma Centre of Yiga Chödzin, forming profound connections [with people] for the purpose of the teaching [in accord with their] own wishes. [He then] travelled to Italy. In the capital city Rome, [he] founded a new Dharma centre named Tashi Chökyi Ling. [He] had an audience with the Pope. [Then, he] returned to France. Mr Benson took the responsibility of offering land for the purpose of building a new monastery for the teaching. Later, [p.383] while [having] a health check in Switzerland, [the Karmapa] bestowed the empowerments and teachings necessary to tame beings on the Tibetans [who lived] there and the Europeans who had faith [in] the Dharma. [He] appointed both his nephew Gendun Gyatso (dGe 'dun rgya mtsho) and Sharse Tenzin Chönyi (Shar sras bsTan 'dzin chos nyi) to commence the grand undertakings of constructing new monasteries for the teaching in France and New York [respectively]. Hence, [he] sent [them] away specially [for that purpose]. [He] returned to Delhi by plane. After meeting with those who had a connection [with him, he] arrived safely at [his] own monastic seat together with his retinue, without any obstacle.

In the earth hare year [1975], according to the appeal [made] by Drupön Dechen Rinpoche, [and] in connection with [his own] advice [to] Situ Rinpoche and his disciples for the purpose of the teaching, [the Karmapa] commanded that [Situ] must visit Ladakh. Hence, [Situ Rinpoche] left [accordingly]. [The Karmapa] advised Drupön Dechen Rinpoche and Lama Chime Dorje that [they] must make the teaching spread and flourish in the Ladakh area. As a compliment on [their] best achievements in the past, [he] gifted [them] with the main representations [of the enlightened body, speech and mind] with splendid blessings as well as excellent offering utensils; [he then] sent [them] to [their] respective monasteries in Ladakh.

Thereafter, [the Karmapa helped] the six fully ordained monks who were to travel to the United States and France [obtain] passports and gave [them] representations of the enlightened body, speech and mind as well as offering utensils, thereupon sending [them] away specially [for the purpose of building monasteries].[60] Then, as [he] was invited to the conference in Darjeeling on the development of the Asian Dharma centres and the Himalayan Buddhist [Society, he] travelled [there] specially [for that purpose]. [During the conference, he] made generous suggestions that it was absolutely necessary to take practical measures to [safeguard] the Dharma. [He] met with the great Dalai Lama, [and] had relaxed and detailed conversations [with him]; [they] were pleased [with one another, in a way] none other than close friends. [He] returned to [his] monastic seat [afterwards]. [p.384] As Mr Shen promised [to be his] patron, [the Karmapa] printed textbooks of the Kagyu [teachings and] treatises of the Sūtra and Tantra in Delhi. Meanwhile, the Karmapa specially sent workers and [money to cover] the expense for the printing of the precious Kangyur of the Buddha, based on the Derge red-ink edition [produced under] the instruction of Situ Chökyi Jungne. [He did so] by means of specially dedicated virtuous deeds, [using] the offerings [made to him for] dedication requests for the living and the deceased [that he] personally reserved, as well as the courageous bodhisattva vow to cause the precious teaching of the Buddha [which was like] a sinking sun to rise and shine again. [In this way, he] lived [his] life maintaining the enlightened activity with profound and vast aspirations of *bodhicitta* that the source of benefit and happiness of all beings, the precious teaching of the Buddha, [would] not decline, [but rather,] spread, flourish and remain forever.

To sum up:

In the presence of the protector who has become [an] worthy [object] of homage
With skilful speech from limitless emanations
Shouldering the weighty task, discussing the multitude of [his] qualities
Worn out, [my] five limbs are resting on the ground

For this, clearly from the beginning, with the commitment to composing [this text]
In the middle, [through] unwavering diligence with sincerity
In the end, [having] joyful smile for perfecting [the text] successfully
By the pure virtue [that I have accomplished as] the source [of] liberation [for] many

May all conflicts: shaken by blood, eyes turned, eyebrows overly twisted
Sound of hardships, unbearable sharp weapons being fired
[p.385] Killings with violent roars [filling] the sky, the earth and in-between
[All these] that cause disaster, become pacified!

Likewise, may all beings devote [themselves] to the right view
Thoroughly delighted to partake of contentment with splendid freedom
Having embraced the qualities of friendship and loving-kindness
May [they] rest in the joyful laughter [of] the Gesar family!

May the tree of life in all the lives of all [beings]
Having the complete branches of leisure and wealth perfected
Be beautified by the fully ripened fruits of qualities
Among abundant leaves of listening, contemplation and meditation!

As [I was] leaving [for] India from the monastic seat,[61] with signs of auspicious interdependence, Sharse Tenzin Chönyi who worked for [the Karmapa] closely encouraged [me] by writing to [me] three times from New York in the United States. For this reason, even though from [my] own point of view, [my] qualities are as thin as a lotus root, [the Karmapa's] deeds of skilful means have guided [me, his] disciple held by the iron hook of his compassion. In the fire male mouse year [1936], at the age of thirteen, [he] identified [me] by [knowing my parents'] names [through divination]: father Kunga (Kun dga') or Tsephel (Tshe 'phel), mother Kalzang (sKal bzang) or Drönma (sGron ma), after which [he] comforted [me, treating me] as a tulku. [I,] one who is called Thrangu by all those close [to me], remembering the qualities of the Three Secrets[62] of the Karmapa, wrote [them down] afresh. At that time, Tenzin Namgyal (bsTan 'dzin rnam rgyal) [who used to] write letters for the Karmapa made efforts to record [my] words in writing, for which I am grateful. By the power of the merit of composing [this text] in this way, may the precious teaching of the Buddha remain [in this world] for long. May all be auspicious!

[p.386] Furthermore, Zhangu Atro (Zhang 'gu a gro) Rinpoche, [one] who holds the treasury of the teachings of scriptures and realisation, encouraged [me] by saying: 'Since the supreme Buddha, the Great Sixteenth [Karmapa], was endowed with incredible deeds of the enlightened body, speech and mind, as well as activity, [you] must write a *namthar* with three sections—the outer, inner and secret.' Although [he] had the wish to ask [me to] compose [such an account], recently [I] have been busy, pretending to [strive for] the purpose of the teaching, and dominated by laziness. Hence, [this task] has not been accomplished. Because of that, in order for the life stories of successive Karmapas in the past to be complete, [I] have written [down an account about] the time when myself served [the Karmapa] closely when he was alive. If the greater qualities of the extraordinary form [of the Karmapa] were read out loud, apart from [what is] widely known [about him] in the perception of ordinary [people, he] would not be very pleased. Thus, even though [I did] nothing other than writing down briefly [his perceivable] deeds [in] stages, this time [I] had this very [edition] printed. This *namthar* of successive Karmapas in the past has been printed in Thrangu Tashi Chöling (Khra 'gu bkra shis chos gling) and distributed without charge. Due to the request from those who need the pecha [edition, I] also have the pecha [version] bound together. Such matters have been taken care of as well as possible. [For] the less important [matters] and the sale through the idea of merchandising, [I] shall call for helpers. Yours respectfully. Thrangu Tulku.

NOTES

1. Among the *namthar* texts of the Sixteenth Karmapa, this account is the most authoritative and widely recognised within the Karma Kagyu school. It contains the most elaborate detail and key features of the literature, hence in many ways, serves as the representation of the Sixteenth Karmapa's *namthar*, in both content and style.

The text has three main editions: (1) the *dpe cha* edition: Karma blo gros chos dpal bzang po, "rgyal ba'i dbang po dpal karma pa rang byung rig pa'i rdo rje mchog brgya phyed la zung gi 'phel ba'i 'grang bya byon pa yan gyi rnam thar/_(16)," in *karma pa sku 'phreng bcu drug pa tshun rim par byon pa'i rnam thar phyogs bsgrigs*, TBRC W1KG3815 (New Delhi: konchhog lhadrepa, 1994), 595–762 (Karma blo gros chos dpal bzang po is another name of Khra 'gu rin po che); (2) the book edition: Khra 'gu rin po che, *rgyal ba'i dbang po*, 321–389; (3) the compiled edition: Khra 'gu rin po che, "rgyal ba'i dbang po dpal karma pa rang byung rig pa'i rdo rje mchog brgya phrag phyed la zung gis 'phel ba'i bgrang byar byon pa yan gyi rnam thar bzhugs so," in *rgyal dbang karma pa bcu drug pa chen po'i gsung 'bum 1*, ed. Jo sras bkra shis tshe ring (Dharamsala: Tshurphu Labrang; The Amnye Machen Institute, 2016), 69–132. The Chinese translation, published in 2016 in 上師之師:歷代大寶法王噶瑪巴的轉世傳奇, received official recognition from the Karma Kagyu school: the Seventeenth Karmapa, Ogyen Trinley Dorje, contributed a foreword (See 鄔金欽列多傑, "序言," 3); Khenpo Karthar Rinpoche wrote the Introduction (See 堪布卡塔仁波切, "前言," 8–14). To the best of my knowledge, no English translation of this text has ever been published. My English translation here is based on the book edition (Khra 'gu rin po che, *rgyal ba'i dbang po*, 321–389).

2. Tibetan: Khro bo gnam lcags 'bar ba. In Sanskrit: *Krodharājagujvarājavajramaṇḍala vidhī-nāma*.

The Chinese translation:《耀燃忿怒天鐵尊》密續 (See 勉東倉巴仁波切:八蚌欽哲仁波切:堪千創古仁波切, 上師之師, 350).

Here, I use Martin's English translation: *The Tantra of the Blazing, Wrathful Meteorite* (See Martin, "*Music in the Sky*," 271).

3. That is, Padmasambhava.

4. That is, the Fifteenth Karmapa. See 勉東倉巴仁波切，八蚌欽哲仁波切, 堪千創古仁波切, 上師之師, 258, 351.

5. That is, the Seventeenth Karmapa. See 勉東倉巴仁波切，八蚌欽哲仁波切, 堪千創古仁波切, 上師之師, 258, 351.

6. That is, the Eighteenth Karmapa. See 勉東倉巴仁波切，八蚌欽哲仁波切, 堪千創古仁波切, 上師之師, 258, 351.

7. Tibetan: Ri bo ta la, that is, Mount Potalaka, the mystical residence of Avalokiteśvara.

8. According to Tenzin Namgyal and Nydahl, 'ox' refers to the month and 'mouse' refers to the year. See Zhanag Dzogpa Tenzin Namgyal, "The Wondrous Activities of His Holiness the 16th Gyalwang Karmapa," in *The Miraculous 16th Karmapa: Incredible encounters with the Black Crown Buddha*, comp. Norma Levine (Arcidosso: Shang Shung Publications, 2013), 40; Ole Nydahl, *Entering the Diamond Way: My Path Among the Lamas* (Nevada City, CA: Blue Dolphin Pub, 1985), 72.

9. *Lugs* in this text may be a typographical error or variant spelling of *lug*.

10. That is, Karma Kagyu.

11. The First Karmapa, Düsum Khyenpa, founded three main monastic seats, Tsurphu Monastery, Karma Monastery and Kampo Nenang, which are also called the upper, middle and lower seats of the Karma Kagyu. Among them, Karma Monastery is the middle seat. See 噶玛钨金, "杜松虔巴," 16.

12. *Geg* in this text may be a typographical error or variant spelling of *gegs*.

13. *Rtog* in this text may be a typographical error or variant spelling of *rtogs*.

14. *Sa chigs* may be a typographical error or variant spelling of *sa tshigs*.

15. *Yon dge* may be a typographical error or variant spelling of *Yongs dge* as in the name Yongey Mingyur Dorje (1628/1641–1708), the Tertön who discovered this practice.

16. *Smig* may be a typographical error or variant spelling of *rmig*.

17. *Kheng* may be a typographical error or variant spelling of *bskang*.

18. The Chinese translation adds: 這裡有蓮花生大士以神通開啟的泉水 (Here, Padmasambhava created a spring through his miraculous power). See 勉東倉巴仁波切, 八蚌欽哲仁波切, 堪千創古仁波切, 上師之師, 367.

19. The Chinese translation specifies this as 阿底峽上師相應法 (The sādhana of Atiśa guru yoga). See 勉東倉巴仁波切, 八蚌欽哲仁波切, 堪千創古仁波切, 上師之師, 367.

20. The Chinese translation adds: 這是龍千巴曾經閉關修行的地方 (This is the place where Longchenpa once practised in retreat). See 勉東倉巴仁波切, 八蚌欽哲仁波切, 堪千創古仁波切, 上師之師, 367.

21. According to the Chinese translation, *lo chen* refers to 龍千喇嘛 (Lama Longchenpa). See 勉東倉巴仁波切, 八蚌欽哲仁波切, 堪千創古仁波切, 上師之師, 367.

22. The Chinese translation adds: 這是蓮師降服許多鬼神的地方 (This is the place where Padmasambhava subjugated many gods and spirits). See 勉東倉巴仁波切, 八蚌欽哲仁波切, 堪千創古仁波切, 上師之師, 367.

23. The Chinese translation adds: 施身法祖師瑪姬拉尊的主座 (The main seat of the founder of the Chöd practice, Machig Labdrön). See 勉東倉巴仁波切, 八蚌欽哲仁波切, 堪千創古仁波切, 上師之師, 367.

24. The Chinese translation adds: 這些各是蓮師、蓮師弟子和馬爾巴的聖地 (These are the holy places of Padmasambhava, his disciples and Marpa, respectively). See 勉東倉巴仁波切, 八蚌欽哲仁波切, 堪千創古仁波切, 上師之師, 368.

25. The Chinese translation adds: 洛查卡曲過去曾是南開寧波的修行地 (In the past, Lhodrak Kharchu was once the place where Namkhai Nyingpo practised). See 勉東倉巴仁波切, 八蚌欽哲仁波切, 堪千創古仁波切, 上師之師, 368.

Appendix B

26. The Chinese translation adds: 鐵普巴天女的佛殿 (The shrine hall of Iron Kīlaya Goddess). See 勉東倉巴仁波切，八蚌欽哲仁波切，堪千創古仁波切，上師之師, 368.

27. The Chinese translation adds: 密勒日巴曾經修行的 (Where Milarepa once practised). See 勉東倉巴仁波切，八蚌欽哲仁波切，堪千創古仁波切，上師之師, 368.

28. The Chinese translation adds: 過去格薩王曾經打敗敵人並將他的劍收起來，後來這把劍成為噶瑪巴所有，是嘎千大營的聖物 (In the past, King Gesar of Ling once conquered his enemies with this sword, and then put it away. Later, the sword came into the possession of the Karmapa and became a sacred object of the Great Encampment). See 勉東倉巴仁波切，八蚌欽哲仁波切，堪千創古仁波切，上師之師, 370.

29. The Chinese translation adds: 堪布卡塔仁波切說，因為這是一把極為貴重的劍，所以它被偷走後使護法不悅，而引起大火 (According to Khenpo Karthar Rinpoche, since it was an extremely precious sword, once stolen, the Dharma protectors were displeased, which led to a big fire). See 勉東倉巴仁波切，八蚌欽哲仁波切，堪千創古仁波切, 上師之師, 370.

30. *Mtshams* may be a typographical error or variant spelling of *'tshams* as in *gang la ci 'tshams*.

31. *Gangs ri* may refer to *gangs ri chen po ti si* on page 346 line 11.

32. According to the Chinese translation, *sgrol ma* refers to 度母隘口 (Tara Mountain Pass). See 勉東倉巴仁波切，八蚌欽哲仁波切，堪千創古仁波切，上師之師, 371.

33. The Chinese translation adds: 這是他和其他家人休閒的地方 (This is the place where he and other members of his family spent their leisure time). See 勉東倉巴仁波切，八蚌欽哲仁波切，堪千創古仁波切，上師之師, 372.

34. According to the Chinese translation, this means the Karmapa enthroned the reincarnation of Palpung Khyentrul (之後法王為八蚌欽哲仁波切的轉世舉行坐床大典). See 勉東倉巴仁波切，八蚌欽哲仁波切，堪千創古仁波切，上師之師, 372.

35. *Dmang* may be a typographical error or variant spelling of *dmangs* as in *'go dmangs* which appears in the last sentence.

36. The Chinese translation adds: 西藏十二女地神之一 (One of the twelve local goddesses of Tibet). See 勉東倉巴仁波切，八蚌欽哲仁波切，堪千創古仁波切，上師之師, 373.

37. *Brugs pa* may be a typographical error or variant spelling of *brug pa*.

38. The meaning of *dpa' bstod* and *tsho pa'i spyi rim* is not clear. In the Chinese translation: 說法 (To give teachings). See 勉東倉巴仁波切:八蚌欽哲仁波切:堪千創古仁波切, 上師之師, 374.

39. The Chinese translation adds: 八蚌寺蔣貢康楚仁波切的總秘書 (Jamgon Kongtrul Rinpoche's general secretary in Palpung). See 勉東倉巴仁波切，八蚌欽哲仁波切，堪千創古仁波切，上師之師, 376.

40. The Chinese translation explains the meaning of *bkra shis rtags*: 吉祥誌：即八吉祥，所以指一家八口 ('Auspicious mark' refers to the eight auspicious symbols, which means there were eight members in the family). See 勉東倉巴仁波切，八蚌欽哲仁波切，堪千創古仁波切，上師之師, 376.

41. The Chinese translation explains the meaning of *shes rab*: 【智慧】指他的母親，【蓮花】指母親的名字中有【蓮花】一字 ('Wisdom' refers to the child's mother, and 'padma' means that the mother's name contains the word 'padma'). See 勉東倉巴仁波切，八蚌欽哲仁波切，堪千創古仁波切，上師之師, 376.

42. The Chinese translation adds: 德格的薩迦派大寺院貢千寺 (The great monastery of the Sakya school in Derge, Gönchen monastery). See 勉東倉巴仁波切，八蚌欽哲仁波切，堪千創古仁波切，上師之師, 378.

43. The Chinese translation adds: 蔣貢康楚仁波切的紮札仁千查閉關中心 (Jamgon Kongtrul Rinpoche's retreat centre, named Tsadra Rinchen Drak). See 勉東倉巴仁波切，八蚌欽哲仁波切，堪千創古仁波切，上師之師, 379.

44. The Chinese translation adds: 作為迎接達賴尊者來訪之用 (For hospitality for the Dalai Lama's visit). See 勉東倉巴仁波切，八蚌欽哲仁波切，堪千創古仁波切，上師之師, 380.

45. The Chinese translation adds: 請求噶瑪巴代表政府到昌都，以祈平撫動盪不安的時局 (To request the Karmapa to go to Chamdo on behalf of the government in the hope to ease the disturbance there). See 勉東倉巴仁波切，八蚌欽哲仁波切，堪千創古仁波切，上師之師, 380.

46. The Chinese translation adds: 一位格魯派的夏巴確傑仁波切 (Sharpa Chöje Rinpoche from the Gelug school). See 勉東倉巴仁波切，八蚌欽哲仁波切，堪千創古仁波切，上師之師, 383.

47. The three main monastic seats that Düsum Khyenpa founded represent the three *cakra*s (Sanskrit, meaning 'wheel') of body, speech and mind. Among them, Tsurphu Monastery is referred to as 'the chakra of mind', hence my translation here 'the wheel of the heart'. See Kagyu Office, "Karmapa Reincarnations."

48. *Lag don* may be a typographical error or variant spelling of *lag 'don*.

49. That is, the four primary disciples of the Karmapa: Shamar, Situ, Jamgon Kongtrul and Gyaltsab.

50. *Tshes* may be a typographical error or variant spelling of *tshe* as in *tshe sgrub thabs shes kha sbyor* by Yongs dge mi 'gyur rdo rje.
    According to the Chinese translation, this is Yongey Mingyur Dorje's Terma sādhana for long life (詠給明就多傑的長壽伏藏法). See 勉東倉巴仁波切:八蚌欽哲仁波切:堪千創古仁波切，上師之師, 391.

51. The Chinese translation adds: 7月(The seventh month). See 勉東倉巴仁波切，八蚌欽哲仁波切，堪千創古仁波切，上師之師, 392.

52. The Chinese translation adds: 薈供 (Offering of Tantric feasts). See 勉東倉巴仁波切，八蚌欽哲仁波切，堪千創古仁波切，上師之師, 392.

53. The Chinese translation adds: 這千尊佛像是不丹塑像師，以陶土做成的，剩餘的土由法王和每一位法王子各塑一尊佛像 (These 1,000 Buddha statues were made from clay by a Bhutanese sculptor. The Karmapa and his primary disciples each used the remaining clay to make one statue). See 勉東倉巴仁波切，八蚌欽哲仁波切，堪千創古仁波切，上師之師, 392–393.

54. According to the Chinese translation, *lo mjug dus gtor* refers to 歲末瑪哈嘎拉法會 (The year-end Mahākāla *pūjā*). See 勉東倉巴仁波切，八蚌欽哲仁波切，堪千創古仁波切，上師之師, 395.

Appendix B

55. The Ninth Traleg tulku was born in 1955, the wood sheep year. The Chinese translation also gives the year 1955 (See 勉東倉巴仁波切，八蚌欽哲仁波切，堪千創古仁波切，上師之師, 396). For this reason, *me lug* in the text may be a typographical error.

56. The Chinese translation specifies that the retreat master was Khenpo Karthar Rinpoche. See 勉東倉巴仁波切，八蚌欽哲仁波切，堪千創古仁波切，上師之師, 396.

57. Again, *Yon dge* may be a typographical error or variant spelling of *Yongs dge* as in the name Yongey Mingyur Dorje.

58. That is, Chia Theng Shen 沈家楨. See 勉東倉巴仁波切，八蚌欽哲仁波切，堪千創古仁波切，上師之師, 400.

59. According to the Chinese translation, this monk was American (他特別為一位美國沙彌傳授比丘戒). See 勉東倉巴仁波切，八蚌欽哲仁波切，堪千創古仁波切，上師之師, 401.

60. The Chinese translation adds: 噶瑪巴各派三位比丘到法國和美國建立寺院 (The Karmapa sent three monks to each of the two countries, France and the United States, to build monasteries). See 勉東倉巴仁波切，八蚌欽哲仁波切，堪千創古仁波切，上師之師, 402.

61. According to the Chinese translation, *gdan sa* here refers to Rumtek monastery (隆德寺). See 勉東倉巴仁波切，八蚌欽哲仁波切，堪千創古仁波切，上師之師, 404.

62. That is, the enlightened body, speech and mind.

Bibliography

TIBETAN SOURCES:

Karma rgyal mtshan. "dpal rgyal dbang karma pa na rim gyi mdzad rnam (4)." In *kaM tshang yab sras dang dpal spungs dgon pa'i lo rgyus ngo mtshar dad pa'i padma rgyas byed*. TBRC W27303.: 34–89. khreng tu: si khron mi rigs dpe skrun khang, 1997. http://tbrc.org/link?RID=O1GS75816|O1GS758161GS75833$W27303.

Karma nges don bstan rgyas. "chos rje karma pa sku phreng rim byon gyi rnam thar mdor bsdus dpag bsam khri shing /(1–14)." In *karma pa sku 'phreng bcu drug pa tshun rim par byon pa'i rnam thar phyogs bsgrigs*. TBRC W1KG3815.: 7–478. New Delhi: konchhog lhadrepa, 1994. http://tbrc.org/link?RID=O1PD106813|O1 PD1068132DB105396$W1KG3815.

Karma blo gros chos dpal bzang po. "rgyal ba'i dbang po dpal karma pa rang byung rig pa'i rdo rje mchog brgya phyed la zung gi 'phel ba'i 'grang bya byon pa yan gyi rnam thar/_(16)." In *karma pa sku 'phreng bcu drug pa tshun rim par byon pa'i rnam thar phyogs bsgrigs*. TBRC W1KG3815.: 595–762. New Delhi: konchhog lhadrepa, 1994. https://www.tbrc.org/#library_work_ViewByOutline -O1PD1068132DB105412%7CW1KG3815.

bKra shis tshe ring. "'jig rten dbang phyug mthing mdog cod paN 'chang ba bcu drug pa chen po'i phyi yi rnam thar rgya mtsho ltar tshad med pa las chu thigs tsam gyi sa bon bzhugs so." *Bulletin of Tibetology: Karmapa Commemoration Volume*, no. 1 (1982): 19–54. Gangtok: Sikkim Research Institute of Tibetology & Other Buddhist Studies.

bKra shis tshe ring. "bka' 'bum rim po che thog mar 'tshol bsdu byed pos mjug bsdu'i snyan bsgron ma bcos gnyug ma'i rang sgra bzhugs lags." In *rgyal dbang karma pa bcu drug pa chen po'i gsung 'bum 3*, edited by Jo sras bkra shis tshe ring, 307–326. Dharamsala: Tshurphu Labrang; The Amnye Machen Institute, 2016.

sKyabs gnas dam pa dpal 'byor don grub. *rgyal ba karma pa na rim gyi sngon byung dang ma 'ongs pa dang da ltar gyi tshul mdo rgyud dang gter yig rnams su lung bstan tshul kun gsal me long zhes bya ba bzhugs so*, edited by bkra shis tshe ring. Dharamsala: Library of Tibetan Works & Archives, 1982.

Khra 'gu rin po che. *rgyal ba'i dbang po dpal karma pa sku 'phreng bcu drug pa tshun rim par byon pa'i rnam thar phyogs bsgrigs*. Varanasi: Vajra Vidya Institute Library, 2008.

Khra 'gu rin po che. "rgyal ba'i dbang po dpal karma pa rang byung rig pa'i rdo rje mchog brgya phrag phyed la zung gis 'phel ba'i bgrang byar byon pa yan gyi rnam thar bzhugs so." In *rgyal dbang karma pa bcu drug pa chen po'i gsung 'bum 1*, edited by Jo sras bkra shis tshe ring, 69–132. Dharamsala: Tshurphu Labrang; The Amnye Machen Institute, 2016.

mKha' spyod dbang po. *bka' brgyud rin po che'i rnam par thar pa chos tshan bcu bdun/*. TBRC W3CN2636. 1 vols. [s.l.]: [s.n.], [n.d.]. http://tbrc.org/link?RID =W3CN2636.

mKhas btsun bzang po. "rje karma pa rig pa'i rdo rje ni." In *rgyal dbang karma pa bcu drug pa chen po'i gsung 'bum 1*, edited by Jo sras bkra shis tshe ring, 133–143. Dharamsala: Tshurphu Labrang; The Amnye Machen Institute, 2016.

mKhyen brtse 'od zer. "dpal ldan kun bzang chos kyi nyi ma chen po phrin las mkha' khyab rdo rje'i rnam thar mdor bsdus/_(15)." In *karma pa sku 'phreng bcu drug pa tshun rim par byon pa'i rnam thar phyogs bsgrigs*. TBRC W1KG3815.: 479–594. New Delhi: konchhog lhadrepa, 1994. http://tbrc.org/link?RID=O1PD106813|O1 PD1068132DB105411$W1KG3815.

Grags pa yongs 'dus. "karma pa bcu drug pa rig pa'i rdo rje'i rnam thar." In *kam tshang gser phreng gi rnam thar kha skong*. TBRC W19988.: 368–399. New Delhi: Topga Yulgyal, 1993. http://tbrc.org/link?RID=O1GC1|O1GC11PD120200$W19988.

dGe legs bstan 'dzin. "bod nas 'brug brgyud 'bras ljongs su phebs pa." In *rgyal dbang karma pa bcu drug pa chen po'i gsung 'bum 1*, edited by Jo sras bkra shis tshe ring, 144–161. Dharamsala: Tshurphu Labrang; The Amnye Machen Institute, 2016.

Chos kyi 'byung gnas, Tshe dbang kun khyab. *sgrub brgyud karma kaM tshang gi brgyud pa rin po che'i rnam par thar pa rab 'byams nor bu zla ba chu shel gyi phreng ba*. TBRC W24686. 1 vols. kun ming: yun nan mi rigs dpe skrun khang, 1998. http://tbrc.org/link?RID=W24686.

'Jam dbyangs tshul khrims. "karma pa rig pa'i rdo rje." In *karma pa sku phreng rim byon gyi mdzad rnam*. TBRC W18133.: 246–255. Lan kru'u: kan su'u mi rigs dpe skrun khang, 1997. http://tbrc.org/link?RID=O2DB98584|O2DB985842DB9860 3$W18133.

'Ja' tshon snying po. *rgyal dbang karma pa'i che brjod mdo rgyud lung 'dren padma'i chun po 'ja'i ming can gyis sbyar ba bzhugs so*. [n.d.]

'Ju chen thub bstan rnam rgyal. "rgyal dbang karma pa sku phreng 16 pa rang byung rig pa'i rdo rje mchog dgongs pa chos dbyings su thim pa'i tshul bstan pa." In *'Ju chen thub bstan gyi sku tshe'i lo rgyus* (9), 315–326. Chauntra: Juchentsang, 2014.

Blo gros don yod. "karma pa rang byung rig pa'i rdo rje'i rnam thar." In *dus 'khor chos 'byung indra nI la'i phra tshom*. TBRC W00EGS1016994. 1: 562–573. Mirik: 'bo dkar nges don chos 'khor gling gi bla spyi spar bskrun zhus, 2005. http:// tbrc.org/link?RID=O3JT201|O3JT2013JT291$W00EGS1016994.

Mi pham rgya mtsho. "thub chog byin rlabs gter mdzod kyi rgyab chos padma dkar po." In *gsung 'bum/_mi pham rgya mtsho*. TBRC W2DB16631. 8: 13–1054. khreng tu'u: [gangs can rig gzhung dpe rnying myur skyobs lhan tshogs], 2007. https://www.tbrc.org/?locale=en#!rid=W4PD506.

TBRC. "karma nges don bstan rgyas (b. 18uu,)." TBRC P926., 2011. http://tbrc.org /link?RID=P926.

TBRC. "mkhyen brtse 'od zer (b. 1904, d. 1953/1954)." TBRC P937, 2011. http:// tbrc.org/link?RID=P937.

gTsug lag 'phreng ba. "sgrub rgyud karma kam tshang gi chos byung rgyas pa (pa)." In *chos 'byung mkhas pa'i dga' ston*. TBRC W28792. 2: 5–510. New Delhi: Delhi karmapae chodey gyalwae sungrab partun khang, 1980. http://tbrc.org/link?RID =O4LS1442|O4LS14424LS1460$W28792.

Tshul khrims rgya mtsho. "rgyal dbang karma pa sku phreng bcu drug pa rang byung rig pa'i rdo rje." In *'bras ljongs su deng rabs bod kyi bla ma rnams kyis mdzad pa dang rnam thar bsdus pa*. TBRC W1KG852.: 49–60. Gangtok, Sikkim: Namgyal Institute of Tibetology, 2008. http://tbrc.org/link?RID=O1PD95669|O1PD956692 DB100180$W1KG852.

rDzogs chen dpon slob. "karma pa sku phreng bcu drug pa rig pa'i rdo rje." In *rgyal dbang karma pa bcu drug pa chen po'i gsung 'bum 1*, edited by Jo sras bkra shis tshe ring, 276–289. Dharamsala: Tshurphu Labrang; The Amnye Machen Institute, 2016.

Zhwa dmar. *dpal rgyal ba karma pa rig pa'i rdo rje'i sku tshe'i rnam thar la bstod pa kunda'i phreng ba zhes pa las lo rgyus dang 'brel ba'i tshig don rnams gsal bar bkral ba kunda'i dri bsung shes bya ba bzhugs so*. Kalimpong: Diwakar Publications, 2013.

gZhon nu dpal. "sgam po ba'i dngos slob kyi skabs." In *deb ther sngon po*. TBRC W7494. 1: 414. New Delhi: International Academy of Indian Culture, 1974. http:// tbrc.org/link?RID=O7494|O7494C2O0065$W7494.

Rang byung rig pa'i rdo rje. "rang rnam bsdus pa." In *rgyal dbang karma pa bcu drug pa chen po'i gsung 'bum 1*, edited by Jo sras bkra shis tshe ring, 64–68. Dharamsala: Tshurphu Labrang; The Amnye Machen Institute, 2016.

Rang byung rig pa'i rdo rje. "skabs su bab pa'i snang glu rkang drug bung ba'i lding dbyangs." In *rgyal dbang karma pa bcu drug pa chen po'i gsung 'bum 3*, edited by Jo sras bkra shis tshe ring, 3–4. Dharamsala: Tshurphu Labrang; The Amnye Machen Institute, 2016.

Rang byung rig pa'i rdo rje. "nyams dbyangs dgyes pa'i nga ro." In *rgyal dbang karma pa bcu drug pa chen po'i gsung 'bum 3*, edited by Jo sras bkra shis tshe ring, 10–11. Dharamsala: Tshurphu Labrang; The Amnye Machen Institute, 2016.

Rang byung rig pa'i rdo rje. "gangs ljongs ris med chos kyi tshogs chen thengs dang po'i skabs rgyal dbang karma pa rin po che'i gsungs bshad." In *rgyal dbang karma pa bcu drug pa chen po'i gsung 'bum 3*, edited by Jo sras bkra shis tshe ring, 16–18. Dharamsala: Tshurphu Labrang; The Amnye Machen Institute, 2016.

Rang byung rig pa'i rdo rje. "rgyal dbang bcu drug pa rang byung rig pa'i rdo rje mchog gi bka' slob." In *rgyal dbang karma pa bcu drug pa chen po'i gsung 'bum*

3, edited by Jo sras bkra shis tshe ring, 19–23. Dharamsala: Tshurphu Labrang; The Amnye Machen Institute, 2016.

Rang byung rig pa'i rdo rje. "shing stag 1974 zla 8 tshes 13 'khod zur mang drung pa rin po cher rdo rje 'dzin pa karma sgrub brgyud bstan pa'i rgyal mtshan don brgyud 'chang ba'i mtshan gnas stsal ba'i bka' shog." In *rgyal dbang karma pa bcu drug pa chen po'i gsung 'bum 3*, edited by Jo sras bkra shis tshe ring, 84. Dharamsala: Tshurphu Labrang; The Amnye Machen Institute, 2016.

Rang byung rig pa'i rdo rje. "me 'brug 1976 zla 12 tshes 8 'khod zur mang drung pa rin po che'i zhal slob 'od gsal bstan 'dzin drung pa rin po che'i rgyal tshab tu bskos bzhag rgyab gnyer gyi bka' shog." In *rgyal dbang karma pa bcu drug pa chen po'i gsung 'bum 3*, edited by Jo sras bkra shis tshe ring, 89. Dharamsala: Tshurphu Labrang; The Amnye Machen Institute, 2016.

Rang byung rig pa'i rdo rje. "zur mang drung pa rin po che'i chos tshogs nas bka' brgyud mgur mtsho dbyin bsgyur deb la che brjod." In *rgyal dbang karma pa bcu drug pa chen po'i gsung 'bum 3*, edited by Jo sras bkra shis tshe ring, 49. Dharamsala: Tshurphu Labrang; The Amnye Machen Institute, 2016.

Rin chen dpal bzang. *mtshur phu dgon gyi dkar chag kun gsal me long*. TBRC W20850. 1 vols. pe cin: mi rigs dpe skrun khang, 1995. http://tbrc.org/link?RID=W20850.

Rin chen dpal bzang. "sku phreng bcu drug pa rig pa'i rdo rje byon pa ni." In *rgyal dbang karma pa bcu drug pa chen po'i gsung 'bum 1*, edited by Jo sras bkra shis tshe ring, 270–275. Dharamsala: Tshurphu Labrang; The Amnye Machen Institute, 2016.

Rum bteg (bKa' brgyud 'dzam gling dbus rgyun las khang). "dpal karma pa bcu drug pa chen po'i rnam thar lo rgyus mdor bsdus bzhugs." In *rgyal dbang karma pa bcu drug pa chen po'i gsung 'bum 1*, edited by Jo sras bkra shis tshe ring, 220–223. Dharamsala: Tshurphu Labrang; The Amnye Machen Institute, 2016.

Rum bteg (rGyal yongs bka' brgyud dbus rgyun las khungs). "rgyal dbang karma pa chen po'i dgongs rdzogs mjug mchod." In *rgyal dbang karma pa bcu drug pa chen po'i gsung 'bum 1*, edited by Jo sras bkra shis tshe ring, 233–257. Dharamsala: Tshurphu Labrang; The Amnye Machen Institute, 2016.

Shes bya. "bzod par dka' ba'i ches yid gdung gi gnas tshul." In *rgyal dbang karma pa bcu drug pa chen po'i gsung 'bum 1*, edited by Jo sras bkra shis tshe ring, 224–228. Dharamsala: Tshurphu Labrang; The Amnye Machen Institute, 2016.

Shes bya. "bka' tshogs mchod 'bul grub ste phyir phebs." In *rgyal dbang karma pa bcu drug pa chen po'i gsung 'bum 1*, edited by Jo sras bkra shis tshe ring, 229–230. Dharamsala: Tshurphu Labrang; The Amnye Machen Institute, 2016.

Shes bya. "dgongs rdzogs mchod sprin." In *rgyal dbang karma pa bcu drug pa chen po'i gsung 'bum 1*, edited by Jo sras bkra shis tshe ring, 231–232. Dharamsala: Tshurphu Labrang; The Amnye Machen Institute, 2016.

CHINESE SOURCES:

大寶法王噶瑪巴官方中文網 (Kagyu Office). "《普度明太祖長卷圖》." Accessed March 29, 2022. https://www.kagyuoffice.org.tw/c-reference/pudu-ming-taizu-changjuantu.

噶玛宝阳. "十四世噶瑪巴出生地：噶玛乡达那村." 法露 *(Dharma Nectar)* 4, no. 2 (2017): 56–63. Karmapa Office.

噶玛善宝. "五世噶玛巴出生地：工布江达镇娘当村. 掩藏在枯叶下的圣石." 法露 *(Dharma Nectar)* 3, no. 2 (2017): 80–87. Karmapa Office.

噶玛善宝, and噶玛善莲. "十、十一世噶玛巴出生地：班玛县多日麻村. 莲花藏乡八吉祥." 法露 *(Dharma Nectar)* 4, no. 2 (2017): 30–39. Karmapa Office.

噶玛善池. "十六世噶玛巴出生地：石渠县洛须镇. 每一次峰回路转都是修炼." 法露 *(Dharma Nectar)* 4, no. 2 (2017): 72–79. Karmapa Office.

噶玛善莲."史诗般的相遇：五世噶玛巴与明成祖." 法露 *(Dharma Nectar)* 1, no. 1 (2014): 72–77. Karmapa Office.

噶玛善莲, ed. "灵谷瑞云有迹:《荐福图》实录." 法露 *(Dharma Nectar)* 1, no. 1 (2014): 78–85. Karmapa Office.

噶玛善莲, ed. "穿越六百年的光芒." 法露 *(Dharma Nectar)* 1, no. 1 (2014): 86–91. Karmapa Office.

噶玛善莲. "四世噶玛巴出生地：边坝县加贡乡.世外桃源小山岗." 法露 *(Dharma Nectar)* 3, no. 2 (2017): 72–79. Karmapa Office.

噶玛善莲. "按图索骥：重绘古"哲霍"圣迹地图." 法露 *(Dharma Nectar)* 5, no. 3 (2019): 22–33. Karmapa Office.

噶玛善莲. "历代噶玛巴与则拉岗." 法露 *(Dharma Nectar)* 5, no. 3 (2019): 66–75. Karmapa Office.

噶玛善莲, and噶玛善宝. "九世噶玛巴出生地：卡瓦岭神山达桑山谷. 鹰巢底下手印石." 法露 *(Dharma Nectar)* 4, no. 2 (2017): 20–29. Karmapa Office.

噶玛善莲, and噶玛宝阳. "黑宝冠缘起：杜松虔巴剃度圣地呷拉觉空." 法露 *(Dharma Nectar)* 5, no. 3 (2019): 46–53. Karmapa Office.

噶玛善喜. "七世噶玛巴出生地：扑朔迷离岗巴村. 消失的脚印岩石." 法露 *(Dharma Nectar)* 3, no. 2 (2017): 96–103. Karmapa Office.

噶玛善喜. "七世噶玛巴出生地：边坝县金岭乡金达村. 阿玛拉千诺'." 法露 *(Dharma Nectar)* 4, no. 2 (2017): 6–15. Karmapa Office.

噶玛善喜. "十二世噶玛巴出生地：汪布顶乡卓格村. 隔了十世重回故地." 法露 *(Dharma Nectar)* 4, no. 2 (2017): 40–47. Karmapa Office.

噶玛钨金, 噶玛善莲, 噶玛善宝, and 噶玛善喜, eds. "第一世噶玛巴：杜松虔巴. 开启九百年传承." 法露 *(Dharma Nectar)* 2, no. 2 (2016): 6–19. Karmapa Office.

噶玛钨金, 噶玛善莲, 噶玛善宝, and 噶玛善喜, eds. "第二世噶玛巴：噶玛拔希. 降服外道蒙古汗王." 法露 *(Dharma Nectar)* 2, no. 2 (2016): 20–29. Karmapa Office.

噶玛钨金, 噶玛善莲, 噶玛善宝, and 噶玛善喜, eds. "第三世噶玛巴：让炯多杰. 把爱放在月亮上." 法露 *(Dharma Nectar)* 2, no. 2 (2016): 30–39. Karmapa Office.

噶玛钨金, 噶玛善莲, 噶玛善宝, and 噶玛善喜, eds. "第四世噶玛巴：若必多杰. 持律利苍生." 法露 *(Dharma Nectar)* 2, no. 2 (2016): 40–49. Karmapa Office.

噶玛钨金, 噶玛善莲, 噶玛善宝, and 噶玛善喜, eds. "第五世噶玛巴：德新谢巴. 佛光播撒汉地."法露 *(Dharma Nectar)* 2, no. 2 (2016): 50–61. Karmapa Office.

噶玛钨金, 噶玛善莲, 噶玛善宝, and 噶玛善喜, eds. "第六世噶玛巴：通瓦敦滇. 善逝前往香巴拉."法露 *(Dharma Nectar)* 2, no. 2 (2016): 62–69. Karmapa Office.

噶玛钨金, 噶玛善莲, 噶玛善宝, and 噶玛善喜, eds. "第七世噶玛巴：确札嘉措. 带领嘎千大营去修行." 法露 *(Dharma Nectar)* 2, no. 2 (2016): 70–79. Karmapa Office.

噶玛钨金, 噶玛善莲, 噶玛善宝, and 噶玛善喜, eds. "第八世噶玛巴：米觉多杰. 青绿山水中的不动金刚." 法露 *(Dharma Nectar)* 2, no. 2 (2016): 80–89. Karmapa Office.

噶玛钨金, 噶玛善莲, 噶玛善宝, and 噶玛善喜, eds. "噶玛寺朝圣：月亮山峰前的圣地." 法露 *(Dharma Nectar)* 2, no. 2 (2016): 90–104. Karmapa Office.

噶玛钨金, 噶玛善莲, 噶玛善宝, 噶玛善喜, and 噶玛宝阳, eds. "第九世噶玛巴：旺秋多杰. 广行尊胜佛行事业." 法露 *(Dharma Nectar)* 3, no. 2 (2017): 6–17. Karmapa Office.

噶玛钨金, 噶玛善莲, 噶玛善宝, 噶玛善喜, and 噶玛宝阳, eds. "第十世噶玛巴：确映多杰." 法露 *(Dharma Nectar)* 3, no. 2 (2017): 18–45. Karmapa Office.

噶玛钨金, 噶玛善莲, 噶玛善宝, 噶玛善喜, 噶玛宝阳, and 噶玛善池, eds. "第十一世噶玛巴：耶谢多杰. 八瓣莲花出生智慧金刚." 法露 *(Dharma Nectar)* 4, no. 2 (2017): 88–93. Karmapa Office.

噶玛钨金, 噶玛善莲, 噶玛善宝, 噶玛善喜, 噶玛宝阳, and 噶玛善池, eds. "第十二世噶玛巴：蒋秋多杰. 出世大士无方游乡国." 法露 *(Dharma Nectar)* 4, no. 2 (2017): 94–100. Karmapa Office.

噶玛钨金, 噶玛善莲, 噶玛善宝, and 噶玛宝阳, eds. "第十三世噶玛巴：敦督多杰. 以诸音而说法的伏魔金刚." 法露 *(Dharma Nectar)* 5, no. 3 (2019): 82–89. Karmapa Office.

噶玛钨金, 噶玛善莲, 噶玛善宝, and 噶玛宝阳, eds. "第十四世噶玛巴：特秋多杰. 无量法调无边众." 法露 *(Dharma Nectar)* 5, no. 3 (2019): 90–97. Karmapa Office.

堪布卡塔仁波切. "前言". In 上師之師：歷代大寶法王噶瑪巴的轉世傳奇. Translated by 比丘尼洛卓拉嫫, 8–14. 台灣：眾生文化, 2016.

勉東倉巴仁波切, 八蚌欽哲仁波切, 堪千創古仁波切. 上師之師：歷代大寶法王噶瑪巴的轉世傳奇. Translated by 比丘尼洛卓拉嫫. 台灣：眾生文化, 2016.

全知麦彭仁波切. 释迦佛广传. Translated by 堪布索达吉. 显密宝库.

鄔金欽列多傑. "序言." In 上師之師：歷代大寶法王噶瑪巴的轉世傳奇. Translated by 比丘尼洛卓拉嫫, 3. 台灣：眾生文化, 2016.

ENGLISH SOURCES:

ADARSHA. "Jiang Kangyur." Accessed March 6, 2017. https://adarsha.dharma-treasure.org/kdbs/jiangkangyur.

Akong: A remarkable life. DVD. Directed by Chico Dall'Inha. London: Awareness Media Productions, 2017.

Aldred, Lisa. "Plastic Shamans and Astroturf Sun Dances: New Age commercialization of native American spirituality." *American Indian Quarterly* 24, no. 3 (2000): 329–352. Quoted in Darinda J Congdon, "'Tibet Chic': Myth, marketing, spirituality and politics in musical Representations of Tibet in the United States." PhD diss., University of Pittsburgh, 2007, 72–73.

Almond, Philip C. *The British Discovery of Buddhism*. Cambridge: Cambridge University Press, 1988. Quoted in Robert Bluck, *British Buddhism: Teachings, practice and development*. London and New York: Routledge, 2006, 5.

Anand, Dibyesh. "A Guide to Little Lhasa: The role of symbolic geography of Dharamsala in constituting Tibetan diasporic identity." In *Tibet, Self and the Tibetan Diaspora: Voices of difference*, edited by C. Klieger, 11–36. Leiden: E J Brill, 2002. Quoted in John Robertson, "Semiotics, Habitus and Music in the Transmission of Tibetan Culture in Toronto." MA diss., Liberty University, 2011, 2.

Anand, Dibyesh. "A Contemporary Story of 'Diaspora': The Tibetan version." *Diaspora: A Journal of Transnational Studies* 12, no. 2 (2003): 211–229.

Anand, Dibyesh. *Geopolitical Exotica: Tibet in Western imagination*. Minneapolis and London: University of Minnesota Press, 2007.

Ani Ea, Gelongma. "Karmapa Becomes Vegetarian." In *The Miraculous 16th Karmapa: Incredible encounters with the Black Crown Buddha*, compiled by Norma Levine, 389–393. Arcidosso: Shang Shung Publications, 2013.

Appleton, Naomi. *Jātaka Stories in Theravāda Buddhism: Narrating the Bodhisatta path*. Surrey, VT: Ashgate Publishing, 2010.

Aris, Michael. *Bhutan: The early history of a Himalayan kingdom*. Warminster: Aris & Phillips, 1979.

Aris, Michael. *The Raven Crown: The origins of Buddhist monarchy in Bhutan*. London: Serindia Publications, 1994.

Ato Rinpoche. "Biography." Accessed July 3, 2018. https://www.atorinpoche.com/biography.

Ayang Rinpoche. "The Light of the World." In *The Miraculous 16th Karmapa: Incredible encounters with the Black Crown Buddha*, compiled by Norma Levine, 61–68. Arcidosso: Shang Shung Publications, 2013.

Barker, Diane. "A Shrine Room in the Black Mountains of Wales." In *The Miraculous 16th Karmapa: Incredible encounters with the Black Crown Buddha*, compiled by Norma Levine, 321–326. Arcidosso: Shang Shung Publications, 2013.

Barker, Eileen. "New Religious Movements: Their incidence and significance." In *New Religious Movements: Challenge and response*, edited by Bryan Wilson and Jamie Cresswell. London: Routledge, 1999. Quoted in Robert Bluck, *British Buddhism: Teachings, practice and development*. London and New York: Routledge, 2006, 11.

Barnett, Robert. "Violated Specialness: Western political representations of Tibet." In *Imagining Tibet: Perceptions, projections, and fantasies*, edited by Thierry Dodin and Heinz Räther, 269–316. Boston, MA: Wisdom Press, 2001.

Batchelor, Stephen. *The Awakening of the West: The encounter of Buddhism and western culture*. Berkeley, CA: Parallax Press, 1994.

Baumann, Martin. "Creating a European Path to Nirvana: Historical and contemporary developments of Buddhism in Europe." *Journal of Contemporary Religion* 10, no. 1 (1995): 55–70. Quoted in Robert Bluck, *British Buddhism: Teachings, practice and development*. London and New York: Routledge, 2006, 19.

Baumann, Martin. "Global Buddhism: Developmental periods, regional histories, and a new analytical perspective." *Journal of Global Buddhism* 2 (2001): 1–43.

Baumann, Martin. "Protective Amulets and Awareness Techniques, or How to Make Sense of Buddhism in the West." In *Westward Dharma: Buddhism beyond Asia*, edited by Charles S. Prebish and Martin Baumann, 51–65. Berkeley, CA: University of California Press, 2002.

Bedi, Kabir. "Karmapa and the Gelongma." In *The Miraculous 16th Karmapa: Incredible encounters with the Black Crown Buddha*, compiled by Norma Levine, 73–76. Arcidosso: Shang Shung Publications, 2013.

Bell, Sandra. "Buddhism in Britain: Development and adaptation." PhD diss., University of Durham, 1991.

Bell, Sandra. "'Crazy Wisdom', Charisma, and the Transmission of Buddhism in the United States." *The Journal of Alternative and Emergent Religions* 2, no. 1 (1998): 55–75.

Bell, Sandra. "Being Creative with Tradition: Rooting Theravāda Buddhism in Britain." *Journal of Global Buddhism* 1 (2000): 1–23.

Bennett, M. J. "The Picnic." In *The Miraculous 16th Karmapa: Incredible encounters with the Black Crown Buddha*, compiled by Norma Levine, 107–116. Arcidosso: Shang Shung Publications, 2013a.

Bennett, M. J. "The Last Blessing." In *The Miraculous 16th Karmapa: Incredible encounters with the Black Crown Buddha*, compiled by Norma Levine, 397–400. Arcidosso: Shang Shung Publications, 2013.

Bennett, M. J., and Norma Levine. "Canada and the Three World Tours of His Holiness Karmapa." In *The Miraculous 16th Karmapa: Incredible encounters with the Black Crown Buddha*, compiled by Norma Levine, 157–165. Arcidosso: Shang Shung Publications, 2013.

Bhushan, Nalini, Garfield Jay L., and Abraham Zablocki, eds. *TransBuddhism: Transmission, translation, transformation*. Amherst: University of Massachusetts Press, 2009.

Bishop, Peter. *The Myth of Shangri-La: Tibet, travel writing and the western creation of sacred landscape*. London: Athlone, 1989.

Bishop, Peter. *Dreams of Power: Tibetan Buddhism and the western imagination*. London: Athlone, 1993.

Bishop, Peter. "Not Only a Shangri-La: Images of Tibet in Western Literature." In *Imagining Tibet: Perceptions, projections, and fantasies*, edited by Thierry Dodin and Heinz Räther, 201–221. Boston, MA: Wisdom Press, 2001.

Bluck, Robert. *British Buddhism: Teachings, practice and development*. London and New York: Routledge, 2006.

Bokar Rinpoche. "The Events of Kalu Rinpoche's Life." In *Excellent Buddhism: An exemplary life*, edited by Kalu Rinpoche, 43–51. San Francisco, CA: ClearPoint Press, 1995.

Bokar Rinpoche, Lama Gyaltsen, and Khenpo Lodro Donyo. "Kalu Rinpoche's Last Moments." In *Excellent Buddhism: An exemplary life*, edited by Kalu Rinpoche, 53–59. San Francisco, CA: ClearPoint Press, 1995.

Brauen, Martin. *Dreamworld Tibet: Western illusions*. Trumbull, CT: Weatherhill, 2004.
Brown, Mick. *The Dance of 17 Lives: The incredible true story of Tibet's 17th Karmapa*. London: Bloomsbury, 2004.
Brown, Mick. "David Bowie's Buddhist Master: 'David rang me up and said I have a very big problem'." *The Telegraph*, May 22, 2016. https://www.telegraph.co.uk/men/thinking-man/david-bowies-buddhist-david-rang-me-up-and-said-i-have-a-very-bi/#.
Browning, James C. "Tarthang Tulku and the Quest for an American Buddhism." PhD diss., Baylor University, 1986.
Bu chen bcu gnyis. "bZhad pa'i rdo rje'i rnam thar mgur mchings dang bcas pa." Some passages translated by Andrew Quintman in *The Yogin and the Madman*, 91–104. New York: Columbia University Press, 2014.
Bye, Reed. "The Founding Vision of Naropa University." In *Recalling Chögyam Trungpa*, edited by Fabrice Midal, 143–161. Boston, MA and New York: Shambhala Publications, 2005.
Carlson, Maria. *No Religion Higher Than Truth: A history of the Theosophical movement in Russia, 1875–1922*. Princeton, NJ: Princeton University Press, 1993. Quoted in Poul Pedersen, "Tibet, Theosophy, and the Psychologization of Buddhism." In *Imagining Tibet: Perceptions, projections, and fantasies*, edited by Thierry Dodin and Heinz Räther. Boston, MA: Wisdom Press, 2001, 156, 164.
CBSN. "Modern Masters of Religion." *YouTube* video, 26:55. June 29, 2014. https://www.youtube.com/watch?v=oChBG73iUHI.
Chandler, Jeannine M. *Hunting the Guru: Lineage, culture and conflict in the development of Tibetan Buddhism in America*. State University of New York at Albany, 2009.
Chögyam Trungpa. *Meditation in Action*. Berkeley, CA: Shambhala, 1969.
Chögyam Trungpa, and C. R. Gimian. *Shambhala: The sacred path of the warrior*. Boulder, CO: Shambhala, 1984.
Chögyam Trungpa, and Sherab Chödzin. *Crazy Wisdom*. Boston, MA and London: Shambhala, 1991.
Chögyam Trungpa. *Born in Tibet*. 4th ed. Boston, MA and London: Shambhala, 2000.
Chögyam Trungpa. "Epilogue." In *Born in Tibet*, 251–264. Boston, MA and London: Shambhala, 2000.
Cleland, Elizabeth C. "The Vajrakilaya Sadhana: An Euro-American experience of a Nyingma ritual." MA diss., Carleton University, 2001.
Coelho, V. *Sikkim and Bhutan*. New Delhi: Indian Council for Cultural Relations, 1971.
Coleman, James W. *The New Buddhism: The western transformation of an ancient tradition*. Oxford: Oxford University Press, 2001.
Coleman, James W. "Chapter Eight. The Emergence of a New Buddhism: Continuity and change." In *North American Buddhists in Social Context*, edited by Paul D. Numrich, 185–201. Leiden and Boston, MA: Brill, 2008.
Conermann, Stephan, and Jim Rheingans. "Narrative Pattern and Genre in Hagiographic Life Writing: An introduction." In *Narrative Pattern and Genre in*

Hagiographic Life Writing: Comparative perspectives from Asia to Europe, edited by Stephan Conermann and Jim Rheingans, 7–19. Gottingen: Hubert & Co., 2014.

Congdon, Darinda J. "'Tibet Chic': Myth, marketing, spirituality and politics in musical Representations of Tibet in the United States." PhD diss., University of Pittsburgh, 2007.

Contractor, Didi. "The Meeting of Mahasiddhas." In *The Miraculous 16th Karmapa: Incredible encounters with the Black Crown Buddha*, compiled by Norma Levine, 87–99. Arcidosso: Shang Shung Publications, 2013.

Conze, Edward. *Buddhism: Its essence and development*. Oxford: Bruno Cassirer Ltd., 1951.

Cush, Denise. "British Buddhism and the New Age." *Journal of Contemporary Religion* 11, no. 2 (1996): 195–208.

Dagyab Kyabgön Rinpoche. "Buddhism in the West and the Image of Tibet." In *Imagining Tibet: Perceptions, projections, and fantasies*, edited by Thierry Dodin and Heinz Räther, 379–390. Boston, MA: Wisdom Press, 2001.

Damchu Lhendup, and Needrup Zangpo. *One Hundred Years of Development*. Thimphu: KMT Publishing House, 2014.

David-Neel, Alexandra. *Magic and Mystery in Tibet*. New York: Dover Publications, 1971. Quoted in Peter Bishop, *The Myth of Shangri-La: Tibet, travel writing and the western creation of sacred landscape*. London: Athlone, 1989, 195, 199.

Davidson, Ronald M. *Indian Esoteric Buddhism: A social history of the tantric movement*. New York: Columbia University Press, 2002.

Dodin, Thierry, and Heinz Räther. "Imagining Tibet: Between Shangri-la and feudal oppression." In *Imagining Tibet: Perceptions, projections, and fantasies*, edited by Thierry Dodin and Heinz Räther, 391–416. Boston, MA: Wisdom Press, 2001.

Dodin, Thierry, and Heinz Räther, eds. *Imagining Tibet: Between Shangri-la and feudal oppression*. Boston, MA: Wisdom Press, 2001.

Dorje Dze Öd. *The Great Kagyu Masters: The golden lineage treasury*. Translated by Khenpo Könchog Gyaltsen, edited by Victoria Huckenpahler, 123–144. Ithaca, NY: Snow Lion Publications, 1990.

Dorzong Rinpoche. "As He Is." In *The Miraculous 16th Karmapa: Incredible encounters with the Black Crown Buddha*, compiled by Norma Levine, 401–403. Arcidosso: Shang Shung Publications, 2013.

Douglas, Nik, and Meryl White, comp. *Karmapa: The black hat lama of Tibet*. London: Luzac & Company Ltd., 1976.

Doyle, Arthur C. *The Adventure of the Empty House*. Createspace Independent Publishing Platform, 2012.

Dreyfus, Georges. "Are We Prisoners of Shangrila? Orientalism, nationalism, and the study of Tibet." *Journal of the International Association of Tibetan Studies* 1, no. 1 (2005): 1–21.

Dusum Khyenpa. *The First Karmapa: The life and teachings of Dusum Khyenpa*. Translated by David Karma Choephel and Michele Martin. New York: KTD Publications, 2012.

Dzogchen Ponlop. 2003. "The Sixteenth Karmapa Rangjung Rigpe Dorje." In *Music in the Sky: The life, art & teachings of the 17th Karmapa Ogyen Trinley Dorje*, edited by Michele Martin, 290–293. New York: Snow Lion Publications.

Eldershaw, Lynn. P. "Collective Identity and the Post-Charismatic Fate of Shambhala International." PhD diss., University of Waterloo, 2004.

Ellwood, Robert S. *The Sixties Spiritual Awakening: American religion moving from modern to postmodern*. New Brunswick, NJ: Rutgers University Press, 1994. Quoted in Elizabeth C Cleland, "The Vajrakilaya Sadhana: An Euro-American experience of a Nyingma ritual." MA diss., Carleton University, 2001, 24.

Empowerment: The visit of His Holiness the 16th Gyalwa Karmapa to the United States. Boulder, CO: Vajradhatu Publications, 1976.

Feigon, Lee. *Demystifying Tibet: Unlocking the secrets of the land of the snows*. Chicago: Ivan R. Dee, 1996.

Fields, Rick. *How the Swans Came to the Lake: A narrative history of Buddhism in America*. 3rd ed. Boston, MA: Shambhala Publications Inc., 1992.

Fields, Rick. "Confessions of a White Buddhist." *Tricycle* 4, no. 1 (1994): 54–56.

Finnegan, Damchö D. *Dharma King: The life of the 16th Gyalwang Karmapa in images*. New York: KTD Publications; Himachal Pradesh: Altruism Press, 2014.

Fisher, Ryan. "The Dialogical Construction of Tibetan-ness: Narratives of Tibetan identity and memory." PhD diss., Southern Methodist University, 2011.

From the Roof of the World: Refugees of Tibet. Berkeley, CA: Dharma Publishing, 1992. Quoted in Peter G Harle, "Thinking with Things: Objects and identity among Tibetans in the Twin Cities." PhD diss., Indiana University, 2003, 40.

sGam po pa bsod nams rin chen. "The Biographies of Marpa and Milarepa." Translated by Francis V. Tiso in *Liberation in one lifetime: biographies and teachings of Milarepa*, 240–254. Isernia: Proforma, 2010.

Gamble, Ruth E. "The View from Nowhere: The travels of the Third Karmapa, Rang byung rdo rje in story and songs." PhD diss., The Australian National University, 2013.

Garratt, Kevin. "Biography by Instalment: The Tibetan periodicals *Sheja* and *Trunggö Böjong* on the lives of reincarnate lamas." In *Religion and Biography in China and Tibet*, edited by Benjamin Penny, 189–220. Richmond, VA: Curzon, 2002.

Gelong Thubten, and Gelong Trinley, eds. *Only the Impossible is Worth Doing: Recollections of the supreme life and activity of Chöje Akong Tulku Rinpoche*. Dzalendra Publishing; Rokpa Trust, 2020.

Germano, David. "Encountering Tibet: The ethics, soteriology, and creativity of cross-cultural interpretation." *Journal of the American Academy of Religion* 69, no. 1 (2001): 165–182.

Goodman, Steven D., and Ronald M. Davidson, eds. *Tibetan Buddhism: Reason and revelation*. SUNY Series in Buddhist Studies. Albany, NY: State University of New York Press, 1992.

Gratton-Fabbri, Louise. "At Play in Paradox: The curious space between Tibetan Buddhism and western practice." PhD diss., Arizona State University, 2010.

Gregory, Peter N. "Describing the Elephant: Buddhism in America." *Religion and American Culture: A journal of interpretation* 11 (2001): 233–263.

Gulati, M. N. *Rediscovering Bhutan*. New Delhi: Manas Publications, 2003.

rGyal thang pa bde chen rdo rje. "The biography of Milarepa." Translated by Francis V. Tiso in *Liberation in One Lifetime: Biographies and teachings of Milarepa*, 161–240. Isernia: Proforma, 2010.

Gyaltsen, Lama. "Lama Gyaltsen's Memories." In *Excellent Buddhism: An exemplary life*, by Kalu Rinpoche, 13–41. San Francisco, CA: ClearPoint Press, 1995.

Gyatso, Janet B. "Autobiography in Tibetan Religious Literature: Reflection on its modes of self-presentation." In *Tibetan Studies: Proceedings of the 5th seminar of the International Association for Tibetan Studies NARITA 1989 vol.2*, edited by Ihara Shōren and Yamaguchi Zuihō, 465–478. Chiba, Japan: Naritasan Shinshoji, 1992.

Gyatso, Janet B. "From the Autobiography of a Visionary." In *Religions of Tibet in Practice*, edited by Donald S. Lopez, 275–281. Princeton, NJ: Princeton University Press, 2007.

Hansen, Peter H. "Tibetan Horizon: Tibet and the cinema in the early twentieth century." In *Imagining Tibet: Perceptions, projections, and fantasies*, edited by Thierry Dodin and Heinz Räther, 91–110. Boston, MA: Wisdom Press, 2001.

Harle, Peter G. "Thinking with Things: Objects and identity among Tibetans in the Twin Cities." PhD diss., Indiana University, 2003.

Harris, Vin. "A New Samye – Getting Started." In *Only the Impossible is Worth Doing: Recollections of the supreme life and activity of Chöje Akong Tulku Rinpoche*, edited by Gelong Thubten and Gelong Trinley, 35–60. Dzalendra Publishing; Rokpa Trust, 2020.

Harrison, Paul. "Some Reflections on the Personality of the Buddha." *The Otani Gakuho (The Journal of Buddhist Studies and Humanities)* 74, no. 4 (1995): 1–29.

Hickey, Wakoh S. "Two Buddhisms, Three Buddhisms, and Racism." *Journal of Global Buddhism* 11 (2010): 1–25.

Hilton, James. *Lost Horizon*. London: Pan Books, 1947. Quoted in Peter Bishop, *The Myth of Shangri-La: Tibet, travel writing and the western creation of sacred landscape*. London: Athlone, 1989, 211.

Hirshberg, Daniel A. "Karmic Foreshadowing on the Path of Fruition: Narrative devices in the biographies of Nyang ral nyi ma 'od zer." *Bulletin of Tibetology* 45, no. 1 (2009): 25–51. Quoted in Ruth E Gamble, "The View from Nowhere: The travels of the Third Karmapa, Rang byung rdo rje in story and songs." PhD diss., The Australian National University, 2013, 90.

Hirshberg, Daniel A. "Delivering the Lotus-Born: Historiography in the Tibetan renaissance." PhD diss., Harvard University, 2012. Quoted in Ruth E Gamble, "The View From Nowhere: The travels of the Third Karmapa, Rang byung rdo rje in story and songs." PhD diss., The Australian National University, 2013, 90.

Holmes, Dharmacharya Kenneth. "Chöje Akong Tulku Rinpoche's Role in Bringing Dharma to the World." In *Only the Impossible is Worth Doing: Recollections of the supreme life and activity of Chöje Akong Tulku Rinpoche*, edited by Gelong Thubten and Gelong Trinley, 61–116. Dzalendra Publishing; Rokpa Trust, 2020.

Holmes, Katia. "How the 16th Karmapa Transformed and Saved My Life." In *The Miraculous 16th Karmapa: Incredible encounters with the Black Crown Buddha*, compiled by Norma Levine, 359–380. Arcidosso: Shang Shung Publications, 2013.

Holmes, Katia. "Pioneer of Tibetan Medicine in Europe." In *Only the Impossible is Worth Doing: Recollections of the supreme life and activity of Chöje Akong Tulku Rinpoche*, edited by Gelong Thubten and Gelong Trinley, 233–291. Dzalendra Publishing; Rokpa Trust, 2020.

Holmes, Ken. *His Holiness the 17th Gyalwa Karmapa Urgyen Trinley Dorje*. Forres, Scotland: Altea Publishing, 1995.

Holmes, Ken. "Memories of the Buddha Karmapa." In *The Miraculous 16th Karmapa: Incredible encounters with the Black Crown Buddha*, compiled by Norma Levine, 289–303. Arcidosso: Shang Shung Publications, 2013.

Holmes, Ken. "The 16th Karmapa in Europe." In *The Miraculous 16th Karmapa: Incredible encounters with the Black Crown Buddha*, compiled by Norma Levine, 281–288. Arcidosso: Shang Shung Publications, 2013.

Holmes, Ken. "A Defining Moment: The disagreement between Trungpa Rinpoché and Akong Rinpoché concerning how the teachings should be given in Samyé Ling." 2014. http://akong.eu/AR_CTR.htm.

Holmes, Ken. "A Defining Moment: The disagreement between Trungpa Rinpoché and Akong Rinpoché concerning how the teachings should be given in Samyé Ling: continued . . ." 2014. http://akong.eu/AR_CTR_2.htm.

Holmes, Ken. "Akong Rinpoché and Samye Ling. Part 4: His 'Aims & Objects'." 2014. http://akong.eu/SL_4.htm.

Holmes, Ken. "Akong Rinpoché Establishing Buddha-Dharma. Part Two: An initial hesitation." 2014. http://www.akong.eu/dharma_2.htm.

Holmes, Ken. "Akong Rinpoché Establishing Buddha-Dharma. Part Eight: The Samye Project." 2014. http://akong.eu/dharma_8.htm.

Holmes, Ken. "Akong Rinpoché Establishing Buddha-Dharma. Part Nine: Dharma teachings . . . beginning the task." 2014. http://akong.eu/teachings_1.htm.

Holmes, Ken. "Akong Rinpoché Establishing Buddha-Dharma. Part Eleven: A study programme." 2014. http://akong.eu/teachings_3.htm.

Holmes, Ken. "Biographical Background." 2014. http://akong.eu/biobackground.htm.

Holmes, Ken. "The Finding and Founding of Samye Ling." 2014. http://www.akong.eu/sl_early.htm.

Holmes, Ken. "The Journey West." 2014. http://www.akong.eu/journeywest.htm.

Holmes, Ken. "The Special Connection with the XVIth Gyalwang Karmapa: 3. Rinpoché's Role in the 1974 Visit to Europe of the Gyalwang Karmapa." 2014. http://www.akong.eu/k16_3.htm.

Holmes, Ken. "The Special Connection with the XVIth Gyalwang Karmapa: 4. Rinpoché's Role in the 1977 Visit to Europe of the Gyalwang Karmapa: Part one . . . Preparations." 2014. http://www.akong.eu/k16_4.htm.

Holmes, Ken. "The Special Connection with the XVIth Gyalwang Karmapa: 5. Rinpoché's Role in the 1977 Visit to Europe of the Gyalwang Karmapa: Part two . . . the actual tour." 2014. http://www.akong.eu/k16_5.htm.

Holmes, Ken. "The Special Connection with the XVIth Gyalwang Karmapa: 6. Rinpoché's Role in the 1977 Visit to Europe of the Gyalwang Karmapa: Part three . . . reflections on Rinpoché's qualities." 2014. http://www.akong.eu/k16_6.htm.

Holmes, Ken. "The Special Connection with the XVIth Gyalwang Karmapa: 7. Rinpoché's Role in the 1977 Visit to Europe of the Gyalwang Karmapa: Part four ... founding the first Samye Dzongs and launching Khenpo Tsultrim." 2014. http://www.akong.eu/k16_7.htm.

Holmes, Ken. "The Special Connection with the XVIth Gyalwang Karmapa. A Long-Life Prayer (Shapten) for Akong Rinpoché." 2014. http://www.akong.eu/shapten.htm.

Hopkins, Jeffrey. "Tibetan Monastic Colleges: Rationality versus the demands of allegiance." In *Imagining Tibet: Perceptions, projections, and fantasies*, edited by Thierry Dodin and Heinz Räther, 257–268. Boston, MA: Wisdom Press, 2001.

Huber, Toni. "Shangri-La in Exile: Representations of Tibetan identity and transnational culture." In *Imagining Tibet: Perceptions, projections, and fantasies*, edited by Thierry Dodin and Heinz Räther, 357–371. Boston, MA: Wisdom Press, 2001.

Humphreys, Christmas. *Buddhism: An introduction and guide*. London: Penguin Books, 1951.

Jacerme, Pierre. "Maitri Space Awareness: The need for place." In *Recalling Chögyam Trungpa*, edited by Fabrice Midal, 111–138. Boston, MA and New York: Shambhala Publications, 2005.

Jackson, David P. *A Saint in Seattle: The life of the Tibetan mystic Dezhung Rinpoche*. Boston, MA: Wisdom Publications, 2003.

Jamgön Kongtrul. *La Nature de Bouddha*. Hui, Belgium: Kunchab, 1993. Quoted in Pemo Kunsang and Marie Aubèle, *History of the Karmapas: The odyssey of the Tibetan masters with the black crown*. New York: Snow Lion Publications, 2012, 230–231.

Jamgon Kongtrul Rinpoche. "Life Story of His Holiness the XVI Gyalwa Karmapa." *Bulletin of Tibetology: Karmapa commemoration volume*, no. 1 (1982): 6–20. Gangtok: Sikkim Research Institute of Tibetology & Other Buddhist Studies.

Je Tukyi Dorje, and Surmang Tendzin Rinpoche. *Chariot of the Fortunate: The life of the First Yongey Mingyur Dorje*. Translated by Yeshe Gyamtso. New York: KTD Publications, 2006.

Kagyu Droden Kunchab. "The Kalachakra in America." Accessed August 26, 2018. http://www.kdk.org/lama-lodu-bio-20.html.

Kagyu Office. "Gyalwang Karmapa's Teachings on the Vajradhara Lineage Prayer Session One: Great masters of the Karma Kamtshang lineage." Reported February 26, 2012. https://kagyuoffice.org/gyalwang-karmapas-teachings-on-the-vajradhara-lineage-prayer-session-one-great-masters-of-the-karma-kamtshang-lineage/.

Kagyu Office. "Akshobhya the Undisturbed: Paradigm of patience." Reported August 29, 2015. http://kagyuoffice.org/akshobhya-the-undisturbed-paradigm-of-patience/.

Kagyu Office. "Completing His Teachings, the Gyalwang Karmapa Speaks of the Chakrasamvara Empowerment." Reported January 22, 2017. https://kagyuoffice.org/completing-his-teachings-the-gyalwang-karmapa-speaks-of-the-chakrasamvara-empowerment/.

Kagyu Office. "Four-Session Guru Yoga Session One." Reported February 11, 2017. http://kagyuoffice.org/four-session-guru-yoga-session-one/.

Kagyu Office. "The Life of the Eighth Karmapa. Year One. Day One: The Black Hat Lama." Reported February 15, 2021. https://kagyuoffice.org/life-of-mikyo-dorje/#1.

Kagyu Office. "The Life of the Eighth Karmapa. Year One. Day Four: A Historical Examination of the First Eight Karmapa Reincarnations." Reported February 19, 2021. https://kagyuoffice.org/life-of-mikyo-dorje//#4.

Kagyu Office. "The Life of the Eighth Karmapa. Year One. Day Nine: The Fifth Karmapa Deshin Shekpa and the Ming Emperor Yongle." Reported February 26, 2021, https://kagyuoffice.org/life-of-mikyo-dorje/#9.

Kagyu Office. "The Life of the Eighth Karmapa. Year One. Day Ten: Karmapa Deshin Shekpa, Karmapa Mikyö Dorje and China." Reported February 27, 2021, https://kagyuoffice.org/life-of-mikyo-dorje/#10.

Kagyu Office. "The Life of the Eighth Karmapa. Year One. Day 14: The Great Encampment during the Life of the 4th Karmapa Rölpai Dorje." Reported March 8, 2021. https://kagyuoffice.org/life-of-mikyo-dorje/#14.

Kagyu Office. "The Life of the Eighth Karmapa. Year One. Day 15: Rousing Bodhichitta and the Sacred Gandhola." Reported March 10, 2021. https://kagyuoffice.org/life-of-mikyo-dorje/#15.

Kagyu Office. "The Life of the Eighth Karmapa. Year One. Day 16: Vegetarianism in the Great Encampment and the Three-Fold Purity of Meat in the Vinaya." Reported March 12, 2021. https://kagyuoffice.org/life-of-mikyo-dorje/#16.

Kagyu Office. "The Life of the Eighth Karmapa. Year One. Day 19: Tibetan Art Forms: Menluk, Khyenluk and Gardri." Reported March 16, 2021. https://kagyuoffice.org/life-of-mikyo-dorje/#19.

Kagyu Office. "The Life of the Eighth Karmapa. Year One. Day 20: Personal Reflections, More on Karma Gardri and Homage to the Gurus." Reported March 17, 2021. https://kagyuoffice.org/life-of-mikyo-dorje/#20.

Kagyu Office. "The Life of the Eighth Karmapa. Year Two. Day 1: Remembering Our Good Fortune and the Purpose of Liberation Stories." Reported March 19, 2022. https://kagyuoffice.org/life-of-mikyo-dorje/#21.

Kagyu Office. "The Life of the Eighth Karmapa. Year Two. Day 4: Taking Harm as the Path and the Faults of Sectarianism and Bias." Reported March 25, 2022. https://kagyuoffice.org/life-of-mikyo-dorje/#24.

Kagyu Samye Ling. "Home." Accessed February 13, 2015. https://www.samyeling.org.

Kagyu Samye Ling. "Choje Akong Tulku Rinpoche." Accessed March 12, 2015. https://www.samyeling.org/about/dr-choje-akong-tulku-rinpoche/.

Kalu Rinpoche. *The Chariot for Travelling the Path to Freedom: The life story of Kalu Rinpoche*. Translated by Kenneth I. McLeod. Kagyu Dharma, 1985.

Kalu Rinpoche. *The Dharma: That illuminates all beings impartially like the light of the sun and the moon*. Albany, NY: State University of New York Press, 1986.

Kalu Rinpoche. *Excellent Buddhism: An exemplary life*. Translated by Christiane Buchet. San Francisco, CA: ClearPoint Press, 1995.

Kalu Rinpoche. *The Foundations of Tibetan Buddhism: The gem ornament of manifold oral instructions which benefits each and everyone accordingly*. Ithaca, NY: Snow Lion Publications, 1999.

Kapstein, Matthew. "The Indian Literary Identity in Tibet." In *Literary Cultures in History: Reconstructions from South Asia*, edited by Sheldon Pollock, 747–802. Berkeley, CA: University of California, 2003. Quoted in Ruth E Gamble, "The View from Nowhere: The travels of the Third Karmapa, Rang byung rdo rje in story and songs." PhD diss., The Australian National University, 2013, 42.

Karma Drodül, Lama. *Amrita of Eloquence: A biography of Khenpo Karthar Rinpoche*. Translated by Lama Yeshe Gyamtso. New York: KTD Publications, 2008.

Karma Phuntsho. *The History of Bhutan*. Noida, UP, India; London: Random House India, 2013.

Karma Thinley. "Karmapa Rangjung Rigpe Dorje." In *The History of the Sixteen Karmapas of Tibet*, edited by David Stott, 129–136. Boulder, CO: Prajñā Press, 1980.

Kay, David N. *Tibetan and Zen Buddhism in Britain: Transplantation, development, and adaptation*. London and New York: Routledge Curzon, 2004.

Kernohan, Vivienne. 2020. "ROKPA in Zimbabwe." In *Only the Impossible is Worth Doing: Recollections of the supreme life and activity of Chöje Akong Tulku Rinpoche*, edited by Gelong Thubten and Gelong Trinley, 416–420. Dzalendra Publishing; Rokpa Trust.

Kipling, Rudyard. *Kim*. London: Macmillan, 1963.

Konchog Gyaltsen, Khenpo. Introduction to *The Great Kagyu Masters: The golden lineage treasury*, edited by Victoria Huckenpahler, vii–xvii. Ithaca, NY: Snow Lion Publications, 1990.

Korom, Frank J. "The Role of Tibet in the New Age Movement." In *Imagining Tibet: Perceptions, projections, and fantasies*, edited by Thierry Dodin and Heinz Räther, 167–182. Boston, MA: Wisdom Press, 2001.

Kotwal, Raj. *God's Own Death*. Gangtok, Sikkim: Dr. M. R. Kotwal, M.D. 'Shunyata', 2013.

Kubo, Tsugunari, and AkiraYuyama, trans. *The Lotus Sutra*. Berkeley, CA: Numata Center for Buddhist Translation and Research, 2007.

van der Kuijp, Leonard W. J. "The Dalai Lamas and the Origins of Reincarnate Lamas." In *The Dalai Lamas: A visual history*, edited by Martin Brauen, 14–31. Chicago: Serindia Publications, 2005. Quoted in Ruth E Gamble, "The View from Nowhere: The travels of the Third Karmapa, Rang byung rdo rje in story and songs." PhD diss., The Australian National University, 2013, 90.

Kunsang, Erik Pema, and Marcia Schmidt. *Blazing Splendor: The memoirs of the Dzogchen yogi Tulku Urgyen Rinpoche*. Kathmandu, Nepal: Rangjung Yeshe Publications, 2005.

Kunsang, Pemo and Marie Aubèle. "The Sixteenth Karmapa, Rangjung Rigpe Dorje (1924–1981)." In *History of the Karmapas: The odyssey of the Tibetan masters with the black crown*, 203–233. New York: Snow Lion Publications, 2012.

Kvaerne, Per. "Tibet Images Among Researchers on Tibet." In *Imagining Tibet: Perceptions, projections, and fantasies*, edited by Thierry Dodin and Heinz Räther, 47–63. Boston, MA: Wisdom Press, 2001.

Lavine, Amy. "Tibetan Buddhism in America: The development of American Vajrayāna." In *The Faces of Buddhism in America*, edited by Charles S. Prebish and Kenneth K. Tanaka, 100–115. Berkeley, CA: University of California Press, 1998.

Lavine, Amy. "The Politics of Nostalgia: Social memory and national identity among diaspora Tibetans in New York City." PhD diss., The University of Chicago, 2001.

Layman, Emma M. *Buddhism in America.* Chicago, IL: Nelson-Hall, 1976.

Learman, Linda. "Introduction." In *Buddhist Missionaries in the Era of Globalization*, edited by Linda Learman, 1–21. Honolulu, HI: University of Hawai'i Press, 2005.

Learman, Linda, ed. *Buddhist Missionaries in the Era of Globalization.* Honolulu, HI: University of Hawai'i Press, 2005.

Levine, Norma. *Chronicles of Love and Death: My years with the lost spiritual king of Bhutan.* Kathmandu: Vajra Publications, 2011.

Levine, Norma. "Black Crown, Black Mountains." In *The Miraculous 16th Karmapa: Incredible encounters with the Black Crown Buddha*, compiled by Norma Levine, 327–331. Arcidosso: Shang Shung Publications, 2013.

Levine, Norma. Introduction to *The Miraculous 16th Karmapa: Incredible encounters with the Black Crown Buddha*, compiled by Norma Levine, xvii–xxxi. Arcidosso: Shang Shung Publications, 2013.

Levine, Norma. "Parinirvana of His Holiness the 16th Karmapa." In *The Miraculous 16th Karmapa: Incredible encounters with the Black Crown Buddha*, compiled by Norma Levine, 381–387. Arcidosso: Shang Shung Publications, 2013.

Levine, Norma. *The Spiritual Odyssey of Freda Bedi: England, India, Burma, Sikkim, and beyond.* Arcidosso: Shang Shung Publications, 2018.

Lhundub Sopa, Geshe, and Paul Donnelly. *Like a Waking Dream: The autobiography of Geshe Lhundub Sopa.* Boston, MA: Wisdom Publications, 2012.

Lhundup Damchö. *Karmapa: 900 years.* Himachal Pradesh: Karmapa 900 Organizing Committee; New York: KTD Publications, 2011.

Lief, Judith L. "Transforming Psychology: The development of Maitri Space Awareness practice." In *Recalling Chogyam Trungpa*, edited by Fabrice Midal, 273–287. Boston, MA: Shambhala Publications, 2005.

Lopes, Ana C O. *Tibetan Buddhism in Diaspora: Cultural re-signification in practice and institutions.* London and New York: Routledge, 2015.

Lopez, Donald S. "New Age Orientalism: The case of Tibet." *Tricycle* 3, no. 3 (1994): 37–43.

Lopez, Donald S. *Curators of the Buddha: The study of Buddhism under colonialism.* Chicago and London: University of Chicago Press, 1995.

Lopez, Donald S. *Prisoners of Shangri-La: Tibetan Buddhism and the West.* Chicago: University of Chicago Press, 1998.

Lopez, Donald S. "The Image of Tibet of the Great Mystifiers." In *Imagining Tibet: Perceptions, projections, and fantasies*, edited by Thierry Dodin and Heinz Räther, 183–200. Boston, MA: Wisdom Press, 2001.

Lost Horizon. DVD. Directed by Frank Capra. 1937. California: Sony Pictures Home Entertainment, 2001.

Luyckx, Carlo. 2020. "Akong Rinpoche's Activity in Belgium." In *Only the Impossible is Worth Doing: Recollections of the supreme life and activity of Chöje Akong*

Tulku Rinpoche, edited by Gelong Thubten and Gelong Trinley, 163–180. Dzalendra Publishing; Rokpa Trust.

MacKenzie, Vicki. *The Revolutionary Life of Freda Bedi: British feminist, Indian nationalist, Buddhist nun.* Boulder, CO: Shambhala, 2017.

Manson, Charles E. "Introduction to the Life of Karma Pakshi (1204/6–1283)." *Bulletin of Tibetology* 45, no. 1 (2009): 25–52.

Marie de Voe, Dorsh. "Keeping Refugee Status: A Tibetan perspective." In *People in Upheaval*, edited by Scott Morgan and Elizabeth Colson, 54–65. New York: Center for Migration Studies, 1987. Quoted in Margaret J McLagan, "Mobilizing for Tibet: Transnational politics and diaspora culture in the post-cold war era." PhD diss., New York University, 1996, 210.

Martin, Dan. "Crystals and Images from Bodies, Hearts and Tongues from Fire: Points of relic controversy from Tibetan history." In *Tibetan Studies: Proceedings of the 5th seminar of the International Association for Tibetan Studies NARITA 1989 vol.1*, edited by Ihara Shōren and Yamaguchi Zuihō, 183–191. Chiba, Japan: Naritasan Shinshoji, 1992.

Martin, Dan. "Pearls from Bones: Relics, chortens, tertons and the signs of saintly death in Tibet." *Numen* 41, no. 3 (1994): 273–324.

Martin, Michele. *Music in the Sky: The life, art & teachings of the 17th Karmapa Ogyen Trinley Dorje.* New York: Snow Lion Publications, 2003.

Martinez, Diana. "The Journey of an Image: The western perception of Tibet from 1900–1950." MA diss., The University of Texas at El Paso, 2009.

Maxwell, John. 2020. "The Arrival of Akong Rinpoche in the West." In *Only the Impossible is Worth Doing: Recollections of the supreme life and activity of Chöje Akong Tulku Rinpoche*, edited by Gelong Thubten and Gelong Trinley, 25–32. Dzalendra Publishing; Rokpa Trust.

McGranahan, Carole. *Arrested Histories: Tibet, the CIA, and memories of a forgotten war.* Durham, NC: Duke University Press, 2010.

McKay, Alex C. "'Truth,' Perception, and Politics: The British construction of an image of Tibet." In *Imagining Tibet: Perceptions, projections, and fantasies*, edited by Thierry Dodin and Heinz Räther, 67–89. Boston, MA: Wisdom Press, 2001.

McLagan, Margaret J. "Mobilizing for Tibet: Transnational politics and diaspora culture in the post-cold war era." PhD diss., New York University, 1996.

Mellor, Philip A. "The Cultural Translation of Buddhism: Problems of theory and method arising in the study of Buddhism in England." PhD diss., University of Manchester, 1989. Quoted in David N Kay, *Tibetan and Zen Buddhism in Britain: Transplantation, development, and adaptation.* London and New York: RoutledgeCurzon, 2004, 9.

Midal, Fabrice. *Chögyam Trungpa: His life and vision.* Boston, New York: Shambhala Publications, 2004.

Mila Khyentse Rinpoche. Introduction to *History of the Karmapas: The odyssey of the Tibetan masters with the black crown*, edited by Maureen Lander, 1–25. New York: Snow Lion Publications, 2012.

Morreale, Don, ed. *The Complete Guide to Buddhist America.* Boston, MA: Shambhala, 1998. Quoted in Peter N Gregory, "Describing the Elephant: Buddhism in

America," *Religion and American Culture: A journal of interpretation* 11 (2001): 239.

Mullen, Eve L. "Tibetan Buddhism, American Interests: Influences upon the lay and monastic relationship in New York's Tibetan Buddhist immigrant community." PhD diss., Temple University, 1999.

Mumbie, Sharon. "Dharma In My Bones." In *The Miraculous 16th Karmapa: Incredible encounters with the Black Crown Buddha*, compiled by Norma Levine, 241–244. Arcidosso: Shang Shung Publications, 2013.

Nattier, Jan. "Visible and Invisible: The politics of representation in Buddhist America." *Tricycle: The Buddhist Review* 5 (1995): 42–49.

Nattier, Jan. "Visible and Invisible: The politics of representation in Buddhist America." *Tricycle: The Buddhist Review* 5 (1995): 42–49. Quoted in Elizabeth C Cleland, "The Vajrakilaya Sadhana: An Euro-American experience of a Nyingma ritual." MA diss., Carleton University, 2001, 17.

Nattier, Jan. "Buddhism Comes to Main Street." *Wilson Quarterly* (Spring 1997): 72–80.

Nattier, Jan. "Who is a Buddhist? Charting the Landscape of Buddhist America." In *The Faces of Buddhism in America*, edited by Charles S. Prebish and Kenneth K. Tanaka, 183–195. Berkeley, CA: University of California Press, 1998.

Ngawang Zangpo. Introduction to *Enthronement: The recognition of the reincarnate masters of Tibet and the Himalayas*, translated by Ngawang Zangpo, 15–57. New York: Snow Lion Publications, 1997.

Numrich, Paul D. *Old Wisdom in the New World: Americanization in two immigrant Theravada Buddhist temples*. Knoxville, TN: University of Tennessee Press, 1996.

Numrich, Paul D. "How the Swans Came to Lake Michigan: The social organization of Buddhist Chicago." *Journal for the Scientific Study of Religion* 39, no. 2 (2000): 189–203.

Numrich, Paul D. "Two Buddhisms Further Considered." *Contemporary Buddhism* 4, no. 1 (2003): 55–78.

Numrich, Paul D. "Two Buddhisms Further Considered." In *Buddhist Studies from India to America: Essays in honor of Charles S. Prebish*, edited by D. Keown, 207–233. New York: Routledge, 2006.

Nydahl, Ole. *Entering the Diamond Way: My path among the lamas*. Nevada City, CA: Blue Dolphin Pub, 1985.

Nydahl, Ole. *Riding the Tiger: Twenty years on the road: The risks and joys of bringing Tibetan Buddhism to the west*. Grass Valley, CA: Blue Dolphin Publishing, 1992.

Obadia, Lionel. "Tibetan Buddhism in France: A missionary religion?" *Journal of Global Buddhism* 2 (2001): 91–109.

Oberoi, Goodie. "Dusum Khyenpa." In *The Miraculous 16th Karmapa: Incredible encounters with the Black Crown Buddha*, compiled by Norma Levine, 77–85. Arcidosso: Shang Shung Publications, 2013.

Ogyen Trinley Dorje. Foreword to *Dharma King: The life of the 16th Gyalwang Karmapa in images*, by Damchö D Finnegan, 6–7. New York: KTD Publications; Himachal Pradesh: Altruism Press, 2014.

Paine, Jeffrey. *Re-enchantment: Tibetan Buddhism comes to the West.* New York and London: W.W. Norton, 2004.

Palden, Lama. "Emperor of Love." In *The Miraculous 16th Karmapa: Incredible encounters with the Black Crown Buddha*, compiled by Norma Levine, 131–136. Arcidosso: Shang Shung Publications, 2013.

Pardee, Thomas, Susan Skolnick, and Eric Swanson. *Karmapa: The sacred prophecy.* Edited by Willa Baker, Elisabeth Deran, Robert Kelly, and Jane Madill. New York: The Kagyu Thubten Chöling Publications Committee, 1999.

Peck, Devorah, and the Kagyu Video Project. "Wish Fulfilling Gem, An Interview with H.H. the 16th Gyalwa Karmapa." *The Meridian Trust* video, 48:16. 1983. https://meridian-trust.org/video/wish-fulfilling-gem-an-interview-with-h-h-the-16th-gyalwa-karmapa_dldv000167/.

Pedersen, Poul. "Tibet, Theosophy, and the Psychologization of Buddhism." In *Imagining Tibet: Perceptions, projections, and fantasies*, edited by Thierry Dodin and Heinz Räther, 151–166. Boston, MA: Wisdom Press, 2001.

Percy, Charles H. "Dear Rinpoche." In *Empowerment: The visit of His Holiness the 16th Gyalwa Karmapa to the United States.* Boulder, CO: Vajradhatu Publications, 1976.

Prebish, Charles S. "Reflections of the Transmission of Buddhism to America." In *Understanding the New Religions*, edited by Jacob Needleman and George Baker, 153–172. New York: Seabury Press, 1978. Quoted in Wakoh S Hickey, "Two Buddhisms, Three Buddhisms, and Racism," *Journal of Global Buddhism* 11 (2010): 6.

Prebish, Charles S. *American Buddhism.* North Scituate, MA: Duxbury Press, 1979.

Prebish, Charles S. *American Buddhism.* North Scituate, MA: Duxbury Press, 1979. Quoted in James C Browning, "Tarthang Tulku and the Quest for an American Buddhism." PhD diss., Baylor University, 1986, 181.

Prebish, Charles S. "Two Buddhisms Reconsidered." *Buddhist Studies Review* 10, no. 2 (1993): 187–206.

Quintman, Andrew. *The Yogin and the Madman: Reading the biographical corpus of Tibet's great saint Milarepa.* New York: Columbia University Press, 2014.

Ray, Reginald A. *Secret of the Vajra World: The Tantric Buddhism of Tibet.* New edition. Boston, MA: Shambhala Publications Inc., 2001.

Recalling a Buddha. Memories of the Sixteenth Karmapa: The life and death of an awakened being. DVD. Directed by Gregg Eller. Cambridge, MA: Tendrel Media, 2009.

Rheingans, Jim. "Narratives of Reincarnation, Politics of Power, and the Emergence of a Scholar: The very early years of Mikyö Dorje." In *Lives Lived, Lives Imagined: Biography in the Buddhist traditions*, edited by Covill, Linda, Ulrike Roesler, and Sarah Shaw, 241–297. Boston, MA: [Oxford]: Wisdom Publications, 2010.

Richardson, Hugh. "The Karmapa Sect. A Historical Note." In *High Peaks, Pure Earth: Collected writings on Tibetan history and culture*, edited by Michael Aris, 337–378. London: Serindia, 1998.

Ringu Tulku. 2013. "He Was Always Free." In *The Miraculous 16th Karmapa: Incredible encounters with the Black Crown Buddha*, compiled by Norma Levine, 137–140. Arcidosso: Shang Shung Publications.

Roberts, Peter A. "The Evolution of the Biographies of Milarepa and Rechungpa." In *Lives Lived, Lives Imagined: Biography in the Buddhist traditions*, edited by Linda Covill, Ulrike Roesler, and Sarah Shaw, 181–203. Boston, MA: [Oxford]: Wisdom Publications, 2010.

Robertson, John. "Semiotics, Habitus and Music in the Transmission of Tibetan Culture in Toronto." MA diss., Liberty University, 2011.

Robinson, James B. "The Lives of Indian Buddhist Saints: Biography, hagiography and myth." In *Tibetan Literature: Studies in genre*, edited by José Ignacio Cabezón and Roger R. Jackson, 57–69. New York: Snow Lion Publications, 1996.

Roesler, Ulrike. Introduction to *Lives Lived, Lives Imagined: Biography in the Buddhist traditions*, edited by Linda Covill, Ulrike Roesler, and Sarah Shaw, 1–11. Boston, MA: [Oxford]: Wisdom Publications, 2010.

Roesler, Ulrike. "Operas, Novels, and Religious Instructions: Life-stories of Tibetan Buddhist masters between genre classifications." In *Narrative Pattern and Genre in Hagiographic Life Writing: Comparative perspectives from Asia to Europe*, edited by Stephan Conermann and Jim Rheingans, 113–139. Gottingen: Hubert & Co., 2014.

Roof, Wade C. "A Time When Mountains were Moving." In *Cults in Context: Readings in the study of new religious movements*, edited by Lorne Dawson, 75–104. Toronto: Canadian Scholars' Press, 1996. Quoted in Lynn. P Eldershaw, "Collective Identity and the Post-Charismatic Fate of Shambhala International." PhD diss., University of Waterloo, 2004, 79–80.

Roth, Steve. "When the Iron Bird Flies." In *The Miraculous 16th Karmapa: Incredible encounters with the Black Crown Buddha*, compiled by Norma Levine, 181–194. Arcidosso: Shang Shung Publications, 2013.

Roth, Steve, and Norma Levine. "USA Introduction." In *The Miraculous 16th Karmapa: Incredible encounters with the Black Crown Buddha*, compiled by Norma Levine, 149–156. Arcidosso: Shang Shung Publications, 2013.

Samuel, Geoffrey. *Civilized Shamans: Buddhism in Tibetan societies*. Washington and London: Smithsonian Institution Press, 1993.

Schaeffer, K. R. "Tibetan Biography: Growth and criticism." In *Edition, éditions: L'écrit au Tibet, évolution et devenir*, edited by A. Chayet, C. ScherrerSchaub, F. Robin, and J.-L. Achard, 263–306. Munich: Indus Verlag, 2010.

Scherer, Burkhard. "Conversion, Devotion, and (Trans-)Mission: Understanding Ole Nydahl." In *Buddhists: Understanding Buddhism Through the Lives of Practitioners*, edited by Todd Lewis, 96–106. West Sussex: John Wiley & Sons, Ltd., 2014a.

Scherer, Burkhard. "Trans-European Adaptations in the Diamond Way: Negotiating public opinions on homosexuality in Russia and in the U.K." *Online – Heidelberg Journal of Religions on the Internet* 6 (2014b): 103–125.

Schwieger, Peter. "From Hagiography to Modern Short Story: How to get rid of old social ideals and literary stereotypes." In *Tibetan Literary Genres, Texts, and Text Types: From genre classification to transformation*, edited by Jim Rheingans, 270–278. Leiden; Boston, MA: Brill, 2015.

Seager, Richard H. *Buddhism in America*. New York: Columbia University Press, 1999.
Seager, Richard H. "American Buddhism in the Making." In *Westward Dharma: Buddhism beyond Asia*, edited by Charles S. Prebish and Martin Baumann, 106–119. Berkeley, CA: University of California Press, 2002.
Sera Jey Monastic University. "Re-establishment at Bylakuppe." Published May 1, 2016. https://www.serajeymonastery.org/histroy/5-re-establishment-at-bylakuppe.
Sernesi, Marta. "To Establish the Qualities of the Master: Considerations on early bKa' brgyud hagiographical writings." In *Tīrthayātrā: Essays in honour of Stefano Piano*, edited by Pinuccia Caracchi, Antonella Serena Comba, Alessandra Consolaro, and Alberto Pelissero, 401–424. Alessandria: Edizioni dell'Orso, 2010.
Sernesi, Marta. "A Prayer to the Complete Liberation of Mi la ras pa." In *Narrative Pattern and Genre in Hagiographic Life Writing: Comparative perspectives from Asia to Europe*, edited by Stephan Conermann and Jim Rheingans, 141–185. Gottingen: Hubert & Co., 2014.
Sernesi, Marta. "Biography and Hagiography: Tibet." *BEB*, no. 1 (2015): 734–743.
Shaw, Sarah. "And That was I: How the Buddha himself creates a path between biography and autobiography." In *Lives Lived, Lives Imagined: Biography in the Buddhist traditions*, edited by Linda Covill, Ulrike Roesler, and Sarah Shaw, 15–47. Boston, MA: [Oxford]: Wisdom Publications, 2010.
Sherap Phuntsok, Khenpo. "The Sixteenth Karmapa Rangjung Rigpe Dorje." In *The Illustrated Lives of the Five Kagyu Forefathers and the Seventeen Karmapas*, translated by Michele Martin, 169–176. Kathmandu, Nepal: Thrangu Tashi Choling Monastery, 2014.
Silk, Jonathan A. "The Fruits of Paradox: On the religious architecture of the Buddha's life story." *Journal of the American Academy of Religion* 71, no. 4 (2003): 863–881.
Sood, Shubhi. *Bhutan, 100 Years of Wangchuck Vision*. Noida: S.D.S. Publishers, 2008.
Sperling, Elliot. "'Orientalism' and Aspects of Violence in the Tibetan Tradition." In *Imagining Tibet: Perceptions, projections, and fantasies*, edited by Thierry Dodin and Heinz Räther, 317–330. Boston, MA: Wisdom Press, 2001.
Speyer, J. S. Introduction to *Jātakamālā or Garland of Birth-Stories*. Translated by J. S. Speyer, edited by F. Max Muller, xv–xxvi. Ancient Buddhist Texts, 2010. https://www.ancient-buddhist-texts.net/English-Texts/Garland-of-Birth-Stories/Garland-of-Birth-Stories.pdf.
Stoddard, Heather. "The Development in Perceptions of Tibetan Art: From golden idols to ultimate reality." In *Imagining Tibet: Perceptions, projections, and fantasies*, edited by Thierry Dodin and Heinz Räther, 223–253. Boston, MA: Wisdom Press, 2001.
Surya Das, Lama. "Black Crown Lama: The 16th Gyalwang Karmapa." In *The Miraculous 16th Karmapa: Incredible encounters with the Black Crown Buddha*, compiled by Norma Levine, 3–13. Arcidosso: Shang Shung Publications, 2013.

Swearer, Donald. "Tensions in American Buddhism." *Religion and Ethics Newsweekly*, July 6, 2001. http://www.pbs.org/wnet/religionandethics/week445/buddhism.html.

Tamney, Joseph B. Afterword to *North American Buddhists in Social Context*, edited by Paul D. Numrich, 225–241. Leiden and Boston, MA: Brill, 2008.

Tara Rokpa Therapy. "History." Accessed March 24, 2015. http://www.tararokpa.org/therapy/about/history/index.php.

Tashi Tsering. "A Biography of His Holiness The 16th Karmapa Entitled 'A Droplet from the Infinite Ocean-Like Outer Biography of Lokeshvara: The great sixteenth holder of the black crown'." Translated by Migmar Tsering, edited by Jeremy Russell, *The Tibet Journal* 9, no. 3 (1984): 3–20.

Tashi Tsering. "A Biographical Sketch of the 16th Karmapa." *Tibetan Review* (August 1992): 14–17.

Templeman, David. "The Mirror of Life: The structure of a 16th century Tibetan hagiography." In *Religion and Biography in China and Tibet*, edited by Benjamin Penny, 132–147. Richmond, VA: Curzon, 2002.

Tenpel. "Propaganda: The making of the holy lama Ole Nydahl." *Buddhism Controversy Blog*, June 30, 2014. https://buddhism-controversy-blog.com/2014/06/30/propaganda-the-making-of-the-holy-lama-ole-nydahl/.

Terhune, Lea. *Karmapa: The Politics of Reincarnation*. Somerville, MA: Wisdom Publications, 2004.

The Fortunate Aeon: How the thousand Buddhas become enlightened. Berkeley, CA: Dharma Publishing, 1986.

The Lion's Roar: The classic portrait of the 16th Gyalwa Karmapa. DVD. Directed by Mark Elliott. USA: Festival Media, 2006.

The Nālandā Translation Committee, trans. *The Rain of Wisdom: The essence of the ocean of true meaning*. Boulder, CO and London: Shambhala, 1980.

The Tibetan & Himalayan Library. "Literature." Accessed March 6, 2017. http://www.thlib.org/encyclopedias/literary/canons/kt/catalog.php#cat=d/k.

Tischer, John. "Blessing Power." In *The Miraculous 16th Karmapa: Incredible encounters with the Black Crown Buddha*, compiled by Norma Levine, 259. Arcidosso: Shang Shung Publications, 2013.

Tiso, Francis V. *Liberation in One Lifetime: Biographies and teachings of Milarepa*. Isernia: Proforma, 2010.

gTsang smyon Heruka. "The Treasure Trove of Blessings." Translated by Marta Sernesi. In *Narrative Pattern and Genre in Hagiographic Life Writing: Comparative perspectives from Asia to Europe*, edited by Stephan Conermann and Jim Rheingans, 181–185. Gottingen: Hubert & Co., 2014.

Tsangnyön Heruka. *The Life of Milarepa*. Translated by Andrew Quintman. London: Penguin Books, 2010.

Tsering Namgyal Khortsa. "The Holder of the Vajra Crown: The Sixteenth Karmapa." In *His Holiness the 17th Karmapa Ogyen Trinley Dorje: A biography*, 79–91. New Delhi: Hay House, 2013.

Tsering Shakya. "Who are the Prisoners?" *Journal of the American Academy of Religion* 69, no. 1 (2001): 183–189.

Tsondru, Lama. "The Origins of Dharma in Spain." In *Only the Impossible is Worth Doing: Recollections of the supreme life and activity of Chöje Akong Tulku Rinpoche*, edited by Gelong Thubten and Gelong Trinley, 181–194. Dzalendra Publishing; Rokpa Trust, 2020.

Tuttle, Gray. "Uniting Religion and Politics in a Bid for Autonomy: Lamas in exile in China and America." In *Buddhist Missionaries in the Era of Globalization*, edited by Linda Learman, 210–232. Honolulu, HI: University of Hawai'i Press, 2005.

Tweed, Thomas A. "Night-Stand Buddhists and Other Creatures: Sympathizers, adherents, and the study of religion." In *American Buddhism: Methods and findings in recent scholarship*, edited by Duncan Ryuken Williams and Christopher S. Queen, 71–90. London: Curzon Press, 1999.

Tweed, Thomas A. *The American Encounter with Buddhism, 1844–1912: Victorian culture and the limits of dissent*. Chapel Hill, NC: University of North Carolina Press, 2000.

Tweed, Thomas A. "Who is a Buddhist? Night-Stand Buddhists and Other Creatures." In *Westward Dharma: Buddhism beyond Asia*, edited by Charles S. Prebish and Martin Baumann, 17–33. Berkeley, CA: University of California Press, 2002.

University of Vienna. "Full-text search in electronic versions of the Kanjur." Accessed March 6, 2017. https://www.istb.univie.ac.at/kanjur/rktsneu/ekanjur/.

Vostrikov, A. I. *Tibetan Historical Literature*. Surrey: Curzon Press, 1994.

Wang, Meng. "The Tension Between the Narratives of Mi La Ras Pa as an Emanation and an Ordinary Person in the Mi La rNam Thar Tradition of Tibetan Buddhism." MA diss., SOAS, University of London, 2014.

Waterhouse, Helen J. "Authority and Adaptation: A case study in British Buddhism." PhD diss., University of the West of England, 1997.

Webster, Ross R. "Tibetan Buddhists, Poetry Wars and the Naropa Institute in the People's Republic of Boulder, Colorado." MA diss., The University of Colorado, 2012.

Welwood, John. "Discovering Buddha Nature in Disneyland." In *The Miraculous 16th Karmapa: Incredible encounters with the Black Crown Buddha*, compiled by Norma Levine, 263–268. Arcidosso: Shang Shung Publications, 2013.

Whitehead, Andrew. *The Lives of Freda: The Political, Spiritual and Personal Journeys of Freda Bedi*. Delhi, India: Speaking Tiger Books, 2019. Kindle.

Wilde, Oscar. *Complete Works of Oscar Wilde*. New York: Harper & Row, 1989. Quoted in Donald S Lopez, "New Age Orientalism: The case of Tibet," *Tricycle* 3, no. 3 (1994): 183.

Williams, Duncan R., and Christopher S. Queen, eds. *American Buddhism: Methods and findings in recent scholarship*. London: Curzon Press, 1999.

Willems, Joost. "Under Karmapa's Black Crown." In *The Miraculous 16th Karmapa: Incredible encounters with the Black Crown Buddha*, compiled by Norma Levine, 355–357. Arcidosso: Shang Shung Publications, 2013.

Worley, Lee. "The Space Between: The theater legacy of Chögyam Trungpa." In *Recalling Chögyam Trungpa*, edited by Fabrice Midal, 289–304. Boston, New York: Shambhala Publications, 2005.

Wyler, Lea. "Changing Ourselves – Changing the World." In *Only the Impossible is Worth Doing: Recollections of the supreme life and activity of Chöje Akong Tulku Rinpoche*, edited by Gelong Thubten and Gelong Trinley, 421–426. Dzalendra Publishing; Rokpa Trust, 2020.

Wyler, Lea. "ROKPA of Dr Akong Rinpoche." In *Only the Impossible is Worth Doing: Recollections of the supreme life and activity of Chöje Akong Tulku Rinpoche*, edited by Gelong Thubten and Gelong Trinley, 333–415. Dzalendra Publishing; Rokpa Trust, 2020.

Yeshe Losal Rinpoche, Chöje Lama. "The Early Life of Chöje Akong Tulku Rinpoche." In *Only the Impossible is Worth Doing: Recollections of the supreme life and activity of Chöje Akong Tulku Rinpoche*, edited by Gelong Thubten and Gelong Trinley, 9–24. Dzalendra Publishing; Rokpa Trust, 2020.

York, M. "The New Age in Britain Today." *Religion Today* 9, no. 3 (1994): 14–21. Quoted in Denise Cush, "British Buddhism and the New Age," *Journal of Contemporary Religion* 11, no. 2 (1996): 196.

Yosay Wangdi. "Echoes of an Agonized Nation: Transformations in Tibetan identity in diaspora." PhD diss., University of Nevada, Reno, 2003.

Zablocki, A. "Transnational Tulkus: The globalization of Tibetan Buddhist reincarnation." In *TransBuddhism: Transmission, Translation, Transformation*, edited by Nalini Bhushan, Jay L Garfield, and Abraham Zablocki, 43–53. Amherst: University of Massachusetts Press, 2009.

Zangmo, Lama. "Reflections on Retreat." In *Only the Impossible is Worth Doing: Recollections of the supreme life and activity of Chöje Akong Tulku Rinpoche*, edited by Gelong Thubten and Gelong Trinley, 131–149. Dzalendra Publishing, Rokpa Trust, 2020.

Zhanag Dzogpa Tenzin Namgyal. "The Wondrous Activities of His Holiness the 16th Gyalwang Karmapa." In *The Miraculous 16th Karmapa: Incredible encounters with the Black Crown Buddha*, compiled by Norma Levine, 29–51. Arcidosso: Shang Shung Publications, 2013.

Index

abbot of the Da-Jue Temple, 189
abbot of the Lian-Yin Temple, 189
The Adventure of the Empty House (Doyle), 31
aggressive materialism, 31
Akṣobhya, 60–61, 70, 85
American/European interpretation of Tibet, 39
American/European Metanarrative, 39
Amitābha, 60–61, 70
Anglo-Tibetan imperial encounter, 31–32
anti-Orientalism, 195
Apadāna, 12
arhat, 10, 60, 208
Ashram of Baba Muktananda, 189
Asia(n): Buddhist countries, 46; Buddhists, 41, 45; Buddhist teachers, 40–41, 44–45; culture, 30, 42; Dharma centres, 136; political refugees, 42; religions, 31, 43, 45, 156, 188
Ato Rinpoche, 172n25
Aural Transmission of Saṃvara, first cycle of, 9
autobiographies, 6–7
Avalokiteśvara, 59, 62–65, 84, 87, 88, 106, 195, 207–8, 233, 238, 243, 252

Baker, Richard, 189

Barawa, Je, 11
Barwe Gyaltsen, 63
Bateson, Gregory, 159
Bedi, Freda, 151–56, 162, 189–90, 196–98; bridging the gap between Tibetan tradition and Western culture, 155, 197; Dharma Centre of Canada, 155; Dharma in Southeast Asia, 154; expansion of Kagyu school, 154–55; founding of the Young Lamas' Home School, 152–53; Gandhi's satyagrahi, 151; Karmapa's tours to Europe and North America, 154–55; Missamari refugee camp, 153; mission to Burma with UN Social Services Planning Commission, 151; modern education, 153; non-sectarian monastery, 154; as Sister Palmo, 154–55; social welfare adviser on Tibetan refugees, 151–52; spiritual path in Tibetan Buddhism, 151; Tantric initiations, 154; Tibetan Buddhist centre in England, 153; Tibetan Friendship Group, 152; transmission of Tibetan Buddhism to the West, 151; Trungpa and Akong, 153–54; Young Lamas' Home School in India, 197
Bhadrakalpika Sūtra, 61
Bimbisara, king, 63, 73
biography/biographies, 6–7

Black Crown Ceremony, 83–89, 106, 160, 184–86, 198; belief in the tradition, 83; Buddha succession, 84; crown as 'the ornament of the Buddhas' emanation,' 84; crown for lineage and power, 84; Dalai Lama's perception, 85; experiences of the West, 88–89; history of the material crown, 85–86; invisible crown, 85, 89; method to liberate beings through visual contact, 87; origin of the Black Crown, 84–85; replica to Fifth Karmapa, 85; representation of Thongdrol, 83; revised account by Ogyen Trinley Dorje, 85–86; ritual ceremony, 86–87; sacred Buddhist rite, 88; Second Karmapa, Karma Pakshi about crown, 85–86; Shanagpa, 83–84; six liberating factors, 84; Sixteenth Karmapa on multiple occasions, 87; symbolism of crown by Rangjung Dorje, 86; in the West, 88
Blackfoot in Canada, 189
Blavatsky, Helena, 31, 33–35, 41, 45, 47
The Blue Annals, 16
Bodhi, Ananda, 174n61, 248
bodhicitta, 60–62, 70, 89, 187, 208–9, 240, 249, 253
Bodhisatta, 12; path to buddhahood, 12
bodhisattva, 10, 12–13, 15–18, 59–67, 89, 134, 168, 170, 201, 203, 208, 210, 215, 219, 226, 233, 240, 253; in the Mahāyāna, 10
Bodhisattva Avalokiteśvara, 59, 62–64, 84, 87–88, 106, 195, 207–8, 233, 238, 243, 252
Books: aligned with China, 39; sympathetic to the Tibetan cause, 39
Bowie, David, 156
Bradley, Tom, 191
Buddhavaṃsa, 12
Buddhism: degeneration from the original, 30; in Great Britain, 45–48; in pre-modern Tibet, 197; psychological interpretation of, 34; as shared identity, 37; in United States, 41–44
Buddhist Association of the United States, 189
Buddhist centres: in England, 153; in London, 151; Thai and Sri Lankan, 189; Tibetan, 1; in Western Europe, 153, 156
Buddhist life-writing, 2, 4, 13
Buddhist Lodge, 46
Buddhist Tantra, 189
Buddhist texts, 38, 41, 45, 196

Cage, John, 159
Cakrasaṃvara, 4, 61, 214, 238, 247–48
Cariyāpiṭaka, 12
change (adaptation), 1
Chanyun, founding abbot of the Lian-Yin Temple in Taiwan, 189
Chia Theng Shen, 186, 192n24, 202
Chime Rinpoche, 172n24
Chinese Cultural Revolution, 36
Chinese rule in Tibet, 35, 39, 107
Chokgyur Lingpa, 65–66, 135, 222, 229, 233, 243, 250; Terma prophecies, 65–66; Terma teaching to Minling Chung Rinpoche, 135
Chokyi Nyima, 115, 135, 196
Christian Center of Dialogue in Denmark, 189
Christianity, 31, 45–46, 168–69, 199
Christian values, 169, 189, 198
cinematic myths of Tibet, 32
code of conduct, on Vinaya, 132–33, 243
Cohen, Leonard, 156
Cold War, 35
The Collected Works of the Sixteenth Karmapa, 61, 204n1
colonial government and Tibetan ruling class, relationship, 31–32
communism, 35, 39, 231
A Completely Clear Mirror, the Catalogue of Tsurphu (Palsang), 16
Conermann, Stephan, 7

Conference of all Tibetan Schools, 108, 136
connections with Bhutan, Sikkim and India: building of monasteries, 114–17; flight and resettlement, 113; help during flight into exile, 113; help during illness, 116–17; historical connections with Bhutan and Sikkim, 111; Karma Kagyu monasteries in Sikkim, 112; Karmapa and Indian Prime Minister and President, 115; Karmapa and ruling class of Bhutan, 111; Karmapa conferred on Sidkeong Namgyal monastic vows, 112; Karmapa incarnations and the royal family of Sikkim, 112; lama-patron relationship with Bhutan and Sikkim, 110, 114; monastic community in exile, 114; preservation efforts, 116; Rumtek, headquarters for Dharma centres, 115; Sikkim and India for monastic seat in exile, 114–15; Sixteenth Karmapa and Tashi Namgyal, 113; Sixteenth Karmapa and Jigme Wangchuck, 111–12; thangka of the Fifteenth Karmapa, Khakyap Dorje, 111; visit of the Fourth Shamar, Chödrak Yeshe, 111
consistency (continuity with tradition), 1
Conze, Edward, 31, 46
counterculture movement, 29, 40, 42–43, 47, 156, 158, 162, 184, 188, 197–98
cross-cultural phenomenon, 1, 195; encounter between Europeans/Americans and Tibetans in exile, 36; exchange between Tibetan Buddhism and the West, 38, 155, 183; interaction, 2; transmission as, 1

Dalai Lama: All-Knowing, 222, 227–30; Fifth, 6, 7, 11, 13; Fourteenth, Tenzin Gyatso, 105, 136; perceived tension with, 110; perception, Black Crown Ceremony, 85; Phuntsok Khyilpa hall for the visit, 106, 233; relationship between Karmapa and, 105–9; Tantric empowerment from, 106, 108; Thirteenth, 67, 85, 89, 211, 215
Dass, Ram, 159
David-Neel, Alexandra, 31, 33, 35; Occult Tibet, 33, 35
death and Thukdam, 89–93; ability to control pain through meditation, 90; attainment of the vajra-like *samādhi*, 92; death of Sixteenth Karmapa, 90; demonstration of impermanence to disciples, 89; funeral ceremony, 92–93; miracles, 89; relics as signs of saintly death, 89; symbol of heart transmission to primary disciples, 92–93; Thukdam, description, 91–92
deluded appearance, 11
Derge Kangyur, 131, 196–97
Dezhung Rinpoche, Sakya lama, 189
Dhagpo Kagyu Ling, 165
Dharamsala, 36, 61, 108–10, 136, 237, 241, 245
Dharma, preservation of: emergence of Ganden Phodrang, 129; Great Encampment, 129; Karmapa in Rumtek, 130; Karmapa's duty as spiritual leader, 129; non-sectarian approach, 135–36; re-establishment of monastic community, 131–35; revival of the Dharma, 130; teaching of the Practice Lineage, 129
Dharma centres, 1, 38, 115, 135; in Africa, 162; Asian, 136; of Canada, 155, 174n61; in Europe, 155, 162, 186–87, 195; founding of, 186–89, 198; In France, 164, 186; Rumtek as the headquarters, 115, 186, 196; of Sakya and Nyingma schools, 189; in Scandinavia, 165; Tibetan lamas from India placed in, 169; in United States, 155, 160, 186–87, 195. *See also* monasteries and Dharma centres, founding of
Dharmadhatu, 162, 250
dharmakāya, 15, 18, 60, 90

Dharma Publishing, 38
Dhātuvibhaṅga Sutta, 14
diaspora, 35–39; collective openness within, 29, 35–36, 38; global, transcultural character of the transmission, 1; Jewish, 36; Tibetan, 29, 32, 35–36, 39, 40, 44, 110, 116, 152, 190, 196
Dilley, Barbara, 159
donations of land from devotees, 186
Dönmo Ripa, 15
Dönden, Thongwa, 86
Dönyö, Lodrö, 61, 132
Dorje, Changchub, 112
Dorje, Chöying, 85, 111, 135
Dorje, Dudul, 131
Dorje, Khakyap, 16, 59–60, 66–67, 111–12, 134
Dorje, Mikyö, 10–11, 86
Dorje, Ogyen Trinley, 4–5, 85–86
Dorje, Rangjung, 3, 86, 163
Dorje, Rangjung Rigpe, 1, 4, 16–17, 59–67, 84–85, 87, 90, 105, 110, 111, 113, 132, 134–35, 152, 195, 209, 216; Bodhisattva Avalokiteśvara, 195; as Dharma King, 195; manifestation of Sixth Buddha of Fortunate Aeon Siṃha, 195
Dorje, Rolpe, 86
Dorje, Thekchok, 112
Dorje, Wangchuk, 87
Dorje, Yeshe, 67
Dorje Dze Ö, 15
Dudjom Rinpoche, Nyingma lama, 189
Dzogchen Ponlop, 115, 134–35, 196
Dzogchen Thubten Chökyi Dorje, 66–67, 210
Dzongsar monastery, 87, 220

The Eight Great Chariots of the Practice Lineage, 133, 219, 239
Eighth Karmapa, Mikyö Dorje, 10–11, 86
Eighth Situ Chökyi Jungne, 16, 219, 253
Eleventh Karmapa, Yeshe Dorje, 67
Eleventh Situ, Pema Wangchok Gyalpo, 67, 134, 210, 211, 216, 224
emperor of Jang, 85, 95n18
Empowerment (produced by Trungpa), 190
engagement with governments and politicians, 190–91; connections with Bhutan, Sikkim and India, 190; disinterest in politics, 190; highest protocol reception in Canada, 191; Tibetan diaspora seen by United States, 190; US interest in Karmapa, 190–91
enlightenment, 10, 12–16, 43, 87, 158, 170, 225
Entering the Way of the Bodhisattva (Śāntideva), 163
Entering the Ways of the Wise (Mipham), 163
Ethnic Tibet, 36
European travellers and writers, accounts of, 32–33
Evans-Wentz, W. Y., 31
exile government, dissociation from, 105–10; Avalokiteśvara empowerment to Karmapa, 106; Black Crown Ceremony, 106; Conference of all Tibetan Schools, 108; disinterest of Karmapa in worldly power, 105; Sixteenth Karmapa and Fourteenth Dalai Lama, 105; flight into exile, 107; Gyalo Thondup's reform, 109; offensive in Chamdo by China, 107; perceived tension with Dalai Lama, 110; Phuntsok Khyilpa hall for the Dalai Lama's visit, 106; political tension between China and Tibet, 106; relationship between Karmapa and Dalai Lama, 106–7; Shamar incarnations, 107–8; Tantric empowerment from Dalai Lama, 106, 108; Thirteen Group, 108–9; tulku lineage banned by Lhasa government, 108

fact and fiction, division between, 7
Fifteenth Karmapa, Khakyap Dorje, 16, 59–60, 66–67, 111–12, 134, 208–10
Fifth Dalai Lama, 6–7, 11, 13; *rangnam*, 6, 11; use of his *namthar* in production of *rangnam*, 7
Fifth Karmapa, Deshin Shekpa, 85
First Karmapa, Düsum Khyenpa, 3–4, 61–62, 64, 65, 69n29, 84–85, 87, 207, 208, 220–21; Black Crown, 3–4; crown and name for Karmapa lineage, 3–4; primary disciple of Gampopa, 4; First Karmapa, 3; Karma Monastery, 4; man of karma, 4; Tsurphu Kagyu, 4
Fourteenth Karmapa, Thekchok Dorje, 112, 218
Fourth Karmapa, Rolpe Dorje, 86
France, donation of land in, 186
friendship with other Buddhist traditions and religions, 188–89, 199; Ashram of Baba Muktananda, 189; Blackfoot in Canada, 189; Christian Center of Dialogue in Denmark, 189; counterculture movement, 188; Dharma centres of Sakya and Nyingma schools, 189; friendship with the Catholic Church, 199; Hinduism, 189; Hopi in United States, 189; inclusion of Theravāda and Zen traditions, 188; interfaith conference in Washington, 189; meeting with dean of Westminster Abbey, 189; meeting with Pope Paul VI, 189; non-sectarian approach, 188; spiritual tolerance, 189; Thai and Sri Lankan Buddhist centres, 189; Theravāda, 189; Zen Buddhism, 189

Gampopa, 4, 5, 15, 93, 133, 158, 163, 165, 170, 223–24
Ganden Palace, 67
Geleg Tenzin, 61
Gesar of Ling, king, 66, 209

Ginsberg, Allen, 159
global expansion: Karma Kagyu lineage, 116, 155–56; of Tibetan Buddhist school, 1, 103, 154
glorified self-image, 13
God Save the King (band), 32
Golden Rosaries, *namthar* collection of lineage teachers, 9, 14
Great Encampment, 129, 137n5, 213–14, 217–18, 225, 228, 233–35
Great Game between Britain and Russia, 30
The Great Tibetan Dictionary, 5
Grof, Stanislav, 159
A Guide to the Bodhisattva's Way of Life (Śāntideva), 5
guru-disciple relationship, 188
Gyalo Thondup, 108–9; efforts of modernisation, 109; reform, 109; United Party, 108–9
Gyalthangpa, 15–16
Gyalwa Chokyang, 62, 65–66, 208
Gyalwa Yungtönpa, 11

hagiography/hagiographies, 6–7; bridge between history and symbolic literature, 8; divide between autobiographies, biographies and, 7; European sacred auto/biography, 6; hagiographical dimension, 8, 10, 15; history and symbolic literature, 8; teacher's life, 6, 8, 10
Halifax, Joan, 159
Hayward, Jeremy, 159
Hidden Predictions (Padmasambhava), 64
Hilton, James, 33
Himalayan Buddhist Society in Calcutta, 136, 249
Himalayan dogma, 40
Hinduism, 189
Hindu Tantra, 189
'histories of incarnations,' 13
Holmes, Ken, 63, 157, 163–66, 170, 185
Hopi community, 155, 189

idealisation of Tibet, 29–39; impact on Western adherents, 29; Tibetan contribution. *See* Tibetan contribution; western imagination of Tibet. *See* western imagination of Tibet
identification with enlightened beings, 59–66; as the bodhisattva Siṃhanāda, 63; emanation of Avalokiteśvara, 65; Karma Ngedön Tengye, 59–62, 64; Karmapa and Padmasambhava, 66; Karmapa as *Lokeśvara*, 62; Karmapa as Padmasambhava, 62–63; Karmapa incarnations, as Indian and Tibetan, 62–63; Karmapa incarnations as Avalokiteśvara, 62; Karmapa's twenty-one incarnations, 65; Khyentse Özer, 62–66; Lodrö Dönyö, 61; manifestations of the Karmapa, 62–63; prophecies in Sūtra, Tantra and Terma, 63–66, 73n57, 75n77; with the Sixth Buddha, 62; Sixth Buddha of Fortunate Aeon, 63; spiritual power, 64; in succession in unbroken lineage, 64; Tashi Tsering, 61–65; Terma of Nyang Ral Nyima Özer, 65
India: Indian Buddhism, 14; *jātaka*s, 12–13; Karmapa incarnations, as Indian, 62–63; lamas from India as teachers in Dharma centres, 169; *mahāsiddha*s, 7–8, 10–11, 15–16, 66; monastic seat in exile, 114–15; rebuilding monastic community, 187; refugees resettlement of by Government of India, 37; retreat centres, 170; study of Indian *mahāsiddha*s, 7–8; support for Karmapa from Indian government, 115; Young Lamas' Home School in India, 197. *See also* connections with Bhutan, Sikkim and India
Indian *jātaka*s, 12–13

Indian *mahāsiddha*s, 7–8, 10–11, 15–16, 66
Indira Gandhi, 115, 117, 151–52
Indrabhuti, King, 63
interfaith conference in Washington, 189
interfaith dialogue, 149, 155, 168, 189, 199; with the Catholic Church, 149; with Christianity, 199; on a global level, 189
invisible crown, 85, 89

Jamgon Kongtrul, 66, 88, 90–91, 115, 129, 133–34, 163, 166–67, 211, 214, 226, 227, 229–30, 238, 249
Jātakamālā, 13
Jātaka-Nidāna, 12
jātaka tales, 12–13; form of Bodhisatta- and Buddha-biography, 12; *jātaka*s in *paritta* collections, 12
Jātakatthavaṇṇanā, 12
Je Barawa, 11
Jigme Wangchuck, King, 87, 111–12, 223
Juchen Thupten Namgyal, 61, 110
Jung, Carl G., 34

Kadam school, 13
Kagyu centres, 111, 195
Kagyu International Headquarters/Office at Rumtek, 186
Kalu Rinpoche, 7, 10, 129, 163, 167–71, 197; arrival at Samye Ling, 170–71; Christian values and Buddhism, 169; disseminating Dharma in the West, 167; interfaith dialogue in the West, 168; Kagyu teachings, 197; lamas as resident teachers, 169; retreat centres in Dalhusy, 167; retreat centres in the West, 197; retreat programmes, 170; Tantric Buddhism, 171; three *yāna*s, 170; Tibetan lamas in exile, 167; title of Khenpo, 167; traditional teaching methods, 169–70; transmission strategy, 169; visits in United States, 168

Karma Kagyu, 20n16; centre in Bhutan at Thangbi, 111; dispute between the Gelug, 108; expansion in the West, 110; lineage, 2, 29, 57, 65, 111, 149, 156, 163, 188; model of spiritual perfection, 4; monasteries, 112, 225, 232, 237, 250; multilayered narrative structure, 4; school, 1, 61, 107–8, 112, 116, 133, 135, 187; tradition, 153, 156, 163, 186, 233; tradition of Buddhist life-writing, 4; Trusts, 186

Karma Monastery, 4, 65, 86, 212, 218, 219, 222

Karma Ngedön Tengye, 16–18, 59–62, 64, 84; essence of holy teachers *vidyādhara*s and *siddha*s, 59; source of the Dharma, 59

Karmapa: attainment of buddhahood, 60; *bodhicitta* in ten perfections, 60; description, 60; embodiment of the activity of the buddhas, 60–61; identified as *Lokeśvara*, 62; instant buddhahood, 60; outer, inner and secret aspects of life, 60; performs activity of buddhas, 60; and ruling class of Bhutan, 111; spiritual accomplishment in the Mantrayāna, 60; strategies and success, 195–96; vast deeds of bodhisattva, 61, 208; visit to Bhutan, 75n72

Karmapa and the Dalai Lama, relationship between, 106–7

Karmapa conferred on Sidkeong Namgyal monastic vows, 112

Karmapa incarnation: buddha and bodhisattva manifestation, 59; prediction of own reincarnations, 59; and the royal family of Sikkim, 112

Karma Pakshi, Second Karmapa, 3–4, 85–86, 218, 238, 250, 251

Karmapa lineage, 18n1; ancient lines of tulkus, 3; interpretation by Kagyu tradition, 3; meaning, 3; origin of, 3; tulku lineage, a lama's reincarnation, 3; twelfth-century Tibet, 3

Karmapas: Eighth Karmapa, Mikyö Dorje, 10–11, 86; Eleventh Karmapa, Yeshe Dorje, 67; Fifteenth Karmapa, Khakyap Dorje, 16, 59–60, 66–67, 111–12, 134, 208–10; Fifth Karmapa, Deshin Shekpa, 85; First Karmapa, Düsum Khyenpa, 3–4, 61–62, 64, 65, 84–85, 87, 207, 208, 220–21; Fourteenth Karmapa, Thekchok Dorje, 112, 218; Fourth Karmapa, Rolpe Dorje, 86; Ninth Karmapa, Wangchuk Dorje, 87; Second Karmapa Karma Pakshi, 3–4, 85–86, 218, 238, 250, 251; Seventeenth Karmapa, Ogyen Trinley Dorje, 4–5, 85–86; Seventh Karmapa, Chödrak Gyatso, 3, 86, 135; Sixteenth Karmapa, Rangjung Rigpe Dorje, 1, 4, 16–17, 59–67, 84–85, 87, 90, 105, 110, 111, 113, 132, 134–35, 152, 195, 209, 216; Sixth Karmapa, Thongwa Dönden, 86; Tenth Karmapa, Chöying Dorje, 85, 111, 135; Third Karmapa, Rangjung Dorje, 3, 86, 163; Thirteenth Karmapa, Dudul Dorje, 131; Twelfth Karmapa, Changchub Dorje, 112

Karmapa's institute in Delhi, 115

Karma Rabtenling, 112

Karma Tashi Chokhorling, 112

Karma Thegsum Choling, 186

Karma Thubten Choling, 112

Karma Triyana Dharmachakra (KTD), 186, 191

Kharag Gomchung, 63

Khenpo Tsultrim Gyamtso, 165, 185

Khyentse Özer, 60, 62, 64–66

Kim (Kipling), 31

Kipling, Rudyard, 31, 33

Kongtrul, Jamgon, 66, 88, 90–91, 115, 129, 133–34, 163, 166–67, 211, 214, 226, 227, 229–30, 238, 249

Kotwal, Raj, 90–92, 99n80

Kunley, Drukpa, 11

Laing, R. D., 156
Lama Anagarika Govinda, 31
Lama Gendun Rinpoché, 166
lama-patron relationship, 110–16
lamas as resident teachers in monasteries/Dharma centres, 169, 186
Lama Zhang, 60, 62
Laṅkāvatāra Sūtra, 84
Legpakye, Devaputra, 61, 208
Levy, Mitchell, 90–92, 99n80
Lhasa, 32, 67, 105–9, 111, 152, 210, 215, 222, 227–30, 233–34, 241; intercultural dialogue between British filmmakers and, 32; Karmapa and Dalai Lama meetings, 107; Karmapa's first audience, fourteenth reincarnation of the All-Knowing Dalai Lama, 222; Karmapa's visits, 107; Younghusband expedition, 111, 152
The Liberation of *Śrīsambhava*, 5
liberation of Tibet from oppressive theocracy, 39
life-writing in Tibetan Buddhism: bias towards historical facts, 7; comparison with European sacred auto/biography or hagiography, 6; division between fact and fiction, 7; four sets of perspectives by Schaeffer, 8; hagiographical dimension, 8; literary, other forms, 6; 'Mila *namthar*' tradition, 5, 15, 25n128; mystical aspect, 8; mythological dimension, 8; *namthar* (*rnam thar*), 4–5; *namthar* literature, description, 5; *namthar* prayer, 7, 10; *rangnam* (*rang rnam*), 4, 6; several truths and realities, 8; study of Indian *mahāsiddha*s, 7–8; tantric instructions for empowerment rituals, 6; teacher's *namthar*, 5, 7, 9; use of 'rationality of common sense,' 7;
vimokṣa, complete liberation, 4–5; Vostrikov's description of *namthar*, 7
Lineage Wish-Fulfilling Gem, 9
literature about Tibet, trends in, 39
The Lives of the Eighty-Four Siddhas, 11, 15
Lost Horizon (Hilton), 33

Mahāmudrā, 9, 15, 61, 86, 91–92, 133–34, 159, 170, 203, 216, 217, 226, 247, 250–51
mahāsiddha. *See* Indian *mahāsiddha*s
Mahāyāna, 10, 14–15, 45–46, 61, 63, 84, 203, 212, 248
Mahāyāna sūtra, 14, 59, 61, 63, 84
Mahāyāna Uttaratantra Shastra (Asaṅga), 163, 165
Maitri Five Wisdoms, 158
*maṇḍala/maṇḍala*s, 59–61, 93, 207, 211–16, 219, 241, 244, 247
Mañjuśrīmitra, 15
meditative absorption (Thukdam), 83, 87
metanarratives, 39
method of giving prophecy, 209. *See also* prophecy
'Mila *namthar*' tradition, 5, 15, 25n128
Minchih, abbot of the Da-Jue Temple in New York, 189
Missamari refugee camp, 152–53
modernisation: Asian Buddhist teachers' strategy, 41; aspects of, 40; of Buddhism, 40; and Buddhist reforms, 152; concern about mental health, 40; individualism, 40, 45; in Japan, 41; relationship between the British and Tibetan ruling class, 31–32; religious purification, 40; sense of entitlement, 40; of Theravāda and Zen Buddhist traditions, 40; Gyalo Thondup's efforts of, 109; to Tibet, 152–53; wish for religion to be consistent with one's lifestyle, 40
Modernist Buddhism, 40–41, 45, 197

monasteries and Dharma centres,
founding of, 114–17, 186–88,
198; advice of renunciation and
bodhicitta, 187; donation of land
in France, 186; donations of land
from devotees, 186; importance
of guru-disciple relationship, 188;
Kagyu International Headquarters/
Office at Rumtek, 186; Karma
Kagyu Trusts, 186; Karma
Thegsum Choling, 186; Karma
Triyana Dharmachakra (KTD),
186; lama-patron relationship,
114; lamas as resident teachers
in monasteries/Dharma centres,
169, 186; monastic community in
exile, 114; preservation efforts,
116, 130; rebuilding monastic
community in Indian subcontinent,
187; renunciation and *bodhicitta*
teachings, 187; Rumtek, headquarters
for Dharma centres, 115, 186, 196;
Sikkim and India for monastic seat
in exile, 114–15; support from
Indian government, 115; sustainable
transmission on individual and
organisational levels, 188
monastery in Lhodrak, 129, 236
monastic community: building new
Rumtek, 131; code of conduct based
on the Vinaya, 132–33; construction
of Tashi Choling in Bhutan, 135; in
exile, 114; propagation of monastic
ordinations, 131–32; rebuilding
in Indian subcontinent, 187;
re-establishment, 131–35; restoration
of, 196; revival of summer retreat,
132; sangha. *See* training the sangha;
strengthening monastic discipline,
131; summer retreat at Rumtek in,
1961, 132; supervision of the monks'
conduct, 132; Kangyur and Tengyur,
131; Three Basic Rituals of the
Vinaya, 132
monastic institutions, 37

Mūlasarvāstivādavinaya, 13
mystical image of the teacher, 11–12

Nāgabodhi, 208
Nāgārjunagarbha, 15
Namgyal Institute of Tibetology in
Sikkim, 131
namthar (*rnam thar*), 4–5; as 'a
Tibetan form of novel writing,' 6;
characteristics of, 5; death episode,
89; definition, 5; emphasis on
supernatural phenomena, 83; of
the Fifteenth Karmapa, 16, 60; of
the Fourteen Karmapas, 16, 59;
functions of, 5; Golden Rosaries, 9,
14; inspiring devotion in disciples,
18; life stories of renowned lamas,
5; link between the present and past
lives, 11; literature, description,
5; 'Mila *namthar*' tradition, 5, 15,
25n128; portrayal of Milarepa, 15;
prayer, 7, 10; produced after his/her
death, 10; and *rangnam*, 6, 7, 12,
14, 15; role in spiritual path of the
disciples, 9; of Sixteenth Karmapa,
63, 64, 66, 84; standard *namthar*,
11; in TBRC database, 6; teacher's
former lives, 8, 12; tradition of
Karmapas, 16
Narthang Kangyur and Tengyur, 131,
202, 244
Nehru, Jawaharlal, 115, 151–53
New Age movements, 29, 42–44, 47,
184, 197
New Age Orientalism (myth of Shangri-
la), 31, 44
1965 Immigration Act, 42
Ninth Karmapa, Wangchuk Dorje, 87
nirmāṇakāya, 15, 60
non-sectarianism: approach, 103, 109,
130, 135–36, 188–89, 199; division
as the 'killers of the teaching,'
136; Himalayan Buddhist Society
in Calcutta, 136; measures to
preserve the Dharma, 136; need for

cooperation among Tibetan schools, 136
Nydahl, Ole, 89, 179n153
Nyingma centre, 189

Oberoi, Goodie, 87
Occult science, 31
Occult Tibet, 33, 35
Olcott, Henry Steele, 31
Ornament of Precious Liberation (Gampopa), 163, 165

Padmasambhava: Black Crown, meaning of, 64–65; Karmapa as emanation of Avalokiteśvara, 64; prophecies, 64–66
Pāli *jātaka*, 12
Palpung Khyentse Özer, 16, 213, 230
Percy, Charles H., 155, 190–91
Phuntsok Khyilpa hall, Dalai Lama's visit, 106, 233
politics and patronage: connections with Bhutan, Sikkim and India, 110–17; dissociation from the exile government, 105–10
Ponlop, Dzogchen, 115, 134–35, 196
Pope Paul VI, 155, 164, 168, 189
portrayal of Karmapa, Tibetan perspective, 16–18; *The Blue Annals*, 16; buddha/ bodhisattva, 17; devotion to the teacher, 17, 18; Karma Ngedön Tengye's account of fourteen Karmapa incarnations, 16; Khyentse Özer's account of Fifteenth Karmapa, 16–17; level of Expedient Meaning, 17; perception of the teacher, 17–18; *The Red Annals*, 16; Tibetan chronicles, 16; willingly reborn in samsara, 17
portrayal of teacher in Tibetan life-writing, 8, 15
positivist science, 31
postmodernism, 40; counterculture and new religious movements, 40; Orientalist gaze of Buddhism, 40; revival of myth of Shangri-la, 40

post-modernist Buddhism, 40, 197
Practice Lineage, 129, 161, 166, 212, 219, 238–39
practice of devotion, 9, 18
practice of perfections, 12
Prātimokṣa, 60, 201
preservation of Dharma. *See* Dharma, preservation of
prioritising ritual over verbal discourse, 198
prophecy/prophecies, 11, 14, 59, 63–67, 111, 201, 207–9, 215, 235–36, 240, 250; method of giving, 209
psychotherapy, 34
Pure Buddhism, 31

qualified interpreters/translators, lack of, 184, 185

Radhakrishnan, President of India, 115
Rangjung Rigpe Dorje's *Namthar* (Thrangu), 205–55, 255n1; chapter-1, succession of lives, 207–10; chapter-2, enthronement, 210–16; chapter-3, studies in the presence of teachers, 216–22; chapter-4, pilgrimages and made offerings in the south, 223–27; chapter-5, travel for welfare of beings, 227–36; chapter-6, monastic seat Shedrub Chokhor Ling with shrines and sacred objects, 236–44; chapter-7, lama-patron relationship in India, Nepal, Sikkim, and Bhutan, 244–50; chapter-8, travelling to Western countries, 250–55. *See also* Sixteenth Karmapa, Rangjung Rigpe Dorje
Rangjung Rigpe Dorje's Rangnam–brief autobiography, 201–4, 204n1
rangnam, 4, 6; description, 6; function of, 10; idea of non-self, 6; *rangnam* literature and Tantric tradition, 6; teacher's own spiritual progress, 6; tradition of, 6
rationality, description, 7
rebirth stories in *rangnam*, 13

Index

rebuilding monastic community in Indian subcontinent, 187. *See also* monastic community
The Red Annals, 16
Reddy, Neelam Sanjiva, 115, 117
refugee policy, 197
reincarnation and institution of Karmapas, symbiotic relationship, 3
renunciation, 130, 187
retreat centres, 115, 134–35, 163, 167, 170, 186, 197, 201, 203, 233, 245, 249; in Dalhusy, 167; in Southern Colorado, 186; in Sweden, Canada and the United States, 170; in Tibet and Indian subcontinent, 170; training, three-year retreat of the Karma Kagyu tradition, 186; in the West, 197
Rheingans, Jim, 7, 10
Richang, head of the Fu-Chih Foundation in Taiwan, 189
Richardson, Hugh, 3–4, 87
rigid rational censorship in the West, 30
Rinchen Palsang, 16
ritual over verbal discourse, 184, 198
Robinson, James B, 7, 8
Roesler, Ulrike, 6–8, 11
ROKPA International, 177n119
role model types in Buddhism, 10
romantic image of Tibet, 32, 39
Romanticism, 30, 33
Root Tantra of Manjushri, 62, 84
Roshi, Maezumi, 189
Rumtek: building of, 131; headquarters for Dharma centres, 115; Karmapa's activity in, 196; Monastery, 87, 108, 130, 152, 184, 196, 238, 249; monastic institute in, 135; quality of education in, 133; summer retreat in, 1961, 132

Śākya Śrī, 60, 62
Samādhirāja Sūtra, 63, 71, 207
Sāmaññaphala Sutta, 14
sambhogakāya, 15, 60, 84–85

Samye Ling, 156–57, 161–65, 170–71, 197, 251
Samye Ling Meditation Centre, 156
Samye Project, 164
Sanchez, Ranulfo, 91
sangha, training. *See* training the sangha
Sangye Lingpa, 65, 84
Saraha, 62, 66, 72n51, 85, 208
Schaeffer, K. R., 6, 8
A Scholar's Feast of Doctrinal History, 3–4, 16, 84–85
Second Karmapa Karma Pakshi, 3–4, 85–86, 218, 238, 250, 251
self-deprecation mode, 10–11
self-glorification, 10
self-prediction of rebirth, 66–67, 76n85; Dankhok linked with kings, 66; discovery and eventual enthronement, 67; Karmapa as a bodhisattva, 67; prediction letter, 66, 79n93; prediction letter, Karmapa's parents, 67
self-representation, modes of, 10
Senge Namdzong, 66–67, 210
Seventeenth Karmapa, Ogyen Trinley Dorje, 4–5, 85–86
Seventh Karmapa, Chödrak Gyatso, 3, 86, 135; official enthronement, 3
Shabdrung Ngawang Namgyal, 111
Shamar incarnations, 107–8
Shambhala Publications, 38
Shambhala Teachings, 161
Shangri-La, 33, 35, 39–40, 44
Shenpen Namrol, 60–61
siddha/siddhas, 11, 15, 59, 60, 62, 93
siddha Langkönpa, 67
Sikkim: connections with, 112–15; Karma Kagyu monasteries in, 112, 225, 237; for monastic seat in exile, 114–15; Namgyal Institute of Tibetology, 131; royal family, 112. *See also* connections with Bhutan, Sikkim and India
Sikkim Research Institute of Tibetology, 117
Siṃha/Siṃhanāda, 59–63, 195, 207–8

Sister Palmo. *See* Bedi, Freda
Situ Pema Wangchok Gyalpo, 67, 134, 210–11, 216, 224
Sixteenth Karmapa, Rangjung Rigpe Dorje, 1, 4, 16–17, 59–67, 84–85, 87, 90, 105, 110, 111, 113, 132, 134–35, 152, 195, 209, 216
Sixth Buddha of Fortunate Aeon Siṃha/Siṃhanāda, 59, 63, 195, 207–8
Sixth Karmapa, Thongwa Dönden, 86
Smith, Gene, 131
Snow Lion Publications, 39
Snyder, Gary, 159
Songtsen Gampo, King, 62, 66, 208–9
sources: life of the Sixteenth Karmapa, 195; Tibetan and English language, 2
spiritual and historical, interplay between, 13–16; ability as skilful means by Mahāyāna sutras, 14; Buddha portrayed with miraculous signs and powers, 14; conformity with world by *Lokānuvartanā Sūtra*, 14; *dharmakāya*, 15; emanation of Nāgārjunagarbha or Mañjuśrīmitra, 15; Indian Buddhism, 14; life stories of Indian *mahāsiddha*s, 15; 'Mila *namthar*' tradition, 15; Milarepa, 15–16; multilayered pattern, 14; *nirmaṇākāya*, 15; *saṃbhogakāya*, 15; *siddha* tradition, 15; Tantric Buddhism, 15, 154, 158, 171, 197, 199; Twelve Great Disciples, 16; Vajradhāra, Kagyu teachers as emanations of, 14; yogin's experience of tragedy, 16
spiritual awakening, 83
spiritual materialism, 156
spiritual path, 6, 8–9, 14–15, 44, 47, 89, 151, 183–84
spiritual perfection, 4, 13
spiritual qualities of teacher, 9–13; *arhat* in Theravāda Buddhism, 10; benefits of life stories of lineage teachers, 9; Bodhisatta's path to buddhahood, 12; *bodhisattva* in the Mahāyāna, 10; deluded appearance, 11; first cycle of the Aural Transmission of Saṃvara, 9; function of *namthar* and *rangnam*, 5, 10; Golden Rosaries, *namthar* collection of lineage teachers, 9; 'histories of incarnations,' 13; influence of rebirth stories in *rangnam*, 13; *Jātakamālā*, 13; life stories of lineage teachers, 9; Lineage Wish-Fulfilling Gem, 9; long path of the Bodhisatta, 12; *mahāsiddha* in the Vajrayāna, 10; modes of self-representation, 10; mystical image of the teacher, 12; practice of devotion, 9; practice of perfections, 12; *namthar* and *rangnam*, 12; role models in Buddhism, 10; role of teacher in Tantric tradition, 9; self-deprecation mode, 10–11; self-glorification, 10; spiritual path, 9; standard *namthar*, 11; straightforward mode, 10–11; transmission within context of teacher-disciple relationship, 9; union of wisdom and compassion, 10
spiritual tolerance, 189
standard *namthar*, 11
straightforward mode, 10–11
strategies for tours to Europe and North America. *See* tours to Europe and North America, strategies for
summer retreat, tradition of, 114, 132–33, 135, 196, 202, 240, 243, 247
supernatural phenomena or miracles, 83
sustainable transmission on individual and organisational levels, 188
Sūtra, 14, 59, 61, 63–64, 202, 204, 207, 212, 244, 253

Taizen Deshimaru, 189
Tantra, 59, 61, 63, 64, 84, 134, 185, 189, 202, 204, 207, 212, 219, 225, 239, 243–44, 253
Tantra of the Blazing, Wrathful Meteorite, 60–61, 207

Tantric Buddhism, 15, 154, 158, 171, 197, 199
Tantric empowerment from the Dalai Lama, 106, 108
Tantric instructions for empowerment rituals, 6
Tantric path, 15, 185
Tantric rituals, prioritisation of, 184–86, 198; Black Crown Ceremony, 184–86; counterculture, new religious and New Age movements, 184; lack of qualified interpreters/translators, 184, 185; reasons for focus on, 184; ritual over verbal discourse, 184; Tantric path, 185; 'teaching by being,' 184–86, 198; traditional spiritual image, 185; type of audience, 184
Tantric tradition, 6, 9, 14, 61, 154, 170, 185
Tara Rokpa Therapy, 177n117
Tashi Choling, 112–14, 135, 202, 224, 237, 238, 245–47, 249–50
Tashi Tsering, 17, 60–67, 73n57, 84, 204n1; claim of Karmapa as Sixth Buddha, 61–62; compilation of Karmapa's *Collected Works*, 61; identification with the Sixth Buddha, 61
teacher, spiritual qualities of. See spiritual qualities of teacher
teacher's *namthar*, 5, 7, 9
'teaching by being,' 184–86, 198
Tengyur, 131, 196, 202, 244
Tenth Karmapa, Chöying Dorje, 85, 111, 135
Terma, 59, 63–66, 84, 133, 135, 208, 222, 228, 229, 240, 243, 250
Terma of Sangye Lingpa, 65, 84
Terma prophecy/prophecies, 64–66, 208, 240, 250. See also prophecy
Terma text: of Dorje Drolö practice, 133; Sangye Lingpa's, 65, 84
testament (*zhal chems*), 59, 66–67, 209–10
thangka of the Fifteenth Karmapa, Khakyap Dorje, 111

Thartse Rinpoche, 189
Theosophical Society, 30, 31, 41, 46; comprehensive psychology or science of the soul, 31; 'Oriental wisdom,' promotion of, 31; Pure Buddhism, 31; religious dogma in rational terms, 31
Theravāda Buddhism, 10, 12, 14, 29, 40, 41, 45, 46, 158, 162, 188, 189
Thich Thien-An, 189
Third Karmapa, Rangjung Dorje, 3, 86, 163; formal identification as a tulku, 3
Thirteen Group, 108–9
Thirteenth Dalai Lama, Thubten Gyatso, 67, 85, 89, 211, 215
Thirteenth Karmapa, Dudul Dorje, 131
Thrangu Rinpoche, 16–17, 60–67, 88, 108, 133, 163, 205, 254, 255
Tibetan agency, 1, 29–30, 36, 39, 195
The Tibetan Book of the Dead, 34
Tibetan Buddhism, 196–99; copies of the Derge Kangyur, 196–97; Derge Kangyur project, 196; in exile, 1; training young tulkus, lamas and Western disciples, 196; transmitting the Dharma to the West, 197; victim of the communist hegemony, 35
Tibetan Buddhist centres: in England, 153; in Europe and the United States, 1; traditional, 171; in Western Europe, 153, 156
Tibetan Buddhist schools, 11, 135, 216
Tibetan contribution, 36–39; academic interest in Tibetan culture, 38; American/ European interpretation of Tibet, 39; books aligned with China, 39; books sympathetic to the Tibetan cause, 39; Buddhism as shared identity, 37; Buddhist texts from Tibetan into English, 38; creative negotiations, 36; Ethnic Tibet, 36; liberation of Tibet from its oppressive theocracy, 39; metanarratives, 39; monastic

300 Index

institutions, 37; resettlement of Tibetan refugees by India, 37; support of Western donors, 37; Tibetan culture in American and European universities, 38; Tibetan-ness, 36–37; trends in the literature about Tibet, 39; urgency to save culture, 36; utopian version of Tibet, 39; Western students of Tibetan lamas in exile, 38

Tibetan culture, 31, 35, 36, 38–39, 44, 160, 163; commercialisation of, 44; damage during Chinese Cultural Revolution, 36; interpretations, 31–32; objectives for Samye Ling to preserve, 163; Occult Tibet, 33, 35; preservation in exile, 39; reconstruction of, 39; role in spread of Buddhism in the West, 38–39; translation of texts from Tibetan into English, 38

Tibetan diaspora, 35–36, 39, 110, 152, 190

Tibetan Friendship Group, 152

Tibetan Metanarrative, 39

Tibetan-ness, 36–37

Tibetan perspective: interplay between the spiritual and the historical. *See* spiritual and historical, interplay between; life-writing in Tibetan Buddhism, 4–9; portrayal of the Karmapa, 16–18; spiritual qualities of the teacher, 9–13. *See also specific entries*

Tibetan refugees, 37, 115, 151–52, 190, 245; resettlement of by Government of India, 37

Tibetans' religious practice and knowledge of occult masters, 31

Tibet as hidden place of wisdom of Western civilisation, 33

Tibet Society in Britain, 156

Torch of Certainty (Thayé), 163

tours to Europe and North America, strategies for: cross-cultural exchange between the West and Tibet, 183; engagement with governments and politicians, 190–91, 198; founding of monasteries and Dharma centres, 186–88, 198; friendship with other Buddhist traditions and religions, 188–89, 198; prioritisation of Tantric rituals, 184–86, 198; prioritising ritual over verbal discourse, 198; 'teaching by being,' 184–86, 198; transmission of lineage into the future, 183

traditional spiritual image, 57, 185

training the sangha: empowerment and transmission of *The Treasury of Kagyu Mantras*, 133; identification of the Sixteenth Karmapa, 134; monastic institute in Rumtek, 135; quality of education in Rumtek, 133; re-establishing the lineage in exile, 134; relationship with Situ and Jamgon Kongtrul, 134; retreat centre, 135; Tantra of meaning/ultimate transmission, 134; training of primary disciples, 133–34; Tsurphu and Palpung systems, 133

Traleg Rinpoche/Traleg Nyima Gyurme/Traleg Kyabgon, 115, 129, 135, 185, 196, 221, 235, 239, 245–46, 249

'transcultural space,' 1

transmission: dialogue with Catholic Church and engagement with US government, 149; change (adaptation), 1; consistency (continuity with tradition), 1; within context of teacher-disciple relationship, 9; development of Karma Kagyu lineage in Europe and North America, 149; Dharma tours to North America and Europe, 149; global, transcultural character of, 1; of lineage into the future, 183; strategies, 1

The Treasury of Kagyu Mantras, 133, 219, 239

The Treasury of Precious Instructions, 133, 219
Trungpa, Chögyam, 156–62, 197–98, 222, 250, 251; adaptation and diversification, 158–59, 198; autobiography, 157; Black Crown Ceremony, 160; Dharma centres, 160; Buddhism in the West, 156; discipline at Dharmadhatu, 162; Eleventh Trungpa of Surmang, 156; formalities to train in 'sacred outlook,' 159; formal transmission of the lineage, 162; issue of 'spiritual materialism,' 156; Maitri Five Wisdoms, 158; meditation, 158; Naropa Institute, Buddhist-inspired university in North America, 158–59; Shambhala Teachings, 161; support from Bedi, 156; teaching and spread of Dharma, 156; Tibet Society in Britain, 156; transmission strategy, 157, 160
Tsewang Phuntsok, 67, 209
Tsurphu, 4, 61, 64, 67, 85, 87, 106, 111–12, 129, 132–36, 202, 207, 209, 211–14, 216, 221, 222, 226, 233, 235, 237
Tulku, Akong, 162–66, 197–98, 251; Black Crown Ceremony, 164; Dharma in southern Africa, 166; honorary title *Dharmacharya*, 164; Karmapa's European monastic seat, 165; Karmapa's tours in Europe, 164–66; long-life prayer, 166; role in transmission of the lineage, 165; Samye Ling, 163–64; Samye Project, 164; Second Akong of Dolma Lhakang Monastery, 162; Tantric teachings, 163; tradition of long retreat, 163; transmission of Tibetan Buddhism, 163
Tulku, Tarthang, 189
tulku lineage, 3, 18n1, 66–67, 107–8, 115, 129, 132–36, 152–54, 157, 196–98, 209, 212–13, 215, 232–33, 235–36, 238–39, 244–45, 247–48, 251, 254, 255; ban by Lhasa government, 108
Twelfth Karmapa, Changchub Dorje, 112
Twelve Deeds, 17, 61, 64
Twelve Great Disciples, 16

Ugyen Wangchuck, King, 111
unbroken lineage, importance of, 11, 15, 64
union of wisdom and compassion, 10
UN Social Services Planning Commission, 151
utopian version of Tibet, 34, 35, 39

Vajradhāra, Kagyu teachers as emanations of, 14
vajra-like *samādhi*, 62, 84, 92
*vidyādhara*s, 59, 62
vimokśa, complete liberation, 3–4
von Guenther, Herbert, 159
Vostrikov, on description of *namthar*, 7

Waldman, Anne, 159
Western devotees' perception of the Karmapa, 57, 83, 92
Western donors, support of, 37
Western imagination of Tibet, 30–36; accounts of European travellers and writers, 32–33; Anglo-Tibetan imperial encounter, 31–32; belief in utopian Tibet, 34; Chinese rule of Tibet and communism, 35; 'cinematic myths of Tibet,' 32; Cold War, 35; colonial government and Tibetan ruling class, relationship, 31–32; degeneration from the original Buddhism, 30; diaspora, 35–36; Great Game between Britain and Russia, 30; members of ruling class in Lhasa, 32; myth of Shangri-La, 33, 35; Occult Tibet, 33, 35; psychological interpretation of Buddhism, 34; rigid rational

censorship, 30; romantic image of Tibet, 32; Theosophical Society, 31; Tibetan diaspora, 35–36; Tibetans' religious practice and knowledge of occult masters, 31; Tibet as hidden place of wisdom of Western civilisation, 33

Western perception of the Karmapa, 29; arrival of Tibetan Buddhism in the West, 29; idealisation of Tibet, 29; intercultural exchange with the West, 29

Western students of Tibetan lamas in exile, 38

Westminster Abbey, 155, 189; meeting with dean of, 189; visit to, 155

wisdom of mahamudra or the ultimate truth, 91

Wisdom Publications, 38–39

World War I, 29, 31, 33

World War II, 29, 31

Yangdzom, Ashi Dekyi, 116

Yongle, Chinese emperor, 62, 85–86, 94n14, 94n15, 96n26

Younghusband expedition, 31, 111, 152

Young Lamas' Home School, 152–54, 156, 162, 197

Yungtönpa, Gyalwa, 11

Zen Buddhism, 29, 40–42, 46, 158, 162, 188–89

About the Author

Dr Meng Wang is a postdoctoral research associate at the SOAS Centre of Buddhist Studies. She has been awarded a PhD and MA from the School of Oriental and African Studies, University of London, and a BA from Peking University. Her research interests focus on Asian transmission agency in the cross-cultural interaction between Buddhism and the West during the modern era of globalisation. Her previous publications include 煉心八句, the official Chinese translation of *Finding Genuine Practice* by the Seventeenth Karmapa Ogyen Trinley Dorje.

Lightning Source UK Ltd.
Milton Keynes UK
UKHW041510201222
414057UK00009B/107